For the Sake of Allah

Dear Brother Huseyin,

With Love and Respect,

[illegible]

04/04/2019

For the Sake of Allah

The Origin, Development, and Discourse of the Gülen Movement

Anwar Alam

Blue Dome Press

New Jersey

22 21 20 19   1 2 3 4

Published by Blue Dome Press
335 Clifton Ave.
Clifton, NJ, 07011, USA
www.bluedomepress.com

Paperback 978-1-68206-021-6
Hardcover 978-1-68206-022-3

Library of Congress Cataloging-in-Publication Data

Names: Alam, Anwar, 1966- author.
Title: For the sake of Allah : the origin, development, and discourse of the Gulen movement / Anwar Alam.
Description: Clifton, NJ, USA : Blue Dome Press, 2019. | Includes bibliographical references and index.
Identifiers: LCCN 2018054113| ISBN 9781682060216 (alk. paper) | ISBN 9781682060223 (hardcover)
Subjects: LCSH: Gulen Hizmet Movement. | Gulen, Fethullah--Influence. | Islam--Turkey. | Islam and politics--Turkey. | Islamic renewal--Turkey. | Social movements--Religious aspects--Islam.
Classification: LCC BP63.T8 A395 2019 | DDC 297.6/5--dc23
LC record available at https://lccn.loc.gov/2018054113

Printed in India

To,

Osman, Bülent, Bilal, Ersin, Mustafa, Ali, Tevfik, Engin, Tuba, Zuhal, Ayşe, Fatma, Ahmet, Hakan, Ercan, Furkan, and thousands of other volunteers in the Gülen Movement who are working for the sake of Allah and without any expectations, to make this world more peaceful, non-violent, and livable, and who are currently facing illegal persecution and suffering in various forms under the current Erdoğan-led Turkish government.

Contents

PREFACE AND ACKNOWLEDGEMENTS

For the Sake of Allah: The Origin, Development, and Discourse of the Gülen Movement is a book of an accident. One fine morning in 2008, a journalist of Turkish origin, who was based in Delhi, visited my office at Jamia Millia Islamia, where I was then holding the position of Professor and Deputy Director of the Centre for West Asian Studies. The gentleman invited me along with a senior Indian journalist to visit Turkey for four to five nights. The visit to Istanbul made me slightly aware of something called the "Gülen Movement." I had never heard about the Movement, aka Hizmet, before this visit despite the fact I had been academically engaged with the phenomenon of Islamic religious movements since 1990, particularly in the context of West Asia.

Apart from a whirlwind tour of historical sites in Istanbul, we were also taken to some of the institutions connected with the Gülen Movement: Fatih University, *Zaman* newspaper, two high schools, the Journalists and Writers Foundation and Samanyolu TV. At no stage of this visit to Turkey and to these Gülen-inspired institutions was I briefed or told about the Gülen Movement. We were not even given any literature concerning the movement. However, the visit helped to generate in me an interest in Turkey. A colleague of mine from Mumbai had a similar experience while visiting Turkey in 2015 on the invitation of the Gülen Movement and was baffled that he was neither briefed about the purpose of the visit nor was he ever given the literature related to Movement.

Back home, I retained the interest and did some preliminary reading about the Movement. Further, a constant interaction with Delhi-based Turkish participants of the Gülen Movement made me more interested in conducting research on the Movement. Luckily, I got an opportunity to visit Turkey for a year (October 2010–September 2011) as Visiting Professor at Fatih University, Istanbul, primarily to conduct post-doctoral research on the Movement. Accustomed to understanding Islam in its South Asian form, for the initial six months of my research I could not find anything "Islamic" about the Movement. The very modern outlook of Hizmet institutions along with the liberalized, open environment at the university campus, including open mixing of young men and women was too puzzling to frame them in the context of an Islamic movement. Except for their punctuality and devotion to the five daily prayers, none of their institutions bore any kind of Islamic sign! Moreover, the volunteers of the Movement were steeped in a Western mode of presentation and interaction, which contributed more to my confusion about their claim to be an "Islamic faith-based movement." I owe a deep sense of gratitude to Fatih University (now shut down by the government) and the then colleagues, staff, and students for providing me institutional as well as academic support to carry out this project.

While living in Istanbul, I also interacted with a large number of people of secular leaning including lay public, academics, journalists, bureaucrats, and a few connected with secular parties including the communist and civic organizations with a view to understanding their perceptions about the Gülen Movement. However, I could not sustain the interaction with them beyond a few settings as I found them totally unforthcoming and not open to dialogue or discussion beyond their conviction that the Gülen Movement is a threat to the secular, modern identity of Turkey without ever describing *how* the Movement is a threat. Their conclusions lacked any credible evidence or narrative. Moreover, they would often proceed from a simple, fixed position: *Islam is bad and secular is good.* On the other hand, I found intellectuals, journalists, and other people connected with the Gülen Movement very much open to talk, relatively transparent and prepared to discuss their arguments, democratic enough to engage with all my questions and queries.

I had a second opportunity to visit Turkey to further renew my research on the Gülen Movement from September 2013 to June 2016, when I was posted at Zirve University, Gaziantep, as full professor in the Department of International Relations, Faculty of Economics and Administrative Science. This gave me additional opportunity to conduct more interviews and endless informal talks with a good number of volunteers of the Gülen Movement, in addition to visiting the Kurdish parts of Turkey, which enabled me to get some idea of Kurdish perceptions of the Gülen Movement. I came across a number of Turks with Kurdish ethnic background working in the Gülen Movement, but participation by Turks with an Alevi ethnic background in the Movement is very low. It was during this second visit that I managed to finish most of the writing of this book, in which I try to capture a holistic narrative of the Movement beginning from 1960s till the failed military coup of July 15, 2016. I owe a special thanks to my esteemed colleagues in the Department of International Relations and others teaching and non-teaching staff in Zirve University (also shut down by the government), who were mostly non-Hizmet, for providing me valuable support and making my stay comfortable in Gaziantep.

A couple of pressing problems at a personal level, as well as fast changing developments in Turkey, delayed somewhat the book's publication. However, it has become more relevant since the Erdoğan regime's brutal crackdown on the Movement, the extent of which has hardly been witnessed in the recent history of Turkey or in the region. Even the Kemalist regime did not display such brutality to the Muslims or any other section of Turkish society.

The title "*For the Sake of Allah*" reflects two strands of thought. First, this is meant to capture the genuine collective aspirations of volunteers of the Gülen Movement, who are directed towards the creation of a peaceful and non-violent world without expectation from others. Second, terrorism by "Muslim actors" often appropriates the phrase "*for the sake of Allah*" to justify its barbaric action. This book attempts to present the real meaning of this term: peace, justice, freedom, service ethics—all values that are activated in the everyday praxis of the Gülen Movement. It is indeed a sad commentary that while the movement with its educational and interfaith discourses constitutes the most important ethical and moral resource to fight the current global specter of terrorism prevailing among a section of the Muslim youth, the Turkish government has called the Movement a "terrorist" organization (FETO) and has violently crushed its tens of thousands of volunteers who are either currently languishing in jail or suffering from various kinds of legalized discrimination, which can be termed as "social and economic genocide."

From 2008 until the writing of this preface a large number of friends and colleagues have contributed immensely to making this book a reality. Although it is too difficult for me to list each individual here to express my gratitude and thanks, as they are countless, they all hold a special place within my heart. Special thanks to İhsan Yılmaz, Erkan

Togoslu, Hakan Yeşilova and to the anonymous scholars who took pains to review the manuscript and suggested very valuable modifications. A very special thanks to Ruth Woodhall for meticulously doing editing, copy editing, and providing valuable academic inputs, which helped me in improving the manuscript.

I am indebted to all those interviewees who gave their precious time, patiently talked to me for many hours, and genuinely attended to all my queries and questions. Some of them have since passed away. May Allah accept my prayers for them, bless their souls, and keep them in peace.

Finally, I owe a great sense of gratitude to my wife, Zuby, and daughter, Sanober, for providing me with comfort and peace of mind during all these troubled years and constantly motivating me to complete this research project.

Anwar Alam
August 5, 2018
New Delhi

GLOSSARY

adhan: the Islamic call to prayer.

adillah: proof or evidence in legal regards; plural of the Arabic word *daleel*

ahl al-dhimma (*Dhimmi*): Christians and Jews living in Islamic societies, such as the Ottoman Empire, who were protected and enjoyed certain rights and privileges

ahl al-kitab: "people of the book," followers of any faith tradition with a divine book, primarily Jews and Christians

Alawites or *Alawi*: member of a sect mostly located in parts of West Asia and North Africa with substantial numbers in Syria and Turkey. Many Alawis consider themselves a separate branch of Islam, neither Shiite nor Sunni.

'alim (pl. *'ulama*): religious scholar who is knowledgeable in almost all Islamic disciplines, gives opinions or issues rulings (*fatwa*s) on religious questions

bid'ah: innovation or deviation from the existing Islamic practices some of which can be considered heretical

da'wah: propagation of the Islamic faith with the intent of educating non-Muslims

dar al-harb: countries that are not under Islamic rule

dar al-Islam: lands that are ruled by Muslim governments

dersane: apartments or other places of residence where followers of the Gülen Movement stay together, usually during their college years, or meet for their reading circles.

dhikr: an act of remembrance usually by reciting prayers, Qur'anic verses, or the names of Allah, a practice more pronounced in mystic/Sufi traditions

faqih (pl. *fuqaha*): a legal expert, jurist

fatwa (pl. *fatawat*): authoritative religious injunction without legal binding

fiqh: Islamic jurisprudence based upon the Qur'an and Sunnah

fitr: a form of *zakat* given to the poor in the month of Ramadan

fitra: the pure state every child is born with that is innately dispositioned to compassion, love, and faith according to the Islamic belief

furu': rulings in Islamic jurisprudence that are secondary in significance to *usul* that deal with the essentials of faith

halal: that which is lawful, permitted, good, and praiseworthy

Hanafi school: one of the four religious Sunni Islamic schools of jurisprudence. It is named after the scholar Abu Hanifa an-Nu'man ibn Thabit (d. 767).

Hanbali school: one of the four orthodox Sunni Islamic schools of jurisprudence. It is named after the Iraqi scholar Ahmad ibn Hanbal (d. 855).

haram: actions that are unlawful and forbidden in Islam

hijab: clothing for the purposes of modesty and dignity according to Islamic dress code

Hijrah: the migration of Prophet Muhammad from Mecca to Medina in 622 CE, which marks the beginning of the Islamic calendar

ijtihad: independent reasoning. It is recognized as one of the legal methods of reasoning in Islamic law (Sharia'), which is completely independent of any school (*madhhab*) of jurisprudence (*fiqh*).

ijma': the consensus of either the *ummah* or just the '*ulama* in Sunni Islam – one of four bases of Islamic Law

ikhlas (ihlas): sincerity in all actions be them religious or worldly. Prayers that are lacking in sincerity are less likely to be accepted.

islah: to reconcile or restore balance and order. It is mostly used in connection to acts of reform.

iman: faith and belief in God and religion

Jamaat-e-Islami: a Sunni Islamic political movement founded in 1941 in India by Abul Ala Maududi. It has substantial influence in South Asian countries.

jihad: "struggle." There are two main definitions of *jihad*. The primary one is the major *jihad*, which is a person's inner struggle against temptations and striving for purification. The minor *jihad* is when Muslims have to defend themselves physically in a battle against oppressors.

kafir (pl. *kuffar*): literal meaning is "something that covers." Farmers, for example, are called *kuffar* in Arabic for they cover seeds under the soil. It refers to disbelievers, infidels, and generally non-Muslims, for they cover the truth.

madhhab (pl. *madhahib*): school of legal thought or jurisprudence that interpret the Qur'an and hadiths for followers. There are four main *madhahib*; Hanafi, Maliki, Shafi'i, and Hanbali.

makruh: actions that are not explicitly *haram* but are frowned upon and disapproved. Omitting these actions results in a reward, but participating in them does not necessarily require a punishment.

Maliki: one of the four major Sunni schools of Islamic Law. It was named after Malik bin Anas in the 8th century

Maturidi school: one of the two major Sunni creeds in Islam (the other one is Ashari school). It was named after Abu Mansur Al Maturidi (d. 944).

mujaddid: a renewer, who appears once in one hundred years to revive the Islamic faith by restoring it based on its authentic elements

mujtahid: an Islamic scholar who is competent in interpreting *sharia* by *ijtihad*.

munafiq: a hypocrite who outwardly practices Islam while inwardly concealing his disbelief, perhaps even unknowingly.

mustahab/mandub: a virtuous action, which is not compulsory, but recommended to do

Muslim Brotherhood: a transnational Sunni political Islamist organization founded in Egypt by Hassan al-Banna in 1928

Naqshbandi: one of the largest Sunni spiritual Sufi orders, which is traced back to Baha-ud-din Naqshband (d. 1389).

qada: God's execution of events, and creation of all things, as they were pre-ordained to happen. Humans are able to make their own choices via free will, but it is God that creates and executes our wishes into reality.

sadaqa: voluntary charity in Islam. It is a highly praised act of generosity.

Sahaba: companions of the Prophet

Shafi'i: one of the four religious Sunni schools of Islamic law. It was named after Imam al-Shafi'i who lived in the early 9th century.

sohbet: conversation, companionship. In the context of the Gülen Movement, it indicates a meeting usually at a participant's home, one of the halls of a school or any other institution affiliated with the Movement or at a public place, to read a book together or listen to a lecture, and also to socialize, drink tea and use the meeting as a platform to discuss charitable projects and activities they were involved with.

Tablighi Jama'at: an Islamic religious movement started in 1927 by Muhammad Ilyas al-Kandhlawi in India

tafsir: exegesis; an interpretation of the Qur'an

tajdid: renewal. In Islamic context, *tajdid* refers to the revival of Islam in order to purify and reform society.

tamsil: parable; fable; representation; using a story or lesson to teach a topic

Tanzimat: an era of reform in the Ottoman Empire which lasted from 1839 to 1876. Its goals were to Westernize the nation, increase centralization, and increase revenue.

taqlid: the unquestioning acceptance of the legal decisions of a scholar without knowing the basis of those decisions

tariqa: a Muslim religious order, particularly a Sufi order

tasawwuf: the inner mystical dimension of Islam; Sufism

tawhid: the core belief in Islam that there is only one God and that He has no partners

ummah: nation; community. It is a synonym for *ummat al-Islamiyah*, and it is commonly used to mean the collective community of Muslim peoples across the planet.

vaaz (*va'z*): sermon delivered in the mosque

Wahhabism: a puritanical Islamic religious movement originated in Saudi Arabia and named after Muhammad ibn Abd al-Wahhab (d. 1792).

wajib/fard: religiously obligatory

zakat: obligatory distribution of a minimum of 2.5 percent of annual saving to the needful, preferably in the month of Ramadan

CHAPTER 1

INTRODUCTION AND PRELIMINARY OBSERVATIONS

Contemporary Turkey has witnessed a silent transformation from below in the form of an Islamic movement called "Hizmet"[1] or the "Gülen Movement," named informally after Fethullah Gülen, a profound Islamic scholar and thinker of Turkish origin who is respectfully called Hodjaefendi.[2] His ideas and writings, spanning more than five decades, have influenced, inspired, and motivated millions of Muslims, predominantly Turkish,[3] to engineer a voluntary, peaceful, faith-based, civic-social movement that has become global in scope. Today the Movement, which originated in Turkey in the 1970s, has spread to many other countries and succeeded in registering its presence in the social field, particularly in education, health, interfaith dialogue, relief work, and peace building. By a conservative estimate, the Movement in pre-mid-2016 period (when the Erdoğan regime violently crushed the Movement following the government's allegation of orchestrating the military coup to overthrow the government) used to run thousands of socio-cultural institutions including schools, dormitories, university preparatory coaching centers, universities, hospitals, dialogue centers, relief organizations, mass media, publishing houses, and associations around the world.[4] The Movement is best known for its educational activities. As one young, Turkish boy in Gaziantep in response to my query stated, "It is a good Movement. It is about education and educating people." Not surprisingly, one scholar has mistakenly called the Movement "educational Islamism"[5] in order to highlight the Movement's acceptance of the open-ended universal value of education, unlike political Islamism, where education or other activity is primarily conceived as a part of a political project. Gradually, at least in Turkey, the Movement had come to signify a "developmental discourse" parallel to modern notions of development and a social engineering of re-centering Islam's ethical and moral values in public life by raising several generations from a section of historically marginalized Anatolian Muslims who over the years would rise through educational programs to serve in public and private sectors.

Late public recognition

The Movement, despite becoming visible as early as the 1970s and 1980s, went largely unnoticed outside Turkey, as evident from its near absence in global academic production on Islam and Islamic movements at least until the early 2000s. Its study was largely confined to Turkish scholarship. There are several factors that hampered the global public recognition of the Movement. First, Orientalism, the dying discourse of colonialism in studying "other cultures," particularly Islam, received a new lease of life with the development of the Islamic revolution in Iran (1979) and Islamic militancy across the globe since the mid-1970s, which reinforced the deeply flawed idea of a nexus between Islam and violence and Islam as "threat" to the "secular-civilized order." The re-invigorated Orientalism along with Huntington's thesis of the "Clash of Civilizations," the United States' paradigm of the "War on Terror," and "Islamophobia" in the European continent paved the way for the development of a discourse of "securitization of Islam" that sees Islam as "potential security threat" to the Western social order in particular and to global order in general. As a result, while fringe, anti-Western Islamic movements or "Political Islam" received the lion's share of public attention in the Western mass media, think tanks, strategic community and state institutions; the large, peaceful, non-violent, Islamic social movements or "social Islam"[6] have largely been ignored.

Second, the delayed public recognition of the Movement partly also owes to the nature of the modern knowledge system. The modern knowledge system not only tends to privilege secular knowledge formations over religious ones but it has also developed a dismissive attitude towards the ability of religious organizations and movements, particularly Islamic ones, to produce the "social good." Further, the dominance of instrumental rationality in modernity and its fragmented and utilitarian approach hinders a fuller understanding of religious phenomena.

A third factor is to do with the Turkish origin of the Movement.

Under the long spell of the Kemalist regime, Turkey gradually faded away from the site of Islam and Islamic imagination. For a large number of Western and non-Western intellectuals, Turkey was a successful example of Western modernization[7] which had recently moved to the category of "moderate Islamic nation" under the political leadership of the AKP (Justice and Development Party), at least until 2012, when the AKP transformed itself into a full-fledged authoritarian-Islamist Party. For this reason, for a large part of the Muslim world, Kemalist Turkey represented anything but Islam. On the other hand Islamic religious academia throughout the Muslim world, partly under the influence of "Gulf-Wahhabi-Petro-Islam," has long been suspicious about the "Islamic" origin of any Turkish Islamic movements in the contemporary period.[8] Thus even in the literature that appeared on the theme of "civic-social Islam" in the backdrop of development of "post-Islamism,"[9] the focus remains mostly on non-Turkish Muslim nations, particularly those identified as sites of Political Islam such as Egypt, Iran, Pakistan, Afghanistan, and the Arab world. Not surprisingly, Gülen and Bediüzzaman Said Nursi have not figured in books dealing with the important personalities of contemporary Islam.[10] In fact, if one looks at the scholarly production on Islamic reform and revivalism since the mid-1970s it has mostly been focused on Iran, the Arab world, Southeast Asia, and South Asia.[11] Turkish Islamic reformist movements and thinkers hardly figure except in the Turkish scholarship.

It is only in recent years that the Movement has received public attention due to a combination of factors:

1. The sheer magnitude of its civil-social works across many nations, particularly in the field of secular education. The contrasting image of the Movement—an "Islamic" movement imparting high-quality "secular education"—appears to be a novelty in the modern era and thus has attracted the attention of scholars in recent years. Though Christian missions have long been involved in running secular educational institutions, this was considered normal as Christianity itself has undergone the process of secularization and conforms to a modern vision of life and a modern understanding of religion as a private, personal entity, and a social organization in the service of humanity. The idea of an Islamic movement or organization running secular educational institutions appears to be puzzling for the modern mind.

2. The development of post-modernism that questions the foundational principles of modernity itself has helped in making intellectuals more receptive to the issue of religious phenomena and the need for a fresh approach towards religion and religious movements.

3. Though Islam began to resurface in the European discourse in the context of Muslim immigrants, the Movement attracted the attention of European scholars in dealing with the issue of "integration" of Muslim immigrants as the Turkish Muslim diaspora is one of the largest in Europe.

4. The political rise of the AKP, an Islamist Party in power since 2002, and its *perceived* alliance[12] with and later violent breakup with the Movement has greatly increased the public visibility of the latter both within and outside Turkey.

5. Finally, though not least, is the frantic search of the Western world for a "moderate Islamic voice" to tame the tide of Islamic radicalism following the 9/11 incident as well as to manage its "Muslim immigrants."

Probably the last two have been the most significant in drawing the attention of the Western world and "critical public" across the globe towards the Movement.

A Movement without name

The Gülen Movement has consciously avoided naming and prefers to call itself "Hizmet" (meaning "service") and thus differs from all other Islamic organizations and movements that have originated in modern times. There is a plethora of Islamic organizations and movements in modern times that consciously choose names and symbols to represent their ideology and mission as well as to differentiate themselves from others, for instance, Tablighi Jamaat, Jamaat-e-Islami, Ikhwan al-Muslimin, Ahle Hadith, Jamiat al-Ulama Hind. Though Gülen has not elaborated any reason for not naming the Movement in the formal sense, his preference for the term "Hizmet," a term coined by Nursi in Turkish setting,[13] is clear from the following passage:

> "Even though some call it the 'Gülen Movement,' I prefer to call it sometimes 'service-Hizmet,' sometimes 'the Movement for Volunteers,' sometimes the 'souls dedicated to humanity,' and sometimes 'a movement that sets its own examples ... .' Even if it may sound

> somewhat lengthy, to do justice to its encompassing character, it may be also called 'a movement of people who are gathered around high human values.'"[14]

The term "Hizmet" exists only at informal, popular level and does not connote any legally formalized naming of the Movement. The Movement is also popularly referred to within Turkey as "the Jamaat," although at times this is used, mostly by the secular-oriented person or its opponents, in a derogatory sense to malign the movement. However, the term "Jamaat" is strongly resented within the Movement. Kerim Balcı, one of the strongest voices in the Movement, consider Jamaat as a reflection of "congregations of Muslims in the mosque,"[15] or as a "sociological and ideological homogeneity"[16] with a fixed target; as Walton puts it, it is a thoroughly inadequate expression that does not capture the spirit and diverse global action-oriented programs of Hizmet. Walton has rightly described Hizmet as discourse of "practice and activity, rather than belonging and identity"[17] or what Akin has called a "contextual action"[18] to indicate the diversity of the Movement's works according to the capacity of the space where the Movement is located. Of late, Gülen himself has preferred a term "Camia" in Turkish, or "Community" in English, to stress the diversity of actions and peoples in the Movement.[19]

It appears that there are deep Islamic as well as pragmatic reasons for avoiding giving a formal name to the Movement. First, the Movement, like all other Islamic movements, derives its inspiration from the works, deeds, and conduct of Prophet Muhammad and the classical age of Islam, and aspires to emulate the Prophetic model as far as possible. The Prophet did not establish any organization or name its mission in order to spread the "Message of God" to humanity. He served God, Islam, people, community, and humanity through his exemplary conduct of trustworthiness, truthfulness, tolerance, compassion, love, dialogue, forgiveness, honesty, and dedication to work. Neither did the Prophet ever directly preach about the values of Islam to others. His personal conduct itself became the source of attraction of Islam for others. Thus, for Gülen, serving the cause of God, Islam, or humanity does not require establishment of any formal organization or direct preaching (*dawa*) about Islam. By focusing on the exemplary conduct and actions of the

Prophet and his Companions, the Movement attempts to adopt the Prophetic attitude to serve humanity, Islam, and God.

Second, the non-naming of the Movement perfectly blends with the pre-modernist Islamic traditions wherein Islamic movements emerged without bearing formal names. This enables the Movement to retain the image of representing the authentic Islamic tradition in the modern age—an age, according to Gülen, characterized by profound moral, ethical and spiritual crisis. For instance, "Wahhabism"—the Islamic puritan movement of the eighteenth-century Arabia and currently the official Islamic creed of the Kingdom of Saudi Arabia—is a term that itself was not given by the founder of the movement, Abdul Bin al-Wahhab, but by non-Muslim European scholars. The followers of "Wahhabism" prefer to call themselves "Salafi." The term "Gülen Movement" has also come to exist in the literature through a similar process. The volunteers in the Movement prefer to identify themselves as the "Hizmet" Movement, while deriving inspiration from the Islamic ideas of Fethullah Gülen.

Third, Gülen believes, in the light of his understanding of the classical heritage of Islam and the times and history of the Ottoman Empire, in the role of the individual, rather than the organization or the masses, in effecting change and making history. He remarks, "To date, all renaissances worldwide have been the result of the efforts and work of the few individual geniuses who are regarded as their architects; they did not arise from the efforts and movement of the masses."[20] The thrust of his teaching aims at the Islam-led (not "Islamism" as it makes Islam a fixed entity) moral and ethical transformation of the individual through exemplary conduct and actions. Gülen has repeatedly emphasized that Islam is essentially a religion of good morals and conduct. It is for this reason that the Movement is called "*tabligh* in the form of *tamsil*"[21] or what İhsan Yılmaz has described as "*ijtihad* and *tajdid* by conduct."[22]

Fourth, Muslims carry a voluntary, moral burden of representing Islam; hence the individual's conduct impacts the representation of Islam in society. Gülen is profoundly concerned about the image and representation of Islam in the public sphere: "What is lacking in the Islamic world is not science, technology, or wealth... All of these have influences of their own; but the most important aspect of all is the image that we give out as a believer. The interpretation of Islam (by others) depends on our behavior and conduct."[23] He reiterated the same concern very recently: "The question that we should ask ourselves as Muslims is whether we have introduced Islam and its Prophet properly to the world. Have we followed his example in such way as to instill admiration? We must do so not with words but with our actions."[24]

This is indeed significant and makes the Movement completely different from other Islamic movements in the modern period. Unlike other modern Islamic movements Gülen has focused on both content as well as form. What is important for Gülen is not only the *correct practice of Islam* but also its presentation in the "dominant universally acceptable form." This partly explains the Movement's thrust on building "secular" educational institutions as this has become a universally dominant form to impart quality education. The import of this sentence is that in today's world the term *madrasa*s has come to denote a "religious school," a religious space or a religious identity for Muslims; hence even the quality teaching of secular subjects in *madrasa*s would not enjoy the reputation and legitimacy in the global market as much as the same educational activity is conducted by the secular educational institutions.

Gülen's thrust on "image and representation" may be partly due to the ethos of Turkish society where, according to Berdal Aral, "image is everything . . .; you may be a wonderful person but with beard that image has gone. The controversy over the headscarf, which appears to threaten the republic, is about politics of a particular image of the nation. Symbolism, particularly linguistic symbolism, is the bane of Turkish politics."[25] A cursory observation of the present-day Turkish generation also confirms this trend that in general they are highly conscious about their presentation and appearance whether in the private or public sphere. This may be in part due to the Kemalist emphasis on bodily reform, which over the years has become a part of everyday life, a habitus, particularly in the public domain.

Thus, an organization bearing the name of Islam does more harm to Islam if its conduct is not upright and is perceived as dysfunctional; whereas an organization without an Islamic name but performing better, having established a name for itself through hard work, and maintaining its moral standards, would serve the interest of Islam far better as it takes no time for others to recognize that the said organization is run by "good Muslims."[26] It is not without reason that all organizations within and outside Turkey inspired by Gülen's ideas do not bear Islamic names. One may understand the non-Islamic names of Gülen-inspired organizations within Turkey in view of the Turkish notion of secularism and the political and legal culture of the Turkish republic that does not allow religious visibility in the public sphere. But what prevents the Movement from prefixing Islamic names to its organizations in those countries, such as India, where there is no such legal bar or political culture that discourages the proliferation of organizations bearing religious names?

Fifth, historically speaking, *hizmet* as social value has a special place in the Turkish social fabric. Serving the community, nation or state, or family, friends and others is a powerful, ingrained Turkish value, nurtured from the Ottoman times until today. However, this does not mean that Turkey does not have a violent past and present. Though service or *hizmet* is certainly not a monopoly of the Turkish nation and such organizations exist across nations, what accounts for the special place of *hizmet* in Turkey is the fact that unlike other countries and societies, *hizmet* is a part of social behavior or collective social consciousness or the collective social ethics of the Turkish society and people. Without going into the details here of the historical formation of "discourse of hizmet" in Turkey, suffice it to state that *hizmet* in Turkish lexicography serves as a "root paradigm" having multiple meanings with overtones of moral goodness or sacredness.[27] Within the Gülen Movement, *hizmet* is generally understood in terms of religious and spiritual, rather than cultural-social value, although there are also some participants who act upon simply for humanitarian reasons, because they trust Hizmet and value it above similar groups.

Sixth, the authoritarian, hegemonic Kemalist establishment that did not tolerate any public expression of religion might also have deterred Gülen from naming a formal Islamic organization, lest the same became an issue for unwarranted confrontation with the Kemalist state. Since the establishment of the Kemalist order in Turkey in the 1920s hardly any organization in Turkey has operated with a prefixed "Islamic" name.

Finally, the non-Islamic naming of Gülen-inspired institutions partly owes to the deep Sufistic Islamic values that have considerably shaped Gülen's worldview. What matters for Gülen is not the outward manifestation of Islam as marker of identity as reflected in a particular designation, or physical attributes and naming, but the inner spirit of Islam—confined to the domain of the inner self of the individual—which enables Muslims to work in the most hostile environments for the common good, for the sake of Allah, without any fear of compromise of their faith. Moreover, Gülen is highly legalistic in his orientation and given his legal sensibilities shaped by the model of Prophet Muhammad, early heroes of Islam, and the high legal tradition of Ottoman Islamic culture, he prefers to work with respect to national tradition and within the existing legal structure of the nation.[28] The issue of legal sensibility for Gülen is a moral issue. Like Gandhi, he firmly believes in the dictum, *the means justifies the ends.* Thus, for him, one cannot secure higher moral and ethical ends by immoral, unethical, and illegal means. In other words, *for Gülen, like Gandhi, the very selection of rightful means is an end in itself.*

Structure of the book

There is overall scholarly consensus that the Movement is a religiously inspired social movement. However, a large number of academic works place the Movement within the frame of "civic-social" with a view to projecting the Movement as a contributory factor in deepening the historical process of the "modernization and secularization of Turkey," and so its Islamic roots and roles are de-emphasized. On the other hand, most of the critical works emphasize the Islamic roots of the Movement, albeit without highlighting the Islamic narratives of the Movement, and with an eventual conclusion: the Movement aims at the Islamization of the Turkish society and state and poses a threat to the modern, secular identity of Turkey. This work exposes this conflation of Islam and civic-social-secular, and argues that the Movement's robust engagement with "civic-social-secular activities" flows from Gülen's orthodox vision of Islam[29] in which this world is as real, and rather more important than the other world, as it is human conduct and action in this world that will ensure the individual's place in the other world. However, contrary to many works that see a "secularizing process at work" in Gülen's "this-worldly orientation," or "Islamicizing process at work" flowing from Gülen's Islamic ideas, this work discounts both possibilities. In this context, the book draws insight from the works of Talal Asad[30] and Casanova[31] and argues that Gülen's Islamic vision has its own conceptualization of secular and asserts its moral and ethical right to guide "the secular" without undermining the secular principle of state governance.

Thus, one of the principal assumptions of this work is that the Movement is essentially an orthodox Sunni Islamic movement. The Islamic content, sources, and representation of the Movement are sufficiently explored and run throughout the book without attempting to classify the Movement into any kind of category (such as conservative, traditionalist, reformist, modernist, progressive, etc.). In fact, it strongly rejects the characterization of the Movement as representative of moderate or liberal Islam. Chapter 2, which provides a comprehensive survey of literature on the Movement, reflects on this aspect of the work among others.

A second important argument of this book is that it dismisses the dominant understanding of the Movement that it acts as a bridge or seeks a late-nineteenth-century Islamic (liberal-modernist) model of reconciliation between Islamic traditions and modern values or advances the agenda of modernity. Rather than aspiring to "wholesome modern values" or creating a synthesis between Islamic and modern values or Islamicizing modernity, Gülen's writings and the activities of the Movement seek a reflective engagement with modernity. To this extent the movement shares the concerns and aspirations of post-modernism: the discourse of identity, recognition, representation, pluralism, diversity, individual rights, and human rights, while rejecting its conception of relative truth.

Thus, this work critically analyzes the various modernist frameworks including the social movement theory, political economy perspective thesis of Turkish Islam, and Weberian Protestant ethic that have been predominantly applied to the Movement and finds them deficient in fully exploring and explaining the various contours of the Movement. A part of the limitation of these theories is that they bring in a dimension of the "notion of other"—directly or indirectly—which is otherwise missing in Gülen's Islamic discourse, while engaging with the phenomenon of the Movement. This is the subject matter of Chapter 2 that broadly deals with a critical review of literature on the Movement.

Having demonstrated the limitation of the modernist framework, the book situates Gülen's Islamic discourse within the framework of "non-traditional and non-modern" that underlies the perspective of "continuity and change" and allows cross-fertilization of Islamic and modern ideas *without* essentializing each other. Chapter 3 broadly lays down the perspective of non-traditional and non-modern that treats "tradition" and "modern" as a discursive process with each having elements of the other as developed by Talal Assad, MacIntyre, and others.

Third, having identified the shortcoming of the secular-modernist framework of analysis, the book locates Gülen and the Movement firmly within the traditions of Islamic movements. There are some scholarly works that highlight the Islamic roots of the Movement, but without any attempt to place Gülen and the Movement in the wider comparative frame of contemporary Islamic discourses and movements. As the dominant scholarship has analyzed the movement within the discourse of the relationship between Islam and modernism, Chapter 4 revisits the late nineteenth-and twentieth-century discourse of Islamic modernism/reformism in order to place the Movement in a comparative frame within the wider field of Islamic movements.

Chapter 5 provides Gülen's approach towards Islam and describes the Mujaddidi tradition, highlights its distinction from Islamic reformism/modernism and demonstrates how the Mujaddidi tradition, unlike Islamic modernism, facilitates the interaction of Islam with the changing social, political, and economic structure of society on the basis of the classification of content (Islamic) and form (modernity). The Mujaddidi model of Islam provides an integrated *Sunni–Sharia–Salafi–Sufi* approach to Islam, which runs contrary to the dominant representation of the movement as primarily a Sufistic Islamic movement in the majority of Western scholarship. In this chain of the Mujaddidi tradition it appears that Gülen built his Islamic discourse primarily upon the philosophical terrain of four great Mujaddid: Imam Ghazali, Imam Rabbani, Imam Khalid and Bediüzzaman Said Nursi, though there are plenty of other Islamic and non-Islamic sources that have influenced Gülen's thinking.

In this context it is pertinent to note that even though the book acknowledges the contribution of Bediüzzaman Said Nursi in shaping and influencing the Islamic discourse of Gülen, unlike the pervasive discourse that reduces Gülen to the shadow of Nursi or confines him to mere practitioner or implementer of Nursi's ideas, it highlights the subtle principal difference between the two in terms of their approach to notions of service, the public sphere, the state, education, and dialogue, which partly explains the success of Gülen's Islamic ideas.

Certainly, there is the context of the Turkish political economy that has contributed to the development of the Movement. This includes the decline of Kemalism, a depoliticized public culture as a consequence of the 1980 military coup, Turgut Özal's neo-liberal economic reform and the gradual emergence of Islam in the public domain since the 1950s owing to the introduction of multi-party democracy and the development of the Turkish-Islam synthesis in the 1980s. However, the book does not rely upon the reductionist approach of a political economy framework, but rather asserts the role of the individual and the transformative power of ideas in shaping the significant political, social and economic changes in societies.

Thus, Chapter 6 provides a detailed analysis of the life trajectory of Fethullah Gülen and highlights the role of his Islamic ideas in shaping the upward mobility of the periphery (the marginalized Anatolian Muslim masses) in a peaceful and non-violent manner, reflects on the reason for the breakthrough of Hizmet Movement in the Westernized parts of Turkey (Edirne, Izmir) and not in the conservative Islamic heartland of Anatolia, and touches upon the impact of the Kemalist revolution in shaping Turkish Islam and Gülen's articulation of the Kemalist phenomenon and its implications for the emergence of the movement. In this regard, unlike some scholarship that highlights the context-specific Islamic positions of Gülen and even bifurcates his legacy between old Gülen (pre-America: Islamo-nationalist) and new Gülen (post-America: Islamo-liberal-universalist-humanism), this book highlights the unity of his Islamic moral and ethical discourses irrespective of context, circumstances, and changes in his physical location.

In conjunction with Chapter 6, Chapter 7 analyzes the national context including the statist economy, rural-urban migration, the constitutional regime of 1961 and 1982 that guarantees civil and political liberty, ethnic, religious and ideological cleavages, and the opening of political and economic spaces in 1980s, the role of agencies such as the mosque and Islamic micro-structures such as *ikhlas*, *hizmet*, *himmet*, *sohbet*, *iman*, *jihad*, *dawa*, *hijrah*—and how these together play an important role in the development and expansion of Hizmet Movement at a global level. In short, the interplay of the forces of economic and political liberalization and an inclusive understanding of Islam partly account for the development of the Movement. It is through this process that Hizmet Movement in Turkey became a national as well as international reality in a short span of time.

Chapters 8 and 9 deal with educational and interfaith discourse—the two most visible aspects of the Movement. These are the two dominant instruments of social change in Gülen's Islamic philosophy in terms of raising ethical and moral individuals by following a bottom-up approach. The twin discourse of education and interfaith dialogue aims at the creation of a golden generation that will guide humanity. The whole gamut of democracy, pluralism, tolerance, service ethics, compassion, and other humanistic values enshrined in Gülen's Islamic philosophy is realized through the discourse of education and interfaith dialogue.

Unlike much of the literature on the educational discourse of Gülen, this chapter argues that Gülen's educational discourse is neither based on classical Islamic education, nor imitates the modern Western education system. Rather it provides a critique of both and aims to combine Western professionalism with Islamic humanism based on the principle of altruism. The chapters further highlight the general features of Gülen's educational discourse and interfaith dialogue and reasons for its emergence within the Turkish educational field and its later transformation into the social movement. An earlier version of Gülen's discourse on education has been published as "The Roots and Praxis of Fethullah Gülen's Educational Discourse," *Hizmet Studies Review, Vol. 2, No. 3, Autumn 2015, 9-30.*

Within this trajectory, the Movement (at the social level), along with Muslim political formations ranging from Milli Görüş to the AKP, came to represent the aspirations of millions of Anatolian Muslims for equity, social justice, fair treatment, and dignity and keeps alive the hope of upward mobility that was denied to them by the Kemalist state, and more particularly by what is called in the Turkish political vocabulary the "Deep State." In other words, the Movement is also a faith-based action movement for equity and recognition in the public sphere within Turkey. The Movement gave a new identity, a new sense of confidence, a new meaning and goal of life and respect to many who had been hitherto excluded under the Kemalist political dispensation. In this context, although considerable literature has highlighted the roots and links of the Anatolian bourgeoisie and petty bourgeoisie with Sufi orders to account partly for the rise of Islam in the Turkish public domain, it is primarily Gülen that reformulated Sufistic principles to suit the modern conditions characterized by disintegration of social collectivities and individualized consumerist life styles.

One intriguing aspect of the Movement concerns its political role. The political aspect of the Movement has been, of late, subject to intense speculation and discussion in view of the government's crackdown on it. The critics, mostly secularists, Kemalists, and other modernists, often suspect a hidden political agenda of the Islamization of Turkish society and polity behind the Movement's supposedly liberal-democratic face. On the other hand, Turkish Islamists ranging from Milli Görüş to the AKP accuse the Movement of playing into the hands of American-Jewish imperialism. Chapter 10 dwells on the role of the "political" in the Movement and its implications for the democratic transformation of Turkey. Within this, the chapter analyzes the four aspects of democratization: upward mobility of marginalized Anatolian Muslim groups, pluralization of the political-public sphere, the majority-minority relationship, and gender justice. The chapter also reflects upon Movement-AKP relations. Chapter 11, the last chapter of the book, as a part of concluding remarks, throws some light on future challenges for the Movement.

Methodological notes

In terms of methodology the book broadly operates within the dominant frame of political sociology and political economy, while avoiding their reductionist trap. Thus, it acknowledges the role of the larger processes of the social, economic and political transformation of modern Turkey in the development of the Movement; however, it places special emphasis on the individuality of Fethullah Gülen in shaping and influencing the Movement in order to underline the role of the subjective factor in the transformation of society. The work has drawn its methodological inputs from interviews and informal conversations with a large number of volunteers connected with the Hizmet Movement. More than sixty face-to-face structured interviews were conducted over a period of five years between 2010 and 2015; the majority of them were conducted during my visiting professorship at Fatih University, Istanbul, from 2010 to 2011. Later a few more interview were conducted during 2014 and 2015, when I was posted as faculty member in Zirve University, Gaziantep, from September 2013 to July 2016. This form of interview was conducted within and outside Turkey. Within Turkey the interviews were conducted in Istanbul, Edirne, Izmir, Erzurum, Bursa, Gaziantep,

Kayseri, Ankara, Konya, Hatay, and Diyarbakır. Outside Turkey the interviews with volunteers were conducted in Delhi (India), Atlanta, New Jersey (USA), Freiburg, Berlin (Germany), Abuja (Nigeria), Tirana (Albania), Bangkok (Thailand), and Bishkek (Kyrgyzstan). During the initial round of interviews, I focused on conducting interviews with contemporaries of Fethullah Gülen (in the age group of 55–80) in order to get some information concerning his life style, activities, and engagement with contemporary issues and important events connected with Gülen. Later face-to-face interviews were also conducted with the younger generation, mostly associated with the Movement for fifteen to twenty years. This helped me to develop an inter-generational perspective on the Movement.

In addition, I also had the opportunity to interview women volunteers connected with the Movement. Further, I have been involved in countless interpersonal informal discussions with the volunteers of the Movement that have helped me in developing an insider-outsider perspective. It was during this process of conducting interviews and my informal discussions and observations that I became aware of the foundational Islamic roots of the Movement. Among the Hizmet institutions that were represented in my interviews were the Journalists and Writers Foundation, Fatih University, Zirve University, Akademi (Istanbul), PASIAD (Istanbul), Indialogue Foundation (India), *Zaman* newspaper, *Today's Zaman*, Atlantic Institute (USA), and Kimse Yok Mu (Istanbul). I have further visited several Gülen-inspired schools within and outside Turkey. I have also participated in many academic conferences on the Movement, often organized by Hizmet organizations within and outside Turkey.[32] This provided me an additional opportunity to interact with some academics, journalists, and businessmen involved in the Movement. Further, my own observations by virtue of having lived in Turkey are also reflected in this work.

The interviews and personal observations were supplemented by readings of the literature on the movement in English including books, articles in journals, conference proceedings, dissertations and theses, and Website materials. Hakan Yavuz has classified the literature on the Movement into four types: academic, journalistic, promotional and apologetic, and critical of the Movement.[33] Though this classification of literature on the Movement has its own value, the works of intellectuals associated with the Movement cannot be dismissed merely on the grounds of being promotional and apologetic; rather by virtue of their long association with the Movement, they provide inside understanding of the Movement and also are very helpful in explaining the ideas and notions of Fethullah Gülen.

Although the book locates the Movement within the traditions of Islamic movements, there is no uniform theoretical perspective that has been applied to the various chapters. Rather the approach and perspectives vary from chapter to chapter. Thus, a critical-analytical approach has been applied while undertaking the survey of literature in Chapter 2 in order to highlight the deficiencies and limitations of the approaches and perspectives underlying various works on the Movement. As the primary concern and orientation of the Movement is post-modernist in nature, the framework of post modernism broadly underlies the non-traditional and non-modern perspective as described in Chapter 3 to locate the Movement. Chapters 4 and 5 employ a comparative and historical approach while dealing with the issue of Islamic modernism and Gülen's approach to Islam. Chapters 6 and 7 combine the framework of the interplay of ideas, political sociology, and political economy while sketching the life trajectory of Fethullah Gülen and analyzing the Turkish national context. Chapters 8 and 9 use a combination of the analytical and historical method to explain the educational and interfaith discourses of Fethullah Gülen. Chapter 10 also uses the analytical method to decode the "political" in the Movement and its role in the democratic transformation of Turkey.

Wherever required from ethical point of view, the names of the interviewees and places have been changed.

CHAPTER 2

LITERATURE ON THE MOVEMENT: A DIALOGUE

What are the central concerns of the major works on the Gülen Movement? How have they conceptualized this Movement?[1] How has the Gülen Movement been represented in the literature? Which aspect of the Movement has received most attention in the various writings on the Gülen Movement? From which perspectives has the Gülen Movement mostly been analyzed? These are indeed relevant questions one needs to pose in order to have a meaningful dialogue with the literature on the Gülen Movement and identify gaps, if there are any, which this work intends to fill. The literature under discussion is mostly that is published in the English language, including works translated from Turkish to English.

Modernity as dominant frame

One dominant pattern in the majority of the literature on the Movement is the "framework of modernity" with variations in thrust and focus that has been heavily employed to understand and analyze this movement. Within this framework the Movement is considered a kind of "epistemological breakthrough" in the history of Muslim societies and capable of attaining the goals of (European) modernity: economic development, nationalism, democracy, freedom, pluralism, equality, civil society, and the secular state. This paradigm has been forcefully represented in the work of Yavuz (2013): *Towards Islamic Enlightenment: The Gülen Movement*. Portraying the modernist thrust of the Movement he concludes, "In short, Gülen's action and readings are preparing the intellectual ground for the conditions of modernity. The problem of Turkish modernity was that it did not have religious foundations. With the Nur movement, and especially with Gülen, the Turks are developing the religious foundations for modernity."[2] He further remarks, "the significance of the Gülen Movement is that it has not only vernacularized the ideas of Enlightenment, but that it has also turned them into a religio-social movement."

Mehmet Enes Ergene's *Tradition Witnessing the Modern Age: An Analysis of Gülen Movement*, though it provides Gülen's critique of positivism, pursues a similar line of argument: how Gülen is harnessing the resources of Islamic tradition to meet the values and challenges of modern civilization. Doğu Ergil says, "When his discourse and actions are observed over an extended time and period, the obvious conclusion is that Gülen's aim is to reconcile tradition with modernity."[3] Bülent Aras and Ömer Çaha state, "Gülen's goals are simultaneously to Islamize the Turkish nationalist ideology and to Turkify Islam."[4] Gülay concluded the same: "In a broad sense then, Gülen's community arises to reject the Kemalist equation of modernization with Westernization. As the Kemalist revolution once tried to 'Turkify' Islam and cultural identity, the Gülen community tries to Islamize modernity and national identity by promoting religious values and practices culled from Islam's 'golden age.'[5] Ahmet T. Kuru detects the middle ground in Gülen's writings that combines the moderate interpretation of tradition with modernity and which explains, according to him, Gülen's success in closing the gap between Muslim (a religious identity) and modernity (a secular identity) and bringing the two together without being apologetic.[6] İhsan Yılmaz says, "The Hizmet Movement successfully continues its critical engagement with modernity and the secular, and constructs creative syntheses between the secular and the sacred."[7] Drawing a parallel between the Protestant missionary movement and the Gülen Movement, Elisabeth Özdalga finds a paradox in the secularizing tendency inherent in the Gülen Movement and its Islamic foundation: "The followers of Fethullah Gülen may well be very fervent believers. Nevertheless, the way in which they formulate their mission—as a humanistic project—undermines and weakens their own theological foundations as Muslims—a development that has meant that the role of religion, Islam, has become destabilized."[8]

How true is the above representation of the Movement, particularly in the views of practitioners in the Movement? Is the Gülen Movement merely about Islamic legitimation of modernity or seeking reconciliation of Islamic traditions and modern values? If so, does the Movement differ from earlier Islamic attempts to reconcile Islam and modernity? Or does the Movement have implications beyond the issue of reconciliation or synthesis between Islam and modernity?

To answer these questions first requires an exposition of Gülen's approach towards Islam and Islamic history, as well as his approach to modernity, which is completely missing in the majority of the literature dealing with the Movement. Except for İsmail Albayrak's *Mastering Knowledge in Modern times: Fethullah Gülen as an Islamic Scholar* (2011), there is hardly any holistic treatment of Gülen's thought, approach and methodology towards the Qur'an and Hadith. What is dealt with in the majority of the literature on Gülen's approach to Islam is his exposition of the Sufi (*tasawwuf*) dimension of Islam—which is but one aspect of Islam, which Gülen has called "the spiritual dimension of Islam." Nowhere in his writings or interviews he has ever described *tasawwuf* as "the" Islam; rather he has always emphasized that Islam is the religion of heart (*tasawwuf*) and mind (legal, rational) and it is the imbalance between the two that has created the problem in Muslim societies. Yusuf and some other senior volunteers associated with the Movement from early days have lamented this somewhat excessive focus on Sufism in the study of Gülen Movement as coming from the Western sources and emphasized the balanced and holistic understanding of Islam.[9]

The reason for the selective focusing on Gülen's exposition of Sufism is that it helps "modern scholarship" in fitting Islam within the framework of a modernist understanding of religion as a private, personal, de-politicized affair between the individual and God, as opposed to an "Islam of politics," thus creating a symbiosis of Islam and modernity in the Gülen Movement. Second, this also helps in projecting the Gülen Movement as a liberal, moderate Islamic modernist movement, particularly in the West.

Second, if Gülen seeks a harmony or a synthesis between Islam and modernity, then in what ways do his attempts and/or model follow similar Islamic attempts in the past or differ from them? The encounter between Islam and modernity is historical. There have been varied Islamic responses to modernity or the process of modernization, ranging from uncritical imitation to accommodation to rejection of modernity. Therefore, if Gülen is responding to modernity, which appears to be the case as evident from the above scholarly engagement on the Movement, then any study focusing on the Movement needs to locate it within the Islamic paradigm of Reform and Renewal (*Islah* and *Tajdid*) in order to reveal its similarity to or differences from similar Islamic attempts in the past in order to understand the "continuity" and "newness" that the Gülen Movement offers. This is important in order to understand the "Islamic breakthrough" of the Gülen Movement or conversely the failures of earlier similar Islamic attempts.

Though Yılmaz's "*Ijtihad* and *Tajdid* by Conduct" (2003) and Ergene's *Tradition Witnessing the Modern Age*[10] highlight the Islamic frame of reform and renewal of the Movement but without any reference to such attempts in the past by such Islamic personalities as Sir Syed Ahmad Khan, Muhammad Abduh, Jamal al-Din Afghani, Rashid Rida, Muhammad Iqbal and so on. Yavuz's *Towards an Islamic Enlightenment* (2013) sufficiently highlights the Islamic roots and structure of the Movement but devotes only four or five lines to these Islamic personalities in the entire book, while placing Gülen within the Islamic modernist/reformist traditions as represented by these Islamic personalities. Similarly, Ali Bulaç places Fethullah Gülen under the genealogy of the Islamic *'ulama* tradition representing the conception of "Civil Islam" authored by Muhammad Abduh as against the tradition of "State Islam" represented by Afghani but without any significant comparative study of ideas of Gülen with other Islamic personalities within the tradition of Civil Islam.[11] Erol Nazım Gülay's *The Theological Thought of Fethullah Gülen: Reconciling Science and Islam* (2007) explores Gülen's theological understanding, though in a limited way, in the larger discourse of Reason-Revelation divide in Islamic tradition.[12] However Erkan Togoslu's "Hizmet: from *futuwwa* tradition to the emergence of movement in public space" (2008) is one significant attempt to locate Hizmet discourse within the grand Islamic narrative of *da'wa.*[13]

In fact, the bulk of the literature does not even place Gülen within Turkish Islamic history, where the movement originated and grew, except for linking it with the Nur movement as some kind of background or basis for the emergence of the Gülen Movement. In this context, it will be worthwhile to reflect upon the relationship between Nursi and Gülen as discussed in the literature on the Gülen Movement. First, there is no detailed study on the relationship between the two, nor comparative analysis of their ideas and actions, despite the fact that they are the two most dominant faces of contemporary Islam in Turkey. The Turkish scholars associated with the Gülen Movement generally appear to be evasive on detailed discussion of Nursi and his influence and impact on the Gülen Movement, partly to avoid the image or "Nursi tag" on the Gülen Movement. This is partly due to the fact that Nursi symbolizes Islamic revivalism and the anti-establishment face in Turkey. Çetin's *The Gülen Movement* (2010)—one of the most comprehensive works on the Movement—does not even refer to Nursi as having any influence on Gülen and the Movement. However, Nursi is revered among the volunteers of the Movement and the writings of Nursi are regularly read collectively in the *dershanes* and *sohbets* of the Movement. Yavuz's *Towards an Islamic Enlightenment (2013)* is one good attempt that throws some light on the views of Nursi and Gülen in a comparative way.

In most of the literature that does examine the relation between the two, Gülen and the Movement are represented as "followers" of Nursi and a faction of the Nursi movement respectively. There are many within and outside the Movement who consider Nursi to be the "real architect" and Gülen to be an activist or implementer of Nursi's vision. As such there is no difference between the two. The differences between the two are considered to relate to the difference in times and conditions, and not in thought and ideas. As Yavuz writes, "If Said Nursi was the architect of religious enlightenment in Turkey, Gülen is both the contractor and engineer of these ideas in terms of their actualization and implantation.[14]" This is indeed the dominant sentiment one finds within the rank and file of the Movement with regard to the relationship between the two. My own interviews and informal discussions with many volunteers confirm this trend. However, they do not consider the Gülen Movement to be a faction within the Nur movement, but a distinct Islamic movement. Emphasizing the distinct identity of the Gülen Movement, "Notes on Gülen Movement"[15] states that "the Movement is no extension of the Nur movement, Revivalists, or of Milli Görüş. It is not a continuation of any Middle Eastern movement or is similar to anything from that region." Notwithstanding the above romanticization of unity between Gülen and

Nursi, I believe there are fundamental differences between the two, as this book will highlight, that range from the very conceptualization of Islam to ideas of educational reform and interfaith, as well as engagement with modernity.

Thus, the holistic treatment of Islamic subjective matter and a comparative framework are completely missing in various works on the Gülen Movement. There are two possible reasons for the failure to place the Movement in a wider Islamic framework. First, it has to do with a general indifference, antipathy or hostility of Turkish scholarship towards the Arab world[16]—the center of Islamic reform and renewal movements—notwithstanding the fact that the Gülen Movement has launched *Hira* magazine to establish communication with the intelligentsia of the Arab world. This may be partly due to the fact that Turkish modernity and nationalism, to a large extent, is historically built upon anti-Arab discourse. Second, the Turkish intelligentsia—mostly confined to study on Turkey[17]—tends to avoid the "Islamic tag" on the Gülen Movement for two reasons: (1) as a marker of differentiation to claim Turkish exceptionalism that privileges "Turkish Islam" or its equivalence "Turkish Muslimness,"[18] (the meaning of this twin interrelated concept will be explored later) which is in tune with the secular-modern tradition of the Turkish state, over other national varieties of Islam[19] and (2) to escape the secular hostility of the state towards the public assertion of Islam.

In addition, there is hardly any attempt to explore *what Gülen means by "modernity."* What is his conceptualization of modernity? Further, no attempt has been made to establish whether modernity remains an "external object" to Turkish society and therefore its internal acceptance requires Islamic legitimation. In this context, it may be noted that unlike the majority of Muslim and other non-Western nations, Turkey did not undergo the humiliating political experience of colonial modernity, in which modernity was experienced in the form of a high degree of political authoritarianism, economic exploitation, aggressiveness, racial arrogance, divisive politics, and disrespect of the other culture, identity and tradition. Rather the idea of modern and modernity (such as the political equality of all nationalities, Ottomanism as form of nationalism etc.) and the modernization program (administrative and legal reform etc.) crept into Turkish society in a piecemeal, gradual fashion, not abruptly, beginning with the Tanzimat as a part of the internal process, not an externally imposed one, which was primarily intended to strengthen and preserve the Ottoman Empire and the later Turkish republican state.[20]

Although Kemal Atatürk commissioned historians to dig out a "secular basis" (language, race and culture) for the construction of the "Turkish Republic" and later imposed a series of modernizing programs aimed at "Europeanizing" Turkey, these measures were broadly considered internal processes having a continuity with the past and therefore did not evoke any widespread protest. The "Sheikh Sait rebellion" and other sporadic small-scale Islamic protests were confined to the Eastern Kurdish area, and that too only in the initial years of the Republic. Also, although the AKP, an Islamist political party, has been in power for more than a decade and half, it has not attempted even to re-visit or re-examine the foundational political principles of Kemalism (republicanism, laicism, nationalism, secularism, statism and populism)[21] despite the growing visibility of Islamic signs in the public sphere, such as the increasing use of the headscarf and a phenomenal growth in the number of mosques[22] and Imam-Hatip schools.[23] This testifies to the broad national consensus over the modern course of development.

For the above reasons "political modernity" and its dominant aspects such as secularism and nationalism, if not democracy, have become the dominant facets of Turkish public life or what Dipankar Gupta called "root metaphors"[24] that historically exist and do not require any legitimation, Islamic or non-Islamic. They have become an inalienable part of Turkish Muslimness. Hence, there are no deep political contestations over these "modern" values except in the domain of interpretation that ranges from exclusive to inclusive. Unlike the Kemalists, secularists, communists, and Islamists, Gülen provides inclusive interpretations of these modern values without necessarily legitimizing them in Islamic terms or even using the term "modernity." Indeed, Gülen himself hardly uses the notion of modernity.

In fact, the term "modernity" does not even occur in *The Statue of Our Souls*—probably the most important book of Fethullah Gülen that outlines his thinking, philosophy and vision of Islam. And wherever the term "modernity" has occurred in Gülen's discourse it carries a negative overtone. Making a distinction between civilization and modernity he calls modernity a "mislabeling," a "misuse of concept" in order to dupe people with false promises:

> "Civilization is different from modernism. While the former means the changing and renewal of man with respect to his views, way of thinking and human aspects, the latter consists in the changing of his life style and bodily pleasures and the development of living facilities. Although this is the truth, the new generations, who have been bewildered through misuse of concepts, have first been misled in their way of thinking and then made to degenerate in belief, language, national thoughts, morals and culture. Apart from this, those Western people enjoying technical facilities more than others, and the so-called 'intellectuals' who have emerged among Eastern peoples, and who consider themselves civilized and the others as savage, have committed, through such mislabeling, a grave, unforgivable sin against civilization and culture: … [A]ll these, together with many other signs of savagery prevailing worldwide, show decisively that the 'developed' peoples of the world have not founded a true civilization, and nor have their 'developing' imitators been able to do so. How pitiful it is that the intelligentsia of 'developing' countries have deceived their people into believing that they could be civilized through modernization of their life style."[25]

"The act of naming" is always political as it has an inherent tendency to privilege or dis-privilege one's culture, tradition, value system, and civilization. The discourse of modernity privileges its own conception of the good life vis-à-vis other conceptions of the good life. It is probably for this reason Gülen has termed modernity a "mislabeling." Highlighting this dimension of Gülen, Şeref Hancı, a student of Gülen, states that "Gülen has never used such terms as 'Kemalists,' 'Secularist' or 'Islamist' or any kind of 'ism' for describing people or thought, which is in accordance with Prophetic traditions. Prophet Muhammad lived with '*munafiqun*' for ten years but never used this term."[26] In other words, Gülen's Islamic hermeneutics is the discourse of social change without any fixed ideology, target, or objective. To be more precise, Gülen's discourse is not about "Islamizing modernity" (that would amount to appropriating and internalizing the Western values, mode of thinking and everyday life practices in Islamic terms), which many scholars like to emphasize in order to present the Movement as the "modern" face of Islam,[27] but about making Islam relevant in changing (modern) times and conditions.

While the major thrust of most academic works on the Gülen Movement is about the reconciliation of Islam and modernity or Islamic legitimation of modernity, such an understanding is totally missing among the volunteers of the Movement, based on my interviews and long informal interactions with many of them within Turkey and in India over the span of five years. For them, the Gülen Movement or Hizmet is about "being in the footsteps of Prophet Muhammad" or a "reasonable way to practice Islam"—in the words of four doctors who were interviewed.[28] Another trend that comes out through my interviews and close informal interaction with many volunteers is that they maintain a sharp differentiation between modernity as Western science and technology and modernity as Western *individualistic* social and political values. While they demonstrate a keen interest and receptivity and remain open towards the former, the attitude to the latter ranges from indifference to a degree of accommodation to outright rejection.[29]

Explaining the relationship between Hizmet and modernity, Tahsin Koral, a volunteer in the Movement, stated, "to preserve our culture and religion with European science and technology. Europeanization of Turkey in terms of imitation of European life style was a mistake, while Europeanization in terms of science and technology is acceptable." Citing the relevance of Europeanization of science and technology, he posed a question: "Are we supposed to use the camel and horse—the vehicles of Prophet Muhammad?"[30] This is indeed the dominant sentiment one finds among the volunteers in their approach to modernity. Looking at their life styles one may call their approach "conservative modernity" but they prefer to describe this approach as striving for a balanced life style characterized by a Westernized appearance combined with a high degree of modern professional work attitudes and interaction in the public sphere on the one hand and a strong inner commitment to what Gülen calls the "essentials of Islam"(which not only includes the five fundamental Islamic rituals and practice but a conception of ethical and moral Islam to be practiced in daily life) and the maintenance of conservative family morality, which does not mean seclusion of women or segregation but a respectable distance between genders.

In many ways Gülen offers an Islam-led moral and ethical critique of modernity, particularly its hedonistic tendency, and attempts to retrieve the universal principles of ethics and morality—what he considers the core of Islam—both to regulate modern life and to save Islam from modern, ideological and politicized versions of Islam.[31] It is not difficult to find out from his writings that he is more critical of the modernist vision of life and aspires to a "humanization and spiritualization of modernity" that allows one to maintain the balance between private and public, religious and secular, individual and group, and science and morality. In other words, this requires a moderate, balanced approach towards life—both material and spiritual—and avoidance of excess—what Ahmet T. Kuru has called "Gülen's philosophy of the middle way."[32] In fact, the entire project of Gülen is to retrieve the moral and ethical vision of Islam with a view to ethical and moral transformation of the individual and society and to produce a "golden generation," which can provide leadership in every walk of human life. Gülen's discourses on education, dialogue, interfaith, peaceful coexistence, pluralism and tolerance flow from his understanding of Islam as essentially a moral and ethical enterprise. However, not much scholarly output on the Movement has explored the Islam-inspired ethical philosophy of Gülen, except for referring to them in passing. One good attempt is a piece by Erkan Togoslu, "Gülen's Theory of Adab and Ethical Values of Gülen Movement."[33]

Representation of the Gülen Movement: Islamic vs civic-social

One consequence of the study of the Gülen Movement as a bridge between Islam and modernity is that one gets a blurred picture of the representation and identity of the movement: whether the Movement is an Islamic or a purely civic-social-secular movement (that renders the conception of Islam a private-personal entity) or a combination of both. The resulting confusion regarding the basic character of the Movement led the Pew Forum on Religion and Public Life to conclude that "a classification of the Movement is difficult since it does not easily fit into existing categories of religious organizations in the Muslim world."[34] Notwithstanding the difficulty of appropriate nomenclature, there is a general consensus that the Gülen Movement is a faith-based civic-social movement inspired by Islamic ideals. The core volunteers of the Movement are unmistakably guided and motivated by the Islamic ideas of Bediüzzaman Nursi and Fethullah Gülen. However, its identification in the form of religious *jamaat*, or sect or an organization is strongly denied or resisted or underplayed, and emphasis is placed more on its "civic-social" character than on its Islamic character. Thus, Muhammed Çetin, a former member of the Turkish parliament and closely associated with Hizmet, states, "The Movement cannot be identified as religious sect. It does not form a distinct entity within Islam or Turkey... Movement participants are not recognized as a distinctive religious group either in Turkey or abroad."[35] Highlighting the "civic" character of the Movement he further states that "the Movement's projects and institutions, in terms of both their nature and scale, constitute important civic initiatives, they are not narrowly 'religious or 'Islamic'—the 'meaning' that the protectionist elite wish to impose upon them. The Movement's services are integrative, inclusive and form part of a continual negotiation of meaning within the mainstream of society."[36] Enes Ergene, another intellectual closely associated with the Movement, also notes, "In contrast to the most common misperception, the Gülen Movement is not a solely religious movement."[37] Berdal Aral, a Turkish academic, who is not associated with the Gülen Movement, also concurs, "Gülen Movement is no longer a religious movement, it has become a cultural-educational movement. It is a religious movement to the extent of observing Islamic rituals and values such as 'non-smoking' and five times prayer."[38] Drawing a distinction between Nursi and Gülen, Yavuz comments, "Nursi's movement remained a faith movement from the beginning to the end. Gülen's movement started as a faith movement but evolved into socio-political movement with the goal of shaping modern institutions and spaces."[39] According to Kenan Çamurcu, a Turkish Muslim intellectual, the Movement has "succeeded in shifting the discourse from the foundational concepts of Islam such as faith, *umma*, *dawa*, *jihad*, and morality to secular concepts of tolerance, democracy, civil society, dialogue and peace."[40]

This trend is becoming institutionalized, as evident from the document "Notes on the Gülen Movement"[41] that delineates the basic orientation and features of Hizmet. According to this document,

> Hizmet is a transnational civil society movement calling upon everyone to collaborate around a common ideal of good work for humanity. The movement aims to facilitate an environment in which all can work together in a pluralistic, peaceful, all embracing spir-

> it and voluntary altruism, regardless of subscription to a certain faith.

The document further states,

> Even though the movement has its origin in a framework of reference based on Islamic values, it is not a movement that espouses superiority through nationalistic or religious identities. It's not Pan-Turkish or Pan-Islamist. It is not a religious sect, fraternity, or cult; nor is it an extension or a branch of any of the above. The movement celebrates the universal moral dynamics and values that were exemplified by the Sufis of the early Islamic history and continue to be universally appreciated today; nonetheless, the movement is by no means a Sufi order, either in its classical or modern definition. The movement encapsulates a faith-inspired peace-invoking service. It promotes universal values, superiority of the law and human rights along with freedom of belief, freedom of religion and freedom of expression.

It is important to stress here that throughout the Notes, which comprise 26 paragraphs, the reference to "Sufi" or "Islamic" is found only once in the above paragraph.

This growing intellectual exercise to project Hizmet as "civic-social movement" and underline the "secularity" of the Movement is in contrast to millions of volunteers who are involved in this Movement with an un-mistakably Islamic motivation and aspirations, as evident from the role of Islam in their daily lives as well as their conception of Islamic mission of service. Many consider their moving to different countries and cities around the world as a form of *hijrah*.

The degree may vary from one volunteer to another, but many see their involvement in Hizmet as parallel to the origin, circumstances, and expansion of Islam and its associated doctrines, narratives, discourses, and principles during the time period of Prophet Muhammad and his closest Companions. In other words, they try to place themselves in the footsteps of Prophet Muhammad and his Companions. The tendency to stress the Islamic dimension of the Movement is more pronounced among the first generation of the Movement.[42] This is one serious gap that one confronts between the Islamic articulation, motivation and aspiration of participants of the Movement and the presentation of the Movement in most English-medium literature as a "civic social movement" in which the role of Islam is de-emphasized, if not totally ignored.

Whether this gap is on account of the interchangeable use of the terms "Islam," "God," "Universe" and "Humanity," which is embedded in the Islamic discourses of Said Nursi and Gülen or because of the elaboration of Islamic values as universal values (more pronounced in the writings of Gülen) or driven by a strategy to make the Movement more universal and acceptable, particularly in the Western hemisphere,[43] or to escape the suspicious gaze of a hostile Kemalist establishment, particularly in the military and judiciary, which has a dubious history of "denigrating, criminalizing and de-legitimizing" Islam and Muslim practices as well as threatening and overthrowing religion-friendly governments in the name of violation of secularism, or due to the combination of these factors is difficult to assess. What could be a plausible explanation for such conflation or the ambiguity about the precise nature of the Movement—whether Islamic, religious, civil-social or combination of all—is the post-Reformation, Western-modernist construction of the meaning of religion in which religion is considered a private, specialized activity with a focus on the transcendental world. A more recent work on Gülen Movement by Joshua D. Hendrick[44] that sharply highlights the ambiguous character of the Movement by focusing on what appears to be "paradoxical gap" to the author between the seemingly "this worldly market essence" of the Movement and its claim of representing Islamic ideals (which for author stands for other world) flows from this lopsided modernist understanding of religion.

However, there is plenty of new research that has debunked this modernist understanding of religion and conclusively demonstrated that secularization as a process has not resulted in the privatization of religion, only shifted or displaced its location from public-political to public-social.[45] Following Talal Assad, many good works have appeared in recent years detailing the specific public character of Islam, its history of public reasoning, and its own conception of public sphere.[46]

Is the Gülen Movement a representative of moderate Islam?

Another consequence of the conflation of Islam and modernity is that a good number of academic works and media coverage, particularly in the West, has portrayed the Movement as representative of liberal, moderate

Islam. Thus, Helen Rose Ebaugh subtitled her work on the Gülen Movement "A Sociological Analysis of a Civic Movement Rooted in *Moderate* Islam" [emphasis mine] and remarked, "One response to Islamic radicalism on the part of Muslims worldwide has been the growth and visibility of 'moderate' or non-violent Muslim movements. One such movement that is experiencing rapid growth in Turkey, its country of origin, and also in the former countries of the Soviet Union, Europe, Australia, Canada, Africa and recently in the United States is the Gülen Movement."[47] She makes two significant claims here: first she describes the Gülen Movement as "representative of moderate Islam" and second she links the Movement with a "response" to Islamic radicalism. However, she is not alone in depicting the Gülen Movement as "moderate Islam"; there are many who have linked the success of the Movement to Gülen's exposition of a moderate version of Islam, notwithstanding the fact that Gülen does not subscribe to such representation of Hizmet. As İhsan Yılmaz states, "[Gülen's] discourse represents a kind of 'moderate Islam' even though he strongly rejects such a definition, as in his view, Islam is already moderate."[48]

However, such a description not only simplifies but also obfuscates and distorts the thrust of Gülen's philosophy and the movement. By all accounts Gülen considers Islam essentially as a religion of moderation. This does not mean that he is highlighting the moderate dimension of Islam. According to him, "Islam, being the middle way of absolute balance between all temporal and spiritual extremes and containing the ways of all previous Prophets, makes a choice according to the situation."[49] The conception of "moderate Islam" is inherently political as it exists in relation to the conception of radical Islam. Moderate Islam entails a conscious political strategy to contain radical Islam.[50] This goes against the basic non-political ethos of Gülen's philosophy. In fact, in an interview he categorically stated, "Islam has no political prescriptions. Moderate Islam implies political Islam."[51]

In fact, categories like "liberal," "moderate" or "radical" are the function of Western, modern scholarship in which social groups, the individual, the community, leaders and opinion makers are categorized with the above labels depending upon the nature of the value system vis-à-vis the prevalent Western, modern value system. Thus, social groups that are peaceful, non-violent and accommodating vis-à-vis dominant modern values and norms can be labeled as "moderate," while groups that do not exhibit such traits are labeled as "radical" or "militant." However, such classification does not exist within the Islamic knowledge tradition. It has only one criterion: Islamic or non-Islamic. Within this broad parameter the individual Muslim's action, behavior, and ritual practice is judged as Islamic or non-Islamic according to well established Islamic legal traditions of (1) mandatory (*fard* or *wajib*), (2) recommended (*mandub*), (3) reprehensible (*makruh*), (4) permissible (*mubah*), and (5) prohibited (*haram*), though application of these five principles varies from one School of Law to another, save for those actions or ritual practices that are explicitly stated in the Qur'an.

Similarly, it would be wrong to consider the Gülen Movement as one of the responses to the prevailing fringe movement of Islamic radicalism as claimed by Ebaugh. Such an understanding of the Movement would make it reactive and ideological—both tendencies that go against the basic tenet of Gülen's philosophy. In fact, the Movement is devoid of any conception of "other"—whether internal or external—against which it conceives its role. Moreover, any keen observer would easily identify and locate its origin in the mid-1970s in Turkey, a period marked by left radicalism in Turkey and certainly not by Islamic radicalism. Rather, Gülen's engagement and repeated emphatic condemnation of terrorist acts became widespread and visible only in the post-9/11 period.[52]

Modern vs. universal values

Another serious lacuna in the literature that deals with the Movement within the framework of Islam and modernity is the conflation of the term "modern" and "universal" vis-à-vis Gülen and the Movement. In fact, the bulk of the literature first identifies a set of values *intrinsic* to (Western) modernity such as the market economy, individualism, reason, rationality, democracy, secularism, pluralism, human rights, tolerance, diversity, science and now peace, then marks them as "universal" and examines the ideas and writings of Gülen vis-à-vis these values in order to pronounce judgment on how the Gülen Movement is promoting modern or universal values. For instance, Yavuz is emphatic in his remark, "On the basis of the writings of Gülen, one could argue that the ideas of the Enlightenment helped inform and shape the idea and practices of the new Islamic thinking in Turkey. Gülen has been more successful than some secularist intellectuals who have sought to promote the ideas of Enlightenment. By casting these *universal ideas* [emphasis mine] in Islamic terms, Gülen has made them more accessible to ordinary Muslims."[53] He even includes toleration, pluralism, science, and political participation as essentially "Enlightenment ideas,"[54] which implies that these ideas and values do not have any roots in the Islamic past.[55] In other words, the basic structure of Gülen's ideas or thinking, according to him and many others is "Western and modern" couched in Islamic terms.

First, such an approach reduces Gülen merely to a "conscious historical agent" in the field of Islamic hermeneutics whereby Islamic principles, doctrines, norms, history, hero, and myth are consciously reinterpreted by Gülen to suit modern-day requirements, problems, and challenges in Muslim societies. However, reducing Gülen to the level of a historical agency only to "Islamicize" modernity not only entails a denial of his individuality or autonomy to have an independent vision but also implies an "interplay of instrumental rationality with political-ideological undercurrent" inherent in the writings of Gülen to achieve a particular target/project (such as modernity), which is contrary to the basic ethos, spirit and action of the Gülen Movement. Dismissing the relevance of such an approach to engaging with the Movement, Kerim Balcı stated, albeit metaphorically, "A rose does not have a reason and target to grow."[56]

Second, the universal approach of modernity and Islam is one thing but the projection of localized European or Arab experiences and values as universal—modern or Islamic values respectively—is quite another. It is difficult to deduce from the writings of Gülen that he subscribes to the universalization of local culture and values. What Gülen considers universal values broadly pertain to the moral and ethical values of individuals, and not to the domain of political modernity:

> Such moral standards as truthfulness, chastity, honesty, respect for elders (especially parents), compassion, love, and helpfulness are always universally accepted values. Also, it is universally accepted that people should refrain from adultery and fornication, robbery,

> deception, alcohol, gambling, and indecent ways of making a living. Accepting and considering such standards and values while making laws is not dogmatism.[57]

The *Notes on Gülen Movement* also underlie similar values as universal values: "It is for this reason the movement envisions a bottom–up rather than a top-down projection so as to re-invigorate universal values that are subject to erosion such as truthfulness, honesty, justice, mutual respect, tolerance and peace."[58] It is this set of values, though not exhaustive in itself, that Gülen wishes to restore in everyday life that has been eroded by modernity in the name of progress and material advancement. Trudy D. Conway provides a comprehensive exposition of Gülen's and the Movement's view of the meaning of these and other universal values.[59]

Third, apart from the problematic of projecting (Western) modern values as universal values, what has also been ignored in the literature on the Movement is the deep cultural contestation that exists over the meanings of these modern/universal values. This has serious implications for examining the issue of whether Gülen's exposition of Islam merely appropriates and endorses the meaning of modernity as it is dominantly understood in the Western hemisphere or he undertakes a critical review of the nuance and meanings of the same in order to provide a more inclusive and richer understanding of modern/universal values, a subject matter that will be explored in a later chapter. A glance over the writings of Gülen easily indicates the latter position. Taking a critical look at the legacy of the Enlightenment, Gülen states,

> Enlightenment movements beginning in the eighteenth century saw human beings as *mind only* [emphasis mine]. Following that, positivist and materialist movements saw them as material or corporeal entities only. As a result, spiritual crises have followed one after another. It is no exaggeration to say that these crises and the absence of spiritual satisfaction were the major factors behind the conflict of interest that enveloped the last two centuries and reached its apex in the two world wars.[60]

What Gülen highlights in this passage is the destructive and violent legacy of the Enlightenment, the roots of which he traces to the materialist understanding of human nature upon which rested all power-centered discourses and theories ranging from Darwin's Theory of

Evolution to Machiavelli's dictum of "the end justifies the means" that were invented in modern Europe/the West to legitimize domination at all levels: individual, group and nation. The phenomenon of colonization in non-European parts of the world and development of Hitler in Germany with their embedded violent legacy only points out to limitation of emancipatory potential of Enlightenment. In many ways modern social science is a power-centered discourse in which moral, ethical, and humanistic aspects of society have been crudely marginalized, if not completely eliminated. It would be highly improbable that modernity with its embedded aspect of violence and destruction along with its fixed principle of uniformity and homogeneity, mechanical application of science and technology, masculinity, aggressiveness, consumerism, disrespect for tradition, non-religious prescription of the "good life" and "development" could have inspired Gülen, a man who has constructed a powerful Islamic theology of love, peace and compassion, to warrant his undertaking an exercise of vernacularizing the ideas and ideals of Enlightenment as Yavuz and others would like us to believe.

However, Gülen does not completely reject the legacy of modernity, nor associate it with a particular region (the West), nor attempt to establish a symbiosis or harmony between Islam and modernity—the three dominant approaches that characterize the intellectual debates on the relationship between Islam and modernity—but makes the public critically aware of the "harmful effects" of the dominant narrative of modernity that produces a chasm between religion and the secular, the heart (ethical and moral values) and mind (reason and science), the human being and nature, and the individual and group, leading to a fragmented, blinkered understanding of human history. In this regard Kuru has rightly concluded that

> Gülen does not try to create an eclectic or hybrid synthesis of modernity and Islam or to accommodate to the hegemony of modernity by changing Islamic principles. What he does is reveal a dynamic interpretation of Islam that is both compatible with and critical of modernity and Muslim tradition.[61]

Rejecting the contention that Gülen Movement bridges the gap between Islam and modernity, Kerim Balcı also stressed that the Gülen Movement is creating its own modernity.[62]

What Gülen decisively rejects is the partisan, fetishistic, dogmatic and ideological reading of modernity, as well as of Islam, and attempts to build a more inclusive narrative of Islam and modernity that provides a holistic, inter-related and balanced understanding of the life process and human history. Thus, unlike individualized, materialist readings of human beings and human nature, Gülen offers a far more inclusive understanding of human beings: "We are creatures composed of not only a body or mind or feeling or spirit; rather, we are harmonious compositions of all these elements."[63] Thus, all facets of human beings need to be paid attention for the composite, balanced growth of the human personality. The ignorance of any aspect of human beings would result in deformed personality. This partly explains why Gülen successfully escapes the Orientalist paradigm of "Spiritual East vs. Material West" whereby the material loss was compensated by projecting a vibrant spiritual life on the East and contrasting the same with loss of spirituality in the West. Rather "East" and "West" emerge in Gülen's discourse as an integral part of a single humanity and he calls for dialogue and cooperation between the two to achieve a happier world. As he states, "In my opinion the West and East each represent an aspect of humanity. The West represents the mind and activism, while the East represents the heart and spirit. So, giving up their centuries-old clashes, these two worlds should come together for a happier, more peaceful world."[64]

It is from this point of view that Gülen rejects the contention that science belongs to modernity and rightly asserts that "science is humanity's common heritage, not the private property of a specific nation."[65] European civilization, which itself benefited from the scientific legacy of many civilizations, particularly from Muslim civilization, can at best be credited for further enriching the scientific tools and methods for the purpose of observation, discovery and experimentation and certainly not for developing science as a discipline, which was and is embedded in every culture and tradition of human societies. The two dominant ideas that (a) link the origin of science with the development of secularism and (b) represent religion as being opposed to science have their genesis in the specific European setting of bitter struggle between Church and State. Since Church became synonymous with religion in the post-Reformation thinking that was subsequently applied to all religious traditions, religion including Islam came to be portrayed as anti-science. One consequence of this process is that science and secularism became arrogant, heartless, dominating, developed a dismissive attitude to other perspectives and world views, and appropriated the mantle of Truth. Gülen in many of his writings and speeches draws the attention of the people and scholars—whether Muslims or non-Muslims—to the consequences of such a reading of modernity and in the initial years gave special focus to encouraging Gülen-inspired educational institutions to excel in the field of sciences so as to dispel the public impression that Islam is antithetical to science.

Similarly, it is hard to demonstrate that Gülen would accept the thesis that the notions of "tolerance," "diversity," and "pluralism" belong to the genealogy of modernity alone. European modernity might have discovered the political notions of "secularism" and "citizenship" as the basis for achieving social and political tolerance after putting an end to long years of religious war. However, the much celebrated virtue of liberalism and tolerance in Europe is imaginable only in the form of the homogenized nation state, which itself came into existence at the cost of destroying the internal social and religious diversity of the European nations. This partly explains why the European nation-state is currently experiencing difficulty in managing its emerging diversity in the wake of post-World War II immigrants, particularly Muslims. Gülen neither subscribes to this vision of tolerance that requires a homogenous population as a basis to sustain internal tolerance; nor does he derive any inspiration from the model of modernity that has destroyed much of the internal social and religious diversity of Europe.[66] On the contrary, his model of tolerance is heavily colored by the experience of the early Islamic tradition and the Ottoman tradition of multiculturalism.

In the same fashion, it would be problematic to argue that Gülen envisions the notions of "equality," "liberty/freedom" and "fraternity" in a modernist form because the contrast between the emancipatory goals of the Western Enlightenment and the inequality, un-freedom and humiliation in the daily lives of individuals, groups, and nations of the "modern" world is too palpable for him not to recognize the limited contours and meanings of these values in the modernist form. For this reason, Gülen does not consider democracy and secularism as a "closed, fixed political project" or "perfect form of governance and polity" but rather an "open-ended process" capable of further evolution towards achieving the higher ethical and moral goals of humanity, which is possible if the discourse of democracy and secularism is combined with spirituality.

Other modern perspectives on the Movement

The simultaneous rise of the Gülen Movement and the economic development of Turkey since the mid-1980s have given birth to five inter-related dominant perspectives on the Movement within the modernist framework: civil society and social capital, social movements, political economy, the Weberian protestant ethic, and Turkish Islam.

Civil society and social capital

Much research has found the Gülen Movement working in the direction of strengthening democracy and civil society in Turkey. Two inter-related perspectives—Civil Society and Social Capital—have dominated these discussions.[67] Employing the framework of Social Capital, particularly that of Robert Putnam,[68] these writings highlight how the Islam-inspired Gülen Movement consisting of thousands of voluntary associations has harnessed the social value of trust, norms of reciprocity, and networks for civic engagement for promotion of the group or community's cooperation and solidarity and resource mobilization for the social good. The individual participation in these collective works is considered to indirectly strengthen the process of formation of democracy and civil society in Turkey, as evident from the moderate Islamic politics represented by the AKP at least until 2012. To this extent and within the broader framework of civil society and social capital, the notion of "civil Islam" has in recent years been increasingly employed to demonstrate how the Sufistic conception and practices of the Gülen Movement encompass an internal separation between the sacred and the secular and thus advance democratic pluralism.[69]

The attraction of Putnam's theory of Social Capital for these scholars, mostly Turkish, is due to its non-political approach, which empirically demonstrates that the nature of democratic governance is dependent upon the nature of civic engagement. In other words, a society with a strong culture of civic engagement and networks ensures strong and effective democratic governance and vice–à–versa. Thus, the notion of "political" in terms of "political mobilization or "politics of street" (if not in terms of generating political opinion through network of civic associations including media and participating in general political process) has been excluded from playing any role in the democratization of state and society. This means social intervention, rather than direct political intervention, is crucial for the democratization of state and society. The nature of the Gülen Movement—a peaceful, non-violent, non-confrontational, civic-social movement with a network generating political opinion, if not directly participating in power-politics—easily fits into Putnam's theory of Social Capital. However, what is lacking in the works of these scholars is that none of them empirically demonstrate that the Movement's civic engagements have a positive impact on the democratic governance of Turkey (at least up to December 2012) or have any role in the democratic transition of Turkey. Support for the democratic process is one thing, but to demonstrate the linkage between civic-social engagement and democratic governance in Turkey is another. While there is enough research that shows the orientation and commitment of the Movement to the former, the literature on the second aspect is negligible. On the other hand, contrary to the notion of civil society that has been traditionally conceived as being in opposition to the state—whether authoritarian or democratic—Berna Turam's *Between Islam and the State: The Politics of Engagement* (2007) provides a rare insight by exploring a "zone of cooperation" between the Gülen Movement and the Turkish state in education and other matters of national interest with *unintended* consequences for strengthening civil society and democracy within Turkey.[70]

Social movements theory

Though attempts have been made to apply Social Movements Theory (SMT) to Islamic movements,[71] and the framework has been used in bits and pieces in many of the works on the Gülen Movement,[72] there have been few direct applications of SMT to the study of the Gülen Movement except those of Helen Rose Ebaugh (2010) and Sanaa El-Banna (2014). A major thrust of these applications of SMT, particularly its theory of political opportunity structure and resource mobilization, is to demonstrate how the Movement has been the beneficiary of the opening up of legal, political and economic opportunity spaces in Turkey in the Turgut Özal period (1980–1993). In particular, the support of the Turkish state is considered a significant factor in the expansion of the Movement. In a more recent article, Sabine Dreher noted, "upon Turkey's Justice and Development Party (AKP) coming to power in 2002, Hizmet expanded globally."[73] Similarly, Gary Wood and Tugrul Keskin link the growth and decline of the Movement with the favor and disfavor of the Turkish state, ranging from the 1980 military coup to the AKP government.[74]

Though the state is a significant factor and its behavior does impact on the internal dynamics of the social movement, the idea that the origin, expansion, and decline of the social movement is linked with the favor and disfavor of the state lacks credible, empirical evidence. On the contrary, this work demonstrates that, more than any favor, how Gülen in person and the Movement—both in terms of participants and resources—have suffered from time to time on account of adverse state actions and yet registered growth. Although the Erdoğan-led Turkish state's crackdown, increasing hostility, illegal harassment, confiscation of resources and systematic persecution of the volunteers of the Movement at least since 2013, which intensified in the wake of the failed military coup on July 15, 2016, has significantly affected the "economic fortunes" and activities of the movement within Turkey, it has not led to its disintegration. The Movement survives and continues to carry out its activities at a global level, albeit on much reduced level. Moreover, these perspectives do not explain why the Gülen Movement and not other Islamic movements have been the beneficiary of the opening up of economic, social and political spaces within Turkey. Yavuz and Kuru underline the pro-globalization outlook of the Gülen Movement in its success.[75] However, they do not explain why predominantly the middle and upper middle class are mostly predisposed towards Gülen's Islamic discourse, considering the fact that most Islamic movements—whether society- or state-centered—support liberalization of the economy, partly due to the sanctity of the notion of private property in Islam and Prophet Muhammad's being a trader.

Part of the difficulty with this perspective lies in the fact that while explaining Islamic social formations or movements from a purely secular or outside perspective by applying a post-Reformation understanding of religion to Islam, these theories fail to take into consideration the internal reasoning, rationality, and historicity of Islam that shapes the Movement's normative concerns and vision as well as people's multiple reasons for identification with the Movement.

Second, although SMT's treatment of the Islamic actor as "rational, normal, calculative," and its recognition of the "autonomy of ideas" and emphasis on an interdisciplinary approach is a welcome move in the understanding of Islamic movements, its articulation of "mobilization" and "collective action behavior" is not free of the notion of "other"—whether this is state, West, secularization, or individual or form of Islam, directly or indirectly—that limits its application in comprehending the multi-faceted aspects of the Gülen Movement as there is no "other" in Gülen's Islamic discourses. Thus, Yavuz's *Islamic Political Identity* (2003), which partly employs this theory to explain the rise of Islamic phenomena in Turkey, treats all forms of Islamic collective mobilization in contemporary Turkey, including the Gülen Movement, as inherently anti-Kemalist. He states categorically, "Thus, the large Sunni periphery embraced Islam as a way of challenging the policies of the center. This "oppositional Muslimness" of the periphery tried to develop a new language to counter Kemalist positivism."[76]

What is clear from this passage is that Yavuz believes a large number of Muslims in Turkey see Islam as being in opposition to Kemalism. Certainly, Kemalism is a living reality in Turkey, as is Islam, but the idea that they are necessarily antithetical to each other is a problematic proposition. A large number of Muslim Turks have not participated in the Kemalist project or remain indifferent, partly due to fear that it would compromise their Muslim conception of life/faith, or do not send their children to government public schools partly in order to save their children from what they consider the "corrupting influence" of "anti-religious," Kemalist, secular schools, but to assume their neutrality or indifference as "active or even passive opposition" to Kemalism is another thing. Politically oriented Islamist movements might construct or represent this "state of indifference" to Kemalism—neither participating nor opposing—as "Islamic opposition" with a motive to replace Kemalism as the value system at an appropriate time and juncture. However, all Islamic formations do not have similar reading of history.

Similarly, many in the Gülen Movement are highly contemptuous of the Kemalist treatment of the Ottoman Islamic heritage and derive inspiration from the "Ottoman model of Islam" in order to be a "good Muslim"; however, a reading of the "Ottoman sensibilities" of many

Movement volunteers as essentially constructed in opposition to Kemalism with the objective to establish an "Ottoman Islamic order" would be an extreme, misplaced interpretation of the collective aspirations and feelings of Hizmet volunteers. Kerim Balcı rightly cautions against such a reading and states, "Yes, many in the Hizmet movement idealize the Ottoman. It was a paradise in that time but not a paradise in today's context. A return to the idea of neo-Ottomanism would be a betrayal to today's Turkey."[77] In fact, many of the volunteers refused to talk to me about Kemal Atatürk, saying, "as Muslims we do not discuss someone who is deceased." It may be noted that the Hanafi legal tradition of Islam, which is dominant among Turks, strongly prohibits Muslims from commenting on the deceased person. Thus, given these limitations of West-centered SMT, Çetin has rightly observed, "there has been little research into peaceful, faith-inspired social movements arising from Islamic backgrounds."[78]

Political economy framework

Scholars working within the frame of political economy have primarily analyzed contemporary Islamic movements in terms of "identity politics" or the "politics of counter mobilization" as an integral part of the forces and process of modernization. The turn towards Islam is considered a function of people's search for collective identity arising out of their migration from localized rural life to mass urban life. Hakan Yavuz's *Islamic Political Identity* (2003) and more recently Rainer Hermann's *Where Is Turkey Headed? Cultural Battles in Turkey* (2014) reflect this perspective while analyzing Islamic political and social movements, including the Gülen Movement in Turkey. A full-fledged application of this approach to the Gülen Movement is reflected in Joshua Hendricks's *Gülen: The Ambiguous Politics of Market Islam in Turkey and the World* (2013). Locating the Gülen Movement within the framework of "Muslim Politics," as developed by Eickelman and Piscatori,[79] the author analyzes the movement primarily in terms of advancing its own share in the Turkish national, secular market in the name of Islam, which produces a culture of ambiguity within the Movement arising out of a contradiction between the Movement's emphasis on Islamic ideals and goals and its everyday participation in the secular market realities. Thus, in all these works, Islam emerges as an "instrumental, "oppositional" category and flourishes on the notion of "other"; hence, like much of SMT, this research is not very helpful to decode the contours of Islamic movements like the Gülen Movement, notwithstanding the merit of these perspectives on other accounts.

The Protestant Ethic

One is indeed surprised to see a large number of works, mostly produced by Turkish scholars, employing the Weberian thesis of Protestant ethics to account for the material success of the Gülen Movement in Turkey. Yavuz (2013) even titles one of his chapters "Islamic Ethics and the Spirit of Capitalism: Pietistic Activism in the Market," which closely resembles Weber's seminal work *The Protestant Ethic and the Spirit of Capitalism.*[80] In this model, hard work, self-regulation, accountability, ascetic life, trust, solidarity, self-sacrifice, honesty, fairness, equity, and service—all traits considered to be intrinsic Protestant ethics—are re-discovered in the Islamic writings of Gülen and transformed into everyday Islamic values which prove to be vital for capitalist development along with the democratic transformation of Turkey in recent years, at least until 2012. Though these writings are important and have merits of their own, a critical engagement with the application of the Weberian framework to the Gülen Movement raises more questions than answers about the relationship between the Gülen Movement and the recent capitalist development of Turkey, even if both share a similar sociological process.

First, the pertinent question, for Weber, was why capitalism/modernity was able to develop in "Christian" Europe and not in "Arab" Islamic lands, the answer to which he found in the "Protestant Ethics" of Christianity that he found lacking in Islam. Whether Weber intended it or not, one consequence of this exercise was that Weber forever de-recognized the Islamic contribution to the development of modernity and placed the origin of modernity exclusively within the genealogy of Christianity.[81] The subsequent writings of European scholars have transformed the Weberian thesis into the "authoritative universal discourse of development" as Edward Said put it in *Orientalism* (1978). Second, the Weberian discourse was situated in the context of a rising (Christian) Europe and declining Islamic world and therefore could not free itself from the framework of "self (Christian West) vs. other (Islamic East)." On the other hand, the Weberian element of comparison is certainly found missing in Gülen's ethical and moral construction of Islam, and this brings into question the application of the Weberian thesis to explain the linkage between the Gülen Movement and the capitalist development of Turkey.

Second, the doctrine of Protestant ethics rests on the idea of "Calling," wherein engagement in worldly affairs is considered the highest form of fulfillment of the individual's obligation as commanded by God, and material success was understood as a "sign of God." However, in the Hizmet Movement every act of the believer is done for the sake of Allah *without expectation of return*. In Islamic tradition, Muslims should do all that is necessary for success, yet with full acceptance that it is only God who knows and determines success or failure, which cannot be made known to human beings. Moreover, Gülen's discourse nowhere appropriates the Weberian–Protestant idea of "Calling" or "Elective Affinity" in Islamic terms, notwithstanding the fact that some of the volunteers in the Movement consider themselves "elected" or "chosen" by God to serve Islam.[82] In fact, it would be tantamount to the basic foundations of Islam as Muslims are expected to work ceaselessly to obtain "God's pleasure" without in any way getting to know whether God is pleased with them or not. Gülen himself states, "God's will is unknowable, and His predetermined fate for each believer cannot be foreseen… In the face of uncertainty, the Muslim must be tireless in performing as many good deeds as possible."[83] Rejecting any parallel between Hizmet and Protestant ethics Kerim Balcı states, "the latter framework cannot be applied to Hizmet as it works on the Islamic principle of the "unexpectability of expecting success."[84]

Third, Protestantism gave birth to two contradictory trends: the emergence of Protestant fundamentalism based upon the individualized, authoritative reading of the Bible at the cost of undermining the role of tradition in interpreting the religious text, and second, the individualization of religious experience leading to the secularization and democratization of Christian societies. Although there are a very few writings that portray the Gülen Movement as an "Islamic fundamentalist movement," a large proportion of scholarship—both Turkish and non-Turkish—associates the latter trend with the Gülen Movement. In fact, the idea that the Protestant movement led to the secularization and democratization of Western societies and a similar process has been unleashed by the Gülen Movement rests on three assumptions: (a) Protestantism broke the monopoly of Church authority over religious resources by vernacularizing the religious texts and challenging the legitimacy of the Church to function as intermediate agency between individual and God, leading to the individualization of religious experience and democratization of religious knowledge and authority, (b) it introduces a this-worldly orientation to Christianity which in turn promotes the idea of secularization, and (c) the location of religious authority shifted from clergy to text.

However, there is no Church in Islam and neither is the *'ulama* the functional equivalent of Church as has been claimed by many Western scholars. Unlike the Church, which is *of* society, the *'ulama*, at least the Sunni, if not Shia, is a diffused, decentralized entity with localized influence and is embedded within the Muslim society.[85] It has never blocked or denied the individual's inalienable (Islamic) right to have access, read, interpret and vernacularize the Islamic religious text. In fact, the development of various Schools of Law and Sufism, along with streams of various discordant Islamic voices against Islamic orthodoxy that have kept emerging throughout Islamic history, testifies to continuous intra-Islamic competition over Islamic normativity that remains open-ended. Moreover, despite the concentration of religious authority in the *'ulama* and Sufi Sheikhs during medieval times, the ultimate authority resides with the Qur'anic text. Thus, the forces that were unleashed by the Protestant movement have been an integral part of Islamic doctrine and history, yet did not result in the Western kind of democratization and secularization of Muslim societies.

In fact, the strength of the Protestant movement does not lie in its vernacularizing or translating the religious text into the native language and its mass circulation but in making them as legitimate and authoritative as reading the religious text and performing the rituals in Latin.[86] In the Islamic imagination, the Arabic language—in which the Qur'an was revealed—remains a sacred language that has never been questioned. Attempts at the "Turkification of Islam" and "Persianization of Islam" could not jolt the Arabic monopoly on Islam, but rather were considered un-Islamic by pious Muslims, including Turkish and Persian Muslims. In fact, Arabic came back to Iran under the government of the Islamic Republic of Iran and has now, under the AKP government, been re-introduced in Turkish elementary schools as one of the foreign language options along with English, German, and French.[87] All important Islamic thinkers, including Gülen, have greatly stressed attaining mastery of

Arabic in order to develop the "*correct*" understanding of Islam, notwithstanding the translation of Islamic religious texts into several native languages. In short, Islamic legitimacy without the Arabic language is near impossible.

Finally, it is difficult to imagine a parallel between Gülen's vision of Islamic capitalism, if he has one, and Protestant capitalism, which unleashed the process leading to the colonization (which Kerim Balcı has described as the "peak of Western modernity"[88]), de-humanization, and enslavement of large parts of the earth by Western industrial culture. Thus, it would be unjust to argue that Gülen's Islamic ethical discourse envisions the development of capitalism, which is disrespectful and insensitive to other cultures and traditions. Sabine Dreher in her study on the Hizmet business community found that on account of Islamic ethics Hizmet Islamic capitalism represents an "alternative globalization project based on service, free markets, education, and outreach through interfaith dialog."[89] Phyllis E. Bernard found Hizmet's model of business similar to the nineteenth century Quaker Capitalism in the West which gives priority to "human welfare" than profit.[90]

If the relevance of the Protestant movement for the Gülen Movement lies in transformation of the human consciousness from an other-worldly orientation to this-worldly orientation, then Gülen finds the inspiration for the same within the tradition of Islam, particularly in Imam Rabbani's theory of two *mims*, and not in the European history of Protestantism. Imam Rabbani saw the crisis of Islam in terms of growing imbalance between the human (material) and spiritual dimensions of the tradition of Prophet Muhammad and sought to overcome the same by restoring the balance between the two. According to the records of Sirhindi's correspondence, *The Maktubat*:

> [The Prophet] Muhammad had in his life time two individuations (*ta'ayyun*): the bodily human and the spiritual-angelic. These two individuations were symbolized by the loops of the two *mims* of his name. The bodily individuation guaranteed the uninterrupted relationship between the Prophet and his community and consequently ensured its spiritual well-being. The spiritual one, on the other hand, directed itself toward the Divine and received the continuous flow of inspiration emanating from that source. A proper

> balance was thus maintained between the worldly and the spiritual aspects of Muhammad's personality, and the Islamic community was continuously under guidance both prophetic and divine. Since the Prophet's death, however, his human individuation has been gradually weakening while the spiritual one has been steadily gaining strength. Within a thousand years the human individuation disappeared altogether. Its symbol, the first *mim* of Muhammad, disappeared along with it and was replaced by an *alif* standing for divinity (*uluhiyat*). Muhammad came to be Ahmad. He was transformed into a purely spiritual being, no longer interested in the affairs of the world. The disappearance of his human attributes … had … an adverse impact on his community which lost the lights of prophetic guidance emanating from Muhammad's human aspect…. Sirhindi … agrees that the ideal prophetic period was followed by a gradual decline caused by the growing imbalance in the performance of prophetic tasks.[91]

What attracts most of Turkish scholars to draw a parallel between the Weberian thesis of Protestant ethics and the Gülen Movement, when a good number of scholars have not only successfully questioned the Weberian contention that Islam lacks elements of Protestant ethics but found this parallel between the two deceptive at best and without much basis? For example, Turner, a distinguished scholar, writes, "When Weber attempted to show that, in addition, Islam as a religion of warriors produced an ethic which was incompatible with the 'spirit of capitalism,' he was hopelessly incorrect in purely factual terms,"[92] and further states:

> [I]t is ironic that when Islamic reformers in the nineteenth century came to define a new set of motives for Islam in the modern age, their analysis of the problem of social change was almost entirely Weberian. There was a parallel between the values of Islamic Reform and those of the Protestant Ethic. Yet, as I hope to show, this parallel is deceptive and should not be treated as any direct confirmation of the Protestant Ethic thesis.[93]

Maxime Rodinson in *Islam and Capitalism* (1978) examines the Weberian thesis and finds it untrue as Islam possesses all features and qualities of Protestant ethics. Peter Gran's *Islamic Roots of Capitalism:*

Egypt 1760-1850 also arrived at the similar conclusion, that Islamic ethics are not an obstacle to the development of capitalism. Ira M. Lapidus also cautions the reader against drawing any parallel between eighteenth- and nineteenth-century *tajdid* movements in the Muslim world and Protestant ethics:

> *Tajdid*, then, is the type of religion which directs the believer toward commitment to abstract symbols and to social action in the interest of social reform. It turns highly developed intellectual and moral capacities and unfulfilled emotions into the commitments to worldly action. However, this is not quite the same as the "Protestant Ethic." *Tajdid* favors dynamic worldly activity, but such activity is not directed to economic accumulation. Rather it is channeled in prescribed ways into religious devotion, control of emotion, pious good works, and the dynamic aggrandizement of the Muslim community, or warfare to expand the realm of Islam. The worldly activity called for by the Islamic ethos is not the systematic reconstruction of the world, but the correct practice of Islam and the extension of the boundaries of Islamic domination.[94]

One plausible explanation for the attraction of the Weberian Protestant thesis to a large number of scholars, mostly Turkish, working on the Gülen Movement is that the framework legitimizes (or fits into) their Euro-centric, nationalist-oriented discourse of development as well as the discourse of Turkish exceptionalism or Turkish Islam to explain the linkage between the Gülen Movement and the economic development of Turkey.

Tasawwuf, Turkish Islam, and Turkish exceptionalism

No dialogue with the scholarly works on the Gülen Movement would be complete without reference to *tasawwuf* (Sufism) and the formation of Turkish Islam. Love and Tolerance—the two attributes of Sufism and Turkish Islam that underpin Gülen's philosophy of Islam—are celebrated among Turkish intellectuals to the extent of transforming them into an inter-related analytical category to explain the success of the Gülen Movement. Many Turkish scholars genuinely believe that the Gülen Movement—an Islamic breakthrough in terms of harnessing the resources of tradition and modernity for the purpose of serving humanity with a vision of peaceful co-existence—was and is possible only within the Turkish zone. Identifying the Gülen Movement as a moment of "Islamic Enlightenment," Yavuz poses a question in a Weberian sense: *Why did the Islamic Enlightenment take place in Turkey and not in other Muslim societies*? He found the answer to this question in the Turkish-Sunni-Hanafi and Sufi tradition of Islam, the reforms of Kemal Atatürk, and the historical pattern of relationship between Islam and the state in Turkey. Kerim Balcı emphatically stated at the end of my interview with him, "Hizmet could not have found a better cultural context than that of Modern Turkey, with its unique historical experience with juxtaposition of Islam and secularism, Sufism and religious Orthodoxy, Christianity and Islam and the relatively a-political mindset free of the torments of Colonialism which poised the Muslim-Arab mindset, who would have reservations about the dialogic approach of Hizmet."[95]

Though of late Fethullah Gülen is trying to lift Islam above its national-cultural attributes, the romanticization of the Ottoman past and nationalist current is quite palpable in the majority of writings of Turkish scholars on the Gülen Movement, as well as among the volunteers in the Movement. But the moot question here is: what is so specific about the Turkish Sufi tradition and Islam, which is not found among other Muslim societies? In what ways does the Turkish-Islamic social formation differ from Arab or Iranian or South Asian Islamic social formations? Is the Hanafi tradition of Islam specific to Turks and not found in other Muslim societies? South Asia is another geographical region where the Hanafi tradition of Islam is the most dominant and where a "functional democracy" continues to survive despite interruption by military or civil forces. Is the Turkish history and past free of violence and if not, then did Islam have any role in that violence? Does the Naqshbandi Sufi orientation espouse an understanding of a more action-oriented Islam than the Sufi tradition in other Muslim nations, which is mostly of a speculative nature? Moreover, as the Erdoğan-led AKP government has resurrected the Kemalist authoritarian structure and is dismantling the democratic gains that Turkey achieved during the last two decades, it raises more questions on the linkage between the thesis of Turkish exceptionalism or Turkish Islam and the democratic development of Turkey.

CHAPTER 3

LOCATING GÜLEN AND THE MOVEMENT: BEYOND TRADITIONAL AND MODERN

What comes out of the preceding analysis of literature on the Gülen Movement is the problematic of locating it within the discourse of Islam and modernity. Notwithstanding the desirability of a "modernist" framework on account of its historical and contemporary relevance, at least in the Turkish setting, this framework poses two specific problems in terms of analysis of religious phenomena in general and the Gülen Movement in particular. First, scholars working within the paradigm of modernity tend to employ a "modern" understanding of religion to analyze religious movements, including the Gülen Movement, despite the fact that contemporary religious movements are directed towards the "unsettling" of this "modern" understanding of religion. The post-Reformation, modern understanding of religion not only privatizes and spiritualizes religion, reduces it to the level of a set of fixed principles of spirituality, mostly related to ethics and morality applicable to the private realm, and makes it unfit for producing any "useful social good," but also determines the particular form in which religion has to exist and to be practiced.

In other words, religion must be subjected to a secular disciplinary process in order to give effect to a secular modern world. Thus, the modern understanding of religion is the product of a power relationship between the religious and modern secular world, not a consequence of an evolutionary process of human civilization from religious to secular as emphasized by the theories of modernity. It was only when scientific rationality became authoritative as the sole universal form of reasoning—singularly allowed to conceptualize the temporal world we live in and to regulate its economies and societies—that religious forms of reasoning became irrelevant and non-rational. The idea of progress embedded in the theory of Evolution has at best legitimized the hegemony of secular modern discourse.

Beneath this modernist thrust of regulating and controlling religion lies a modernist desire to eliminate religion as a counter source of political loyalty which is exclusively demanded or reserved for the secular nation-state. The birth of the modern state—which means the "All-Knowing State/Sovereign"—has replaced the notion of the All-Knowing God/Sovereign. The religious upsurge in recent years throughout the globe (Islamic resurgence in the Muslim world, Moral Majority phenomenon in the United States, New Religious Movements in Europe, Liberation Theology in Latin America, Sinhala Buddhism in Sri Lanka, Hindutva in India, etc.) in part is also a reaction to the secular's treatment of religion.

This modern articulation of religion emerged in the context of the bitter sixteenth-century Church-State struggle in the European zone, leading to the separation of religion and politics as the "modern" principle of statecraft that continues to shape and influence the political elites' perception of religion across all cultural contexts. The *specific* religion, religious tradition, and religious problem (Christianity and Church) of a *specific* cultural-political context—Europe—was generalized and universalized and uniformly applied to all religions and religious traditions irrespective of whether other non-Christian religious traditions (or for that matter Christian traditions in non-European contexts) have ever functioned as "Church" or ever witnessed anything similar to the "Church–State struggle." In other words, "Church" became synonymous with "religion."

One implication of this modernist process is to simplify not only the notion of religion in terms of spirituality with a common doctrine of God, Prophet, Book and rituals, but also the development of the "scientific" outlook that treats tradition (meaning religious tradition for all practical purposes) as a homogenous, fixed, closed, static entity and, an obstacle to the development of modernity. Guided by this notion of religion, tradition and idea of progress, the modernized political class of most of the post-colonial or semi-colonial nations embarked on the "reform" of religious and cultural traditions in the name of equity, justice, development, and progress. In terms of effective public policies, the measures range from establishing control, regulation, and supervision to elimination of religious influence with variations in degree. The underlying idea of reform was to strengthen the state as well as to modernize "traditional" societies. Though certain reforms, particularly related to women, did help in the elevation of women, the political process resulted in "disfiguring" religion, dislocating it from its place in society, marginalizing religious forces, and finally unsettling the historically evolved forms of interaction between religion and the political establishment, which in turn became one factor, among many, in politicizing the religion and religious resistance.

It does not require any anthropological insight to debunk this modernist understanding of religion and tradition. A cursory look at the history of religion demonstrates how the imagination and meaning of the notions of God, Prophet and Book not only differ from one religious tradition to another but also from one sect, denomination or school to another within the same religious tradition. Islamic history is perennially pregnant with a discourse on the Islamic doctrine of *Tawhid* (monotheism) and *Iman* (faith). There is no finality and consensus on the interpretation and understanding of various Islamic doctrines and principles. Thus, Islam, or for that matter any religion, is the name of a whole gamut of traditions of religious practice. Talal Assad has called this religious practice a "discursive tradition" consisting of historically evolving discourses embodied in the doctrines, practices, and institutions of communities.[1] A discursive tradition is a formation that has produced historically contingent categorizations of doctrine and practice. In this sense, a tradition is continuously constituted, formed, modified, or rejected through an open-ended process of rational, interpretative debates and arguments centered on texts as well as oral practices. A religious tradition is continuously formed and modified in a similar process. This contrasts with such categories as "reformism" and "scripturalism," which many, including anthropologists, have too often taken for granted as fixed, knowable forms. This way of understanding of Islam makes more sense than Geertz's conceptualization of Islam between High (Urban, *'ulama*) and low Islam (Sufi, rural)[2] as what is called an "Islamic tradition" is arrived at or constituted out of this interactive process between the two.

Asad, a noted anthropologist of religion, provides a comprehensive definition of a tradition and an Islamic tradition:

> A tradition consists essentially of discourses that seek to instruct practitioners regarding the correct form and purpose of a given practice that, precisely because it is established, has a history. These discourses relate conceptually to a past (when the practice was instituted, and from which the knowledge of its point and proper performance has been transmitted) and a future (how the point of that practice can best be secured in the short or long term, or why it should be modified or abandoned), through a present (how it is linked to other practices, institutions, and social conditions). An Islamic discursive tradition is simply a tradition of Muslim discourse that addresses itself to conceptions of the Islamic past and future, with reference to a particular Islamic practice in the present.[3]

Similarly, Alasdair MacIntyre, a moral philosopher and a critic of modernity, has defined tradition as

> an argument extended through time in which certain fundamental agreements are defined and redefined in terms of two kinds of conflict: those with critics and enemies external to the tradition who reject all or at least key parts of those fundamental agreements, and those internal, interpretative debates through which the meaning and rationale of fundamental agreements come to be expressed and by whose progress a tradition is constituted.[4]

Asad also rightly questions the modernist attempt to provide the universal definition of religion: "There cannot be a universal definition of religion, not only because its constituent elements and relationships are historically specific, but because the definition is itself the historical product of discursive processes."[5] He further highlights the fallacy of bundling all regions and religious traditions in a single conception of religion and states:

> Anyone familiar with what is called the sociology of religion will know of the difficulties involved in producing a conception of religion that is adequate for cross-cultural purposes. This is an important point because one's conception of religion determines the kinds of questions one thinks are askable and worth asking.

> But far too few would-be anthropologists of Islam pay this matter serious attention. Instead, they often draw indiscriminately on ideas from the writings of the great sociologists (e.g., Marx, Weber, Durkheim) in order to describe forms of Islam, and the result is not always consistent.[6]

Asad, MacIntyre, and similar works by others help in escaping the binary framework of modernity vs. tradition as well as overcoming the orientalist, essentialist paradigm of Islam and modernity, which is most common in the many writings dealing with the issue of the relationship between Islam and modernity or Islamic movements including the Gülen Movement. Many, particularly Islamic reformist intellectuals and leaders, have sought to avoid this trap by making a distinction between modernization and Westernization; the former representing Western science and technology, while the latter stands for Western cultural values. One can find traces of this framework operating among Muslim reformist leadership and intellectuals ranging from Jamal al-Din Afghani to Bediüzzaman Nursi. The Islamic synthesis/modernist model of the late nineteenth century (premised on the synthesis of Western science and technology and Muslim culture and values), which is associated primarily with Egyptian Muhammad Abduh and which became the dominant discourse of post-colonial states in the Muslim world, could not succeed as it was not perceived as a sufficiently authentic Islamic model by many Muslims. With the all-round failure of this model in addressing the material as well as spiritual grievances of the Muslim community in the major parts of the Muslim world, Islam in its politicized, orientalist form, or what is called "Islamism," came back as an intellectual discourse claiming to represent the "authentic" Islam.

One way of escaping "essentializing" Islam as well as "essentializing" modernity is to treat tradition and modernity as a continuous interactive process in which each contains elements of the other. This interacting process between tradition and modernity, or what is called "continuity and change," received a blow from the construction of a notion of modernity that transforms "tradition" into "traditional" and thereby introduces a mental block between tradition and modernity, making them two distinct process and discourses and antithetical to each other. This was due to the modernist reading of tradition in ideological terms. However, this way of conceptualizing modernity and tradition has received a serious blow in many recent writings that have demonstrated the futility of the modernist framework to understand the process of social change. This comes out clearly in the definition of tradition provided by Asad and MacIntyre in which tradition is more appropriately conceptualized as discourses extended through time, as a framework of inquiry rather than a set of unchanging doctrines or culturally specific mandates. MacIntyre points out how liberalism constitutes a tradition of modernity itself.[7] Brown also notes,

> A tradition emerges from the prism of modernity as multi-colored responses. Some responses will show the effect of modernity much more dramatically than others, but none will be entirely untouched. At the same time each color of the spectrum, each different response, is clearly rooted in tradition. All responses to modernity from a religious tradition and even those that seem to have left the tradition altogether behind, maintain certain continuity with the tradition, just as each band of spectrum is present in the light entering a prism.[8]

Earlier, John O. Voll also highlighted the pitfall of the binary framework of modernity vs. tradition and examined modern intellectual Islamic styles in the Muslim world from the perspective of continuity and change.[9]

Making a distinction between "tradition" and "traditional," Haj defines the former as relating "not simply to the past or its repetition but rather to the pursuit of an ongoing coherence by making reference to a set of texts, procedures, arguments, and practices," something parallel to the history of modernity, and says that

> this body of prescribed beliefs and understandings (intellectual, political, social, practical) frames the practices of Islamic reasoning and provides a useful framework for understanding how the function and the meaning of Islamic arguments change over time and in response to both internal and external challenges facing the tradition. It is these collective discourses, incorporating a variety of positions, roles, and tasks that form the corpus of Islamic knowledge from which a Muslim scholar (*'alim*) argues for and refers to previous judgments of others. It is from within this tradition of Is-

> lamic reasoning that claims are made and evaluated and are either rejected or accepted as Islamic.[10]

It is within the above theoretical framework that one needs to situate Gülen's discourse. Gülen first comes from an Islamic tradition of scholarship, draws his inspiration from Islamic ideas and history, particularly from the life and conduct of Prophet Muhammad, articulates his thinking in Islamic terms, and mostly speaks from within the Islamic tradition. It is from within the paradigm of Islamic tradition that he engages himself with the issues of religion, revelation, reason, science, secularism, democracy, pluralism, human rights, women rights, terrorism, interfaith, education, and so on. He is certainly a part of the Islamic tradition of Reform and Renewal (*islah* and *tajdid*). As Gülay rightly observed, "Gülen's religious worldview is internally consistent and does not utilize scientific facts or historical examples as crutches. It derives its authenticity from the proclaimed divine authority and absolute truth of the Qur'an. The encounter with modernity does not compel Gülen to compromise the pillars of faith."[11]

The cosmos of Gülen is that of Islam ranging from Prophet Muhammad to Bediüzzaman Said Nursi, from where he derives his inspiration, his moral strength, and his vision of the good life. Thus, he states,

> From the philosophical thinking to the truth of Sufism, from the established view of religion to its moral dimension, we will take our models from the most enlightened, the brightest era, of each we are always proud, and which we consider to be golden slice of time, and we will leave the tapestry of our future, thread by thread, on the canvas of time. In this tapestry Jalal al-Din Rumi will come together with Taftazani, Yunus Emre will sit on the same prayer mat with Mahdumguli, Fuzuli will embrace Mehmed Akif, Ulug Bey will salute Abu Hanifa, Hodja Dehhani will sit knee to knee with Imam Ghazali, Muhy al-Din ibn Arabi will throw roses to Ibn Sina, Imam Rabbani will be thrilled by the glad tidings for Bediüzzaman Said Nursi. From such a great past, with its wide panorama, the men of stature will come together and whisper to us the charm of salvation and revival.[12]

What is crucial to understand here is that unlike the earlier modern Islamic reformers and thinkers with a few exceptions (such as Muhammad Iqbal and Nursi) Gülen's structure of thinking is not Western; nor does he utilize Islamic discourses to legitimize or appropriate Western/ modern discourses and values. He primarily dwells upon the universal value of humanity as an integral part of Islam's fundamental doctrine and values.

If some of Islam's universal values are today celebrated as "modern" values, it does not mean that Gülen is legitimizing modern discourse in Islamic terms. Yavuz's *Towards an Islamic Enlightenment* is one such classic attempt, notwithstanding the fact that "Enlightenment" in the Muslim imagination occurs with Prophet Muhammad, which remains the blueprint of development for all successive Muslim generations. It would be utterly disrespectful and misleading to interpret Gülen's Islamic vision as a "modern" vision because in many ways Gülen's Islamic thinking is highly critical of modernity or the consequences of modernity, particularly its violent legacy and "commodification of life." More than Gülen himself, it is other scholars who have interpreted his ideas in terms of Islam and modernity or more precisely as an "Islamic response" to modernity or modern conditions. One scholar bitterly complains of this scholarly tendency while reflecting upon Nursi,

> [A]ccording to Mardin [referring to Şerif Mardin's work on Nursi], Bediüzzaman's message was shaped by the modernizing world into which he was thrust. There is no place in Mardin's study for theological concepts such as sincerity in worship, devotion, God's approval, Knowledge of God, and love of God. This should not lead us to discuss the facts of Nursi's life. Yes, he lived in modern times. However, Nursi's main concern was neither to oppose, nor support modernity.[13]

This statement, I believe, is equally relevant for a balanced understanding of Gülen. Therefore, it is of the utmost importance to locate and understand Gülen's ideas and praxis within the tradition of Islamic reasoning.

Looking from this perspective and in my understanding of Gülen's thought, it appears that Gülen espouses a non-traditional and non-modern perspective that prescribes an Islam-inspired, ethically and morally guided, modern, life process. This perspective is different from a great deal of literature on "alternative modernity" or "multiple modernity" that has been applied to what are called "transitional societies," including Muslim societies.[14] In these works, focus has shifted from a discourse of doctrinal complementarity between Islam and modernity to the *ways* of experiencing modernity in everyday lives and in the process creating diverse forms of living as modern and Muslim or what is called "Muslim modernities." A good number of such studies pertain to Muslim women's experience of modernity,[15] partly because women remain a site of interaction between traditional and modern values or an indicator for the measurement of "progress" in transitional societies.[16] More recently Bacık and Kurt applied a perspective of "amodernity" to understand the apolitical orientation of the Gülen Movement.[17] Although these writings are significant and at least have debunked the uniform application of Western modernity, they continue to treat "tradition" and "modernity" as two different, specific sets of ideas and processes without cross-fertilization of ideas of each other with an eventual result that most of these studies end up pointing to a trajectory of social change in Muslim societies from traditional to modern, notwithstanding the multiple overlapping layers of discourses of being modern.

On the other hand, the perspective of non-traditional and non-modern entails a "discursive space" that combines a continuum of tradition and modernity within each category. For instance, what is called "modern" ideas of equality, equity, liberty, freedom, justice, rights, human rights, women rights, pluralism, tolerance, and so on are deeply embedded within Islam since its inception. Both Islam and modernity have a long inclusive as well as exclusive tradition of interpretation of these ideas. Hence the relationship between the two is didactic and interactive, not antagonistic as is commonly understood. At best the difference between the two lies in terms of framing, articulation, and institutionalization of these ideas, which reflects a difference of tradition, time, and space not a difference over the ideas. Thus, "modernity" and "West," unlike in the writings of modern-day Islamists, do not appear as "other" in Gülen's narrative of Islam and Islamic history. Free from any perceived burden of threat from the West/modernity, Gülen is able to construct a non-political, non-ideological, non-homogenized, non-apologetic, and humanistic understanding of Islam.

More specifically, "non-traditional" refers to a conceptualization of tradition in the formation of "virtuous community" without following the routes of excessive focus on ritual and identity discourse, whereas "non-modern" reflects an approach that seeks an engagement with modern institutions, ideas, and values without internalizing the discourse of Western modernity. Thus, Gülen's Islamic discourse does not hinder his followers from interacting and working in a modern setting. As Eşref Potur explains, "what is important in Hizmet is *iman*. One can move into any structure with *iman*."[18] Similarly the Gülen Movement engages itself with the institutions and idea of modernity such as secularism, democracy, human rights, nationalism, and gender justice without indulging in the exercise of "Islamizing modernity" and without accepting the ontological and normative vision of modernity. Being primarily a "discursive space," as Gülen understands it, both Islam and modernity are subject to multiple interpretations that allow them to freely interact and cross-fertilize each other's ideas. This kind of articulation of Islam and modernity is clearly revealed in Gülen's position on the *complementarity* of Islam and democracy, a position that strives to be a bridge between a moderate interpretation of Islam with a moderate interpretation of democracy. Gülen does not attach to Islam or democracy, the most important attribute of modernity, any fixed, closed values but sees each as an open entity subject to interpretation for achieving higher moral ends.

The perspective of non-traditional and non-modern also helps in unearthing Gülen's inclusive vision of Islam that prescribes diverse ways of being Muslim in everyday modern settings. The problem of how to be Muslim and modern together, which has eluded many Muslim philosophical minds over the last two centuries, is resolved in Gülen's paradigm of Islam, not due to any attempt to "Islamicize modernity" or due to any synthesis between Islam and modernity, but partly due to the fact that this paradigm does not attempt to "singularize" Islam or Muslim identity and various experiences of modernity but offers multiple ways of being Muslim on the basis of classification of "form" and "content." The "forms" (externalities, mode of physical appearance, ways of working, modes of representation) may be modern, but the content remains Islamic—Islam's universal values and essentials of faith.

CHAPTER 4

ISLAMIC MODERNISM/REFORMISM: REVISITING THE DEBATES

Having laid out the necessity to locate Fethullah Gülen and the Movement within the trajectory of Islamic tradition, it is important to ask: what is Gülen's approach to Islam, the Qur'an and Islamic history? Does his approach reflect a continuity of the late nineteenth-century framework of what is called "Islamic modernism" or "Islamic reformism"? Or is his approach more akin to the pre-modern Islamic framework of *ijtihad* and *tajdid* that continued till the mid-nineteenth century? Or does Gülen offer a new paradigm of *ijtihad* and *tajdid*? One needs to examine these questions in order to understand the complex facets of the Gülen Movement that defy, to my understanding, the parameters of the "traditional or modern" framework of analysis of a social phenomenon.

However, a brief revisit to the discourse of modernity and the nature of its challenges to the Muslim, as well as Muslims' varied responses to it, is essential in order to mark out the similarities and dissimilarities of the Gülen Movement to pre-modern or modern Islamic movements.

Modernity and its challenges to Muslim societies

Certainly, over the last five hundred years, Modernity has been a hegemonic secular discourse and knowledge formation that has deeply affected all other knowledge systems, life styles, values, and thinking patterns. It has transformed conceptions of time, space, property, work, identity, marriage, gender relations, body, nation, authority, government, and state, as well as relationships between individual, family, community, and state.[1] Modernity encapsulates four inter-related aspects: (1) the principle of structural differentiation; (2) the principle of functional specialization; (3) the principle of cultural secularization; and (4) the principle of rationalization of rights and authority. The first two are inter-related and broadly belong to the cultural face of modernity—the legacy of reason, humanism, science, and technology. They concern the movement of human life from simple (traditional—marked by undifferentiated structure, roles, and functions) to complex (modern—marked by differentiated, specialized structures, roles, and functions). This aspect of modernity has not been a contested issue in the Muslim world and is normally accepted as a natural course of development. The Muslim world itself underwent the process of differentiation and specialization. This is reflected in the development of specialization in the study of natural and physical sciences—mathematics, astronomy, logic, Algebra, medicine; in the study of Islam—Qur'an, Hadith, Sunna, Tawhid, Sharia, law and theology; and in the study of humanities and literature—philosophy, theology, and Arabic philology. The science of hermeneutics was well developed in Muslim societies before it travelled to Europe and became a "modern" method of analysis and description. More than any other Muslim empire, it was the Ottoman Empire that demonstrated the marked feature of a highly developed bureaucracy and other specialized structures and functions, though the pace of differentiation and specialization might not have been as fast as it occurred in the West. Modernity in this physical form is therefore not new to the Muslim world in general and Turkey in particular. Reflecting upon the general development in Muslim societies, W. C. Smith notes, "Much of what characterizes other Muslims in the nineteenth and twentieth centuries, the Turks underwent in the eighteenth and nineteenth."[2]

It was the last two aspects of modernity, cultural secularization and rationalization of rights and authority—broadly pertaining to the domain of political modernity—that had a more recent direct bearing on the Muslim societies and therefore have been subject to fierce contestation and debates. Modernity in the form of the principle of cultural secularization refers to a unilinear movement of human history from religious to secular or what Weber called "disenchantment of the world," while rationalization of authority and rights implies a fundamental shift in the legitimization of all forms of authority and rights, particularly political authority, from God to human. In this form, modernity not only celebrated rationalism, democracy, liberalism, nationalism, scientism, secularism, and positivism as the "truth," and as the only pathways to achieve human freedom and material advancement, but also indulged in the demonization of non-Western cultures and peoples, particularly Islam, Muslims, Arabs, and Turks who lie in the neighborhood of European modernity. Centered on Islam and Muslims, it created a new discourse called "Orientalism"—an essentialist method of study about the "other" culture, people, and history.[3]

Modernity in this form or political modernity became overtly ideological; it announced the "death of God" and privileged a materialist conception of the "good life" over the religious conception of the good life. An aggressive Western modernity posed an existential dilemma to the Muslim world, whose understanding of progress and development was contingent upon the "correct practice of Islam." It posed a fundamental challenge to Muslims' conceptions of faith, identity, worldview, life styles, authority and sovereignty, justice, and social, political and economic relations. The dilemma of Muslims was best captured by W. C. Smith: "The fundamental spiritual crisis of Islam in the twentieth century stems from an awareness that something is awry between the religion which God has appointed and the historical development of the world which He controls."[4]

As political modernity intensifies its efforts to transform the world in its own mold—through the combination of persuasion, coercion, and imposition—various reactions, whether secular or religious, in the form of accommodation, rejection, violence, revolt, and acquisition with variations in degree emerged across various societies of the world—a process that continues to date. The responses were contingent upon how modernity was experienced within the various segments of societies that were affected by modernity, the nature of the relationship between the colonial powers and colonized societies, and the perception of the dominant elites—political, social, economic, religious and intellectual—of the subjugated societies about the Western colonial powers. Thus, the French assimilationist variety of modernity evoked a more violent response from the French-dominated colonies than the British somewhat accommodationist model of modernity drew from its colonies.

Further, if certain features of political modernity—liberty, equality, dignity, democracy, progress, and scientific achievement—were the source of attraction for the emerging Westernized elites, its other characteristics—political subjugation, denial of freedom, inhuman treatment, and demonization of the subject's culture and religion—appeared to them repulsive. This "dual colonial self" of the political elites of subjected societies vis-à-vis the dominant West was best captured by Ashis Nandy in his book *Intimate Enemy*—an enemy which was and is both an object of temptation and distress.[5] Owing to this duality of the colonial self, the response of dominant, mainstream elites to Western modernity was often marked by contradiction and ambiguity with apologetic overtones.

The Muslim world is no exception to this trend and witnessed diverse forms of Islamic responses to modernity. In fact, having been once at the power center of the world, scholars and leaders of the Muslim world have grappled far more seriously with the phenomenon of modernity than any other civilization in order to find answers to the "crisis of Islam," the "loss of power, prestige, and influence," and to save and restore the glory of Islam, state, and empire. This partly explains the recurrence and pervasiveness of the discourse of "Islam and modernity" in the Muslim world compared with the relationship between any other religious tradition and modernity. Nowhere was this scholarly engagement with modernity more intense than in Ottoman Turkey, which, as the political center of the Ottoman Empire and being geographically close to the center of modernity (Europe), was the first Muslim land to feel the overwhelming impact of modernity.[6]

Nature and responses of Islamic reformism/modernism

Islamic reformism or modernism emerged at the center stage of Islamic discourse in the late nineteenth century to address this "crisis of Islam." It was an attempt to overcome the internal malaise—the social, political, moral, and economic stagnation—of Muslim societies and the external political challenges of modern Europe. The model seriously reflected upon and debated the issue of reform and modernization (of Islam), particularly dealing with the prevailing state of education, the nature of politics and government, the condition of women, and the "corruption" of Sufi orders, so as to achieve the goal of Islamic modernity that entails ways of living as Muslim and modern together. Gülen is also considered to address the same dilemma of the Muslim community of combining Islam and modernity and is considered by many to successfully resolve this dilemma through his philosophy of education. It is for this reason many consider the Gülen Movement to be a continuum of Islamic modernism and have attempted to analyze the Gülen Movement within the perspective of Islam and modernism as discussed in the preceding chapter.

Though the genealogy of Islamic modernism can be traced to the reformist ideas of Khayr al-Din al-Tunisi, and the Tanzimat program of the Ottoman Empire, the representative figures of this trend were Jamal al-Din Afghani, Muhammad Abduh, Rashid Rida, Ali Abd al-Razik and Taha Hussein in the Arab world under the Ottoman Empire, and Sir Syed Ahmad Khan, Shibli Nomani, Muhammad Iqbal, Amir Ali, and Maulana Abul Kalam Azad in the Indian subcontinent under the British Empire, and Namık Kemal and Ziya Gökalp in Ottoman Turkey. In its liberal form Islamic modernism remained an intellectual movement without much impact on the Muslim masses and was characterized by al-Nahda and Salafism in the Arab world and the Aligarh and Nadwa movements in India respectively. In the Ottoman Turkish land, as the state itself had represented the trend of Islamic modernism since the Tanzimat era, it could not generate a "liberal" socio-religious movement from below as in the Arab parts of the Ottoman Empire or in the Indian subcontinent.

In terms of social support, it drew strength from a significant section of the Westernized middle class, who were aspiring to a relatively liberalized version of Islam than the then-existing Islamic orthodoxy. In terms of public policies, Islamic modernism came to be associated with the social reformist agenda, particularly concerning women, of post-colonial Muslim states. On the other hand, in its overtly politicized form Islamic modernism was manifested in the development of Hasan al-Banna's Ikhwan al-Muslimin (Muslim Brotherhood) and Mawlana Maududi's Jammat-e-Islami. They constructed a political theology of the Islamic state, a derivative of the European nation-state, as a pre-condition to overcoming the all-round crisis in Muslim society.

Despite coming from diverse national, class, and sectarian backgrounds these advocates of Islamic modernism display a common concern, approach, and outlook, notwithstanding the differences in their overall thrust. The first noticeable thing is that their structure of thinking was very much "Western" and was heavily influenced by the political reading of the West. In other words, it is the "Political West," rather than "Cultural West," that informs and shapes their Islamic articulation of the "idea" as well as the "direction" of the reform required for the re-generation of Muslim societies. The Muslim Reformers did not engage with the West directly through European liberal thought and its political theoretical order, but rather, they acknowledged it in a political context characterized by Western foreign domination, occupation, and colonial administration.

Almost all Islamic modernists including Sir Syed Ahmad Khan, Muhammad Abduh, Muhammad Iqbal, Jamal al-Din Afghani, and others had personally experienced the West by sojourn in the European countries.[7] They discovered the material success of the West primarily in political terms: a strong military, effective administration, institutions of justice, advanced fiscal regulation, homogenized and unified nation, strong leadership and democratic form of government and separation of religion and politics. In particular, they identified four elements behind the rise of Europe: evolutionism, nation-state, representative form of government, constitutionalism and rule of law, and scientific and technological development. And conversely, they attributed the under-development of their societies, by comparison, to the "backwardness" of the traditional political system: autocratic and unjust ruler, illiteracy, ignorance, disunity, non-application of Sharia, etc.

Referring to the nineteenth-century Islamic modernists Aziz al-Azmeh has underlined the "Western" structure of their polemics, "Classical Islamic reformism was a curious mixture of organicist historicism and evolutionism, with a liberal-constitutionalist and utilitarian interpretation of the scriptures."[8] It is this vision that directed their approach towards Islam and Islamic history, in selecting the themes and precedents of Islamic history and in identifying the agenda for Islamic reform, which mostly concerned the state of governmental affairs, education, improvement in the status of women, science, and Sufi orders, as well as shaping their discourse on the complex issue of the relationship between revelation and reason, Islam and science, and Islam and democracy.

The interpretive efforts of these scholars, as gleaned from their writings, was aimed at "imagining" Islam in the Western form or bringing Islamic doctrine and practices closer to "modern" social (liberalized gender/sexual morality), economic (capitalism and market-centered economy), and political (nation-state and representative government) realities. Not surprisingly, their discourses focused upon reformulating Islamic doctrines and practices to underline the "correct" (modern) practice of Islam: monogamy as opposed to polygamy (the Qur'anic position of a man's entitlement to have four wives is only possible under certain conditions including equal treatment of all wives, which is not humanly possible), equal status of women, "sanctity of private property," and the principle of democratic governance in the form of *shura* (consultation, representative government), *maslaha* (public interest, principle of welfarism), *Ijma* (*'ulama*'s consensus, people's opinion or consent) and *ijtihad* (right to interpret the Islamic text or reasoning), as against the principle of *taqlid* (imitation of past practice).

Second, most Islamic modernists saw the solution to the "crisis of Islam" primarily in political and educational reform. Ideas of political reform ranged from Afghani's[9] advocacy of the political unity of the global Muslim community under one strong leadership—whether Indian, Iranian, Egyptian, Sudanese, or Ottoman—to the political ideas of justice, equality and freedom, consultation, delegation of power and some kind of representative government, albeit couched in Islamic terms and idioms, as advocated by a large number of political elites and scholars across the Muslim empires.[10] The obsession with the "reform of state" in the light of political developments in Europe was more palpable among the Ottoman Turkish scholars and elites than in other parts of Ottoman land. The prominent reformist voices were Namık Kemal (1840–1888), Abdullah Cevdet (1869–1932), Mansurzade Said (1864–1923), Ziya Gökalp, (1864–1923), Ali Suavi (1839–1878) and Şemseddin Sami Frasheri (1850–1904). This tendency drove Turkey towards Kemalism, under which Turkey underwent the most intense political experience of Westernization ever witnessed. This was not without reason as in the Ottoman Islamic discourse "the reform of state" emerged as the essential condition and agency to protect Islam, the empire, the republic and the "life, liberty and property" of the people. Development was not conceivable without factoring in the state—a political tradition that continues to date in Turkey and continues to tilt the balance in favor of the state in the case of conflict between state and civil society.[11]

The "idea of educational reform" was primarily intended to secure reconciliation or harmony between Islam and modernity by bringing the necessary reform in the field of higher education, whether through reform of the existing curriculum, focus on science, adoption of modern methods of teaching and examination systems, or establishment of modern higher educational institutions. The two prominent names associated with this aspect of Islamic modernism were Muhammad Abduh[12] in the Arab world and Sir Syed Ahmed Khan[13] in the Indian subcontinent. The former devoted himself, without much success, to reforming the educational curriculum of Al-Azhar university; the latter mobilized the resources of Muslim nobility in addition to the support of British colonialists to establish Muhammadan Anglo-Oriental College, which later was transformed into Aligarh Muslim University. Nursi pushed hard, without success, to open up an Islamic university in the Kurdish-dominated Eastern part of Turkey, both to benefit the Kurdish population and to demonstrate the compatibility between Islam and modernity.

Third, the approaches and methods of Islamic modernists were very much influenced by the inter-related sources and development of modern Europe: Protestantism, supremacy of reason, personalization/privatization of religion, the Western thesis of Muslim backwardness in terms of Imam Ghazali's (supposedly) declaration of the closing of the gate of *ijtihad* and the structure of the centralized, homogenized secular nation-state. The development of Protestantism in Europe in the sixteenth century is considered to have released the historical forces of the Reformation and Renaissance, which resulted in the present-day prosperity of European nations.

In the paradigm of Protestantism, the "Biblical text," not the Church or Clergy, emerged as the "central authority," the real meaning of which was considered to be distorted by the mediatory role of Church and Clergy. According to this paradigm, human reason is capable of discovering the true meaning of Christianity by having direct access to Bible—the Book of God—without any mediatory role of any agency. It identifies the excessive ritualism of Catholic Christian tradition as a source of corruption of the original Message of Christ. It "personalizes" the Christian religion by reconfiguring the Christian doctrines in terms of relationship between God and individual and making attainment of "salvation" reliant upon God's Calling and Election without the mediatory role of Church and Clergy. This trend led to the individualization of Christianity and is considered to have helped in the development of secular-democratic Europe and the West.

Influenced by the discourse of Protestantism, as outlined above, and its ensuing political development in Europe, the Islamic modernists resurrected the Qur'an as the site or the central text/authority for demonstrating the compatibility of Islam with reason, rationalism, science, democracy, secularism, and liberalism, on the one hand, and de-emphasized, diluted, or ignored, if not completely eliminated, the role of mediatory agencies—whether recorded or oral traditions (Hadith and Sunna) or School of Law or '*ulama* or Sufi saints—in discovering the correct meaning and practice of Islam as contained in the Qur'an, on the other hand. The Islamist modernists (particularly those coming from Arab backgrounds such as Muhammad Abduh, Rashid Rida and others) greatly stressed the philology of the Arabic language (what is called the Nahda movement—the revival of Arabic literature in the Arab world in late nineteenth century), its syntax, grammar, and the standardization of Arabic letters, in exploring the "correct" meaning and understanding of the Qur'an and Islam as practiced during the period of Prophet Muhammad and the Four Rightly Guided Caliphs.

The underlying thrust of "Back to the Qur'an" was to discover the "unadulterated" or *original* meaning and practice of Islam that was considered to be "adulterated" or "corrupted" over the period of many centuries through the process of "*localization* of Islam." This modernist spirit was best captured by Allama Iqbal: "the universal and impersonal character of the ethical ideals of Islam has been lost through a process of localization. The only alternative open to us, then is, to tear off from Islam the *hard crust* [emphasis mine] which has immobilized an essentially dynamic outlook on life, and to rediscover the original verities of freedom, equality, and solidarity with a view to rebuild our moral, social, and political ideals out of their original simplicity and universality."[14]

To this end, almost all Islamic modernists asserted the application of the principle of *ijtihad* (right to interpret and deduce analogy based on Islamic sources) and rejected the principle of *taqlid* (blind imitation by Muslims of past Islamic practices in general and of the words, interpretations, and practice of the imams of the four established schools of Islamic law—Hanafi, Shafii, Maliki and Hanbali). In their exercise of the principle of *ijtihad* they were broadly guided by the Western thesis that "Muslim backwardness" and "stagnation in Islamic thought" is the result of the "closing of the gate of *ijtihad*," which has been attributed to Imam Ghazali.

However, the phrase, "the closing of the gate of *ijtihad*" is not historically tenable, as anybody with a general Islamic knowledge can draw up a long list of individual Islamic reformers and scholars, including Ibn Taymiyya, Imam Rabbani, Shah Waliullah, Abdul Bin Wahhab, to name a few, who exercised the option of *ijtihad* in the post-Ghazali period. Also, as Landau-Tasseron points out, "*mujaddid* hadith served as an argument to prove that 'the gates of *ijtihad*' were never closed, since its continuation was guaranteed by the appearance every hundred years of the *mujaddid*."[15] In fact, the phrase "the closing of the gate of *ijtihad*" is, at best, a myth that does not correspond with the realities of Islamic history, though its scale of operation might have been slowed down in particular periods of Islamic history. In this regard, Gülen has rightly called the phrase an "extreme point of view."[16] One fails to understand, if the gate of *Ijtihad* was closed in the twelfth century in the Sunni Muslim world, how Muslim Empires such as the Ottoman, Mughal, and even Andalusia could have flourished in the post-Ghazali period.

However, with the advent of modernity as a discourse of social change that depicted the past traditions and narratives as obstacles to future development and progress, the Western, orientalist scholars invented the "theory of the closing of the gate of *ijtihad*" both as to describe the stagnation of Islamic thought in Muslim civilization, and to differentiate itself as a vibrant, dynamic, Christian civilization from the static, frozen, Islamic civilization. Under the spell of modernity, the Islamic modernists found in the expression of "the closing of the gate of *ijtihad*" a rational framework to diagnose "Muslim backwardness," as well as a solution to the "Muslim backwardness" in the "opening of gate of *ijtihad*." That this framework remained dominant for analyzing Muslim society is evident from a remark in the Foreword to Fazlur Rahman's *Islamic Methodology in History* in 1964:

> It was indeed unfortunate that Muslims during the preceding centuries closed the door of *ijtihad*, resulting in stagnation and lack of dynamism .... We hope that the Muslims, living under the stress

> and strain of modern times, will find enough food for thought in these publications resulting ultimately in rekindling in them the burning desire, nay the longing, for exercising *ijtihad*, the only pre-requisite for recapturing the pristine glory of Islam and for ensuring an honorable place for the Muslim Umma in the comity of progressive, dynamic and living nations of the world.[17]

One consequence of the heightened emerging reformist discourse of *ijtihad* was that all prominent Islamic reformers undertook the exercise of writing *tafsir* (commentary) of the Qur'an. Thus, Muhammad Abduh's *Risalah Tauhid* (The Theology of Unity), Syed Ahmad Khan's *Tafseer ul-Qur'an*, Bediüzzaman Said Nursi's *Risale-i Nur* and many others were all attempts to reinterpret the Qur'an in the light of the modern-day realities of science, rationalism, and democracy with a focus on demonstrating its timeless relevance, particularly to disprove the Western allegation that Islam is anti-rational. Afghani responded to Renan's description of Islam as a non-rationalist religion by resurrecting the rationalist foundation of Islam and introducing a modern method of reading the Qur'an that helped in the creation of a generation of Muslim activists and scholars with a critical outlook and alternative perspectives on such issues as the legitimacy of political rule, justice, the right to protest, humanity, the *umma*, *dawa*, etc. It was due to him that the Qur'anic verse, "Verily God will not change the condition of a people, until they change what is in themselves" became the motto of all Islamic modernists for change and progress.

Even Allama Iqbal provided a brilliant philosophical defense of the Islamic legacy of rationality, science, and freedom by quoting extensively from the Qur'an and called Islam a "religion of inductive intellect."[18] Sir Syed Ahmad Khan found Western/modern scientific discovery as "God's promise in action" parallel to "God's promise in words" as revealed in the Qur'an. Muhammad Abduh evolved a methodology of "essential vs. non-essential" in Islam in order to make Islam compatible with the modern philosophy of science and rationalism. In his zeal to reform Muslim society and make capitalist ethics acceptable to the wider Muslim populace, Muhammad Abduh even went to the extent of issuing a *fatwa* declaring it lawful "to deposit their money in the Postal Saving Banks where it would draw interest."[19] Much later, Nursi dwelt upon "proof" of the fundamental aspects of Islam—the existence of God, Resurrection, Hell and Heaven, Prophethood—from everyday life experience in accordance with the mandate of science.[20] It may be noted here that, among all Islamic modernists, Nursi was the only Islamic scholar who explained *how* Islam is compatible with modernity and science on the basis of logic, allegory, and empirical evidence from the universe or nature, while others boldly asserted the compatibility of Islam and modernity without any empirical or demonstrative effect. On the other hand, the votaries of Political Islam such as Mawlana Maududi, Hasan Al-Banna, Sayyid Qutb and Imam Khomeini based their Islamic reasoning on the Qur'an to reject any compatibility of Islam with any aspects of the West and constructed notion of the Islamic state parallel to the European nation-state.

Consequences of Islamic reformism/modernism

In their zeal to prove the rationalist foundation of Islam under the impact of Western modernity, many Islamic modernists first developed a critical outlook towards the Hadith and Sunna narratives, gradually moving to the position of suspecting the authenticity of many Hadith and Sunna narratives, and finally went to the extent of casting doubt upon the verses of the Qur'an that do not conform to the test of reason. As a result, even though the rhetoric of the superiority of revelation over reason was maintained, in practice the attempted balance between revelation and reason was tilted in favor of the latter.

Thus, Sir Syed Ahmad Khan, who initially defended the role of Hadith and Sunnah in a series in rejoinder to Muir's "Essay on the Life of Muhammad," gradually accepted the subordination of Hadith and Sunna to the Qur'an, then became critical of many of the Hadith narratives, developed a method to deduce the "authenticity" of Hadith narratives and "eventually came to reject almost all hadith as unreliable."[21] He even cast doubt on the authenticity of verses of the Qur'an that do not conform to human reason and nature. He categorically states,

> Thus, the only criterion for the truth of the religions which are present before us is whether the religion (in question) is in correspondence with the natural disposition of humankind, or with nature... After determining this criterion, I clarified that Islam is in full accordance with nature. So, I formulated 'Islam is nature and

nature is Islam.' This is a wholly correct proposition.[22]

For him, the Qur'an can be understood by any sound and enlightened mind: "Modern scientific discoveries are the manifestations of God's promises in reality, while the Qur'an presents God's promises in words." Based on this argument, Ahmad Khan suggested that the Scripture has to come to terms with the law of nature, including scientific discoveries. He therefore rejected miracles, as well as many Qur'anic descriptions, which he considered "supernatural" in their literal sense.[23] Though, unlike Syed Ahmad Khan, Muhammad Abduh did not see the Qur'an as a "Book of Science" but as a "Book of Guidance"[24] to guide human conduct, he eventually developed an ambivalent position on the authenticity of many Hadith narratives.[25]

The same outlook led the Islamic modernists to develop a very critical outlook on Sufi practices and ritualism and held them responsible for the backwardness of Muslim society and corrupting Islamic practices. However, it was not merely the '*ulama*'s traditional disdain for certain practices of Sufi orders (*tariqa*) (such as the *pir-murid* relationship, dance and music, performance of miracles, celebration of the birthdays of Sufi saints, its claim to intercession between God and human beings, grave visitation, excessive ritualism, etc.), but the vision of a "unified Islam" which in turn partly derived from the "success" of the model of the "homogenized nation" in Europe that located in the diversified, localized Sufi orders the source of "Islamic malice" and an obstacle in the "progress" of the unified Islamic *umma* or nation or community.

Thus, the "nation-state-Islam" vision of post-colonial modernizing Muslim states, which represented the creed of Islamic modernism, dealt harshly with Sufi orders across all Muslim countries, ranging from curtailment of their religious activities to altogether outlawing them as happened in Kemalist Turkey in the name of "modernizing" society and purging Islam of Sufi-supernaturalism, miraclism, and obscurantism. The current Sunni Islamic militancy, an off-shoot of the tradition of Islamic modernism, continues to target violently the localized Sufi shrines in the manner of eighteenth-century Wahhabism in various parts of the Muslim world.

One consequence of Qur'an-based Islamic discourses by Islamic modernists is that the Islamic traditions including Sunnah and Hadith received little attention in their narratives about Islam, notwithstanding their rhetoric of deducing the original meaning of Islam in the light of the Qur'an and the Islamic practices of Prophet Muhammad and the Four Rightly Guided Caliphs. This partly explains why none of the prominent Islamic modernists of the nineteenth century chose to write a book about the life-history of Prophet Muhammad and his Companions. As a result, the balance that had existed between the Qur'an, Sunnah, and Hadith—which had guided the balanced interpretation of Islam for so long—broke down in much of the twentieth century. The excessive reliance on Qur'an-based Islamic discourses, along with a free and easy exercise of *ijtihad* by modernist Muslims first transformed the Qur'an from a "revealed Book of Guidance" to a "literary text" which is subjected to multiple selective interpretations. Thus, Nasr Abu Zayd rightly commented that

> the Qur'an was/is reduced to the mercy of the ideology of its interpreter; for a communist, the Qur'an would reveal communism, for a fundamentalist the Qur'an would be a highly fundamentalist text, for a feminist it would be a feminist text and for a votary of political Islam it would be primarily a political text of power, rule, and state.[26]

This process resulted in the development of a fragmented view of the Qur'an and Islam—a tendency that continues to manifest even today as evident from the prevalent discourse of "Meccan vs. Medinan Islam,"[27] using verses that correspond to the social Islam of peace, justice, equality, freedom, reconciliation, love and tolerance, or the political Islam of violence, war, *jihad*, law, order, obedience, community, state respectively—and a steady erosion of ethical and moral perspective and values as embedded in the Islamic tradition of Sunnah and Hadith and Sufism. The latter was also in part a fall-out from the long, sustained campaign by different forces of Islamic modernism—state as well as non-state actors ('*ulama*)—against Sufism, both violently and non-violently, that eventually produced a rupture in the unity of heart and mind which is required for the proper, holistic, and balanced understanding of Islam and the Qur'an.

Allama Iqbal had anticipated such a development in view of the speed of Islamic reformism. He remarked,

> We heartily welcome the liberal movement in modern Islam... Further, our religious and political reformers in their zeal for liberalism may overstep the proper limits of reform in the absence of check on their youthful fervor. We are today passing through a period similar to that of the Protestant revolution in Europe, and the lesson which the rise and outcome of Luther's movement teaches should not be lost on us. A careful reading of history shows that the Reformation was essentially a political movement, and the net result of it in Europe was a gradual displacement of the universal ethics of Christianity by system of national ethics. The result of this tendency we have seen with our own eyes in the Great European War, which, far from bringing any workable synthesis of the two opposing systems of ethics, has made the European situation still more intolerable.[28]

Similarly, the late Fazlur Rahman, an Islamic modernist, writing in 1979, bitterly lamented the absence of an ethics-based narrative of the Qur'an in modern times: "One cannot point to a single work of ethics squarely based upon the Qur'an, although there are numerous works based upon Greek philosophy, Persian tradition and Sufi piety."[29] Against this consequence of the writings of Islamic modernists Fethullah Gülen intends to restore the balance between the Qur'an, Sunnah, and Hadith, and retrieve the universal ethics of the Qur'an and Islam.

Second, as Islam increasingly became bereft of its Sufi dimension (heart), it was reduced to a "function of mind"—rationalization and legitimization of all sorts of private and public actions in the name of Islam. As a consequence, the discourses of Islamic modernists were caught in a vicious circle of their own inner, multiple contradictions and thus failed to arrest the declining fortunes of Muslim societies. Thus, on the one hand, Islam and Sharia was increasingly transformed from an "ethical and moral public discourse" to a fixed, rigid, codified entity applicable mostly to the family sphere. On the other hand, in their zeal to become "modern," Islamic modernists ended up legitimizing West-inspired social, political and economic reforms in Muslim societies. Thus, if the burden of "reform" pushed the Islamic modernists to take a critical look at past Islamic traditions and reject the principle of *taqlid*, the same trajectory pushed them towards *uncritical* imitation (*taqlid*) of Western institutions, values, and practices couched in Islamic terms.

Third, Islamic modernists and modernizing post-colonial Muslim states paid more attention in "educational reform" to the secular component of education without inculcating Islamic values as a "guiding factor" in their engagement with secular education. As a result, the educational system in Muslim societies remained torn between what is called Islamic education or transmitted science and secular education or *ilmi* (rational) science—a division that came to stay in medieval Muslim societies and which became further strengthened under European political hegemony. Under attack by European rationalism and positivism this process led to the transformation of the *madrasa* (originally, an educational space) into a religious institution imparting religious instruction, while governmental schools and private Christian missionary schools became the site of secular education.

The Islamic modernists could not close the increasing social gap between the religious system of education and the masses on one side and the Westernized, secular system of education and the elites on the other; rather the gap between the two qualitatively increased and religious education became increasingly irrelevant in the emerging secular world. Because of its own Western moorings, it could not dispel the public perception and fear of compromising their Islamic identity and values while seeking secular education in public or private educational institutions; thus, it miserably failed in its objective of harmonizing Islamic culture with Western science and technology. In the milieu of the resulting contradiction between the public image of Islam—the ideal (freedom, equity, and justice) and source of legitimation of public policies—and its growing irrelevancy, isolation and marginalization in everyday life process on the other, Islam became a victim of the "politics of Islamic reform," developed an inferiority complex with apologetic outlook and lacked the confidence to engage with the things called "public" and "modern." Islam increasingly became a mechanical, lifeless, identity-centric discourse, and developed an "other-worldly orientation" for the Muslim masses, not on the basis of inherent Islamic principle but principally in opposition to the "this-worldly orientation" of Christianity (Protestantism) and the Western, material civilization that also included the modernizing Muslim states.

The apologetic outlook of Islam was best reflected in Abduh's conceptualization of the rising (Christian) West and declining (Islamic)

East in terms of *"Islam without Muslims" and "Muslims without Islam"* (a phrase which is originally attributed to the Egyptian Islamic scholar Rifa'a al Tahtawi (1801-1873)) respectively, meaning that while one finds the working of Islam in the day-to-day life of Europe, and hence there is development, the same is missing in the Muslim lands, where hence there is backwardness. Even Muhammad Iqbal could not free himself from the paradigm of apologetics while defending Islam, as is evident from the following passage,

> The permanence of the British Empire as a civilizing factor in the political evolution of mankind is one of our greatest interests. This vast Empire has our fullest sympathy and respect, since it is one aspect of our political ideal that is being slowly worked out in it. England, in fact, is doing one of our own great duties, which unfavorable circumstances did not permit us to perform. It is not the number of Muhammadans, which it protects, but the spirit of the British Empire that makes it the greatest Muhammadan Empire in the world.[30]

Similarly, Ziya Gökalp, the father of Turkish nationalism, saw in Protestantism, which brought material success in Europe, an "Islamicized version of Christianity." As he states,

> When we study the history of Christianity, we see that, following the Crusades (11th–13th centuries), a new movement started in Europe, which was then acquainted with Islamic culture. This movement aimed at imitating Islamic civilization and religion. It penetrated Europe with time, and finally culminated in Protestantism as a new religion entirely in contra-distinction to the traditional principles of Christianity. This new religion rejected the priesthood, and the existence of two kinds of government, spiritual and temporal. It also rejected the papacy, the Councils, the Inquisition—in short, all institutions, which had existed in Christianity—as contrary to the principles of Islam. Are we not justified if we look at this religion as a more or less Islamicized form of Christianity? … If these principles taken by Protestantism from Islam were factors in this progress, do they not also constitute an experimental proof that Islam is the most modern and most reasonable religion?[31]

It was due in part to this apologetics, growing privatization and marginalization of Islam accompanied by democratic deficit in governance, inequity, and paucity of social justice that Political Islam emerged in the mid-twentieth century demanding the re-centering of Islam in the political-public life of community, nation, and *umma* in general and the implementation of Sharia in particular. This trend led to the development of the "Islamization" of knowledge and science that seeks the Islamic roots of every discipline and branch of human knowledge and which in turn obstructs free engagement with education and knowledge as a neutral process and reinforced the fear of "Western education" in Muslim societies. As a result, "education" could not emerge as a "value" worth pursuing in Muslim societies until the late twentieth century.

As "image of Islam" in both forms of Islamic modernism came to suffer from "excess"—the "privatization" of Islam in the liberal imagination of Islam and its "politicization" in the radical imagination of Islam—the Islamic modernists were caught in the "private vs. public" dichotomy that does not belong to the Sunni mainstream understanding of Islam, and thus could not transform their objective of "making Islam relevant for this world" into a reality. Owing to multiple contradictions and a lack of clear direction, the Islamic modernists were neither perceived by the majority of Muslims as "sufficiently Muslim," nor by the Westernized minority of Muslims as "sufficiently modern" and thus failed to generate the social forces for change beyond the limited circle of intellectuals. One consequence of this historical process of Islamic modernist reformation is that Islam was "nationalized," "politicized," and "instrumentalized," which led the late Fazlur Rahman, the celebrated Pakistani Islamic scholar, to bitterly remark, "instead of politics serving Islam, Islam has come to serve politics."[32]

Finally, due to the focus on social and political reform Islamic modernist reformation did not present itself as being a movement of religious revival and a resurrector of civilization, but rather as being a movement of political, social, and conceptual reform—even though questions of intrinsic essence and Islamic identity were among the sum total concerns of its thought and the paragraphs of its reformist texts. In fact, it would not be an exaggeration to point out that in its attempt to provide a rationalist interpretation of Islam it could not sustain the balance between faith and reason. Somehow the issue of faith, notwithstanding their rhetoric of maintaining the superiority of revelation over reason, was diluted or eroded or marginalized in the Islamic modernists' imagination of Islam. In fact, Islam at this juncture faced another moment of "serious spiritual crisis," parallel to the two other such moments it had faced in the past, which will be briefly dealt with in the next chapter.

Suffice it here to state that the Islamic modernists responded to this "crisis of Islam" by merely appropriating the Western vision of the good life in Islamic terms and by enlarging the scope of human reason so that it sometimes questions the "truth" of Islamic Revelation and in the process ended in diluting the essentials of faith. As they focused merely on the structural reform—political, social, and legal—connected with the state, they were not perceived as a movement for religious revival but a movement for social and political reform. Shabestari, an Iranian theological intellectual, notes that "the reform movements of the last one hundred and fifty years from Muhammad Abduh to Ali Shariati were not true attempts at reform in the field of religion. They merely represented the foundations for movements towards political and social change that employed religion as a means to an end and a vehicle for their ideas."[33] As a result, they failed to present Islam as a credible source of identity, faith, and motivation for the Muslim community.

CHAPTER 5

GÜLEN'S APPROACH TO ISLAM

Do Gülen and the Gülen Movement belong to this continuum of the Islamic reformist or modernist tradition as explored in the preceding chapters? Any casual reader of Gülen's literature would easily find that Gülen does not belong to this genre of Islamic reformism. Though the idea of Islamic reform does occur in the writings of Gülen, its meanings and emphasis are not similar to those of nineteenth-century Islamic liberals. For Gülen, unlike the Islamic modernists of the nineteenth and twentieth centuries, Islamic reform first and foremost means the revival of Islamic faith, which in turn leads to individual actions in various fields of human life. However, many scholars such as Hakan Yavuz, as well as a few scholars associated with the Hizmet movement, do not consider the Gülen Movement as a strictly faith-based movement. According to Yavuz, "Nursi's movement remained a faith movement from the beginning to the end. Gülen's movement started as a faith movement but evolved into a socio-political movement with the goal of shaping modern institutions and spaces."[1] To establish the difference between the two, he elaborates, "Gülen's main focus is not on inner individual conscience, but rather actions in the public sphere."[2]

Yavuz's attempt to differentiate between the two in terms of faith and public action is erroneous as it is premised on the post-Reformation modern understanding of religion in terms of private faith between individual and God, which does not subscribe to any public role for religion in this world. However, Casanova in his study *Public Religions in the Modern World* has propounded the thesis of the "de-privatization of religion" and demonstrated that religion was never privatized but only shifted its location from political to social.[3] Moreover, Islam does not believe in a private-public dichotomy; rather, in the Islamic imagination, faith is strongly connected with both parts of the world. Muslims are expected to follow the commandments of God (*Sharia*) in this world to earn reward in the other world. In this regard, Fazlur Rahman has rightly noted that "Islam is the first actual movement known to history, that has taken society seriously and history meaningfully because it perceived that the betterment of this world was not a hopeless task nor just a *pis aller* but a task in which God and man are involved together."[4] Similarly, Gülen asserts the indivisibility of Islam by stating that "there is no separation of this world and the next in the believer's life."[5] In essence, the Gülen Movement is a "faith-in-action" movement in which actions in the public domain flow from the spirit of strong faith. Gülen underlines this understanding of the Gülen Movement by stating, "the basic dynamic of our life of action and thought is our spiritual life, which is based on our religious values."[6]

The Gülen Movement and the *Tajdid* tradition

The crucial difference between the Gülen Movement and the Islamic modernist or reformist movement is that unlike Islamic modernists, Gülen comes from the Renewalist (*mujaddidi*) tradition of Islam or what is called the Islamic tradition of *ijtihad* and *tajdid* (Renewal).[7] Though it is difficult to determine the context and period in which the *mujaddidi* tradition in Islam originated, it is strongly linked with the idea of religious renewal (*tajdid*) and the revival of Prophetic practice (*ihya al-Sunna*), which developed at a very early stage of Islamic history on the basis of a famous Hadith, "God will send to this community on the eve of every century a man who will renew its *din* (religion)." The import of this *Hadith* is that a person of vast knowledge will appear with an effort to maintain the faith and revive its tenets by interpretations based upon the changing conditions of the age. A *mujaddid* is thus to appear among them on the eve of every century, not to bring a new *Sharia*, but to revive the existing one. There is no institution within Islam, at least within Sunni Islam, that confers the title of *mujaddid* upon an *'alim* in recognition of his service to the Muslim community. *Tajdid* is what every scholar or believer should work for, so that the faith is maintained as fresh as it was first revealed. But whether a person was a *mujaddid* or not is usually an estimation or perception by future scholars looking back on his contributions and struggle. Sometimes individuals (an *'alim* from within the ranks of religious scholars, *'ulama*) assume the position in their self-perception, as well as in the public perception. As a result, one finds the emergence of countless *mujaddid* in Islamic history spread over different parts of the Muslim world without any universal Muslim consensus over them.

Gülen makes it clear that the term "Renewal" has a specific connotation only for "*din*" without being in any way connected with any other kind of reform: "Self-renewal takes place in the metaphysical, not the physical, realm and is a revival of the spirit and of spiritual life; the term 'renewal' is not seriously used for any other kind of renovation."[8] He believes that *tajdid* is an intrinsic part of Islamic dynamism without which regeneration of Muslim societies would not be possible. As he states, "the fundamentals of our spiritual life are religious thought and imagination. Not only have we sustained our life with these, but we have also taken action by relying on them."[9]

Tajdid can only be undertaken by a *mujaddid*. A *mujaddid* in his effort to renew (*tajdid*) religion will use a tool called *ijtihad* (reasoning) and in doing so also become a *mujtahid*. Thus, in order to be *mujaddid* one has to be a *mujtahid* in the first place. Hence while all *mujaddid* must be *mujtahid*; not all *mujtahid* are *mujaddid*. According to Enes Ergene, one of the important intellectuals in the Hizmet movement, "a *mujaddid* must combine four kinds of profiles in his personality: classical scholarship of Islam, knowledge of Sufism, knowledge of philosophy, and knowledge of *dawa*. While to be a *mujtahid*, one of these four profiles is sufficient. Hodjaefendi [Gülen] combines all these profiles unlike the majority of Islamic scholars in the past."[10] In fact, after examining the legal and religious qualifications of Gülen to be recognized as *mujtahid*, Ismail Acar concurs that, "Gülen has the capacity to be a *mujaddid*, but he deliberately regards himself as a regular pious Muslim because of his humility."[11] However, he further clarified that "in Islamic tradition, especially among religious scholars who were trained in Sufi tradition, it is common not to declare their scholarly qualifications. In the history of Islamic law, very few jurists declared that they were *mujaddid*. Jalal al-Din al Suyuti (d. 911/1505), an Egyptian Jurist, was one of the few."[12] Thus, what is important for a person to be recognized as *mujaddid* is the public perception built over the years on the basis of his religious qualification and legitimacy and not the declaration by himself. Though there is no source that confirms that Fethullah Gülen considers himself *mujaddid*, what is certain is that he is considered *mujaddid* not only by many volunteers of the Gülen Movement but also in wider Islamic circles.[13]

Mujaddidi tradition vs. Islamic reformist tradition

There is a substantial difference between the approach of the *mujaddidi* tradition of Islam or Islamic tradition of *ijtihad* and *tajdid* and the Islamic reformist tradition. In the *mujaddidi* tradition, *ihya al-Sunna* (revival of the Sunna) assumes special significance as the Islamic faith is renewed on the basis of understanding the Qur'an in the light of Prophetic guidance and examples. It limits the role of human reason in the interpretation of Qur'anic verses: reason assumes a secondary position in relation to revelation as a source of knowledge and faith, and is required as aid to uphold the Qur'anic truth.[14] There is a heavy emphasis on imitating the Prophetic model of conduct in the everyday life process and on internalizing what I would call the process of "heartization of Islam" (Islam by heart). This model believes in the unity of mind (rational or reason) and heart (ethics and spiritual) or balanced, judicious, harmonious application of mind and heart together in understanding the Qur'an, Hadith, Sunna, and dominant Islamic practice which demands a controlled exercise of the principle of *ijtihad* and *taqlid*. In the Islamic reformist model the main thrust is the application of human reason in the interpretation of Qur'an, Hadith, Sunna, and Islamic practice so that the meaning of Islamic texts and practices should conform to the basic structure of human reason in order to be considered "Islamically" legitimate. The unfettered exercise of *ijtihad* and its almost blind rejection of *taqlid* along with its tendency to "historicize" or "contextualize" Qur'an within a particular time-space sometimes leads to contradicting the fundamentals of Islamic faith, notwithstanding its rhetoric of acknowledging the superiority of Revelation over reason or complementarity between Revelation and reason.

Second, in the *tajdid* tradition of Islam, though the principle of Sufism is retained, it decisively rejects the concept of authority flowing from a Sufi Saint or his right to intercede between the individual and

God with a promise to fulfill material expectations. Rather, it invests authority in text: the Qur'an and Hadith. According to Lapidus, "this form of Islam stresses intellectual knowledge, hard work, self-discipline, and communal responsibility. A believer in this frame of mind is prepared to direct his energy towards rationally defined causes and to adopt rational-legal means of action to achieve his/her goal. Pent-up emotional force can be directed into commitment to ideals and to worldly activity to remake the world in the image of what it considers universal/ultimate Truth."[15] In other words, the *tajdid* tradition of Islam transforms highly developed intellectual and moral capacities and unfulfilled emotional needs into commitment to world action for the sake of Allah without expectation of return.

Third, in the *mujaddidi* tradition of Islam the focus is on renewal of faith in the individual, whereas the Islamic reformist tradition is more broadly concerned with reform of structure: social, economic, and political.

Fourth, as Enes Ergene points out, "*Tajdid* does not feel obliged to explain itself because it refers only to renewal from inside; reform, on the other hand, has to explain itself to the masses. Because it has no relation with the tradition, neither at the intellectual level nor on the basis of collective inherent references, it has to resort to evidence from outside tradition in order to legalize itself. Between reform and tradition there is an epistemological and ontological incompatibility and gap. Reform has an ideological nature, rather than an epistemological or methodological nature."[16]

Fifth, whereas the impulse and inspiration in Islamic modernism for "reforming" Muslim societies came from the conceptual apparatus of modernism and its geographical center—Europe, for Islamic renewalists, the impulse and inspiration for "renewing," not "reforming" the faith is rooted in the Islamic principle of *ijtihad* and *tajdid* and primarily based on the Prophetic model.

Last, if not the least, a crucial difference between the two lies in their approach to Sharia. The scope of Sharia ranges from Qur'an, Hadith, Sunna to four school of Islamic laws. The Islamic modernists of both varieties—liberal and radicals—tend to take a formalistic, textual, literalist, and legalistic view of Sharia, though degree of literalism is far greater among the radical factions of Islamic modernists. Whereas in the *mujaddidi* tradition Sharia is predominantly understood in terms of normative values and moral and ethical principles derived from its understanding of God's such attributes as justice, equity, compassion, mercy, forgiveness, love, peace, brotherhood, tolerance, harmony, non-interference in personal belief etc. Muzaffar Alam, a distinguished Indian medieval historian, has highlighted this understanding of Sharia with reference to moral and ethical training of sons of Mughal rulers and how such normative values of Sharia had guided the administrative actions of successful Mughal rulers in India during much of medieval period.[17] Gülen too provides a holistic understanding of Sharia consisting of two complimentary aspects: outward (methods of religious worship including ritual rules, governance, penalties etc.) and inward (normative values associated with God's attributes including love, justice, and peace).[18] One serious implication of this understanding of Sharia is that whereas in the hand of Islamic modernists the Islamic *fiqh* (law) itself becomes an expression of divinity, in *mujaddidi* tradition the Islamic *fiqh* is just a "human means/construct" the relevance and utility of which is measured in terms of conforming to God's attributes and purpose of creation as noted above.

This difference in the approach between the *mujaddidi* tradition of Islam and the Islamic reformist tradition has significant bearing on their response to modernity. While in the latter discourse the attempt is to "Islamicize" modernity, in the former the attempt is to engage with modernity without compromising the foundations of Islamic faith. In other words, in the Islamic reformist tradition modernity is imagined in Islamic terms—which means Islam becomes a "form" within which the essence/content of modernity is practiced. However, in the Islamic renewalist/*mujaddidi* tradition, "Islam" is imagined in "modern"/universal terms and values (with focus on the dominant meaning of the universal values)—which means modern becomes a "form" within which the essence/content of Islam in moral-ethical terms is practiced. Thus, whereas the discourse of Islamic modernists invariably results in adjusting Islam with the demands and value of modernity, in the renewalist tradition of Islam the attempt is to remain steadfast in practicing the normative ideal and essence of Islam within the dominant form of modernity. Thus, modernity does not become an "appealing object" or a "threatening object" to Islam in the renewalist tradition of Islam, unlike in the discourses of Islamic modernism, wherein modernity either evokes a "deep appreciation" and "wholesome imitation" in the liberal version of Islamic modernism or "repulsion" and "rejection" in its radical, politicized version. As a result, grounded in the "truth" of Islamic faith, the Islamic renewalist tradition has better capacity to utilize the doctrinal resources and practice of Islam to deal with any new challenges such as modernity than the Islamic modernists, whose engagement with modernity has been marked by contradiction, apologetics, and lack of clarity as detailed earlier in this chapter.

Genealogy of Gülen's Islamic thought

Having differentiated the basic contours of the difference between the Renewalist (*mujaddidi*) tradition of Islam within which I place the Gülen Movement and the modern Islamic reformism, it is important to delineate Gülen's approach to the Qur'an and Islam, its history, and doctrines in order to understand the normative and philosophical dimensions of the Gülen Movement. Though there are many Islamic and non-Islamic sources, figures, and personalities that have helped in shaping Gülen's conceptualization of Islam, its history, and its doctrine, it appears to be Imam Ghazali (1058-1111), Ahmad al-Faruqi al-Sirhindi (1564-1624) (also known as Imam Rabbani), Mawlana Khalid al-Baghdadi (1779-1824) and Bediüzzaman Said Nursi (1877-1960) who have decisively influenced the thinking pattern of Fethullah Gülen. In addition to these figures, many other Islamic personalities such Mawlana Jalaluddin Rumi, Shah Waliullah Dehlawi and Muhammad Iqbal frequently occur in his discourse and appear to have contributed to shaping his ideas. However, it appears that Gülen has built his Islamic thought on the sub-terrain of the first four Islamic thinkers mentioned above. All of these four Islamic figures acquired the honorific title of *mujaddid* and are deeply revered in the Sunni Muslim world. Imam Ghazali has been called the "Proof of Islam," while Imam Rabbani has been hailed as *mujaddidi alf-i-thani* (Renewer of the Second Millennium), Mawlana Khalid al-Baghdadi as "Caliph of all *Mujaddidi* Order," and Bediüzzaman Said Nursi is considered among some Turkish Sunni Muslims to be the thirteenth and perhaps the most important in the chain of *mujaddid*.[19]

What is important to underline is that all these four important figures of Islamic history are credited with reinforcing or re-establishing the mainstream Sunni creed or *Ahl al-Sunna wa'l Jamaat* that has been jolted from time to time. The first credible challenge to the Islamic faith emerged in the ninth and tenth centuries in the challenges of Greek rationalist thought as championed by Ibn Sina and others. Ibn Sina and many others like him were pious Muslims, but, as Allama Iqbal noted, since their "structure of thinking was Greek,"[20] they tended to provide a kind of rationalist interpretation of Islam that resulted in diluting the essentials of the Islamic faith, which consists of the six principles: (1) Belief in the Unity of God (Allah—Doctrine of Tawhid), (2) Belief in the Angels, (3) Belief in the Revealed Books, (4) Belief in the Messengers (Prophets) and Prophet Muhammad as last Messenger, (5) Belief in the resurrection and the events of the Day of Judgment, and (6) Belief in the predestination of all things and events (*qadar*) and God's decree. The first and the last two were considered to be diluted in the interpretations of Ibn Sina and others of the Islamic faith. It is Al-Ghazali, *the Proof of Islam*, who is credited with having restored the supremacy of Faith (of Sunni Islam) and Revelation over reason and an emerging "deviationist" tendency within Islam.[21]

A second moment of spiritual crisis that Islam faced was during the fifteenth and sixteenth centuries when various form of Islamic syncretism—the mixing of the Bhakti movement into Sufism, the expansion of Shiism, the Mughal Emperor Akbar's Din-i-Ilahi—all combined posed challenges to Sunni Islamic Orthodoxy. It is Imam Rabbani, the *Mujaddid*, whose *Maktubat* (Letters) are considered to have restored the supremacy of the Sunni Islamic faith over emerging what was/is considered Islamic deviationist tendencies. Similarly, Mawlana Khalid al-Baghdadi is considered to have provided crucial support to the then-Ottoman Empire in the eighteenth century, which was representing the Sunni Islamic Orthodoxy in the face of the emerging challenges of Wahhabism and growing activities of Christian missionaries.

The third moment of crisis for Islam came during the mid-nineteenth to mid-twentieth century when European rationalism and positivism posed a serious challenge to the Islamic creed both as a faith and a rationalist faith. While during the first two crises Islam was the dominant power and challenges were coming from within the fold of Islam so the crisis did not appear to be an "existential dilemma of identity," the third moment of crisis occurred during the period when Islam was no longer the dominant power and challenges were coming from outside the Islamic fold. This generated a serious existential dilemma for the Islamic identity, faith, history, and civilization.

It is at this juncture that Bediüzzaman Said Nursi's *Risale-i Nur* performed the task of Imam Ghazali and Imam Rabbani by resurrecting the "Truth" of mainstream Sunni Islam by demonstrating the compatibility between Islam and science and reason and faith, at least in the Turkish setting, where among all the Muslim nations the Islamic faith faced the most severe challenge from European positivism and Kemalism. However, Nursi could not emerge as a *mujaddid* like Ghazali and Rabbani partly on account of his Turkish nationality that was rapidly undergoing the process of secularization at the cost of "Islamic" Turkey, the hostile Kemalist state, and the historical conflict between Arab and Turks—the combination of which obstructed the dissemination of Nursi's works throughout the Muslim world.

The underlying reason for the success of the *mujaddidi* model in coping with the "crises of Islam," at least in the Sunni setting, is that this model treats Islam in a holistic manner and strikes a harmonious balance between theology and philosophy, revelation and reason, heart and mind, materialism and spiritualism, this world and the other world, and the Qur'an, Universe, and humanity with an underlying tone that the practice of *Sufism is an essential component to lead a* "Muslim" life. In other words, this model lays down an integrated *Sunni-Salafi-Sufi-sharia* or what Lapidus has called "Sunni-Sharia-Sufi"[22] approach towards Islam.[23] Describing this approach to Islam Lapidus wrote,

> This synthesis includes a commitment to the Qur'an and hadith (the sayings of the Prophet) as the scriptural sources of Islam, to the four schools of Islamic law, to the mystical teachings in the tradition of al-Ghazali which emphasize correct ritual and legal practice joined to an ethical pious inner life, and to the theological school that balance reason and faith. Institutionally this religious position was represented by the schools of law and numerous "conservative" Sufi brotherhoods.[24]

Asad also points out that "it is not as if there were only two options in Islam—Sufi or Salafi. Abduh, one of founders of the Salafi (Reform) movement, always accepted the Sufi tradition. The great medieval reformer, Imam Ghazali, was at once a scripturalist (an elitist, if you like) and a Sufi."[25] Underlining the integrated *Sunni-Salafi-Sufi-Sharia* approach Gülen himself remarked, "Figures like Ghazali, Imam Rabbani, and Bediüzzaman Said Nursi are the 'revivers' or 'renewers' of the highest degree, who combined in their person both the enlightenment of sages, knowledge of religious scholars and spirituality of the greatest saints."[26] Within this framework the Sunni Islamic creed is delineated by the following features: fundamental principles of faith; emphasis on literal interpretation of the Qur'an wherever possible; reliance on tradition in explaining the text; use of reason within limits; respect for the Companions of the Prophet collectively as the most important source of religious authority after the Prophet; acceptance of a set of theological positions on God's attributes, religious doctrines, prophecy and revelation; recognition of Sufism as the spiritual dimension of Islam, the Qur'an as the Speech of God, the definition of a "believer" (Muslim), and sources of authority in law; and rejection of positions held by rationalist theologians known as *Mu'tazilis*. Gülen broadly operates within this Islamic structure of *Ahl al-Sunna wa'l Jamaat* as laid down by these *mujaddids*.

In particular, Gülen appears to clearly adopt Ghazali's doctrine of the Mean, rules concerning reconciliation between Reason and Revelation, God as the ultimate cause of every happening and action and rejection of the materialist model of "cause and effect" to explain the developments in the world, and Sufism as the "necessary component" to practice the essence of Islam.[27] All these Ghazalian doctrines were in varying degrees also adopted and endorsed by Imam Rabbani and Bediüzzaman Said Nursi. Gülen's central idea of "hizmet," meaning "service to humanity," can be traced back to Imam Rabbani's notion of "*abdiyat*,"[28] or "service to God," which has become coterminous with "universal" and "humanity" for a large number of Islamic scholars since the mid-nineteenth century in response to modernity's claims over the "universal" and "humanity."[29] Moreover, Rabbani's broad classification of "form and essence" or "Formal Islam vs. Essential Islam"[30] based on *Sufi* categories such as outward (*zahir*), inward (*batin*), form (*sura*), and essence (*haqiqa*) while interpreting *Sharia* appears to have influenced Gülen's thinking on resolving the tension between modernity (form) and Islam (inner essence) as outlined in the preceding pages. Mawlana

Khalid al-Baghdadi's idea of reviving the strict path of the Prophet's Sunna along with his contribution of transforming the Naqshbandi *tariqa* into an action-oriented program for the purpose of mobilization of Muslims and its spread in Anatolia[31] appear to influence Gülen's conceptualization of action and intervention in the world without any expectation of material rewards.

Said Nursi holds a special position among the Turkish Muslim masses, Islamic scholars and reformers partly because he enjoys the reputation of "saving" Islam from the secularizing zeal of Kemalist Turkey and partly because his treatise, the *Risale-i Nur*, is considered to be the most important Islamic text in modern times that deals with the whole gamut of issues confronting Muslims today, ranging through faith, education, poverty, harmony, tolerance, backwardness and other challenges of modernity. Even the Gülen Movement was initially considered a Nur faction; however, the Movement has dissociated itself from such identification in recent years, although Nursi remains a revered figure and *Risale-i Nur* a revered text among the volunteers of the Gülen Movement.

Although Gülen never had an opportunity to meet him, he has called Nursi "the number-one figure of the modern age who succeeded in presenting Islam's vast ocean of faith, moral values, and conscience in the most efficient and purest way."[32] Nursi's contribution to Gülen's thought is evident in the following principles: (1) politics is divisive in nature while education serves the purpose of unity; (2) there are three enemies of Muslims: poverty, ignorance and disunity; (3) religion and science are complementary to each other and there is no contradiction between Islamic and rational-scientific values; (4) persuasion rather than imposing while teaching about faith, and referring to science as one among multiple methods to understand and discover the signs and laws of God; (5) introducing Islam back into the people's lives while being careful not to give a false impression of reforming Islam; (6) everything in the universe is a sign of God, and the Qur'an, universe, and humanity are three books of the same meaning; and (7) human nature is essentially good and cooperative.[33]

Basic paradigm of Gülen's Islamic thought

In line with many Islamic thinkers Gülen also unequivocally asserts the

Islamic doctrine of Pre-destination and believes the Qur'anic message cannot be fully comprehended by only rationalist interpretation, notwithstanding the fact that due to his *Sunni-Hanafi-Maturidi* tradition[34] the role of reason is much greater in his Islamic cosmology in comparison to these *mujaddids*. Thus, Gülay has rightly observed that "Gülen's Islamic reasoning represents a uniquely reflexive combination of reason and revelation. Unlike the syntheses of reason and revelation struck in the past by reformers like Sirhindi and Nursi, Gülen's reconciliation redefines the philosophical foundations of both concepts. ... Reason is reconstructed along Islamic, *harfi* lines. Revelation is reinterpreted according to natural theological and rationalist principles and obtains more resonance and coherence with modern historical circumstance and intellectual standards."[35]

It is from within this Islamic tradition, which *harmonizes* Islamic orthodoxy with mysticism, and reason with revelation, that Gülen espouses an organic, integrated, holistic view of Islam in which various dimensions (such as material—Islamic law, and spiritual—Sufi practice) are interrelated in a cooperative and balanced manner. A proper, balanced understanding of each part requires understanding of its linkage with other parts and of its specific position within the whole. It is from this Islamic perspective that Gülen sees inner balance and harmony endowed with the purpose of mutual help and cooperation in God's creation—whether human, nature or non-human—and aspires to restore this balance, which is under severe strain due to excessive materialism or even spiritualism. As Gülen observes,

> There is an obligation for us to realize conception in order to view creation and events from the Islamic perspective and to examine everything with Islamic reasoning. To achieve this, our knowledge about humanity, life, and the universe should first be sound and in accord with the essence and reality of matter, on the same course and orbit as its origin and objectives; all its parts should support one another and collaborate; the whole and the parts should be related or interconnected like different voices expressing the same theme, like a composition with a single rhythm and meter, like a central embroidered motif encircled by a repeating pattern.[36]

It was this inbuilt balance within Islam that led Gülen to consider

Islam essentially a "religion of moderation" and remark, "Islam, being the middle way of absolute balance between all temporal and spiritual extremes and containing the ways of all previous Prophets, makes a choice according to the situation."[37] The integrated, balanced outlook of Gülen is visible from many of his narratives with regard to exposition of Qur'anic verses, Hadith and the relationship between the Qur'an (God's Attribute of Speech), Universe (God's created book) and humanity (God's vicegerent on earth). Considering the Qur'an essentially a "Book of Guidance," like Egyptian Islamic reformer Muhammad Abduh, he approaches it mostly from a thematic point of view (such as justice, freedom, equality, welfare, women's rights, human rights, etc.), deduces the multiple meanings of a single verse, and establishes a balance between a particular meaning of a Qur'anic verse and its relationship with other Qur'anic verses and the overall objectives of the Qur'an. In deducing the meaning of Qur'anic verses to address the contemporary problems of Muslims in particular, as well as human civilization in general, Gülen, heavily utilizes the Hadith and Sunna in the interpretation of verses, adopts the method of three-tier meaning (following Imam Ghazali and Imam Rabbani's inner vs. outer meaning of the text) of the text—*lafzi* (literal meaning), *aqli* (intellectually) and *dhawqi* (inner) as well as drawing on the four Sunni schools of law in order to deduce the meaning of the verse that would be acceptable to the present age without anyway compromising or losing the sanctity of the Qur'an.

Gülen asserts the timeless and universal character of the Qur'an and calls for renewal of its meaning and interpretation in new contexts. In the words of Nursi "*The Qur'an grows new and younger with every new age.*" Similarly, following Nursi, Gülen sees an essential unity between God, Universe, Qur'an, and humanity. He says, "The Qur'an, like the universe and humanity, is an organic entity, for every verse is interrelated with the others. Thus, the first and foremost interpreter of the Qur'an is the Qur'an itself. This means that a complete and true understanding of a verse depends on understanding all other relevant verses."[38] Thus, for Gülen, only a balanced, holistic reading of Islam—its foundational texts, its dominant practice, principles, values, and norms—can enable a Muslim to understand that the Universe, Qur'an, and Humanity are all interrelated and manifestations of a single Truth having the same value. According to him, individuals and nations have suffered when these three have been separated from each other, while conversely peace and development have been established when these three were close. Exploring the linkage between them, Gülen, like Nursi, rejects any conflict between religion and science; instead, they complement each other. However, unlike the Islamic modernists, Gülen does not subscribe to the thesis of "Islamization of science" that traces the roots of every scientific theory to Islam because he considers such an attitude as a sign of an inferiority complex that will eventually put the Qur'an in the secondary position. In fact, Gülen considers scientific explanations to be of transient, and hence of lower value, in decoding the various "signs" of the Universe as science keeps changing, unlike the transcendental truth.[39]

Role of *hadith* and *sunna* in Gülen's thought

An excavation of Gülen's work in totality reflects that the *Hadith*, *Sunna*, and Companions of Prophet Muhammad (up to three generations) are central to his ethical and moral narratives of Islam. This is clearly visible in many of his sermons and speeches made both in his capacity as government-appointed imam of various mosques within Turkey and as private person while living in the United States of America. For Gülen, the Qur'an and Islam are best represented in the life history of the Prophet and the first-generation Companions. As Halim Çalış states, "Gülen picks examples mostly from the life of Prophet and his Companions because he considers them the most relevant models for all Muslims."[40] It is not without reason that one of his first works is a biography of the Prophet,[41] probably one of the best biographies of Prophet Muhammad that I have come across. He also supervises Qur'anic *tafsir* studies with his students, which can eventually become a separate work later on[42]—an act which many leaders of Islamic movements—political or social—preferred to perform first in order to establish their Islamic credentials and gain legitimacy among Muslims. For Gülen, the Prophet and his Companions represent the perfect balance between Qur'an, Hadith, and Sunna and this accounts for the success of the early generation of Islam as well as parts of the later period when these three were combined in Muslim practice. Conversely, periods of Muslim civilization stagnated and became backward on account of the gradual separation of these three. Thus, whereas in much of the late-medieval Muslim period the Hadith along with *tariqa* (Sufi orders) had emerged as the primary source of Islamic knowledge and everyday Islamic practices and conduct, and the Qur'an was safely placed on the high *thakht* (high corner-shelf of the House), in the modern period from the mid-nineteenth-century, Islamic reformers emphasized the centrality of the Qur'an as the primary source of Islam and everyday Muslim practices and conduct and had a critical outlook on Tradition (Hadith and Sunna) and Sufi orders. In contrast, Gülen, following Imam Rabbani's theory of two *mims*,[43] also stresses the different dimensions of the Prophet and strongly emphasizes the unity of the physical and metaphysical realms in the personality of Prophet Muhammad.[44]

Sufism in Gülen's Islamic thought

This brings us to the role of Sufism in the construction of Gülen's Islamic thought. The Sufi (*tasawwuf*) dimension of the Gülen Movement has attracted much attention in the literature, particularly in the English-medium literature, on the Gülen Movement. Much of this literature has examined the role of Sufism in the Gülen Movement or in the construction of Gülen's Islamic philosophy either from the point of view of presenting Gülen's Islamic thought as advocating the cause of "personal/private Islam," or highlighting the Gülen Movement as a liberal and democratic social movement, or even going to the extent of presenting Gülen's exposition of Sufism as *the* narrative of Islam. These explanations of the role of Sufism in the Gülen Movement partly emanate from the scholar's desire to place Gülen's Islamic thought or the Gülen Movement as a bridge between Islam and modernity, which does not correspond to Gülen's imagination of Sufism and its place in his Islamic cosmology. For Gülen, Sufism is important but only one dimension of Islam.

Certainly, Gülen accords a very high importance to the practice of Sufism in a Muslim's life, which is evident from the fact that he calls Sufism the "Spiritual Dimension of Islam" and the "heart of Islam." In recognizing the service of Sufism to Islam, Gülen mostly draws inspiration from Naqshbandi Sufi discourses as expounded by Imam Rabbani, Khalid al-Baghdadi and Bediüzzaman Said Nursi,[45] and has penned three volumes on Sufism under the title "*Emerald Hills of the Heart: Key Concepts in Practice of Sufism* (Vol 1, 2 and 3),[46] which is a detailed exposition of major principles of Sufism revolving around the inner qualities of human being in order to attain God's consciousness." The centrality of Sufi ideas in the Gülen Movement can be gauged from the fact that the movement has recently produced two separate volumes, *Qualities of a Devoted Soul* (2013)[47] and *Inner Dynamics of the People of Hizmet* (2013)[48] which contain most of the Sufi ideas and practices for the purpose of the socialization and moral training of Hizmet volunteers.

Though Gülen comes from a community setting where the tradition of the Naqshbandi Sufi *tariqa* was dominant, following Nursi's dictum that "this is not the age of *tariqa*," he did not establish any *tariqa* in the tradition of Sufi orders, probably for two reasons: first, he saw the Sufi *tariqa* had itself become empty of the "Muhammadi spirit" on account of its excessive ritualism, miraclism and *piri-muridi* culture, and thus it was no more capable of renewing the task of *dawa*; second, the institutional form of *tariqa* that suited the localized feudal economy had become irrelevant in the modern setting characterized by mass communication, the national economy, and the lonely individual. For him, it is the principles of Sufism, rather than the *tariqa* form, which is important. As he stated in reply to a query about the relationship between *Risale-i Nur* and Sufism, "I think the mistake here is due to mixing Sufism with dervish orders (*tariqa*). Sufism is Islam's inner life; dervish orders are institutions established in later centuries to represent and live this life."[49]

For Gülen, Sufism is a multilayered concept and operates at multiple levels in an individual Muslim life. Broadly, Sufism complements by "humanizing" and "spiritualizing" other branches of Islam such as *kalam* and *fiqh*, thereby ensuring the balance in the practice of Islam. In other words, much like Imam Ghazali and Imam Rabbani, Gülen builds his Islamic narratives through integrating Sufism into the Sunni-Hanafi frame of reference. Through the regular practice of *dhikr* (remembrance of God)[50] and attaining various Stations (a Sufi term for attaining higher levels of consciousness one after another), the individual attempts to internalize the moral and ethical conception of Islam or "state of Godly consciousness" at the level of heart. In other words, values attached to Islam are not perfected in day-to-day life except through a Sufism-inspired process of what I call the "heartization of Islam." At a more practical level, it is a *life-centered discourse*, which is aimed at the ethical and moral transformation of an individual based on the Prophetic model of *insan-i kamil* (perfect human). For, according to Gülen, "Morality is the essence of religion and a most fundamental portion of the Divine Message… The Prophet, who is the greatest embodiment of moral principles, said: 'Islam consists in good morals; I have been sent to perfect and complete good morals.'"[51] Gülen saw in every Muslim a potential to be transformed into an "*insan-i kamil*" through the method and principles of *tasawwuf*.

As a discourse and a method Sufism intends to imitate the Prophetic model of *insan-i kamil* by overcoming the egoistic, carnal, and hedonistic desires of human beings; by harnessing the ethical and moral energy of human beings such as altruism, trust, love, compassion, courage, honesty, loyalty, peace, cooperation, self-disciplining, asceticism, goodness, thankfulness, forgiveness, helplessness, and so on, it channels them into collective action to serve God and humanity with sincerity, responsibility, and humility under the constant guidance of God's presence, for His sake only and without any expectation of return. It is about "living among people, but constantly being with God."[52] In short, Sufism is a regulatory theological power that prevents human beings from committing excessive indulgence in materialism and guides human action from an ethical and moral perspective. It inculcates God-fearing consciousness and an attitude of loving, caring, and respect towards God's creation by absorbing and dissolving the self into the "Muhammadi spirit" and God-consciousness.[53] In this regard, it may be noted that Ali Ünal, an Islamic scholar and one of the Islamic intellectuals of the Gülen Movement, was referring to this "lack of Muhammadi spirit" and "God-consciousness" when he said that "we [meaning Muslims in general and Turkish Muslims in particular] were defeated in ourselves, not by enemies."[54]

In fact, Gülen's entire Islamic discourse is geared towards retrieving the inner balance between the physical and spiritual dimensions of Islam, which is considered to have once prevailed during the period of the Prophet, what Gülen, following Imam Rabbani, has described as *al-asr al-saadah* (Age of Happiness),[55] the imbalance of which in the later periods is considered to have led to the qualitative decline of Muslim civilizations. Gülen's balanced, integrated approach towards Islam not only rests on the Islamic idea of inherent order in God's creation but also stems from the Islamic conception of human nature. Unlike the dominant Western materialist philosophy that primarily sees human nature in terms of materialistic, negative attributes—selfish, egoistic, aggressive, conflictual—probably in line with the Christian doctrine of Sin (in which "the Fall of Adam" was considered a depraved, immoral, sinful act so the human being is essentially a sinful entity and earth a corrupting place) that constructed a power-centered social science discourse for explaining and analyzing human development, Islam treats the human being primarily as a moral entity and considers goodness, cooperativeness, and altruism as his/her basic nature.[56] Further, Islam takes a holistic view of the human being in which the person is composed of spirit, soul, and body. As Gülen states, "We are creatures composed of not only a body or mind or feeling or spirit; rather, we are harmonious compositions of all these elements."[57] Thus, the different branches of Islam, in harmony with each other, are geared to develop a composite, balanced growth of the human personality. The ignorance of any aspect of human beings will result in a deformed personality.

It is from this perspective of Islam that Gülen constructs a powerful but flexible inclusive Islamic theology of peace, love, tolerance, dialogue, cooperation, altruism, social action, human rights, and pluralism that emphasizes, rather celebrates, common universal values. As he puts it,

> Regardless of how their adherents implement their faith in their daily lives, such generally accepted values as love, respect, tolerance, forgiveness, mercy, human rights, peace, brotherhood, and freedom are all values exalted by religion. Most of these values are accorded the highest precedence in the messages brought by Moses, Jesus, and Muhammad, upon them be peace, as well as in the message of Buddha and even Zarathustra, Lao-Tzu, Confucius, and the Hindu Prophets.[58]

The inclusiveness of Gülen's Islamic thought is further evident from his definition of a Muslim: "As a Muslim, I accept all Prophets and Books sent to different peoples throughout history, and regard belief in them as an essential principle of being Muslim."[59] Similarly, he imagines a "golden generation" that will manifest the best of values exalted by all faiths: "the loyalty and faithfulness of Adam, the resolve and steadfastness of Noah, the devotion and gentleness of Abraham, the valor and dynamism of Moses, the forbearance and compassion of Jesus."[60] In fact, the volunteers in the Gülen Movement do organize special *sohbets* (community gatherings to read together or for lectures), keep fasts and offer special prayers on some of the important dates connected not only with Prophet Muhammad and Companions but also Prophets of other monotheistic traditions, such as Noah's pudding. This is also a common practice among a good section of Turkish Muslims, however, Hizmet's contribution in this regard is to take it further to celebrate them with non-Muslims, too.

The flexibility inherent in his Islamic approach allows Gülen to conduct *ijtihad* to meet the modern-day social, political, and economic requirements of Muslims on the basis of the principle of Essential and non-Essential dimensions of Islam without in anyway compromising the basic structure of Islamic faith, unlike Abduh and many other modern Islamic scholars/reformers who also invoked the thesis of essential vs. non-essential Islam to facilitate modern changes. Thus, Gülen firmly takes a position on the headscarf issue in Turkey. According to him,

> "This issue is not as important as the essentials of faith and the pillars of Islam. It is a matter of secondary importance (*furu*) in *fiqh*... In the sixteenth and seventeenth year of Muhammad's Prophethood (peace be upon him), Muslim women's heads were still not covered (in the prescribed way). It was not included in the pillars of Islam or the essentials of faith."[61]

Though he did not issue a fatwa on this issue, he advises Muslim girls to seek education opportunities even if the state prohibits the wearing of headscarf.[62] He considers the issue of dressing and keeping a beard as "personal choice," for Islam does not impose a certain type of dressing nor is beard an obligatory (*fard*) Muslim practice.[63] Similarly, he does not endorse the practice of polygamy in the Muslim family on the grounds that it is neither a part of faith nor a *sunna* of the Prophet Muhammad:

> "There is no record in the Qur'an or the *hadith* that it is *sunnah* to marry more than one woman by means of religious ceremony. In the Chapter of Women (Sura al-Nisa), permission to marry more than one woman under special circumstances is mentioned only as a license or a special permission. However, marrying just one woman is encouraged to the degree of being mandatory. Thus, no

> one can consider marrying four women a matter of fulfilling a *sunnah*, they cannot claim to have fulfilled any religious law by doing so."[64]

Some of his other bold *ijtihad* includes permitting artificial fertilization by a childless couple with a warning to be vigilant as this might be misused, allowing the would-be marriage partners to check each other's medical background before tying the knot to avoid future medical problems on the ground of public health, permitting autopsy for the purpose of identification of a killer, and allowing pig products in bait for fish, for fish change the nature of pig products in their digestive systems.[65]

The above flexibility in Gülen's Islamic positions vis-à-vis modern-day problems flows from his treatment of Islam as "discourse," not as a matter of identity to be preserved in a particular form: behavioral or institutional. Accordingly, Muslims can maintain their faith even while operating in the hostile, secular milieu without bothering about the form in which Islam has to be practiced. From this perspective Gülen does not consider the veil or the beard as essential elements of faith or as indispensable to the accomplishment of Muslim life. As he remarked, "I see the robe, turban, beard and loose trousers as details. Muslims should not be drowning in detail… Choosing not to wear then should not be construed as weakening the Muslim Turkish identity. No one should be categorized as sinner because of such things."[66] Thus, the volunteers of the Gülen Movement are indistinguishable from secular Turks in terms of Westernized appearance, clothing, manners and mode of social interaction, but are die-hard Islamic in ethos and conduct. The absence of Islam as primarily identity discourse, which otherwise characterizes almost all modern Islamist political and social movements, has allowed the volunteers of the Gülen Movement to operate with ease within the secular-modern structure and participate and compete in the West-dominated global opportunity structure. Tahsin Koral, a volunteer then working in India, on being asked what the Gülen Movement has given to him, stated, "I can move freely throughout the globe without being fearful of anything on account of my Muslim identity.[67]" In fact, the Islamic narrative of Fethullah Gülen attempts to form "a virtuous, global, Muslim community" without exclusive focus on identity and ritualistic dimensions of the process of community formation. Unlike Islamic traditionalists' emphasis on the ritual purity of Islamic practice and post-modernists' celebration of the discourse of identity, Gülen's construction of "Muslimness" is reflexive and flexible and does not hinder interacting and working in a modern setting or engaging with the institutions and ideas of modernity such as secularism, democracy, human rights, nationalism, gender justice, without necessarily accepting the ontological and normative vision of modernity.

The treatment of Islam as discourse allows Gülen not to identify modernity and Islam with a fixed set of values, but to see them as a living discourse, a specific knowledge formation without the conflict between the two that the conventional understanding suggests and thus facilitates the modern changes in Muslim societies. From this perspective Gülen comes close to Iranian philosopher Abdolkarim Soroush's distinction between religion and religious knowledge[68] and echoes the position of Jürgen Habermas, one of the most important philosophers of the twentieth century, who has characterized religion and modernity as two "complementary intellectual formations." According to Habermas,

> This modern reason will learn to understand itself only when it clarifies its relation to a contemporary religious consciousness, which has become reflexive by grasping the shared origin of the two complementary intellectual formations in the cognitive advance of the Axial Age. In speaking of complementary intellectual formations, I am expressly rejecting two positions: first, the blinkered enlightenment which is unenlightened about itself and which denies religion any rational content, but also, second, Hegel's view for which religion represents an intellectual formation worthy of being recalled, but only in the form of a "representational thinking" (vorstellendes Denken) which is subordinate to philosophy. Faith remains opaque for knowledge in a way which may neither be denied nor simply accepted. This reflects the inconclusive nature of the confrontation between a self-critical reason which is willing to learn and contemporary religious convictions. This confrontation can sharpen post-secular society's awareness of the unexhausted force (das Unabgeholtene) of religious traditions. Secularization functions less as a filter separating out the contents of traditions than as a transformer which redirects the flow of tradition.[69]

Gülen's conception of Islamic history

Any description of Gülen's approach towards Islam is not complete unless one also deals with his understanding of Islamic history; for his approach towards Islam partly derives from his imagination of Islamic history. What is Gülen's imagination of Islamic history? How does he represent Islamic history in modern times? How does "Turkish Islam" affect his imagination of history and Islamic history in particular? Though there is hardly any literature that reflects upon Gülen's conception of history, particularly Islamic history, one can deduce his orientation by analysis of his vast speeches and writings on the Islamic past.

First, unlike many Islamic traditionalists and modernists, Islamic history, for him, does not become frozen in a particular time—the period of Prophet Muhammad or the Four Rightly Guided Caliphs, or the three generations of Companions or the period of the four Sunni schools of Islamic law. Since it is God who is at the center of human history, history is always in continuous motion and ever present in human lives. Hence, the Islamic view of history is neither time- nor space-bound. Gülen not only keeps reminding Muslims about the Prophetic model of Prophet Muhammad and his Companions but also about many bright spots, such as famous Muslim personalities, rulers, empires, *'alim*, and Sufis of the Islamic past and projects them not only as "relevant" but as integral to constructing an enlightened Islamic future in which,

> Mawlana Jalal al-Din Rumi will come together with Taftazani, Yunus Emre will sit on the same prayer mat with Mahdumguli, Fuzuli will embrace Mehmed Akif, Ulug Bey will salute Abu Hanifa, Hodja Dehhani will sit knee to knee with Imam Ghazali, Muhyi al-Din ibn Arabi will throw roses to Ibn Sina, Imam Rabbani will be thrilled by the glad tidings for Bediüzzaman Said Nursi.[70]

Second, Turkish Islamic history is an important ingredient in Gülen's conception of Islam. In this context it is worth quoting Gülen's use of the term "Turkish Islam" and "Turkish Muslimness":

> "The Hanafi understanding and Turkish interpretation dominates more than three-fourths of the Islamic world. This understanding is very dear to me. If you like, you can call this Turkish Islam. Just as I see no serious canonical obstacle to this, I don't think it should

> upset anyone. Actually, I think the world needs an interpretation of the Qur'an and Sunna that explains, addresses and belongs to everyone. Societies that have never founded states, never known the spirit of Sufism, never experienced the events that the Turkish nation has faced because of the great states it has founded, and have never gained the centuries of experience it gained cannot really say anything in the name of universality. Therefore, when evaluating the Turkish version and experience of Islam, and why it accepted the Hanafi school of law as its formal code of law, the history of Islam in general and Turkish history in particular should be kept in mind. … Turkish Islam is composed of the main, unchanging principles of Islam found in the Qur'an and Sunna, as well as in the forms that its aspects open to interpretation assumed during Turkish history, together with Sufism. More than any other Muslim country, Sufism has spread among the Turks in both Central Asia and Turkey. This is why Turkish Islam always has been broader, deeper, more tolerant and inclusive, and based on love. If we can breathe this spirit into the modern world's carcass, I hope it will revive. The Turkish nation interpreted Islam in the areas open to interpretation. From this viewpoint, it attained a very broad spectrum and became the religion of great states. For this reason, I think the term Turkish Muslimness is appropriate. Another aspect of this is that in addition to profound devotion to the Qur'an and Sunna, the Turks always have been open to Sufism, Islam's spiritual aspect. Sufism has spread among Turks more than others."[71]

Further, in an interview, he made clear his preference for the Turkish language:

> "Had I been given the ability to write to the same extent in both Arabic [the language of Qur'an] and Turkish, I would choose Turkish, because we must make Turkish the language of the future."[72]

Thus what is evident from his expression of "Turkish Islam" or Turkish "Muslimness" or his preference for Turkish language is that since he believes that Sufism has far deeper roots in Turkey than in other parts of the Muslim world, in addition to the fact that the Ottoman-Turkish-Hanafi interpretation of Islam has dominated three-fourths of the Islamic world in the past, the Turkish version of Islam is far balanced, broader, deeper, more inclusive, and tolerant in terms of "historical memory of lived Islamic practices" irrespective of the language (Ottoman-Arabic or Ottoman-Turkish) in which Islamic discourses and practices were expressed, recorded, and debated. Therefore, one should factor in Turkish Islamic history, language, and understanding while examining matters related to Islam. This partly explains why Gülen's narrative of Islam involves the life-histories of important Islamic personalities of Ottoman Turkey—rulers, *'alim*, architects, poets, and so on, in addition to his general emphasis on the life-experience of the Prophet and his Companions.[73]

Third, Islam exhorts a Muslim to see not only the outward manifestations of the different happenings of human life, but to study the undercurrent of ideals and motives, which have shaped those happenings. It is for this reason that Gülen considers Mehmet II as a great man for his vision and not for his conquest of Istanbul. He states, "For those who submitted their hearts to the ideals of the Prophet, the opening of Istanbul is as insignificant as the conquest of a little village. Fatih [Mehmet II] was great in his ideals, not with the thing he did."[74] Here, teleologically speaking, Gülen echoes the position of Imam Rabbani. According to Friedmann,

> After his release from prison, Sirhindi wrote one letter to Jahangir. He wishes success to the imperial armies and then proceeds to apply the Sufi dichotomy of form (*sura*) and essence (*haqiqa*) to military affairs. He makes a distinction between "formal victory" (*surat-i-fath*), which can be achieved by the "army of war" (*lashkar-i ghaza*) and "real victory" (*haqiqat-i-fath*), which can be achieved by "the army of prayer" (*lashkar-i dua*). He has no doubt in his mind that the army of prayer is the stronger one, because prayer, not the sword, is the only way to avert the divine decree.[75]

Fourth, Gülen judges historical events mostly from a moral point of view and sees the rise and fall of civilizations as integrally related to the rise and fall in value consciousness in these civilizations. However, unlike others, according to Gülen, the motion of rise and fall in history is neither linear, nor a cyclical one that revolves around liberal-reformist-synthesis Islam and fundamentalist-rejectionist Islam, nor circular, but a spiral which may be "imagined as the connection of open-ended circles through which it is both possible to rise up and to fall down continuously. History moves like a 'spiral curve' and represents the opposite motions of rising and falling. Spirals of time and space reminds not only of the rise and fall but the processes of construction, deconstruction and reconstruction."[76]

Fifth, Gülen's spiral notion of Islamic history provides Muslims with "a state of optimistic hope" of once again reaching the stage of perfection by means of "renewing" the faith within themselves without waiting for any messiah (or Mehdi) to come. Thus, in Islam hope is intrinsically connected with faith. The Qur'an, according to Fazlur Rahman, "condemned *hopelessness* [*emphasis mine*] as one of the gravest errors, charged man with limitless potentialities and made him squarely responsible for discharging this 'trust.'"[77] Gülen too underlines this interconnection between faith and hopefulness: "The one who is a believer is hopeful and the [extent] of his hope is as much as his belief. Those who have been defeated in the practicality of the world are those who have failed in the realm of hope. The individual lives by means of hope, and it is also by means of hope that a collectivity gains life and sets about prospering."[78] It is on the basis of this twin interrelated maxim of "hope and faith" that Gülen intends to build his "golden generation" who collectively will be a panacea for the ills of the modern world. The idea of a golden generation is premised on the model of *insan-i kamil* (perfect human) anchored in the model of the Prophet, who symbolizes the "balance" of all virtues and wisdoms—love, compassion, tolerance, peace, faith, reason, order, loyalty, trust, altruism, leadership, family and action, mind and heart, and so on. Thus, it is in this sense that Gülen remarked, "It is undoubtedly clear that today the conquest of the world can be realized … by penetrating into people's hearts with the Qur'an in one hand and reason in the other."[79]

Finally, history is about representation and presentation. Gülen is profoundly concerned about the image and representation of Islam in the public sphere. He attributes the ills of the Muslim world to a deficiency in the act of representation. According to him, "What is lacking in the Islamic world is not science, technology, or wealth… All of these have influences of their own; but the most important aspect of all is the image that we give out as a believer. The interpretation of Islam (by others) depends on our behavior and conduct."[80] He further said, "Our deficiency is with regards to a Muslim-like image. Because of this deficiency, we do not have people today like Sadreddin Konevi, Rumi, Naqshband, Hasan Shadhili, Ahmad Badawi, Imam Rabbani, Mawlana Khalid or Bediüzzaman… Even if the Qur'an is kept on high shelves in velvet covers but is not represented by people, then the Qur'an cannot speak for itself.[81] He reiterated the same concern as follows: "the question that we should ask ourselves as Muslims is whether we have introduced Islam and its Prophet properly to the world. Have we followed his example in such way as to instill admiration? We must do so not with words but with our actions."[82]

In Gülen's paradigm the issue of representation is centrally linked with the issue of communicating faith (*dawa*). The effectiveness of *dawa* depends upon how one represents and conducts oneself. As he states, "Without conscious and strong-minded representatives, the Holy Qur'an experiences a pathetic situation… A perfect team of representatives, a team that devotes itself completely to communicating God's name and to becoming a part of the religion will be able to illustrate properly the ways in which the Qur'an finds expression."[83] Thus, words without actions are a poor form of representation and conduct and often harm the image of Islam if words are not matched by actions. Hence, direct preaching or advocating (*dawa*) does not have a place in the Hizmet Movement. The Movement strongly believes in the universal language of conduct and exemplary actions as the most effective source of *dawa* through which Islam has conquered millions of hearts since its inception. As a Guide Book for Volunteers of the Hizmet movement notes: *"being is important; preaching and advocating is not important but living and role modeling is important."*[84] A cursory look at volunteers of the Hizmet movement (mostly Turkish that I have interacted with and observed) indicates how conscious they are in terms of both their bodily representation (a Westernized form of clothing and presentation) and conduct (Islamic ethical and moral sensitivity) with a developed sense of becoming a role model while engaging with the world every day. It is this very conception of Islam that has produced one of the largest Islamic movements (Hizmet) based on the Islamic philosophy of altruism within a short span of four decades. Though a *tajdid* movement is not a unique phenomenon in Islamic history,[85] a "*tajdid* by conduct"[86] on such a global scale is certainly a novelty in Islamic history.

CHAPTER 6

GÜLEN'S LIFE TRAJECTORY AND EMERGENCE OF THE MOVEMENT

As the preceding chapters assert the Islamic roots of the Gülen Movement and discuss Gülen's approach to Islam and its differences from the tradition of Islamic modernism/reformism, a number of related questions emerge at this juncture. How does Gülen's Islamic approach influence the development of the Gülen Movement? What was/is the material and ideological context that has shaped the Gülen Movement? Is the emergence of the Gülen Movement a local Turkish phenomenon or was it also influenced by the revivalist trend of Islam since its inception? How has the life experience of Gülen shaped the emergence of the Gülen Movement?

Situating Gülen

Almost all scholarly works on the Gülen Movement have attempted to locate Gülen's Islamic ideas within the contemporary local-national context of Turkey. The Islamic legacy of Said Nursi along with the Kemalist reforms, the political context of the Turkish-Islam synthesis during the 1980s, the policies of Turgut Özal, and the Naqshbandi tradition of Anatolia, or what is called "Turkish Islam," often constitutes the national-material context for the development of Gülen's humanist, Islamic discourse. İhsan Yılmaz's paraphrasing of the Gülen Movement as a "child of the Kemalist Revolution"[1] and the dominant thinking among Turkish intellectuals, as well among the rank and file of the Gülen Movement, that "Gülen is an executioner of Nursi's ideas" sums up this trend of localizing Gülen and the Gülen Movement. A sharper localization of Gülen's ideas and discourse appears in the analysis by Hakan Yavuz. He highlights how the Frontier Islamic culture of Erzurum, called *Dadaş* culture, shaped Gülen's masculine, anti-Shia, homogenized, statist and nationalist understanding of Islam during much of his life in Turkey.[2] Bekim Agai also concurs that "Gülen's earlier writings, based on conspiracy theories against Turkey, are full of anti-missionary and anti-Western passages."[3]

There is also a growing attempt to divide Gülen's ideas and legacy into two phases: 1960–1999 (the Turkish context) and post-1999 (the American context) periods. It has been argued that it is only with his migration to the United States and his exposure to American/Western liberalism that Gülen began to utilize the universal discourse of human rights, democracy, liberalism, interfaith dialogue and tolerance in Islamic terms. Yavuz has even called the post-American phase of Gülen's life the birth of the "New Gülen."[4] Others such as İhsan Yılmaz and Recep Kaymakcan also shared this sentiment and consider Gülen's sojourn in America as qualitative change in his thinking making a second stage in the Gülen Movement,[5] as if to draw a parallel with Said Nursi, whose life trajectory is predominantly studied with reference to "Old Said" (–1923), "New Said" (1923–1950 or 1960) and sometimes also Third Said (1950–1960).

The above has its own merits in the explanation of social phenomena. However, a mere contextual reading of a phenomenon suffers from reductionism on the one hand and denial of the autonomy of ideas and its transformative role in societies on the other. This approach also renders injustice to the transformative role of the important personality in history who moves and rules over millions of hearts. For instance, Bekim Agai appears to be dismissive of the original contribution of Fethullah Gülen and considers his success due to the "packaging" of ideas in different ways suited for the respective audience.[6] According to him, "Gülen shows a distinct readiness to adapt his messages, theorized in writings, to the targeted audience. One specific strategy used to attract people is the presentation of his ideas without stressing their Islamic background."[7] Thus, what is clear from the above statement is that Gülen's success is not due to any *epistemological breakthrough* but due to the "packaging" and "mode" of presentation of his ideas. Yavuz treats Gülen in a more or less similar fashion: "Today, when Gülen talks about Islam, one hears the voice and message of Nursi."[8]

A part of the problem with such work on the Gülen Movement is that it miserably fails to explain what makes it the most dominant Islamic movement within Turkey, outstripping the reach and influence of other Islamic movements, if it lacks original idea and praxis. Why could other Nur groups, if one considers the Gülen Movement a faction of the Nur movement, not be as successful as the Gülen Movement? Moreover, Gülen's distance to the left and Middle-Eastern regimes has been much exaggerated, partly in order to portray his Islamic thoughts as "narrow" and primarily to locate, rather confine, him within the Turkish-nationalist trajectory so as to deny him a place in the annals of Islamic cosmology and heroes.

Gülen himself once conceded: "I think belonging to a race does not have any intrinsic value... Like all the people from Erzurum, I might have some influence of nationalism on me."[9] The young Gülen was soon to discard conspiracy theory and, along with Turgut Özal, since the mid-1980s significantly contributed towards lifting the nation from sterile statism and populism entwined with an inward-looking mentality fearful of external conspiracy and injected a new sense of confidence to participate and compete in the fast-emerging opportunity structures thrown up by the process of globalization. Moreover, had Gülen been a prisoner of his Turkish nationalist identity—an identity that is partly derived from the anti-Arab construction of Turkish nationalism—the Movement would not have launched *Hira* Magazine, which is targeted to reach out to the Arab intellectuals and people to enhance dialogue and understanding of each other.

Beyond the local-national context

In order to engage with various facets of Fethullah Gülen's ideas and praxis and the Gülen Movement, it is imperative to situate them within the combined *interactive and interpretative* process of the Great Tradition of Islam and the Little Tradition of Islam so as to understand the Islamic positions of Fethullah Gülen on the range of issues affecting the social, economic, and political life of Muslims including Turkish Muslims.[10] For, following Talal Asad, the discourse of Islam is essentially a discourse of "correct" Islamic practice subject to the understanding of the *'alim* (plural: *'ulama*).[11] Gülen's engagement with both traditions of Islam has been explored in great detail in the preceding chapter. The subsequent pages will demonstrate the interplay of the Great and Little Tradition of Islam in Gülen's ideas and thought while reflecting upon the ensuing problems of "modern" Turkey.

For Gülen, Turkey appears as a part of the organic whole of Islam; hence, its problems can only be addressed in the light of Islam's experience and history, which also includes the Turkish experience of Islam. *The Statue of Our Souls*, which is a collection of his most important articles that taken together contain a vision document of his life process, reflects this approach of Gülen towards addressing the problems of the Muslim world in general and Turkey in particular. It is not, as the case has been made out, that the then-prevailing local, Turkish, material context was instrumental in shaping his outlook on Islam, Turkish nationalism, and other contemporary debates. Rather, the interplay of the Great Tradition and Little Tradition of Islam have shaped the *life-in-context-responses* of Gülen on the range of issues in the political, social, and economic realms.

Early childhood

[Syed] Muhammed Fethullah Gülen[12] was born in the Korucuk village of the eastern Anatolian province of Erzurum in 1938[13] in an impoverished family of eleven siblings (eight brothers and three sisters). Gülen is the third eldest among all his siblings and eldest among sons. It was an extended family consisting of 30 members.[14] From all accounts, including my field interview with Gülen's relatives, it appears that Gülen's immediate and extended family was deeply religious. Both his father, Ramiz Efendi, and mother, Refia Gülen, were secretly teaching Qur'an to the boys and girls of the village. Ramiz Efendi, was also an imam in the village mosque, in addition to being a shepherd.[15] Today Erzurum hosts a mosque named after Gülen's father, Ramiz Efendi.[16] He also had sufficient knowledge of Islamic and Ottoman history, which he used to share with family members.[17]

According to Seyfullah Gülen, younger brother of Gülen and other relatives, "Many *alims*—both from our mother's and father's side—used to frequent our house and our house had virtually turned into a center of debates and discussion about Islam, Islamic history, and Ottoman history. Unlike us, Gülen used to keenly participate and listen to these scholarly discussions."[18] Gülen spent up to nine years in the village. Thus, Gülen's early exposure to Islamic values, teachings, and socialization took place within the Islamic milieu of his extended family, where he was initiated into the culture of Qur'an reading and ritualistic aspects of Islam and learnt the Islamic values of love, cleanliness, respect, and cooperation. He was recognized as a "special child"— all members of the family were respectful and loving to him. The family members used to wait for Gülen to join the family dinner and did not eat food without him.[19] He is reported to have finished a reading of the Qur'an at the age of four and his mother organized a community feast both in the recognition of exceptional talent of her child and also due to prevalent local tradition.[20] Since that age Gülen has never missed performing daily prayers (*namaz* in Turkish, *salat* in Arabic), according to his biography.[21]

Gülen became *Hafidh* (one who has memorized the Qur'an) when he was around the age of ten. He also attended a public primary school for three years in his native village. Subsequently, by the age of ten he moved to Alvar along with his father, who was appointed imam by the community in a mosque. He remained in Alvar for around five years receiving Islamic education in a *madrasa*[22] under the guidance of Muhammed Lutfi Efendi, a Naqshbandi Sufi Sheikh, who was also known as "Alvarlı Efe"—the most famous *'alim* in that region at that time.[23] From Lutfi Efendi, Gülen learnt the Sufi-spiritual-humanistic dimension of Islam. On several occasions, he has personally acknowledged his indebtedness to and admiration for Lutfi Efendi for the latter's contribution in shaping his understanding of Islam. He found in his death a "void that could not be filled."[24] Another contribution that Gülen has acknowledged in the making of his Islamic personality is that of his grandmother whom he has described as "more than a hundred *'alim*."

During his childhood years Gülen displayed a different characteristic from other children. According to a family source, he was never found playing with other village children of his age group. Unlike other children, there was a sense of aloofness in him and at times he would point out "cheating" and "wrong doing" committed by children while playing.[25] At the age of fourteen, Gülen started giving speeches in the villages on Islam, the Prophet's life and the Companions, and expected others to call him "Hodja." He even asked his brother Seyfullah not to address him as "Abi" (elder brother) but as "Hodja."[26] These were some of the early signs that at a very early age Gülen was becoming aware of his "self" and started giving shape to his life in search of one of the most fundamental questions that has haunted many thinkers in all ages: *what is the meaning of life*? By this time, he used to frequent *'alim*'s graves for both a source of inspiration and mark of respect to the departed souls due to prevailing local custom and tradition.[27]

Religious education in Erzurum

At the age of fourteen or fifteen Gülen moved to a *madrasa*/Sufi tekke (officially banned but still existing underground) in Erzurum for higher Islamic education and training. He stayed there from 1954–1959 before moving to Edirne, according to Mehmet Kırkıncı (born 1928, now deceased), one of the most respected Islamic scholars in Turkey in recent time,[28] who was (at the time of interview in 2011) looking after the *madrasa*/Sufi lodge where Gülen stayed. It must be highlighted here that, notwithstanding the Kemalist attack on Islamic institutions, traditions and values, the Islamic religious and cultural infrastructure managed to survive in much of central and eastern Anatolia. *Madrasa*s and Sufi lodges used to function secretly and illegally. Mehmet Kırkıncı narrated how Islam was preserved in Erzurum and in much of Anatolia:

> "We in much of Anatolia including Erzurum neither accepted nor opposed the Kemalist state. People learnt Islam secretly and continued with the Islamic Ottoman history and memory. When *madrasa*s and tekke (lodge) were closed down, Allah sent *Risale-i Nur* and then *Risale-i Nur madrasa*s came into existence. There was one *'alim* from every *madrasa*, which was closed down by the government, for every three villages in Anatolia. After the Democratic Party came into power in 1950, there was much religious freedom; the government opened *imam-hatip* and Qur'anic schools with the support of the community. On June 16, 1950 *adhan* started to be pronounced in Arabic again.[29] It was *asr* time. People, particularly women, came out and were crying at hearing *adhan* in Arabic. Islam was returned to our life. Since then Islam in Turkey is growing."[30]

Erzurum in Anatolia holds a special position from the Islamic point of view. The province has the distinction of defending Islam against the Russians, (Shia) Iranians, Armenians, and Greek Christian Orthodox through much of modern history. Kemal Atatürk organized the First Nationalist Congress in Erzurum to mobilize the Muslim masses against the European occupation. It was here that Said Nursi camped for thirty-five days to explain his concept of a university to the city's elites and peoples.[31] The province was also at the forefront of fighting the communist threat during the 1950s and 1960s. Gülen himself, after returning from military service in 1963, participated in the anti-communist movement.

This geo-strategic politics of Erzurum is considered to have shaped a particular conception of Islam, what Yavuz, has termed "Frontier Islam" or "Dadaş culture" in which Islam is historically articulated and conserved in a masculine, community, statist, and nationalist form. Yavuz believes Gülen carried this statist and nationalist conception of Islam until he moved to the United States, where he began to interpret Islam in terms of the universal discourse of human rights, liberalism, democracy, individualism, and secularism. Though I do not want to undermine the geo-strategic importance of Erzurum or the statist and nationalist tradition of Islam in general that otherwise prevails in Turkey, in my interviews with most people including intellectuals and *'ulama* from this city, they all emphasized the high tradition of *tasawwuf* (Sufi tradition) as the cultural identity of Erzurum as well as a factor in withstanding the onslaught of the Kemalist attack on Islam.[32]

It was in this political culture of Erzurum that Gülen received his religious education. According to Mehmet Kırkıncı, "We, including Gülen, were sleeping, eating and reading together in this *madrasa*. It was here that Gülen was learning Arabic language in a class of eight students from Osman Bektaş and came to be acquainted with Said Nursi's work, *Risale-i Nur*.[33]" As the government had placed a ban on *Risale-i Nur*, taking the name of Bediüzzaman Said Nursi and teaching *Risale-i Nur* directly was not possible. Nonetheless, according to Kırkıncı, Gülen became aware of Nursi and *Risale-i Nur* in these *madrasas*: "Once Gülen asked, 'We see everything but we cannot see God. Why?' I said, "Because of the glaring brightness of His manifestation" and added, 'This is not my word but that of Bediüzzaman Said Nursi.' Gülen was shocked to hear this and became aware of Nursi for the first time at this point of his life."[34]

The exposure to Nursi's ideas and teachings provided a different perspective to Gülen to understand Islam and also expanded his horizon of Islamic understanding, according to Kırkıncı. "He took everything from *Risale-i Nur*. He is implementing ideas of Nursi," asserts Kırkıncı. However, he also acknowledges that over the years, "Gülen has enriched and expanded the interpretation of *Risale-i Nur*." Reflecting upon some of his personal qualities, Kırkıncı said that Gülen has four special attributes: "good memory, persuasive capacity, power of speech and a habitual reader of Islamic texts, especially reading of the Sahabas' lives (lives of the Prophet's Companions)."[35] Whether Gülen was or is conscious of these qualities or not, he rose to fame on the basis of his power of speech while delivering sermons (*vaaz*) before daily prayers *namaz* and on Fridays in the mosques. We will explore the content of his speeches and lectures at a later stage. Suffice it to state here that by the end of his stay in the Erzurum *madrasa*, Gülen came to develop a strong sense of devotion and service to Islam with a commitment to ethical and moral regeneration—a conviction that grew more firmly within him as he moved to Edirne and later to Izmir, the two most Westernized cities of modern Turkey, where in view of the mixing of the sexes and the growth in Western lifestyles, the perceived decline of Islamic ethical and moral values would have become more visible and palpable to him. It is not without reason that Hizmet under the leadership of Gülen began its journey from most Westernized parts of Turkey.

Early signs of commitment to Islam

Gülen's emerging sincerity of intention, determination, endurance of hardship, and conviction to serve Islam, God, and Muslims (later humanity) is evident from his many statements, actions, and personal anecdotes. First, from a number of interviews it becomes clear how subject matter such as Qur'an, faith, education, and the issue of bringing Islam to the youth has preoccupied Gülen right from his Erzurum days to date.[36] Second, despite family pressure he refused to marry as he was clear about his role in this life from a very young age. In this context, it is worth recalling some of his statements when he visited his home in Korucuk. On being repeatedly asked for marriage from his family members he escaped himself by arguing, "As a rule and tradition the eldest of the family looks after the family. Hence, I am not the eldest. Seyfullah [Gülen's younger brother] is the eldest as he takes care of the family; hence, he should marry."[37] Third, on another occasion when Gülen visited home, he gave a speech and asked everybody to say "Amin" after his speech: "'How do you accept me?' I [Seyfullah] replied, 'You are my brother.' On this he said, 'If you accept me as brother, are you ready to face with me any tribulations, be it pressure from the state, jail, and other hurdles? If you are ready to live with this pressure, then I accept belonging to the family. Otherwise I will go away."[38] In the same speech, he asked every family member to join him in a prayer and say 'Amin.' He said. 'O God, as long as I am alive, let my brothers become neither rich nor poor.' Everybody said 'Amin.'"[39] Fourth, on the occasion of visiting Ankara for giving test to become an imam in a mosque and looking at the crowd gathered for the test, Gülen reportedly stated, "There is no test that I cannot undertake, but it is not the test that is important but how to save humanity."[40] Fifth, Fahri Hayırlı also testifies that unlike other imams, "Gülen was never interested in the existential questions like job, house, or money and never accepted any kind of gift. His condition was worse than mine. He had nothing to eat day after day."[41] Finally, the commitment to serve Islam also flows from his faith in individual agency, which he might have learnt from his life-trajectory and study of prominent figures in Islamic history: "To date all renaissances worldwide have been the result of the efforts and work of the few individual geniuses who are regarded as their architect; they did not arise from the efforts and movement of the masses."[42]

Early public life: Edirne and Kırklareli (1959–65)

Thus, Gülen was already a soul determined to serve the cause of Islam when he came to Edirne in 1959 to take up a position of imam and preacher in Üç Şerefeli mosque after having successfully passed the required examination administered by the Turkish State's Presidency of Religious Affairs in 1959.[43] He lived in Edirne on and off for almost five years, including two years of military service. For most of his life in Edirne in 1960–61 he stayed inside the mosque and confined himself to study of the Islamic texts and worship. He had rented an apartment where he stayed for a few weeks, but later, he left the apartment and moved into the mosque to keep himself safe from sin. He used to sleep at the window of the main hall of the mosque for more than two years. From the available written sources and my interviews, it appears that Gülen hardly ventured out of the mosque. Part of the reason for his self-isolation was his internal fear of being corrupted in the Westernized lifestyles and culture of Edirne outside. As he himself reportedly said, "I do not want to harm my eyes by witnessing the 'lifestyle' in the streets of Edirne."[44] However, he used to conduct religious classes for girls [elementary school kids] within the mosque upon request from the families of girls.[45] In 1961–63 Gülen completed his military service in phases on account of his poor health. During this period, he also had an opportunity to read many Western classics that was given to him by a military officer.

After completion of military training in 1963 he returned to his home in Erzurum and started "preaching everywhere"[46] in Erzurum on Islam-related issues. In 1964, he was posted to another mosque in Edirne as imam and preacher. By this time Gülen had started to attract public attention for his preaching and vast knowledge on Islam and other subjects. People started approaching him inquiring about questions related to Islam and Islamic practices. One such encounter with Gülen is worth recalling here. Two boys with a secular-Kemalist background met Gülen and told him, "We do not believe in God, but we do not know what to do after a person dies [meaning burial rituals]." While living in Edirne Gülen developed a band of eight to ten students who used to meet in his house to read and discuss *Risale-i Nur*.[47] By this time he had also developed good and close relations with the city's mayor (who was from Erzurum) and the city mufti, which might have helped him in conducting Islamic activities in the form of meetings and interactions with students. With this, the process of Hizmet was set in motion in Edirne.

Though the breakthrough for Hizmet came during Gülen's stay in Izmir, Gülen has reportedly claimed that Edirne shaped him: "Had I not stayed in Edirne, I would not have chosen Izmir."[48] It can be safely argued in the light of his own statement that while living in the secularized and Westernized public culture of Edirne he was able to experience the moral and ethical decline of Islam and the Turkish nation which he would have escaped while living in the socially conservative Islamic milieu of

Erzurum. This is because of the fact unlike parts of Edirne, Izmir, Antalya, Istanbul, and other coastal peripheral areas, the Kemalist modernizing reforms hardly affected the everyday Islamic life, what Şerif Mardin calls the "micro structure" and "life worlds," of large parts of Erzurum, eastern and central Anatolia.

The mosque attendance in these cities in the 1940s, 1950s, and 1960s was very sparse. In 1960s' Edirne there were only a small number of mosque-going people (Edirne has many historic public mosques) out of its 30,000 population.[49] Several of my interviewees in Izmir also confirmed this trend that during the 1950s and 1960s the mosque used to be empty. As Muin points out about the state of daily prayers (*namaz*) in Izmir, "During Ottoman times the mosque was full. After the republic the mosque was empty. With Hizmet, the mosques near all the universities are now full,"[50] emphasizing the large participation of youth in *namaz* compared to earlier Republican times. While living in Edirne Gülen started becoming aware of challenges that Islam faces in the modern world. The central questions for him, which other Islamic thinkers had also posed in the modern age were: how to save the Muslim youth from the aggressive Western philosophy and culture of materialism, excessive individualism, sexual license, and communism, and how to make Islam relevant for people's lives and the Turkish nation. These issues became clearer and sharper to him when he moved to Izmir, where he was to witness the clash of two cultures—Islam vs. secular—in the context of the migration of Muslim peasants from Anatolia to the Western part of Turkey.

However, before moving to Izmir in 1966, he worked in Kırklareli in 1965 for almost eight months as a preacher. As the authorities had already placed a ban on his speech in the mosque[51] and were planning to dismiss him in 1964 in Edirne on account of his growing popularity,[52] he volunteered to be transferred to Kırklareli, probably not to cause any further discomfort. It was only after moving to Izmir in 1966, partly thanks to a friend who became the deputy director of the Diyanet and who vacated his position in Izmir, that Gülen started serious preaching along with public actions.

As the young Gülen was becoming aware of the national-political context shaped by the Kemalists, it is imperative to explore in what ways the Kemalist discourses, state system, and emerging national-context shaped Gülen's understanding of Islam, including the Islam-state relationship. How did young Gülen look upon the Kemalists' reforms? How did Gülen articulate and respond to these contexts? Did the Kemalist revolution impact on the normative structure of Islam? Has the Kemalist state system any role to play in Gülen's supposedly liberal and moderate construction of Islam? Did the Kemalist state system shape the evolution of the organizational structure and strategies of the Gülen Movement? An examination of these questions has an important bearing on understanding Gülen's Islamic discourse, action, and praxis in Izmir and the emergence of the world-wide global movement.

The Kemalist Revolution, modern Turkey, and Gülen

Among the boldest modernizing laws that the Kemalist Republic promulgated were those abolishing the Caliphate and establishing the Presidency of Religious Affairs (1924), closing traditional seminaries (*madrasas*) in favor of a unified educational system (1924), abolition of *Sharia* courts (1924) and banning of *Sufi* orders (1925), prohibiting the wearing of fez and veil (1925), adopting European criminal, civil and commercial codes (1926), replacing the Arabic script with Latin (1928), removing Islam as state religion in Turkey (1928), forbidding polygamy and other laws equalizing women—in divorce proceedings, inheritance rights, and later in parliamentary elections (1934), introducing secularism as a constitutional principle in 1937, repealing the public ban on alcohol, prohibiting the wearing of clerical dress outside of mosques and other venues of religious ceremonies, Sunday as the day of rest (the only Muslim state to decree this), the Gregorian calendar instead of the *Hijri,* pressure for European clothing, and moving the capital from the Islamic- Istanbul to a more neutral Ankara.

These reforms, which otherwise appeared revolutionary to the non-Turkish modernist world, from the Turkish point of view were part and parcel of a "reform" process that was unleashed in the Tanzimat times and only acquired greater momentum during the Kemalist period. It is important here to note that the process of secularization that was launched by the Ottoman leadership in the first half of the nineteenth century took place under Islamic auspices and was an *endogenous and not an exogenous* one, which was a key factor in making the reforms acceptable to the Turkish population. Under Ottoman rule, a civil code (*kanun*) always ran parallel to the religious code (*sharia*). In fact, particularly in the nineteenth century, the civil code had become gradually more dominant in relation to the conduct of public affairs, restricting the application of religious code mainly to the private sphere. The "Tanzimat" reforms, which were based on Islamic principles, thus had initiated the end of the centuries-old dogma that "Islam is religion and state" in Turkey and formed the social basis for the country's vigorous Euro-centered modernization program under Kemal Atatürk. The Kemalist reforms have deepened this Ottoman tradition of keeping the sphere of religion and state separately in functional terms, if not in legal sense, as well as retaining the overall state's control and supervision over religious organizations.

The abolition of Caliphate by Kemal Atatürk—an event that is considered an end to Muslim or Islamic rule in the Muslim world and which in turn intensifies the "politics of the Islamic state"—neither altered the traditional pattern of relationship between Islam and state nor brought much change in the power relationship between the two, whereby Islam has historically served the state. The power and function of office of the Sheikh ul-Islam of the Ottoman era was shifted to the Diyanet (Presidency of Religious Affairs), which continues to enjoy the second position in the government hierarchy after the office of President of the Republic, and whose powers and functions have tremendously increased under successive governments since its foundation in 1924. With the Diyanet, modern Turkey has moved towards being an exclusive "Hanafi-Sunni Muslim nation" from an inclusive, flexible "Islamic" Ottoman Empire.

Today the Diyanet is one of the largest "public" institutions in Turkey with an estimated 85,000–100,000 employees including muezzins, muftis, imams of mosques and other functionaries. It oversees almost 78,000 state mosques and 5,000 state Qur'an schools with 157,000 students. Other tasks include preparing and distributing the Friday sermons throughout the country, publication of religious texts, designing the content of broadcasts about Islam and of Qur'an recitations in the state media, translating religious texts, writing Islamic legal reports and opinions (*fatwa*) on a range of issues, organizing and regulating pilgrimages to Mecca, and religious care for Turkish Muslims abroad. The institution received TL 3.8 billion in 2012 and TL 4.6 billion in 2013, which was the second largest item in the national budget.[53]

While critics find in the institution of Diyanet a violation of the principle of secularism that does not qualify Turkey as a "full secular state," the majority of religious Turkish Muslims consider it an obligation on the part of the state—whether secular or otherwise— to provide religious services to the people and thus does not consider that the Diyanet compromises the secular character of the state. The majority of Turkish Muslims are accustomed to seeing the Islam-State relationship in this historical pattern, which has hardly been disrupted by the Kemalist state. What is important to observe is that even though the Diyanet serves as an "official Islam" in Turkey, it has never been an object of attack from any quarter of Islamism—whether the radical Milli Görüş and its various avatars such as the National Salvation Party, the Welfare Party or more moderate parties such as the Virtue Party and the AKP—unlike in other parts of the Muslim world, where the development of political Islam is considered a kind of revolt against the official Islam (Al-Azhar in Egypt, Al-Zaytuna mosque in Tunisia and the Wahhabi establishment in Saudi Arabia).

This partly explains why the tradition of political Islam is relatively weaker in Turkey in comparison to other parts of the Muslim world. In fact, Turkish Islam has hardly produced any prominent Islamist radicals or advocates of political activism such as Hasan al-Banna,[54] Sayyid Qutb,[55] Abul Ala Mawdudi,[56] or Imam Khomeini.[57] Even if there exist some discrete groups of Islamic radicals in Turkey, their influence on Turkish society and politics is negligible and therefore irrelevant for the majority of Turkish Muslims. Since the state has historically not been an object of Islamic discourses and speculations among Turkish Islamic intellectuals, Islam in Turkey has not been politicized unlike in other parts of the Muslim world, save for Muslims' concern for public acknowledgement of Islamic symbols and identity in the public sphere.[58] The AKP, which shares the legacy of Milli Görüş, was able to come to power partly on account of shedding much of its political Islamism and embracing the long secular tradition of state, in addition to many other factors. In fact, when the Erdoğan-led AKP moved towards the spectrum of political Islamism after 2013 in order to overcome the corruption charges it faced, it first lost its majority in the June 2015 parliamentary election, before subsequently gaining a majority in the November 2015 parliamentary election due to multiple reasons including the polarized national context induced by the state politics.

From this perspective, Islam has not been dislodged from its public role and position in Turkey, as has been generally thought due to a combined consequence of the *longue durée* secularization and modernization since Ottoman times on the one hand and the Kemalist reforms on the other.[59] Rather, following Casanova's theory of the "de-privatization of religion,"[60] Islam in Turkey and elsewhere in the Muslim world only lost its political clout and influence owing to the gradual replacement of the *'ulama* by the secular intelligentsia in various sectors of life, including politics. This was further perpetuated by the *'ulama* class themselves by internalizing the modernist discourse of religion as private entity and its conscious distance from modern education—a key to participating in the modern opportunity structure—out of a perceived fear of its corrupting influence and partly due also to the way that the emerging secular order discriminated and discouraged the participation of religious personnel in the public opportunity structure. However, the *'ulama* continues to provide public services—whether in the form of education, social service, or general Islamic service.

Where the Kemalist experience differs from past regimes and many present Muslim nation states lies in two discursive fields: the interpretation of nationalism and secularism. This led to a far greater degree of control over religious organizations, Turkification of Islam including the banning of calling *adhan* in Arabic (1932–1950) and Hajj pilgrimage to Mecca and Medina (1934–1947), imposition of Western dress codes, discrimination against Muslims in public opportunity structures, particularly in the military, courts, police, general administration, and a national campaign to delegitimize the discourse of Islam and Muslim identity; rather, it "criminalized" Islam, making it a "symbol of backwardness"—which led to the transformation of Islam into the "internal enemy" of the Kemalist secular nation state. As Yavuz points out, "that Kemalist 'secularism' was meant to represent 'Progress' and 'civilization' against alleged Islamic 'backwardness' and 'Oriental barbarism.'"[61]

Above all, the doctrine of secularism was interpreted by the state authorities with a sole intention to stifle any expression of religion in the public sphere and make the religious individual and groups liable under the notorious Article 163 (repealed in 1991 under Turgut Özal's presidency), which had made the "group reading of *Risale-i Nur*" and "intention to change the secular state" a criminal act to be "punishable by law."

It is worth recalling here an incident concerning how the state authorities interpreted secularism in order to understand its full implications for leading a Muslim life under the then "modern Turkey." Suat Yıldırım, who was posted in Edirne from 1964–1966 as Deputy Mufti, put a banner between the minarets of the mosque containing three phrases from the Qur'an: (1) "Iman (faith) is power," (2) "Return back to Allah" and (3) "Respect the Fast." The then-Governor of Edirne found the public display of these three Qur'anic phrases in violation of the principle of secularism on the following grounds: (1) If faith is power; then faithless (secular) is powerless, (2) it would make people think religiously, and (3) it would put pressure on those who do not keep the fast. He had the banner taken down![62]

Earlier in 1965 in Edirne, immediately after Gülen made a public speech on the occasion of *Kurban Bayram (Eid ul-Adha)* in which he highlighted the meaning and significance of the feast day, a police investigation was launched into whether the speech was in violation of the principle of secularism and whether Gülen could be arrested under Article 163.[63] According to Suat Yıldırım, a large number of the faithful were arrested in the past under the draconian Act 163. The first state investigation against Gülen was also launched under Article 163.

The current president (2014–) and former prime minister (2003–2014) of Turkey Recep Tayyip Erdoğan, was himself put behind bars for reciting a poem that contradicted the principle of secularism in the eyes of the state authority. The poem that he recited while on a visit to his wife's home town, Siirt, in 1997 reads, "The minarets are our bayonets, the domes our helmets, the mosques our barracks and the faithful our army." Interestingly, the poem was penned by Ziya Gökalp, the father of Turkish nationalism, between the defeat of the Ottoman Empire and the Balkan Wars, and the War of Independence of the Republic, and "has been part of every text book; every pupil knows it."[64] In addition, the "deep state" created many legal hurdles to stop Erdoğan from becoming prime minister in 2003.[65] It is thus no surprise that since the inception of the Republic, the Kemalist state has hunted and persecuted many celebrated Islamic intellectuals including Necip Fazıl (1905–1983) and Bediüzzaman Said Nursi. In the case of the latter, the regime went to the extent of disinterring and relocating his mortal remains in an unknown place within Turkey, lest his burial site become a center of attraction and mobilization.

Such instances are countless in the republican history of modern Turkey. Suffice it here to point out that throughout the twentieth century the Kemalist state authorities, principally the Constitutional Court, the State Security Court, the military, and the bureaucracy, have notoriously misused the principle of laicism/secularism, the six principles of Kemalism and "State Security" to deal with non-Kemalist parties and individuals—whether Islamic (Sunni), ethnic (Kurdish, Alevi), or communist. This abuse often involved the imposition of bans on political organizations and illegal confinement of individuals for varying periods including life-bans on individuals' political careers.[66] Thus, for religious Muslim Anatolians, the Kemalist doctrine of secularism was at best an instrument of control, disciplining, domination, subjugation and discrimination against them.

It is, therefore, not Islam, which fears the Kemalist state, but the Kemalist state that lives in constant fear of Islam, in particular "Islam-in-Ottoman-form." It was partly on account of fear of Islam that the one-party state system of Kemal Atatürk deferred twice the introduction of the multi-party system before it was finally introduced by the end of the 1940s as part of the fulfillment of a condition for becoming a member of NATO and a recipient of aid under the Marshall Plan. The fear was not misplaced. The Kemalist Republican People's Party lost miserably to the Democratic Party of Adnan Menderes, which ruled the country until it was overthrown by the military regime in 1960.

Gülen, the Kemalist system, and Nursi

How does Gülen look at the Kemalist revolution and post-Kemalist developments in the country? Though there are not many direct statements from Gülen either supporting or critiquing Kemal Atatürk and the Kemalist state system, which can be relied upon to deduce his position on this question, he has often been accused of supporting an authoritarian state system ranging from Kemal Atatürk to the military regimes on the grounds of his silence. However, an inference can be drawn on the basis of Gülen's Islamic background. As someone trained in Hanafi Islamic jurisprudence and in other branches of Islam and living in the Sufi Islamic cosmology, Gülen refrains from criticizing any individual living or dead, including Kemal Atatürk. Similarly, his understanding of Islamic self and ethics does not allow him to oppose a state/government run by Muslims, which he continues to maintain despite his Movement facing an existential threat from the current Erdoğan government. For a long time, Gülen refrained from launching a personal attack on President Erdoğan, except for critiquing the growing tendency of totalitarianism under the Erdoğan regime.[67] This position comes from the Islamic maxim that "order is better than anarchy and chaos" and "bad government is better than no government."

With regard to the Kemalist state system and reforms, he does not see them as obstructing Muslims from performing the *essential* commandments of Islam. Certainly, the Kemalist state abolished *madrasa*s and Sufi lodges, dervishes, and orders, and for some period tried to Turkify the Islamic rituals along with "reforming the bodily costumes and physical appearance." However, Gülen believes that by the time these reforms came into existence the *madrasa*s and Sufi dervishes, lodges and orders had already lost their "regenerative capacity" and internally "died down." Moreover, these reforms could only affect the "institutional structure" within which Islam had hitherto existed and thus created a "crisis of Islamic identity" for many who were accustomed to imagining Islam in that institutional frame; they did not affect the fundamentals of Islam, its principles, and discourses. In other words, the Kemalist state did not affect the normative structure of Islam.

For Gülen, the basic principles of Islam are unchangeable, but its forms and institutions, and the structures in which Islam has to be represented must keep changing in accordance with the demands and values of the age. In other words, for him, Islam is internal to the individual self, not a thing to be preserved in a "particular format." For Gülen, Muslims should avoid conflict even if the law does not permit its expression and manifestation in the public realm. Moreover, for Gülen, the Kemalist government did not rupture the historical pattern of relationship between Islam and state except by changing its own form and exercising greater control: the Turkish state continues to provide Islamic services to the Muslim. Hence, Gülen did not find it problematic to serve the Kemalist state by becoming imam, preacher and teacher in a government-funded public institution, unlike Nursi, who preferred to withdraw from the Kemalist state structure, and Maulana Maududi, who in the early period of Jammat-e-Islami, asked many of his Indian followers to resign (and many did) from government positions on the grounds that serving a non-Muslim government amounts to *taghut* (idolatry) and thus contradicts the fundamentals of Islam.

The impact of the Kemalist regime on Islam has been primarily analyzed as dislodging Islam from the public realm and adversely affecting the age-old Islamic arrangement between state and society. Thus, Bobby Sayyid found in the Kemalist reforms a process of delinking Islam from the center of the political order and making it free in the civil society for its-interpretation and re-inscription leading to the politicization of Islam, which in turn gave birth to Islamism at the cost of Kemalism.[68] Şerif Mardin saw the impact of Kemalist reforms as dismantling of Islamic arrangements or of Islam as link between Centre and Periphery or between the ruler and ruled.[69] However, for Gülen, the overall impact of the Kemalist reforms and application of principles of secularism and positivism was that Islam ceased to be a motivating force for public action. Islam had become increasingly irrelevant as it was no more a privileged identity, nor a source of social prestige, nor was it connected with wider public employment opportunities. This had led to the development of an attitude of hopelessness, inertia, and fatigue to the future where any change was not possible.

Gülen's understanding of the Kemalist state and its impact on Islam has six major implications in terms of the formulation of principles that were applied in building the Gülen Movement while he was living in Izmir and continuing to guide the Movement. These broad principles also differentiate Gülen from Nursi in many ways, notwithstanding the fact that the two are the most revered sources of inspiration for Hizmet volunteers and they do not see any differences between the two except that Gülen an implementer of Nursi's ideas as indicated in Chapter 2. These are as follows:

(1) Nursi rejected all offers of serving the Kemalist state and dissociated himself from any form of participation within the state structure; rather, he preferred to withdraw, lived an isolated life, and thought to "save Islam" by resorting to writing his *tafsir* (interpretation) of the Qur'an, the *Risale-i Nur*. In this phase, Nursi never indulged in any kind of opposition to the Kemalist state and despite being hunted down by the Kemalist state; he retained the imagery of "political opposition" to the Kemalist state or an idea that the Kemalist form of state is an

"alien" or "threat" to the "mainstream Sunni discourse of Islam". Hence, even though Nursi attempted to make modernity a "normal object" by demonstrating the Islamic roots of the same, he could not remove the Muslims' public perception of the Kemalist state as a "threatening object" to Islam. This eliminated the possibility of a constructive role of Islam in the public domain.

On the other hand, Gülen accepted and served the Kemalist state as he did not find the Kemalist state as "threatening" to his Islamic belief, faith, or the normative structure of Islam. By participating in the Kemalist state structure he not only obliterated the conception of the form of state/government as conditional for Muslim participation in public life but even facilitated the social acceptance of the Kemalist state, which made it possible for the Anatolian Muslims to participate in the opportunity structure of the Kemalist state system without fear of losing Islam. Further, Gülen's Islamic discourse and the participation of Muslims in the Kemalist state structure also helped in developing a more inclusive interpretation of the principles of Kemalism.

(2) Gülen demonstrated through his action and conduct that it is possible to serve Islam within the existing legal structure of any state, irrespective of its form.

(3) Nursi's *Risale-i Nur* is an Islamic philosophical discourse demonstrating the complementarity of Islam and modernity, particularly science, without accepting the ontological premises of positivism. In the Nursian perspective, the "scientific truth" or positivism is time- and context-specific and keeps changing with fresh innovation, discovery, and experiment. The truth of Islam is "transcendental," "permanent" and non-changeable. Science is one among many human methods to understand and discover the "Secrets" and "Laws" of God, the Creator. Nursi's attempt to bring harmony between Islam and science was a continuation of the eighteenth- and nineteenth-century trend of Islamic reformism and modernism, though it differs from many exponents of this trend such as Sir Syed Ahmad Khan, Jamal al-Din Afghani, Muhammad Abduh, Rashid Rida and others in method and rigor of analysis. Thus, Nursi's Islamic discourse was, to a large extent, an attempt at "Islamization of science" in order to preserve Islam from the threat of positivism and therefore is not free of reactive and apologetic tendency.[70] Gülen, on the other hand, though influenced by Nursi's ideas, builds an Islam-inspired

social movement that values the role of science in human progress but without "Islamizing science" and hence is non-reactive and non-apologetic. Moreover, he contributed more to dispelling the fear of science vis-à-vis faith among the Muslim communities of Turkey than Nursi by taking this issue into the public sphere through organizing conferences, media, preaching in public places, cassettes, and so on.

(4) For Gülen, unlike Nursi, the central issue is not demonstrating complementarity or compatibility between Islam and modernity but "representation of Islam" in the public domain. Thus, for Gülen, the discourse of Islam is primarily a discourse of good conduct, morals, values, setting an example and representation. As this Islamic discourse primarily constitutes the "content" of Islam, Muslims can participate and interact with any other discourse or structure such as modernity, which for Gülen is a "form," albeit a dominant one, within which a Muslim has to learn how to conduct and represent himself or herself without fear of "losing faith," which might appear to be happening as a result of interaction with such discourses and structures. Thus, while in the Nursian understanding, learning of science—physics, chemistry, or math—is an Islamic act and value, for Gülen this is not enough: Muslims must set an example by "teaching," "learning," and "representing" science in the public domain.

(5) While Nursi conceives education primarily in terms of Islamic education and sought unsuccessfully to build an Islamic university as a knowledge-site for the reconciliation of Islam and science, for Gülen, education is primarily an "Islamic value," a "lifelong moralizing discourse," and an "equalizing force" to represent Islam in the modern, secular, public sphere.

(6) If school can serve as the ideological foundation of the Kemalist secular state, then a school can also serve Islam and humanity.

Emergence of Hizmet: Izmir (1966–1992)

Gülen arrived in Izmir in 1966 at the age of twenty-eight. In Izmir Gülen was given a position as an imam for Kestanepazarı Mosque and manager of the boarding school adjacent to the mosque, and for preaching in the Aegean region of Western Turkey. Although he regularly traveled to other cities, he retained his association with Izmir until 1992. While living in Izmir, as in Edirne, he confronted the problems of unemployment, poverty, empty mosques, youth falling prey to hedonism, individualism, sexual license, communism and materialism, the emerging clash of values between Anatolian Muslim migrants and modern, secular, Kemalist Turks, and other ideological clashes and conflicts at the cost of national unity. He diagnosed these problems as "lack of high ideals" to motivate the society and nation, "lack of morals and ethics" to regulate individual conduct and cultivate the sense of responsibility and accountability, "lack of hope," "lack of proper guidance, particularly to the youth." He sought to address the same by focusing on the revival of ethics, morals and the educational spirit of Islam and the age-old Turkish, Naqshbandi Islamic tradition of *hizmet*: *living for others, preparing for the next generation—all for the sake of Allah without expectation of any return*. In short, he identified the "problem of lack of motivation" among people, particularly among the youth, to work for society, nation, Islam, God, and humanity, and found the solution in the resurrection of Islam's moral and ethical values, including the Turkish Islamic tradition. For him, Islam is the greatest resource for motivation in this world.

Though Gülen's description of a "sickness" that has afflicted the Muslim world in general and Turkey in particular is akin to Nursi's famous Damascus sermon (1911),[71] it differs in scope, substance, and method, particularly in the conceptualization of "education," "public sphere" and "representation of Islam in the public domain"—the issues that will be dealt later in this book. Suffice it here to highlight that unlike other Islamic thinkers and scholars, who posed similar concerns and questions about Islam and modernity, and who found the solution to the "crisis of Islam" or conversely the "challenges of modernity" in withdrawing from modernity, or violently confronting modernity, or imitating Western education and science, or rejecting modernity, or appropriating some aspects of modernity (education, science and technology) and rejecting others (Western values and culture of individualism and mixing of sexes), or privileging Islamic values and culture over Western values and culture, Gülen recognized that Islam is one among multiple existing discourses in the present world; thus, Islam needs to compete with other discourses in a peaceful manner while remaining at the center of the dominant discourse—modernity. This requires a careful presentation and representation of Islam in the modern world. Thus, for him, what is required is the "true" presentation of Islam's principles as evolved during the period of *al-Asr al-Saadat* (Age of Happiness—Period of Prophet Muhammad and his Companions) both in "words and actions" so that Islam can become an example of good work, conduct, morals, and ethics.

Armed with this diagnosis, Gülen focused on education as ethical and moral discourse, the development of educators and a golden generation (those knowledgeable of the present age)—the combination to help in overcoming or dealing with the challenges of modernity. Convinced of the *sirat al-mustaqim* (the straight path) of Islam, which calls for avoidance of extremes, Gülen embarked upon reconnecting Muslims, particularly the youth, with the memory of the Islamic and Ottoman past in terms of high morals, ethics, honesty, responsibility, trust, cooperation, hard work, education, and other virtues, through his speeches, preaching, Friday sermons, and participation in talks in coffee houses during his stay in Izmir.

However, before his foray into the large field of public action, Gülen, following in the footsteps of Prophet Muhammad, first built his credibility through his exemplary conduct, action, knowledge, preaching, high thinking, and his ascetic, simple way of life. Already known for these virtues from his Edirne days, he lived in a small hut located in the outside open corner of Kestanepazari mosque in Izmir for five years, though he was entitled to live in a dormitory along with a food facility; he refused both on the ground that he was receiving a salary from the government for preaching.[72]

The foundation of the Hizmet Movement as *tabligh* in the form of *tamsil* was laid down during this period. It appears from several of the interviews that I conducted that from 1966–1969 Gülen confined himself to the teaching of students in the Qur'anic school attached to the mosque, conducting five times daily prayer, preaching before *adhan* and Friday sermons (*khutba*) and answering visitors' queries about Islam and Islamic rituals, in addition to continuing with his habits of reading Islamic and other texts, and the performance of *dhikr*. While earlier students had been taught the subject matter of *ilahiyat* and *iman*, Gülen introduced them to the Arabic language, other branches of Islamic science, and methods of understanding the Qur'an, humanity, the universe, and science. His style of teaching was innovative and led to change in the prejudices and fear that the students had about science and also brought significant changes in personal conduct and approaches towards Islam. He used to deliver sermons not only on the mandatory Friday but also after every congregational prayer, mostly to his students.[73]

He wanted the young generation to ask, "What is *salat?*" and "What is *iman*?" instead of his preaching about them. The theme of these sermons during this period (1966–1971) were mostly related to the basic teachings and principles of Islam, the Prophet's life, the lives of his Companions (Sahaba), the heroes of Islam, the history of the Ottoman Empire, education, the notion of community service (*hizmet*), *haram* vs. *halal*, and other Islam related themes.[74] These initial lectures and sermons related to Islam helped in the development of people's confidence in him.[75] One noticeable thing was that in all his speeches, lectures, and sermons there was no reference either to *Risale-i Nur* or Bediüzzaman Said Nursi.[76] This could have been partly due to the government hostility towards Nursi and *Risale-i Nur* movement and the existence of Article 163 (repealed in 1991) that banned the reading of *Risale-i Nur* in groups. However, in private dershane meetings or *sohbet*s Gülen continues to read and discuss aspects of *Risale-i Nur*.

A second noticeable feature of Gülen's sermons was that he used to weep[77] while delivering sermons on the Prophet's life or lives of the Companions and on many an occasion he also moved the people attending to emotion and weeping. Though his critics see his "weeping" as a "demagogic and theatrical strategy" or "melodrama" to mobilize people, in essence it flows from his own complete ethical identification with the "goodness" of deeply held values (i.e. Islam for Gülen) and an awareness of the mismatch between the goodness of that value and its distorted misrepresentation in today's world.

By the end of 1969, Gülen had started drawing public attention for his simple ascetic life, knowledge, sincerity of intention and purpose, and his commitment to serve people and Islam unflinchingly. He started growing a moral and ethical aura around himself and people started reposing trust, faith, and hope in him for gaining a "good life." He was soon to be recognized as "someone special" blessed with divine grace.[78] It was only in the post–1969 period that Gülen got involved in the wider public debates and discussions by visiting cafes, tea stalls, coffee houses, university premises, attending conferences and seminars, and touring and lecturing within Izmir and various cities of the Aegean region, speaking on Islam, science, humanism, Darwinism, positivism, and education. This mode of communication was something new and attractive and was never known in recent Turkish history. It was during this interactive process that the idea of "dormitories," "preparatory coaching courses" and "reading houses" emerged.[79]

From 1969 onwards Gülen started the practice of organizing the "special reading camp" of two to three weeks outside Izmir in which mostly selected students from middle school and high school were participants during the months of July–September when schools, colleges, and universities in Turkey were closed. The purpose of organizing this "special reading camp" was and is to refresh, update, and strengthen the Islamic morale and ethical consciousness through a system of group reading of Islamic texts, including *Risale-i Nur*, or lectures by a senior Abi (elder Hizmet volunteer) who is well versed in Islamic texts so as to prepare the student to deal with the ever-growing complex challenges of this world. Gradually the "Camp System" or "Book Reading Camp" became an *integral* part of the Gülen Movement. With the expansion of the Movement globally and increase in financial support, today the camp is organized by different organizations at convenient times at sites with better social infrastructure and recreational facilities. Today, along with Islamic texts and *Risale-i Nur*, Gülen's writings are also read and discussed in these "book reading camps."[80]

Gülen was arrested following the 1971 military intervention and held behind bars for almost six months. The circumstances were already becoming tense in the country for some time. Gülen had to leave Kestanepazari mosque, as the administration had started fearing his growing popularity and was also not happy with his teaching that reconciled religious belief with scientific thought to students.[81] By 1971–72, Gülen had acquired a small number of dedicated followers who were willing to dedicate themselves to work for his ideas and vision. Turkey was going through a difficult phase of high unemployment, poverty, lack of basic facilities for a decent life, and was becoming internally polarized along fixed cultural, ethnic, ideological, and religious identities and ideas that often resulted in violence, the frequency of which had tremendously increased by the end of the 1970s—partly fueled by the socio-economic crisis, accompanied by the wave of Anatolian "Muslim" migration from the villages to the "Kemalist-secular" cities since the 1950s, a process that has continued till today, and by the lack of a democratic culture of dialogue and negotiation.

It was against this background of emerging socio-economic crisis and civil-ideological strife between Islamists, leftists, and Kemalists that throughout the 1970s Gülen mostly concentrated on the notions of education, family, peace, service, and dialogue within the framework of Islam to build the Turkish nation. In his discourse, "education"—a theme that I will return to in chapter 8—emerged as a key reference point for addressing the national problems. He saw in "quality education" and "educators" a "unifying," "moralizing" and "ethicizing" means to overcome the national crisis by not only providing an alternative perspective on the "good life" but also as the "only" means through which participation in public employment and other opportunity structures could be ensured and thus could address a part of the emerging "problem of integration" of Anatolian immigrants. With this understanding, he initially encouraged the Muslim youth, mostly from Anatolia, to attend Imam-Hatip schools (state-managed religious schools) as it was an expectation that "a good Muslim grows in Imam-Hatip."[82] His initial support for Imam-Hatip schools is partly due to the fact this was only the option available for Muslim children as government schools was still not favored by Muslim parents for fear of their corrupting influence and negative effects on their children's faith.

Gülen continued to support Imam-Hatip schools but gradually shifted his focus from the mid-1970s to building secular schools, reading rooms, preparatory coaching classes for university examinations, dormitories, and "light houses"[83] with the intention to provide better facilities and coach the bright students, mostly Anatolian children from Imam-Hatip schools, to compete at the national level in order to gain access to higher education and to pursue careers in civil and public service. The Hizmet Movement originated in these dormitories and coaching institutes. Towards this end he started persuading businessmen to divert part of the money they allocated for *zakat, sadaqa* and *fitra* as well as a part of their surplus for educational purposes, as education is the most noble Islamic value and goal.

Simultaneously, Gülen launched *Sızıntı* (1979)—a monthly magazine—with the purpose of demonstrating the complementarity between

Islam and science, as well as to deflect the intertwined national perception that "Islam is opposed to science and hence inimical to progress" among the secular leftists and Kemalists, on the one hand, and "fear of modern education or science as a corrupting influence on the Islamic faith" among Muslims, on the other hand. Thus, *Sızıntı*, which was shut down after the July 15 coup attempt in 2016, was addressing the concerns and fears of both groups, secularists and Muslims, and within a short time it acquired a very high national circulation. Each *Sızıntı* edition used to contain an editorial column by Gülen himself despite his busy schedule. The success of *Sızıntı* indicated the shift in national perspective, the weakening of Kemalism, and the emergence of a social constituency supportive of Gülen's ideas and efforts. *Aksiyon* (Action) was another popular weekly magazine that the Movement was going to launch in 1990s.

Gülen enthusiastically mobilized business people to establish the "private foundations" that had become possible in Turkey under new laws enacted during the premiership of Süleyman Demirel. The Kemalist state had banned the establishment of private foundations until 1970. Thus, by Gülen's efforts, the Teacher Foundation and the Technical Staff Foundation were officially registered in 1973. Other foundations, such as the Agricultural Foundation and Doctor Foundation also came into existence in the 1970s.[84]

Additionally, Gülen has shown remarkably flexibility in utilizing modern and popular modes of communication: print and electronic media, CDs, cassettes, videos, and so on, to air his Islamic lecture and put across his point of view in the public sphere. On the other hand, volunteers on their own had already started recording Gülen's Friday sermons and other lectures and made them available on electronic devices such as cassettes and CDs to spread his message. In the process, publication and printing activity became one of the crucial sites for Hizmet to reach out to the people. In focusing on printing, publications, and the utilization of modern electronic gazettes to spread the message of Gülen, the Movement altered the Rumian framework of "everybody is welcome" to "going to everybody" in order to serve the Islamic notion of *dawa*: the dissemination of the message of Prophet Muhammad. Gradually, dialogue became an integral part of the Gülen Movement. In 1977 Gülen was commissioned by the Presidency of Religious Affairs to go to Germany to deliver a series of lectures to the Turkish diaspora. Over the years, Izmir became a center of the Hizmet Movement with the establishment of the first functional dormitory, first preparatory coaching institute, first formation of a board, first middle and high school (Yamanlar School, 1982).

By this time Gülen had acquired a national identity and recognition[85] and large numbers of people who were attracted to his ideas attended his Friday sermons. His national recognition and stature became evident when Gülen was invited to deliver the Friday sermon in the Blue Mosque in 1977, an event which was attended by important state dignitaries including Süleyman Demirel and İhsan Sabri Çağlayangil, the foreign minister. In the late 1970s Gülen had given a call for "national dialogue" as a means to resolve the misunderstandings between ideological groups and the violent conflicts that had marred the national political scene of Turkey, and he had delivered a series of lectures against mindless violence, anarchy, and terror. By 1978–1979, the Hizmet movement had already reached Istanbul, where Gülen would later take up residence on the fifth floor of an apartment building—a number that acquired an informal symbolic value to refer to Gülen in the Hizmet circle. The Movement gradually spread to many parts of Turkey.

Gülen, Hizmet, and the 1980 military coup

In 1980 the military seized power and indulged in a reign of terror that particularly targeted the left. It continued to rule till 1983. According to Yavuz, "The regime of 1980–1983 persecuted anyone who had been involved with any socialist or social democratic organizations or party in the 1960s and the 1970s. Large numbers of intellectuals, students, artists, and politicians who had been involved in leftist politics were imprisoned for long periods of time. Around 650,000 people were arrested; 1,683,000 cases were prepared; and 517 people were sentenced to death, although only 49 of the sentences were carried out. In addition, 30,000 people were fired from their jobs for holding objectionable political views, 14,000 had their Turkish citizenship revoked, and 667 associations and foundations were banned."[86] In this context, the literature is replete with how Gülen forged a close association with the military junta under the framework of a Turkish-Islam synthesis to prevent Turkey from falling into the leftists' hands. It has also been highlighted how the Turkish military regime used Gülen as a moderate Islamic force to contain the influence of radical Islamism and limit the impact of the Iranian Islamic revolution (1979) on Turkish Muslims.

Nevertheless, there is no direct or indirect evidence to indicate that the Gülen Movement forged alliances with other Islamic political forces (Erbakan) or Islamic social forces (various Naqshbandi groupings such as Zahid Kotku) or the military junta either to contain leftist and rightist threats. Gülen had already dissociated himself from other Nur factions on the issue of the formation of political parties and participation in politics during the 1960s on the ground that politicization or ideologization or association with power-politics has an inherent tendency to harm Islam itself. This remains the basic principle of the Movement, while keeping the door open for dialogue and cooperation with everyone in the service of humanity—individual and organization, despite the fact the Movement is currently facing an existential threat from its supposedly one-time ally, the Erdoğan-led AKP party. The left was holding sway in universities, where the Movement did not have any influence at that time. Moreover, all state regimes have used Islam in times of crisis, which is independent of the forging of alliances with this or that group.

On the contrary, the military regime (1980–83) seized all the registered foundations and trusts belonging to the Movement. Though Gülen had already quit the post of imam in 1980, the military cancelled his license to preach, issued a warrant to arrest him, and raided various locations in search of him.[87] Under the circumstances Gülen had to go underground from 1980–1986.[88] The authorities even placed a ban upon his students' preaching. State surveillance of the "Green" or "Islamic" company, as the authority labeled them for their association with the Gülen Movement, was strict.[89] Though the expansion of the Movement was negatively affected, Gülen continued to guide the Hizmet Movement while remaining underground and asked his trusted volunteers to spread to different parts of the country to continue the work of *hizmet*.

By this time the Hizmet Movement had developed a national presence within Turkey and established a good network of volunteers. For instance, both Faruk Karaca and one of the industrialists in Gaziantep[90] testified that Burak Aslan started Hizmet in Gaziantep. Burak stayed in Gaziantep for five years and tried to establish an "Educational Trust," a registered foundation for Hizmet work. By the time Burak left, Hizmet had developed a good social base of volunteers consisting of large and small businesses, teachers, students, and others. It was only in 1986 when the Turgut Özal government promulgated a law on "freedom of movement" that Gülen again resumed his public role of preaching. In the context above it may be fair to state that much of the literature that has pointed to Gülen's support for the military regime under the "Turkey-Islam thesis" and hence as a beneficiary of the military regime does not hold water.

It may be noted that though Gülen had been preaching about the necessity of secular schools, preparatory coaching, dormitories, and so on, since the early 1970s, the breakthrough in the expansion of educational activities began in the mid-1980s and since then it has continued. It took a decade of hard work to achieve the breakthrough. Thus, whereas Hizmet had only a few schools (Yamanlar in Izmir, Fatih in Istanbul) until 1986, it expanded to 300 schools between 1986 and 1996 and since 1996 it has grown to approximately 1,000 educational institutions—both domestic and abroad.[91] A majority of these schools have emerged as "branded" and established credentials for "quality education," which in turn has helped in attracting a section of elites. Although a decade of fertilization of ideas and successful results of educational initiatives such coaching and schools did help in attracting and mobilizing resources from parents and businessmen, it was the emergence of the Muslim *bazaari* middle class and Muslim industrialist class known as the Anatolian Tigers by the mid-1980s owing to Turgut Özal's neo-liberal economic policy that provided the financial impetus to Gülen's educational initiatives. However, behind the emergence of the Muslim industrial class also lies the contribution of Gülen, who through his Islamic discourses had created the national context of "disciplined labor" and "cooperation" between labor and capital since the mid-1980s. The role of "disciplined labor" in the development of the Anatolian Tigers has been noted as follows:

> The rapid expansion of exports of manufacturers played a key role in the rise of the Anatolian tigers, regional industrial centers such as Gaziantep, Denizli, Kayseri, Malatya, Konya, Çorum and others. With craft traditions and non-unionized workforces, these

> industrial centers began to account for a significant share of growing exports in textiles and other labor-intensive industries. Their competitive advantage was bolstered by low wages, long working hours, and flexible labor regimes. Large numbers of small and medium-sized family enterprises played a central role in the rise of these industrial centers. Their rise was achieved with little state support and little or no foreign investment.[92]

It is in this sense that the much discussed "Weberian protestant ethics" is applicable to the Gülen Movement. With the flow of domestic capital Hizmet activities, particularly in the field of education, began to multiply on a rapid scale on account both of demands for its quality education created by a demographic shift in Turkey and of the poor standard of public schools. As the Movement gained momentum and a large section of "Muslim Turkey" began to identify with the "Islam-in-nation" or "nation-in-Islam"[93] cause, support in the form of donations, scholarships, and infrastructure began to flow to Gülen's Hizmet Movement throughout the 1980s, 1990s and 2000s leading to tremendous expansion in dershanes, coaching institutes, schools, colleges, universities, interfaith dialogue centers, relief programs, print and electronic media, book stores, publishing houses, a bank, and more. Gradually, the movement developed a kind of market infrastructure with a large number of exchanges and circulation of services, products, and goods taking place among Hizmet followers and institutions, which led one author to analyze the Gülen Movement primarily in terms of the market principle of demand and supply, albeit coached in Islamic terms.[94]

It must be cautioned here that the "petro dollar" or "Gulf money" of the 1970s had no role in the expansion of the Hizmet Movement as sometimes alleged. The Saudi and other conservative Islamic monarchies and Emirates would certainly be reluctant to support a Turkish-based Islamic initiative given the historical mutual distrust between the two, and more so if the Islamic movement promotes a relatively liberal and moderate vision of Islam. However, whether the global Islamic revivalism that was emerging in the 1970s against the failure of the secular state had any role to play in the emergence of this Turkish, Islamic, political, and social movement needs investigation. Some of the visible faces of the Hizmet Movement in Turkey, before being shut down by the Erdoğan government in the aftermath of December 2013 Corruption exposé and the failed military coup (July 15, 2016), were: the FEM Preparatory Coaching Centers, the Journalists and Writers Foundation (1994), *Zaman* newspaper (1986), Samanyolu TV, Burç FM, Kimse Yok Mu Relief organization, Bank Asya, Şifa Medical University in Izmir, Zirve University in Gaziantep, and Fatih University in Istanbul along with 17 other universities, Sema Hospital in Istanbul, and innumerable "branded" schools and coaching centers, and business associations such as TUSKON, HÜRSİAD and İŞHAD etc.

With such multitudinous activities in "secular domains with an unmistakable modern/Western appearance" and hardly witnessed ever before in the history of Islamic movements, the Hizmet Movement was debated by the outside world, particularly the intelligentsia, as a "civic-social movement" that blends well with the growing "civil society discourse" in the political context of the democratic transition of Turkey from Kemalist authoritarianism since the mid-1980s—a process that has received a setback since 2012 with Erdoğan increasingly becoming an authoritarian-populist leader. Although Hizmet did attract peoples from non-Islamic orientations on account of its inclusive discourse and social activities, it must be brought to light that behind these institutional interventions in the public sphere lies the Islamic principle of *temsil*: setting an example through concrete action and conduct. Once established with credibility, these institutions themselves would be a source of *temsil* and *dawa*. As Suat Yıldırım points out, "the goal of Hizmet is to contribute to raising a new generation in harmony with Islam's universal values using all contemporary means such as TV, media, music, school, NGO, et-cetera."[95] Prior to July 2016 failed military coup, the Hizmet Movement used to bring thousands of people of various faiths to Turkey to showcase their works (schools, universities, media houses, hospitals, Journalists and Writers Foundation, etc.) without preaching to them directly about the relationship between Islam and these institutions.

In 1989 the Turgut Özal government asked Gülen to resume his duties, withdrew the governmental order that had canceled his license to preach, and conferred upon him the title "Emeritus Preacher" allowing him to preach in any mosque within Turkey. From 1989–1992 he preached in the main mosques of Istanbul and Izmir and drew crowds of tens of thousands of people for his Friday sermons and *vaaz* lectures. By this time Gülen had hundreds of dedicated volunteers, mostly students from Anatolia who had passed through Imam-Hatip high schools, been trained in the discipline of education, mostly in science subjects—a topic that I will return to at a later stage—and raised in various dormitories, *dershane*s and light houses to serve his Islam-led vision.

At this juncture, the disintegration of Soviet Union in 1990–91 and the independence of the Central Asian Republics provided a golden opportunity for Gülen to expand his Hizmet work abroad. Although many saw in Hizmet's expansion to Central Asia an escape from a hostile domestic political environment,[96] I believe the expansion into Central Asia had purely Islamic and nationalistic motives. First, Turkish people share their genealogy, history, and race with Central Asia. Second, for Gülen, Central Asia stands second only to Mecca and Medina, as the most famous Hadith (Hanafi) tradition came from this region in addition to the fact that the area has produced a host of classical Islamic scholars. It is these nationalist and Islamic reasons that motivated volunteers of Hizmet who were mostly education faculty graduates—a discipline that Gülen had initially emphasized to produce a battery of teachers—to go there, to work for low wages, and live in inhospitable conditions. Third, Turkish Muslim business houses supported Hizmet's work financially, due to both their Islamic-nationalist sentiment and their business interests. İhsan Yılmaz noted the contribution of Hizmet movement to the Central Asian Republics: "Every Anatolian city was declared a sister city of a particular nation and the Hizmet Movement volunteers of that city mobilized the people both in material terms and human capital."[97] Furthermore, the Turkish government supported Hizmet's efforts as they saw in Hizmet an agency to promote Turkish influence in the region, while the Central Asian republics, lacking money and infrastructure, welcomed Hizmet to build educational institutions. The convergence of interests and the volunteers' hard work and dedication led Hizmet schools to emerge as the "brand" school in Central Asian countries. Being thus branded, these schools abroad soon emerged as a point of contact between Hizmet and the elites of the countries concerned. Additionally, Hizmet, apart from its educational face, began to act as a conduit to promote Turkish business abroad and vice-à-versa. The success gained in Central Asia led the Hizmet Movement to be replicated in other parts of the globe, and it is currently active in almost 165 countries.

At the time of writing, in a large number of countries the educational activity was still financed and supported by the domestic mobilization of resources within Turkey, the largest chunk of which was contributed by small, medium, and large business houses.

From the mid-1990s, as Gülen became more aware of the process of globalization with the tremendous growth of mass-communication that has increased the cross-cultural movement of people, reduced time and space, and brought religions and cultures face to face, he started focusing on interfaith dialogue and met the Greek Orthodox Patriarch, the Armenian Orthodox Patriarch, the Chief Rabbi of Turkey, the Vatican's Representative to Turkey, and the Pope with the purpose of removing misunderstanding of each other and cultivating a culture of mutual living with respect and recognition of each other's cultural and religious differences. The seeds of his vision of dialogue and recognition of pluralism were already present when he gave a call for national dialogue in the mid-1970s. However, it was not until 1994 that the Journalists and Writers Foundation (JWF) officially came into existence to express this vision. Mr. Gülen himself is the honorary president of the JWF—one of the few positions that he has held officially in Hizmet. Following his move to America in 1999 (on the grounds of health as well as to escape political persecution by the military), his views on multiculturalism, pluralism, and the necessity of interfaith and inter-cultural dialogue became firmer, which led to tremendous growth in the dialogue centers of the Hizmet Movement in different parts of the world. The much celebrated Abant Conferences, a project by JWF, were established as a dialogue platform in Turkey in 1997 as a part of this process. With this shift in approach, the historical figure of Rumi, though always present in Hizmet's philosophy, has emerged as an integral part of Hizmet's discourse of love, peace, and tolerance.

Gülen continues to provide moral leadership to the Movement. The Movement has demonstrated remarkable resilience, internal cohesion, and solidarity to resist the ever increasing pressure, hostility, and repression from the AKP government headed by President Erdoğan since December 2013.

CHAPTER 7

GÜLEN MOVEMENT: CONTEXT, AGENCIES AND MICRO STRUCTURES

After sketching out the trajectory of Fethullah Gülen's life in context and the development of the Gülen Movement, there remain certain questions to be probed. What makes the Gülen Movement successful in building a strong presence in education, media, interfaith dialogue, relief and rehabilitation, and other sectors of public life within and outside Turkey, at least before July 15, 2016? What was/is so specific about the Movement that has allowed it to make an impact upon and attract the attention of Turkish people, cutting across the classes and regions of the country? Why do people feel motivated to work for the Hizmet Movement? What were/are the mobilization strategies that have been used by the Gülen Movement? What are the dominant features of the Movement? How does the Movement work?

Role of the mosque

The first important factor is connected with the role of the mosque. The mosque in Islamic history and society has not only functioned as a prayer space, a source of collective Muslim identity, of religious education, and a site of social gatherings and interactions, but also as a site of alternative social and power structure, authority, and influence. The mobilization character and oppositional role of the mosque vis-à-vis state authority have been well documented and need not be revisited here. In recent memory, the mosque with its Friday sermon as an instrument of mobilization played the most significant role in engineering the Islamic revolution in Iran (1979), and in the Arab Spring that resulted in the overthrow of some autocratic regimes of the Arab world that were once considered invincible. It is therefore not without reason that throughout history the authorities in Muslim societies—whether in the form or empire, kingdom, or nation-state—have opted for strict control, supervision, and regulation over mosque functionaries. The contemporary Muslim Middle Eastern states, including Turkey, exercise even greater control over Islamic religious institutions, ranging from the appointment of imams and other functionaries of the mosque to the supply of the Friday sermon. In most Muslim Middle Eastern countries, the government has tried to bring under its control as many mosques as possible. Nonetheless, private, non-governmental, community mosques continue to proliferate in Muslim societies and pose substantial challenges to government authority. Private mosques have been hotbeds of political Islam and its many radical variants in a number of Muslim societies.

In this regard Turkish Muslim experience differs from Arab Muslim history in the sense that the mosque has not been seen by the public as an instrument of politicization, opposition, and mobilization against a particular social/religious/political group or "Muslim state authority," at least until recently.[1] The mosque as "political space" has been alien to Turkish Muslim history and culture. For Muslims of Turkey, it remains a religious, an educational, and a socio-cultural space. Even the Islamists in Turkey have been averse to the instrumentalization of mosques, on account of both the Islamic tradition of Turkey and of the secular-legal-political culture of the Turkish republic. Moreover, there are hardly any private mosques within Turkey. Even where a community has built a private mosque, the functionaries of the mosque including the imam and muezzin are appointed by the Turkish government as government employees.

This partly explains why the Kemalist state, while constricting the Islamic face of the Turkish nation by outlawing the Sufi *tekke*, *madrasa*s, *sharia* courts, caliphate, Islamic education and purging any Islamic insignia from public sphere, did not feel it necessary to institute the centrally administered "Friday sermon" and regulate its time frame until the mid-1990s, particularly after 1997 post-modern military coup, when the military dominated Kemalist state decided to administer the written Friday sermon centrally.[2] The practice of centrally administered Friday sermon remained till 2006. It was then relatively decentralized when the task of preparing *khutba* was first transferred to the regional mufti office before it was further decentralized in 2009 at the level of individual imam of the mosque subject to the approval of local mufti office.[3] Gülen, as legally authorized state preacher and imam of the mosque, did enjoy the advantage of the relative absence of state regulation of the content of the Friday sermon as well as *vaaz* sermons before the *adhan* until the mid-1990s.[4] He constructively utilized this public space for "educating" or "re-memorizing/re-connecting" the "Muslim public" with the exemplary qualities and virtues of Islam and the Islamic Ottoman past of Turkey through focusing on the life of Prophet Muhammad, the lives of his Companions, and the lives of "Muslim heroes" of Turkey—whether belonging to Ottoman times or the period of the Republic.

Ori Z. Soltes has noted the role of the mosque in Gülen's mobilization:

> In Izmir he began to redirect the role of the mosque toward what it had been in Islam's golden age: the center of life, attending not only to the prayer-centered spiritual needs of its constituents, but to their psychological and intellectual needs as well. He did not merely preach Friday Sermons, but conducted discussions which focused on the questions relating to everyday life: both their concerns and the issues about which they were merely curious—to which the Muslim tradition, linked to contemporary thought, offers answers. His deep learning and his psychological acuity combined to help him develop a reputation to expand his following.[5]

Whether Gülen was conscious of the historical role of mosque in serving Islam, the community, nation, and *umma*, or whether he was simply performing his officially assigned duty, the position of state preacher and imam of mosque with the freedom to deliver *vaaz* before the prayer and to choose the theme of the Friday sermon (*khutba*) and deliver the same without the limitation of time did provide an opportunity and legitimate space/forum to establish communication with the wider public. After all, Gülen rose to national prominence only through the agency of mosque. He has mostly delivered long lectures related to Islamic themes during the *vaaz*. However, it must be noted that Gülen has never been involved in coordinating or mobilizing imams or other religious functionaries of mosques at any level, national, regional, or local, to put across his message.

Constitutions of 1961 and 1982

The second important factor in the rise of Hizmet is that in performance of his public role Gülen was also protected by a "regime of social, economic and political rights" established by the 1961 Constitution of Turkey that was further strengthened under the 1982 Constitution, as well as an emerging political culture that was less hostile to the public expression of Islam. Even though the military regime dislodged the Democratic Party from state power on the grounds of misuse of religion for political purposes, the Constitution of 1961, drafted and finalized under the supervision of the military, itself gave constitutional recognition to the role of religion, particularly in the field of education, and to the role of the Diyanet, which was further strengthened in the Constitution of 1982. Gülen's public speeches and actions broadly fall within the scope of the 1961 and 1982 Constitutions. Thus, under the Constitution of 1961, Article 10 enjoins the state to undertake measures for the "development of individual's material and spiritual existence"; Article 19 grants freedom of thought, conscience, and faith; Article 19 and 29 provide the right to form associations; Article 22 and 23 sanction the freedom of the press, publication of books, newspapers, and periodicals; and Article 35 calls for "protection of family, mother and child." Similarly, Article 12-34 of Chapter II titled "Fundamental Rights and Duties" and Chapter III titled "Social and Economic Rights and Duties" of the Turkish Constitution of 1982 further strengthen and elaborate the above articles of the 1961 Constitution. In short, the 1961 and 1982 Constitutions provided a relatively liberal political atmosphere to Gülen to carry out his Islamic mission without much legal and political hindrance.

Rural-urban migration

A third factor in the growth and efficacy of the movement was that Gülen's social Islamic discourse appeared at a critical juncture in Turkish politics in the 1970s, which were characterized by mass migration of peasantry from villages to urban areas. Turkey witnessed a major demographic transformation as a result of this mass migration from the underdeveloped East and South East to the major urban centers of modern Turkey, such as Istanbul, Izmir, Ankara, Antalya, Adana, Gaziantep and so on, that started in the 1950s and has continued to date on account of the industrialization process unleashed in the major urban centers of the country, improved transportation, road infrastructure and communication networks. The population increased from 17,800,000 in 1940 to 44,000,000 in 1977.[6] Today the population has reached approximately 82 million. In 1950, only 25 percent of the population lived in cities; by 1993, this figure had increased to 59 percent. In 2003, the proportion of people who live in urban areas had grown to 65 percent and today it has reached 75.5 percent.[7]

With this migration from rural to urban areas, Turkish witnessed a new social phenomenon called *gecekondu* (or squatting – literally "overnight-built" houses on government lands without permission). According to Tas and Lightfoot,

> by the 1980s, nearly 60 percent of the residents of Ankara, Istanbul, Adana, Izmir, and Bursa lived in new *gecekondu* or in city neighborhoods that had originated as *gecekondu*. In the 1990s, the situation became even more dramatic than before. The largest cities continued to grow, and several towns grew to be classified as cities for the first time. In both the established and new cities, an extraordinary number of *gecekondu* settlements were erected. Currently, out of a total population of 68.5 million in Turkey, it is estimated that twenty million people live in *gecekondu*.[8]

As the rural migrants with their "local, Naqshbandi Islamic self" moved into the urban spaces and came face to face with the state's secular-political-legal culture and Westernized life styles, the perception of relative deprivation or, in other words, "poor Muslims" vs. "rich secular-Kemalists"—a contrast that was not visible in the villages in the absence of secular elites—became deeper among the rural migrants. Even though the "*gecekondu*" areas were not "slums" or "ghettos" as found in some of largest urban cities or metropolises of the South and over the years buildings were legalized or transformed into proper apartment-style houses with the support of the government because of the emerging, competitive, electoral democracy in Turkey, they did share "problems of integration" in the context of city life: unplanned and haphazard growth: cramped housing facilities, overcrowded neighborhoods, lack of basic amenities including proper drinking water, hygiene and sanitation, lack of access to quality education, isolated life, high degree of unemployment among the migrant youth, income inequality, the discriminatory policies towards these migrants' neighborhoods by secular, urban elites who controlled the power structure of the state, and cultural conflicts between rich, urban, secular lifestyles and poor, Muslim rural lifestyles.

Formation of the collective Islamic self: white vs. black Turks

The "Anatolian influx" (rural) into "modern secular Turkey" (urban) brought the rural, religiously oriented, Muslim Turks face to face with the Western lifestyles of modern Turkey, which had not been so directly experienced within Anatolia. The migration into urban areas also made the class differentiation/inequality between Black Turks (Anatolia) and White Turks (non-Anatolian, Westernized, state elites) more visible. The Anatolian Muslim migrants faced the daunting task of integrating themselves with state values. They were faced with alien, hostile laicism and aggressive Western lifestyles and robbed of their legitimate Muslim (Ottoman) heritage, history, language, culture, value and symbols, while at the same time being sensitive to preserving their Muslim sense of history, culture, religion, family and identity—the baggage with which they migrated—and becoming profoundly aware of the discriminatory attitude of the government towards them (mostly against the students of Imam-Hatip schools). They were left with nothing but suffering from an increasing alienation, hopelessness, anxiety, confusion, directionlessness and without any clue how to cope with rapid changes.[9]

As Muslim/Islamic emerged as the "victimized and oppressed identity," it helped in forging the collective bond among migrants that came to the urban centers with a different provincial, sectarian and *tarika* identity. It was in the city that the migrants discovered in Islam/Muslimness a source of unity, pride, tradition, identity, recognition, strength, sharing of a collective life, and an escape from what they considered the immoral life of the city full of treachery, lies, manipulation and exploitation. In this context, Şerif Mardin rightly noted,

> The contrast between the ideals of traditional Turkish society—courage, generosity, equity, mutual help—and the new rules of the game—cunning, miserliness, skewed income distribution—have

> made the young contemptuous of bourgeois society just as German adolescents were contemptuous of Burgerlichkeit in the days preceding Hitler's ascent to power.[10]

On the other hand the political process was also becoming receptive to the public expression of Islamic/Muslim identity on account of competitive electoral democracy that was forcing the political parties, including the Republican People's Party (CHP) to concede to religious demands being made since the late 1940s, such as the introduction of Qur'anic and Imam-Hatip schools, Ramadan festivities, renovations and new constructions of mosques, return to *adhan* in Arabic, the strengthening of the role of the Diyanet, and a greater tolerance of the mushrooming of Sufi orders and *tekke* (lodges)—all combined to strengthen and legitimize the "collective Muslim self" emerging from below in the political sphere. Kemalism could sustain itself only in the state institutions and urban centers under an authoritarian set-up and by force of law and coercion.[11] With the introduction of the multi-party system, it quickly lost political ground.

Also by the 1970s, the Kemalist state was steadily losing its ideological appeal on account of its failure to meet the rising socio-economic concerns of its growing young population that had only a faint memory of Kemal Atatürk. Heinz Kramer noted,

> Like all the state-oriented and latently authoritarian concepts of modernization, Kemalism becomes dysfunctional if the stage of social development has crossed the threshold beyond which the majority of the population is no longer ready to follow but demands to become the master of its own fate. Turkey has reached this point.[12]

The more the Kemalist state faltered and faced a legitimacy crisis, the more it leaned towards Islam. The military interventions of 1960, 1971, and 1980, and their programs testified to this political trend.

It was this national vacuum that increasingly came to be filled by the Gülen Movement and other Islamic actors at societal level and by Islamically oriented political parties at national-political level and which led to due recognition of the role of religion in social-public life.[13] As Gülen remarked, "We must raise Islam to the first and most important point on the agenda, one that is to be dwelt on in every element of life."[14]

Gülen firmly believes that Islam as moral philosophy of life has to compete with other modes of philosophy of life from all possible angles in order to secure respect for Islam in society and it cannot command that respect by living in a private cell. This has become imperative in today's world where "religious truth" and the "religious vision of the good life" is only one among many competing visions of the good life. From this point of view Islam must address the challenges of the Turkish nation and humanity at large.

The process of formation of the "collective Muslim self" in urban Turkey coincided with the decline of Kemalism. The two emerging political streams that filled the national-political space vacated by the decline of Kemalism were Islamism and Leftism—both sharing and competing for the lower-class, urban, social base. All three political discourses—Kemalism, Islamism, and Leftism—were and are, in essence, the "discourse of the state." As the Left and Islamists competed for the same urban, social base—as in many contexts "Muslim" and "class" converge in the city—and Kemalists, Islamists and Leftists competed among themselves for the few public opportunities and control of state in general, the combination led to a "charged national-political atmosphere" that resulted in the worst form of youth violence throughout the mid-1970s that Turkey had witnessed.[15]

Turkey, with a stagnant economy and increasingly polarized society, had all the trappings to slip into vicious, internal, social, and political conflicts. It was in this charged social and political milieu, with extremism, ideological divides, and mutual distrust at national level, that Fethullah Gülen's inclusive, non-ideological "nation-in-Islam" or "Islam-in-nation"[16] discourse, including "peace," "unity" "cooperation," education, "self-sacrifice," "dialogue," "altruism," and "self-discipline" found easy reception and respect among the larger Turkish public at a general level and was an immense help to the Anatolian migrants to discover a new meaning of life, new ways of serving Islam, nation, and humanity, and thus enabled them to cope with modern challenges without being fearful of losing their own identity and faith.

By focusing on the "Muhammadi ethics and morals of Islam" and the Turkish-Ottoman Islamic tradition of service, Gülen was subtly presenting to the "Muslim nation" a way out or a way to overcome this "national crisis" characterized by extremism, under-development, illiteracy, poverty, disunity, and corruption. These morals and ethics of Islam consisted of such human qualities as hard work, trust, solidarity, thrift, honesty, fairness, equity, service, altruism, and welfarism, and a belief that the strengthening of these Islamic values would benefit the progress of the Turkish nation and Umma. In this context, it is worth pointing out that Gülen's stress on the Ottoman past, despite the regime's strong reservations and hostile attitude to it, was not merely an emotional impulse but serve the purpose of reconnecting Turks with Islam via the Ottoman legacy. Islam makes sense to people when it is linked with their history and everyday cultural practice, story, idiom, and norms.

Gülen's new Islamic discourse with focus on work ethics, peace, dialogue, reconciliation, and tolerance provided a lesson to the state-oriented Turkish nation that the interest of the nation and Islam can be served not only through state agency but far more effectively by participating in social sectors: education, health, relief, media, and others. As Gülen states, "Islam does not need a state to survive; in the modern age, civil society can independently maintain Islam even where Muslims are not the majority."[17] This belief in serving Islam and humanity through social agencies became firmer within Gülen as he moved to the United States and traveled in other Western countries. He realized that democracy, freedom, and education are not only the safest means to serve Islam and humanity but they are essential conditions to secure one's faith.

In particular, Gülen's "nation-in-Islam" or "Islam-in-nation" discourse made sense to a section of the "Muslim public," including youth, the business class, the bazaari middle class, women, and students, in the context of an emerging "victimized Muslim collective self," growing pluralization of the public sphere, and increasing critical awareness of *the paradox of living in a homogenized Turkish Muslim nation on the one hand and the exclusion of the Muslim collective self from the national identity and power structure of modern Turkey on the other.*[18] The Gülen Movement along with other Islamic movements is to a large extent a product of this growing imbalance between (once) anti-religious secular nation-state and the predominant homogenized Muslim nation.

While Islamic political forces from Milli Görüş to the AKP used this political context for re-centering "Muslim Turkey" and de-centering "Kemalist secular Turkey" in the political arena, Gülen's inclusive, peaceful, non-violent, Islamic ideal and message and his "theodicy of hope"—

to use Uğur Kömeçoğlu's expression[19]—not only provided a cognitive structure and "meanings" to a vast number of Anatolian Muslims to help them overcome the stress and strains of fearful living in a Godless modern age,[20] but in line with the *tajdidi* tradition of Islam, motivated and channeled the emotional resources of a vast number of Anatolian Muslims, who had become increasingly aware of the mismatch between their marginalized status and poor representation in the power structure and their actual, enhanced capacity resulting from the changing socio-economic-demographic reality of Turkey; these resources were to be put into "positive action" and "ceaseless work," without the notion of "other"[21] and with the hope that it is not merely possible to remove this imbalance or imperfection and gain equal status in Turkish society, but also to resurrect the glory once bestowed on Turkey as cradle of Islamic civilization and transform "Turkish Islam" into a universal Islamic discourse.

As the left was decimated by the 1980 military coup, Anatolian Muslims regained their economic clout from the mid-1980s under the neo-liberal economy initiated by Turgut Özal, and the political context became more "*green*" with the coming of Islamists to power.[22] This diluted the anti-religious meaning of secularism, and along with a post-modernist discourse of identity, the Gülen Movement rapidly expanded both vertically (in the elites) and horizontally (in the masses), cutting across ethnic and class identity. However, the dominant social basis of the Movement remains the lower, middle, and upper middle-class Muslims.

Thus, in this context, it would not be an exaggeration to state that even though it might have been the military crackdown (1980) that created a semblance of law and order (at the cost of many lives, mostly belonging to the left), amidst the intense sectarian and ideological rift in Turkish society, it was the vision of Turgut Özal[23] and Fethullah Gülen that lifted the nation from sterile statism and populism entwined with an inward looking mentality fearful of external conspiracy; their vision injected a new sense of confidence to participate and compete in the fast emerging opportunity structures thrown up by the process of globalization. Mustafa Yeşil, former Secretary General of the Journalists and Writers Foundation (JWF), underlined this contribution of Gülen when he stated, "The Kemalist system of education made us feel that the entire world was the enemy of Turkey; thanks to Hodjaefendi, the young generation is thinking differently."[24]

Thus, a part of the reason for the expansion and national appeal of the Gülen Movement is that it represents the aspirations of millions of Anatolian Muslims for equity, social justice, fair treatment, and dignity, and keeps the hope of upward mobility alive that was denied to them by the Kemalist state, and more particularly by the "deep state." In other words, it is also a faith-based movement for equity and recognition in the public sphere within Turkey. The Movement gave a new identity, a new sense of confidence, a new meaning and goal of life, and respect to many who were hitherto excluded under the Kemalist political dispensation.[25] As Binnaz Toprak aptly puts it, "the Islamic movement not only resolved problems of identity and conservative angst; it became a channel to political power, social status, intellectual prestige, and economic wealth for people who in one way or another had been marginalized by the republican ethos."[26]

It may be stressed here that the rapid integration of volunteers in the opportunity structure created by Hizmet Movement within and outside Turkey is a factor equally important to account for the success of the Hizmet Movement in contrast to other Islamic movements in the world. The Gülen Movement provides employment opportunities to thousands of unemployed, frustrated students, including those from Imam-Hatip schools with mostly coming from low-income religious family background, who felt unjustly discriminated against and excluded from public employment opportunities on account of the state perception of them as coming from a religious background despite receiving a similar education and having the same qualifications as graduates of government schools. They are employed in the rapidly growing Gülen-inspired private schools and preparatory coaching institutions within and outside Turkey, with a new sense of their Islamic identity, role, and mission. In this process Gülen made a great contribution to preventing a situation from developing in Turkey like in Algeria[27] or in Pakistan,[28] where a section of students and youths of religious background, deprived of any access to opportunity spaces or the job market, became foot soldiers to fight in the name of Islam against the state and the West.

Microstructures of the Hizmet Movement

But how does Hizmet work? What is the conceptual apparatus upon which this Movement has emerged and expanded globally in such a short span of time? What are the dominant features and the organizational structures of the Movement? How are decisions reached within the Movement?

The most important Islamic micro cognitive structures of Hizmet Movement are the notions of *hizmet*, *himmet*, *iman*, *hijrah*, and *jihad*.

Hizmet as an Islamic discourse

Literally "*hizmet*" means "service." However, in the Gülen Movement, *hizmet* has a powerful Islamic connotation. It is the most dominant Islamic value and refers to "constant actions in this world to please God without any expectation of return." According to Gülen, "the worldly life should be used in order to earn the afterlife and to please the One who has bestowed it. The way to do this is to seek to please Allah and, as an inseparable dimension of it, to serve immediate family members, society, country, and all of humanity accordingly. This service (*hizmet*) is our right, and sharing it with others is our duty."[29] Thus, in Gülen's Islamic discourse *hizmet* is assumed to be an integral dimension of Islamic faith as well as the core value of the "golden generation." In my interviews and informal interactions with several volunteers of the Hizmet Movement, the idea of *hizmet* as an "Islamic service ethic"—serving people, community, nation, humanity, helping others—all for the sake of Allah without any expectation of return comes out very strongly. Mustafa Yeşil, Director of JWF, made a distinction between "*imani Hizmet*" and "Hizmet" in order to buttress the Islamic dimension of Hizmet.[30] Thus, Hizmet as service value, as Yavuz has rightly observed, "becomes the externalization of an internalized belief system."[31]

However, in order to understand the full import of *hizmet* as a service ethic, it is important to be familiar with the historical formation of this value system in the Turkish national setting, where the Hizmet Movement was born and shaped. The word "Hizmet" in Turkish lexicography served as "root paradigm" having multiple meanings with overtones of moral goodness or sacredness. According to Şerif Mardin, "*Root paradigm* is a term used by Victor Turner to characterize clusters of meaning which serve as a cultural "map" for individuals; they enable the person to find a path in their own culture… [S]uch paradigms affect the form, timing and style of behavior of those who bear them."[32] He considers "gazi" an example of a "root paradigm" and demonstrates the multiple meanings of the Turkish word "gazi" in multiple contexts (conqueror, fighter for faith, one spreading the holy message, struggle within oneself for purity) and concludes that "the *gazi-gaza* cluster makes up a cultural constellation which is still active in contemporary Turkey and which shapes social behavior in important issues."[33]

Similarly, *hizmet* turns out to be a relatively durable root paradigm having multiple meanings ranging from military mission to Turkish nationalism to Islamic *dawa* to government services to altruism that frame the cultural map of Turkish-Muslim society. What underlies these multiple meanings of *hizmet* is its association with mission for noble, sacred purposes. As Berdal Aral points out, "every Turk has a mission to fulfill."[34] Ömer Çaha informs me that, "every Turk is proud of having ruled over one third of the world."[35] Etienne Copeaux's work on *hizmet* provides the multi-layered meaning of this particular root-paradigm in Turkish historical narratives as well as its elevation as national value to denote the Turkish contribution to the world in general and the Muslim world in particular.[36] Another scholar has highlighted the role of *hizmet* in Turkey as a powerful form of legitimation of varieties of public action: "The mission of the state has changed over time. *Çağdaşlaşma* (modernization) replaced the Ottoman ideal of *I'la-yi Kelimetullah* (that is, upholding God's name and conquering new territories for the sake of Islam) as the form of *hizmet*. The concept of *hizmet* has additional avenues of circulation. Every military intervention in Turkey has been legitimized by reference to the "mission of protection" of Kemalist principles. Members of the Turkish nationalist (*Ülkücü*) movement in Turkey identify themselves as "*mabed bekçisi*" (Guardians of the Mosque). The Gülen community movement identifies itself with a mission of *hizmet* (service to the country, humanity, and the world). Any form of work or struggle should have a mission (a form of *hizmet*) to legitimize itself.[37] The idea of "mission" is inherent in the Turkish notion of *hizmet*. My own stay in Turkey for about a year from 2010 through 2011 and from September 2013 through June 2016 made me recognize this "mission" dimension as a cultural trait of Turkish personality.

The Ottoman Islamic history, culture, tradition, myth, stories, and idioms have played an important role in nurturing this Islam-led service ethic that also factored into managing the affairs of the multi-ethnic Ottoman empire relatively peacefully. It was partly due to this altruism/service orientation that the Ottoman State allowed the fleeing, persecuted Jews from Andalusia (modern Spain) to settle in the central provinces in Turkey in the fifteenth century. The Ottomans preferred to call themselves "servants of the Holy Cities of Mecca and Medina" after conquering those cities.[38] The service ethic (or service to the nation and state) also impacted the formation of Turkish nationalism in three ways. First, it blurs the distinction between Islam/Muslim/Turk—all are complementary. This partly explains why the transition from Turkish Empire to Turkish nationalism has been relatively free of any polemical debate between Pan-Islamism vs. nationalism or Islam vs. nationalism—a debate which remains alive in much of the Muslim world today. Unlike in Turkey, the governments of today in Muslim countries continue to feel the heat of Islamic discourses that treat nation and nationalism as antithetical to Islam and global Muslim unity.

Second, *hizmet* as "service ethic" is a factor in maintaining the "social" character of the Turkish nation-state, despite the push factors of globalization and liberalization that demand the gradual withdrawal of the state's service in the social sector. This has partly affected the state's policy of distribution of social wealth, which in turn has mitigated problems of social and economic inequality. Analyzing the growing role of faith-based associations in serving the poor and undertaking other philanthropic activities, İpek Göçmen has observed how religious service ethics have been incorporated in the governance of state institutions:

> [A]t the central level, the establishment of the Social Assistance and Solidarity Fund in 1986 was the first and main step taken by the government to support the parts of population that are not covered by social security services (SYGM, 2012)... It was modeled on *vakif* institutions, which existed long before the birth of the Ottoman Empire. The idea of introducing a social-assistance institution modeled on *vakif*s is significant for two reasons: it is based on Islamic principles and it emphasizes citizens' duty to care for the poor. After the 1990s and particularly the financial crises of 2000 and 2001, both the fund's budget and field of activity expanded dramatically; currently there are more than 900 foundations of the Social Assistance and Solidarity Fund all over the country con-

nected to the central directorate in Ankara (SYDTF, 2012).[39]

Besides, the social value of *hizmet* in Turkey prevented the development of a comprador character in the national bourgeoisie, characteristic of India and many other post-colonial societies. The Anatolian Muslim bourgeois is nationalist par excellence and invests heavily in the domestic sector as well as participating in philanthropic activities. It is not without reason that Turkey was the third largest country in the world in terms of donations and aid to other needy countries in 2014, out of which the private contribution was greater than the state contribution.[40] Evidence for the *hizmet*-inclined social self of the Turkish nation is further buttressed by the fact that Turkey is not only shouldering the responsibility of largest number of Syrian refugees (more than 2.5 million), even at the cost of low intensity localized Syrian-Turkish conflicts, but also providing the best social services, facilities, and security to the refugees, according to the joint report of Brookings Institute and the International Strategic Research Organization (USAK).[41] This appears to be a paradox considering the historical animosity between Turks and Arabs. Further, whereas Arab countries, particularly Gulf Arab nations, closed their border to Syrian Arab refugees, Turkey kept the door open, for refugees coming from both Iraq and Syria.

Thus, historically speaking, *hizmet* as social value has special place in the Turkish social fabric. Serving the community, nation or state, or family, friends and others is a powerful, ingrained, Turkish value, nurtured during Ottoman times, that persists even today. The attempts of the Kemalist state—both persuasive and coercive—to wipe out "anything related to Islam" from the collective memory of the Turkish nation and society, was not able to replace this historically formed Islamic value of social service, though certainly it weakened and maimed it. Over the years it has transformed itself into a collective "service ethic" and national value of Turkish society, which partly explains its wide acceptance and the voluntary participation of people with diverse orientations in the Gülen Movement. It is not without reason that Gülen successfully tapped this "ideational-cultural-material resources of Turkish society" as Islamic mission (*hizmet*) to serve humanity across the various nations of the world in all possible fields: education, health, charity, philanthropy, and dialogue. According to İhsan Yılmaz, Gülen frequently use the notion of

"*Dar ul-Hizmet*" (Abode of Service) in order to buttress the service ethics of Islam as well as to overcome the age-old, negative, conflict-ridden, binary division of Islam into *Dar ul-Islam* (Abode of Peace) and *Dar ul-Harb* (Abode of War).[42] The Gülen Movement has further strengthened the tradition of *hizmet* and has transformed the notion of *hizmet* into an "everyday service ethic" within Turkey. In this regard Gülay has rightly noted that, "[Gülen's] theological emphasis on *hizmet* represents the most important conceptual departure from Nursi and the Naqshbandis. While Nursi and the Naqshbandis do not condemn this-worldly activity, they also do not emphasize it as a foundational principle."[43] In order to underline this specific meaning of *hizmet* some researchers started to name the Movement as the Gülen-Hizmet Movement,[44] rather than the erstwhile Hizmet Movement.

Himmet and resource mobilization

Within the Gülen Movement "*himmet*" refers to the courage and determination of the volunteer to contribute in material terms for the *hizmet*. In other words, *himmet* is an important means to realize the goal of *hizmet*. A *himmet* meeting is a fundraising event locally organized by volunteers who oversee *hizmet* events in a certain locality on a voluntary capacity. Headed by Abi (for all male volunteers) or Abla (for all female volunteers), the *himmet* meeting takes place on a fixed day, either weekly or bi-monthly to discuss and mobilize the resources for the future projects of Hizmet. Though teachers, doctors, engineers, and other service-sector employees participate in *himmet* meetings, it is the bazaari, middle-class business group that constitutes the core strength of the *himmet* meeting. I myself have attended two all-male *himmet* meetings, one in Izmir and another in the Fatih district of Istanbul. A group of thirteen owners of medium-size businesses was present at the Izmir *himmet* meeting (held on March 15, 2011), while the one in Fatih, held on May 26, 2011 in Istanbul, was attended by a group of 20 owners of medium-size businesses.

The *himmet* meetings were started with a recitation of the Qur'an by the Abi or a senior volunteer. In the Izmir meeting there were two specific agenda items: (1) to raise the subscriptions to *Zaman* newspaper and (2) the issue of scholarships for underprivileged students. It was a regular consultative meeting, not a meeting to take up a new project.

One volunteer, associated with construction work, offered five scholarships with a hope to increase next year. Others followed suit, making different commitments. This group made the commitment of raising 500,000 US dollars over the next two years to support educational activities abroad. Interestingly, every member of this group had visited two or three countries to see their own investment in Hizmet as well as to explore the business opportunities through the Hizmet network.

The *himmet* meeting in Istanbul was more structured. The meeting began with recitation of the Qur'an by a senior Abi, followed by a short film on a Hizmet teacher who died in Mongolia and the success of Hizmet schools in science Olympiads.[45] The group, which had been together for the last four months, was given the project of a school in Indonesia and scholarships for 1,000 Indonesian students to study in Turkey. The monthly expenses of this school in Indonesia were estimated to be 31,000 US dollars. The senior Abi, who had come from Germany to attend this Himmet meeting, delivered an emotional speech to motivate the group to donate generously for this purpose. Amongst the things he said were:

> "This opportunity is only for you. In the afterlife there will be some rewards, which you do not know. To support Hizmet, there is no need to be a rich person…Allah has given you the materials and your soul. You give His material in His way. Like *Hadhrat* (the Honorable) Uthman gave seven hundred camels for the sake of Allah during the Tabuk Campaign, *Hadhrat* Abu Bakr gave all his belongings, *Hadhrat* Umar gave half of his belongings…We are investing in this world, we will harvest in the afterlife…The *hizmet* will go on. The important thing is where your position is."

He narrated the story of a businessman based in Germany who is looking after two schools in Germany.

He further added: "There is a Turkish person who went to Taiwan in 1995 for *Hizmet*. Hizmet supported him for thirteen years. Today he has become a successful businessman and has promised to contribute 35,000TL, which is the equivalent of ten scholarships. Tonight, he is the first person who made *himmet*."

Thus, everything from Islamic narratives to concrete examples are utilized to motivate the volunteers to contribute a part of their income for the sake of Allah. The speech was followed by commitments made by those who were present. In this meeting, the contributions ranged from two to thirty scholarships. A teacher from the USA who was present at the meeting, though not a part of this *himmet* group, also contributed 500 US dollars.

It appears that the money contributed in the *himmet* meetings is a combination of *zakat*, *sadaqa* and *fitra*, as well as one's own capacity to contribute for the sake of Allah, though the bulk of money is generated through *sadaqa*. Apart from Islamic calling, faith in Fethullah Gülen's call to service, peer group pressure, and social standing all combine to motivate the meeting participants to contribute money. The members of the *himmet* meetings also compete among themselves to contribute generously for the cause. The contributors are called *mütevelli* (*mutawalli*). The atmosphere in the *himmet* meetings was one of informal discussion and consultation without any formal recording of the minutes of the meeting in writing. It is totally based on trust and cooperation and money collected thus or through other sources is deposited to the local Hizmet foundation or in the name of an individual bank account holder. People used individual accounts especially at times when they feared a possible unlawful government takeover of their charity, just as happened in the aftermath of the 1980 military coup and Erdoğan's government crackdown since 2013. In both crackdowns, all the foundations and trusts were seized and their bank accounts were frozen.[46] This state behavior continues even today, as seen in Erdoğan's persecution on Hizmet which even seized individual accounts.

In addition to *himmet* meetings, resources, money or materials, are also mobilized by approaching a single *mütevelli*. Any volunteer, mostly senior Abis, can approach a potential *mütevelli* for a particular project. The *mütevelli*, having agreed to such a project, either donates a large sum of money or supplies materials and takes the responsibility of constructing a school, dormitory, or, if he/she so wishes, endow such property. Zirve University, Gaziantep, where this author was faculty member, was one such *waqf* property donated by the Nakipoğlu family of Gaziantep and others. Such *mütevelli* are normally big business persons. It is difficult to say whether the big businessmen do conduct their own *himmet* meeting. However, their financial contribution is indeed crucial for Hizmet projects. Helen Rose Ebaugh provides a detailed description of the involvement of big business in Hizmet projects such as *Zaman* newspaper, Bank Asya, Samanyolu TV, Fatih University and so on.[47] Hayri Kafdağlı, the General Secretary of Kimse Yok Mu (KYM), the Hizmet relief organization, also pointed out the role of big business houses in Hizmet projects.[48] According to him, one of the biggest furniture companies in Turkey, donates 1 million TL of furniture every year to KYM. Similarly, one big textile and electrical company donated 200,000TL and 1,000,000TL to KYM for a 2011 flood-relief program in Pakistan. However, these donations by industrialists are also linked with liberal tax exemption introduced in the mid-1990s if donations are linked with education, food, clothing, and other domestic appliances.

In this context, it should also be noted that that these big investors are also tied to hundreds of thousands of Hizmet Movement volunteers. Thus, the circulation of *Zaman* newspaper and viewership of Samanyolu TV is also dependent upon the ready market of Hizmet volunteers. Similarly, the Hizmet schools within Turkey and abroad play an important role for Hizmet-linked universities within Turkey in mobilizing the children of elites who can afford the high fees of these universities. While I was writing this book, when the Erdoğan government was hell-bent upon closing Bank Asya, it was the "critical support" of the Hizmet volunteers and networks that was sustaining the bank.

Through my interaction with several such volunteers of the Movement, it became clear to me that members of the *himmet* meetings are not only there to provide economic support for identified projects, but they also get involved in the execution of the projects by making on-the-spot visits, which in turn satisfy them that their money is being properly utilized. The sense of democratic participation in its execution makes them feel that they are important stake-holders in the Hizmet project. Though the contribution of large business houses has sometimes been highlighted to the extent of pejoratively calling Hizmet a representative of "Corporate Islam," it is these countless *himmet* meetings based in the municipality, wards, *mahalle*, towns, and districts of Turkey, along with thousands of schools and coaching institutions in almost all provinces of Turkey, which are the financial backbone of the Hizmet Movement.

Enes Ergene provides the following operative principles that are kept in consideration while carrying out a Hizmet project:

- Whether it is a reasonable and feasible project;

- Make sure it does not cause any harm in the locality and environment;
- Whether it will present something "new" or add value to an "existing thing";
- Whether it is in harmony or contradiction with local values and beliefs.[49]

Motivational microstructures

Though the horizontal and vertical expansion of the Gülen Movement is built upon the structure of "business-teacher-student," it is the in-built Islamic cognitive structure of the "*ikhlas-iman-hijrah-jihad-dawa*" linkage that provides the motivational resources for the expansion of the movement. *Ikhlas* refers to purity of intention and sincerity to carry out any action or deed for the sake of the pleasure of Allah. This is as important as the achievement of any goal—whether in this world or hereafter. In other words, *ikhlas* is part of the doctrine of means and ends, according to which it is the *nature of the means that determines the nature of goal.* Thus, like Gandhi, in Gülen's discourse the pursuit of legal-moral-ethical means itself constitutes an objective to secure the higher ends or pleasure of Allah, which in turn depends upon purity of intention and sincerity. Thus, intention and sincerity determines the selection of means to achieve the goal.

There is a close relationship between *ikhlas* and *iman. Ikhlas* is a pre-condition for the development of a state of *iman. Iman* refers to becoming conscious or profoundly aware of the commandments, prescriptions, values, and goals of Islam. It transports the Muslim from a "state of Muslimness" to a "state of Islamicness." In other words, it signifies the transformation from Muslim-in-itself to Muslim-for-itself, if paraphrased in the Marxist dictum of class-in-itself to class-for-itself. The imagination of *iman* varies from one Islamic school or sect to another. In Gülen's imagination of *iman*, Muslim/Islam is an inclusive category and even non-Muslims who share the virtues of *iman* in moral and ethical goodness can qualify to be a *mumin in terms of attributes.* It is the ideological construct under which a Muslim visualizes his/her life for Islam-led moral and ethical ideals. From this point of view, though, Gülen shares the ideological act of "objectification of consciousness" but decisively rejects the exclusive, parochial, political construction of the Islamicist understanding of *iman* or the Marxist notion of class-in-itself. In other words, a Muslim develops a state of consciousness to lead a selfless life for the sake of Allah. *Sohbets*, dormitories, light houses, book reading camps, *himmet* meetings, and other elements of the fluid organizational structure of the Hizmet Movement are all geared up to generate a "state of *iman*" among its core volunteers.

The "state of *iman*" propels or motivates a Muslim, mostly young boys and girls, to undertake *hijrah* (migration) for the purpose of *dawa*: spreading the message of Islam. As Eşref Potur, a senior volunteer in the Movement, states, "Hizmet [the movement] is all about delivering the message of the Prophet—the most essential responsibility of today's Muslims."[50] *Hijrah* was performed by Prophet Muhammad when he moved from Mecca to Medina under conditions of extreme hardship. Irrespective of the circumstances under which Prophet Muhammad undertook the *hijrah*, over the years *hijrah* and *dawa* have become the cardinal principles of Islam. When volunteers of the Hizmet Movement move within and outside Turkey in order to take up an assignment of Hizmet, they are considered to have performed a *hijrah*.

The word *jihad* is derived from *jahada*, "exerting oneself or striving." It is a "state of action" to be performed by Muslims only for the sake of Allah and nothing else. All material (movable and immovable) and non-material contribution and means is considered legitimate in the performance of *jihad* if it is used directly for Allah's cause, for one's spiritual growth and serving humanity. *Jihad*, thus, is centrally linked with the doctrine of *dawa*. It has two connotations: (a) *jihad al-nafs*, the struggle against oneself and (b) *jihad al-shaytan*, the struggle against the devil. Both notions imply the struggle against one's bad intentions, inclinations, and against seduction and enticement by proximate pleasures. It is further extended to the struggle for the good of Muslim society and against corruption and decadence. It becomes co-extensive with the concept of *amr bi'l ma'ruf wa nahyi an al-munkar* (commanding what is good and forbidding what is abominable). This form of *jihad* is called "greater Jihad" on account of a saying of the Prophet when returning after conducting a raid on an enemy party: "We are now returning from the Smaller Jihad to the Greater Jihad." When asked what he meant by "Greater Jihad," he answered, "The *jihad* against oneself." Within the Hizmet Movement the notion of *jihad* is associated with Greater Jihad, which calls for the inner struggle to purify one's heart and undertake positive action that is beneficial for Islam and humanity.

The effect of *ikhlas-iman-jihad-hijrah* is to perform the task of *dawa*, which means conveying correctly the message of Islam and Prophet Muhammad to the world. The Hizmet Movement gives special importance to the representation of Islam and enjoins every Muslim to represent Islam through their best possible positive action, manner, words, and conduct. In Hizmet discourse, *dawa* consists both of content and of the form in which Islam is presented.

Even though the Hizmet Movement creates economic opportunities for many volunteers, it is these Islamic motivational structures that primarily motivate the volunteers of the Hizmet Movement to move from one place to another, work hard, even on low wages, endure hardship, and live selflessly for the sake of Allah.

Supportive organizational structures

Sohbet refers to the coming together of volunteers once in a week for a collective reading of Islamic texts, particularly *Risale-i Nur* and the writings of Gülen, whereas *dershane* offers a space, whether at the work place, office, or residential buildings, to organize *sohbet*. *Sohbet* is organized along gender, neighborhood, class, and professional lines almost always on a weekly basis. I have personally attended a few *sohbet* meetings. In my observation, there are two kinds of *sohbet*. One in which a senior volunteer reads a portion of the Islamic text (mostly in Turkish), while others listen, followed by congregational prayer, and the exchange of informal pleasantries with each other. In the other kind, the volunteers gather and each read a different portion of the same Islamic text in turn and also discuss the meanings of what they read. There is a senior Abi (or Abla), normally a student of Gülen, who initiates the program and explains the meanings of the text (mainly in the Turkish) in case of disagreement over the meaning or lack of clarity about a portion of the Islamic text among the volunteers. Further, the senior Abi or teacher relates the relevance of the particular portion of the Islamic text under discussion for the modern-day realities. In addition to the reading of a religious text, matter related to future projects is also informally discussed.

Dormitories are facilities for students to live in while attending the high schools, coaching institutes, and universities set up by Movement participants. It may be noted that many of the high schools are boarding schools. Depending on the conditions of local regulations and cultural values, after-school programs are offered to those students who are willing to learn Islamic universal ethical values. These programs include Islamic literature, including publications by the Hizmet Movement. The dormitory is the place where Muslim students are generally exposed to the basic values of Islam. It is from dormitories that students who show eagerness to be involved with the Hizmet community and/or learn more about Islam are offered accommodation in the "light houses." Each dormitory is managed by volunteers of the Movement.

Light houses are residential flats with three or four bedrooms where eight to ten students live together and usually a senior one among them (*abi* for boys, *abla* for girls) takes charge to put things in order. The living costs in dormitories and light houses are normally borne by the students themselves, though Hizmet also provides support in the form of scholarships to academically promising and financially needy students. The light houses are the most important organic unit of the Hizmet Movement; students consolidate their faith and religious practice in these houses and develop culture of service, and depending upon their willingness some of them move further to take roles in the Hizmet Movement. It is in this space that students undergo the rigorous process of Islamic, spiritual, ethical, and moral training in the light of Nursi and Gülen's writings under the supervision of an Abi or Abla in order to develop the willpower to overcome carnal desires, to cultivate the orientation and capacity to dissolve his or her own self and serve others, and finally to develop God-consciousness or a state of *iman*. In other words, *dershane*s, and particularly the light houses, in the Gülen Movement have been conceived to provide spaces for the volunteers to undergo a moral and ethical training that combines that of the *madrasa* (school, mind), *tekke* (Sufi lodge, heart) and military academy (discipline). The students living in the light houses are expected to be dynamic, action-oriented, and dedicated to the cause of Islamic *dawa*. Gülen has called the light houses "a tree the seed of which was planted in the times of Prophet Muhammad himself."[51]

The other structures, including book reading camps, and *himmet* meetings, are spaces for volunteers to constantly renew themselves with Islamic commitments and values and generate resources for Hizmet projects.

Volunteers, leadership, and the decision-making process

The Hizmet Movement is a loosely structured volunteer movement based on the principle of "free will." This fact came out in most of my structured, un-structured, formal, and informal interviews and meetings with the volunteers, as well as through day-to-day observation: *there is complete freedom to enter, exit, and return within the networks of the Hizmet Movement.* The volunteers identify themselves with the cause of Hizmet and work in their individual capacity or as a part of organization inspired by the ideas and vision of Fethullah Gülen.

The Movement is composed of three kinds of volunteers: the first is the core, permanent ones coming through the routes of Hizmet dershanes, dormitories, and light houses and socialized in the Hizmet environment. Some of these who have professional positions in a Hizmet institution are on the monthly payroll of that institution, mostly occupy leadership positions, and are expected to be ready to move and undertake assignments and responsibilities allotted from time to time. Such permanent volunteers are dedicated to working in the Hizmet network for life and are subjected to transfer from one place to another depending upon the contingencies. They are expected to contribute ten percent of their annual salary to the Movement. Though these permanent volunteers work with the modern, bureaucratic principles of chain of command and functional hierarchy, their transfer from time to time is also a part of Islamic notion of *hijrah*—the most vital aspect of Muslim life to serve *dawa*. The second core component is *mütevelli*s who provide bulk of financial support – both in money and in kind – to the Hizmet projects. Outside these lies the third group, the large periphery consisting of volunteers of diverse orientations, sympathizers, and part-timers, including non-Muslims.

Though the absence of membership criteria, constitution, flag, ceremony, insignia, designated office bearers and so forth in the Hizmet Movement has been much celebrated as the "uniqueness" of the Hizmet Movement, I find this is nothing new or unique in the history of Islamic movements. Except for modern Islamist movements or Political Islam such as the Muslim Brotherhood and Jammat–e-Islami (which is based on membership, with organizational hierarchy, written constitution, and flag), all other Islamic social movements do not exhibit modern organizational membership features and are in essence voluntary movements. Likewise, the absence of *tariqa*, (order), while retaining the principle of Sufism, is considered a novelty of the Hizmet Movement. For this reason, some scholars have labeled Gülen as "neo-Sufi." However, there has been a series of Islamic Sufi scholars without any established order in the annals of Islamic history, such as Rabia, Mansour Hallaj, Hasan al-Basr, Junaid al-Baghdadi, Imam Ghazali, Imam Rabbani, Shah Waliullah Dehlawi and others. The non-modern features of the Hizmet Movement (lack of membership, constitution, etc.) draw heavily upon the Turkish Nur movement, which does not exhibit any membership criteria, initiation rites, *tariqa*, or written constitution; this helps them retain the image of being closer to the Prophetic model.

Though fluid, the Hizmet Movement is not devoid of functional leadership and hierarchy. In terms of function and unity of purpose the Movement is simultaneously centralized and decentralized, hierarchical, and egalitarian. The element of centralization is evident as I observed a similar argument running among the Hizmet volunteers right from Istanbul to Delhi to Bangkok vis-à-vis the Hizmet–Erdoğan-government standoff, as well as on other issues. The centralized leadership is not very visible in terms of designation and structure, and only two informal designations—Abi (brother) and Abla (sister)—appear to form the structure of the Movement. Functionally speaking, each Hizmet-inspired institution or group is headed by individuals who are also either a school director, business owner, head of a foundation, or a regular volunteer who is active in a certain neighborhood, city, or country. These individuals are usually a senior Abi or Abla who supervises and coordinates the Hizmet community, activities, their interactions among themselves, and outreach programs. The informal structure of Abi and Abla at each level of functional hierarchy is marked by a strong sense of accountability, trust, respect, and loyalty of participant volunteers. In the informal parlance, the word Abi or Abla signifies respect and recognition of seniority, which is in fact the same meaning in their Turkish vernacular.

Abis or Ablas, or in whatever form an individual is defined, holds a position of authority based on his credentials, experience in Hizmet, and religious knowledge. Generational seniority and having had lessons directly from Gülen himself are also considered important for recognition within Hizmet circles.

The term "big Abi," used informally, signifies some of those who are like the veterans; they are usually the ones who have been out there for Hizmet from the early days, as well as some of managerial rank who have come to be perceived holding important position within the diffused network of Hizmet Movement. Most of these abis are considered to have good religious knowledge and are often designated as imams (head), keeping with Islamic tradition of leading a group, at each level of functional unit irrespective of its size: nation, region, country, district, neighborhood, institution or group. It appears that the designation of imam is only applied to a senior male Abi. I have not come across any single Abla carrying the designation of imam. Similarly, there is no informal expression like "big Abla" signifying women of religious authority and leadership.

It appears that the practice of appointing imam heads in the Hizmet Movement has come from the tradition of Khalid al-Baghdadi, who used to appoint Khalifa (deputies) to supervise and coordinate activities related to his *tariqa*. This was an innovation in the organizational history of Sufi *tariqa*.[52]

In this Islamic tradition, Gülen's role is more like a position of a philosopher, guide, and source of inspiration and source of inspiration to millions of volunteers, if not the leader of the Movement.[53]

It appears that one is expected to adhere to the Qur'anic dictum: "Obey God and obey the Messenger and those in authority from among you," and the flow of decision and message within the Movement generally appears to be from top–down; however, at each level of Abi and Abla heading a particular organization or country there exists a considerable amount of functional autonomy. Thus, I have often observed how the leadership of the Hizmet Movement in India are free to identify the issues and themes of Hizmet works, select people for visits to Istanbul, organize events, and so on. They do not receive instructions from people sitting in Istanbul in their day-to-day functioning; neither have I ever heard that their decision to organize a particular event or recommendation of individuals for "Hizmet-visit" to Turkey has ever been vetoed by any other higher authority. Mustafa Yeşil, the former president of the Journalists and Writers Foundation, emphatically stated, "We have no authority over dialogue organizations all over the world."[54] At best, it can be safely stated that various Hizmet bodies working in the same field exchange experiences with each other, share skills, and coordinate activities. Thus, by giving autonomy to Hizmet volunteers in the "field," the Hizmet Movement has given to a vast multitude of Hizmet volunteers a "sense of meaningful participation" and of being a "part" of the decision-making process within the Movement. The combination of centralization and decentralization goes a long way in maintaining the cohesiveness, unity of purpose, sense of participation, and discipline within the Hizmet Movement.

Decisions concerning projects or other matters are arrived at through consultation and discussions. At each level of functional hierarchy there exists consultative structure, and consensus is the dominant norm of working. However, the final decision rests with the person heading that unit in case that consensus is not reached or in urgent or exceptional circumstances. It has been reported that there exists a "Council of Wise Men"[55] or "Central Board consisting of thirty full-time advisors or Büyük Abiler"[56] that are in regular consultation with Gülen himself, but during my research investigations, including a visit to Pennsylvania, where Gülen resides, I have not come across such a formal structure within the Movement. Provided his health permits, Gülen spares some time each day for consultation and conducts *sohbet* at least twice in a week through which he reaches out to the Movement. I have often observed that important functionaries of the Hizmet Movement, such as the head of the Hizmet Movement in a particular country and others, often pay a visit to Gülen in America for the purpose of consultation. Gülen considers "consultation" as the most important democratic value and a criterion in order to be recognized as a "full and perfect Muslim" and "believing society" and devoted a full chapter in his book *The Statues of Our Souls* to "Consultation" in order to explain the significance of the Qur'anic verse on consultation for building a democratic society and state, as well as for the future of Islam.[57] Gülen categorically recognizes the necessity of a collective leadership and decision-making process in the modern era: "The place of genius has now been replaced by collective consciousness with consultative and collective decision making."[58] In short, the whole Hizmet Movement runs on the informal principle of consultation, trust, cooperation, and faith.

CHAPTER 8

GÜLEN MOVEMENT IN ACTION: THE EDUCATIONAL DISCOURSE

Education is the most dominant face and identity of the Gülen Movement. There are no official figures about the numbers of Gülen-inspired educational institutions including schools, coaching institutes, student hostels, and universities. Thomas Michel, writing in 2010, provided the estimates of the movement's educational activities: "A recent estimate is that there are about 800 elementary schools, high schools, college preparatory institutions, student dormitories, and more than ten universities in almost 110 countries that are associated with this Movement."[1] Today, the movement is credited with establishing and running schools across 160 countries of the world. An empirical survey or observation of these schools (which onlookers, but not Movement participants, often call "Gülen schools" or "Turkish schools") reveals that they primarily conduct secular education within the national-legal-educational framework of the country where the school is located. The religious instruction is imparted in accordance with the law of the nation. Thus, within Turkey, the Gülen-inspired schools provide mandatory religious instruction for one hour in a week in accordance with the law.

The success of Hizmet in education raises several questions. Muslim scholars and reformers (both Islamic and non-Islamic) have time and again highlighted the central value of education in the Qur'an and Hadith in recent centuries but that has not unleashed the urge in the Muslim community to prioritize the quest for education. What makes Gülen's Hizmet a successful educational enterprise? In what ways do Gülen's interpretation of Islamic history and values resonate with a substantial section of Turkish people, including the section of Anatolian businessmen, and inspire them to become volunteers and make investments in the field of educational activity without expectation of material return? Or was it mere coincidence, the right time and context, that made a good proportion of the Turkish population receptive to Gülen's interpretation of Islam and his appeal for education, a reception which was lacking previously? Or is it that Gülen's writings and speeches provide an "alternative philosophy of life process" that first caught the imagination of a section of the Turkish population and that is gradually making its presence felt in other parts of the world?

Dominant narratives and its fallacies about Gülen's discourse

There are two explanations that have been advanced to account for the success of Gülen's educational discourse. The first broadly locates Gülen's philosophy of education within the historical trajectory of the relationship between Islam and modernity and attributes the educational success to Gülen's attempt to reformulate Islamic doctrines and practices in the light of the values of modernity. In other words, Gülen is considered a part of the long chain of "Islam and modernity" discourse that has successfully resolved the Muslims' paradox of living as "Muslim and modern" together in the modern ages—an issue that has preoccupied the Muslim/Islamic mind for centuries. However, most analysts operating within the framework of Islam and modernity merely *assert* the successful resolution of Islam and modernity via Gülen's Islamic educational discourse without actually demonstrating through logic, empirical facts, and argumentations *how* and *in what manner* Gülen's educational discourse harmoniously reconciles the values of Islam and modernity. The preceding chapters have critically examined the paradigms of the reconciliation of Islam and modernity and found them deficient in explaining the phenomenon of the Gülen Movement.

In fact, Gülen's educational discourse fundamentally differs from the approach of the late nineteenth-twentieth century model of Islamic modernism. First, much of the discourse of Islamic modernism arose in reaction to Western challenges and domination and therefore could not free itself from an apologetic and reactionary outlook. As a result, it either generated a discourse that indulged (broadly speaking) in the Islamic legitimation of modernity, its institutions, values and ideas (such as democracy, parliament, constitution, secularism, nationalism, capitalism, etc.) or an Islamic discourse (the genre of political Islam) that rejected Western modernity, or an Islamic discourse that preferred to withdraw from worldly engagements (secular) on the basis of the reformulation of Islam as a discourse for the *din* (other worldly) as a separate realm from the world (*dunya*). In all these discourses, the superiority of Islam was affirmed and hence they were not free of a power disposition. On the other hand, Gülen's educational discourse in part is a critique of the Western educational system and attempts to address the de-humanizing consequences of Western modernity.[2]

Second, liberal Islamic modernism aimed at the creative synthesis of Islamic values and Western science and technology through "social and educational reform" in Muslim societies. However, "Islamic social and educational reforms" were closely drawn from the Western-modern experiences that resulted either in reforming the existing curriculum, introduction of Western science and education, systems of examination (Abduh's experiment in Al Azhar, Egypt), creating Western-oriented educational institutions (Sir Syed's Aligarh Muslim University, India), or the creation of separate secular schools and universities by the Muslim state, and demonization of Sufi institutions and practices by both Muslim reformers and states. The so-called synthesis was either grossly tilted towards domination of the secular knowledge system over the Islamic educational system, or, at worst, ended in imitation of the Western educational system. One consequence of this process was an ever-growing gap between the secular education system and religious education system (now called *madrasas*) in Muslim societies. This division in the educational system continues to exist in Muslim societies, where graduates of Western, secular education institutions exercise almost complete monopoly over state resources, power, influence, and authority, while graduates of Islamic educational system suffer from a high degree of marginalization in all walks of life. The division was even institutionalized in many post-colonial Muslim nation-states, where science subjects would be only taught either in English, French, or German, while "Islamic" (religious) subjects were imparted either in Arabic or indigenous languages. In other words, English, French, and German were and are recognized as languages of modernity.

Further, the idea of separation between the secular and Islamic education systems was perpetuated by transformation of *madrasas* from a "place of study" into a place of exclusively Islamic religious learning by divorcing them from the subjects belonging to natural science and the humanities as they increasingly came to be identified with the "Western education system." '*Ulama* sought to preserve Islamic identity in the form of Islamic *madrasas*, which gradually became the most important symbol of Islamic identity. In contrast, Gülen's educational discourse aims at obliterating such a *false* distinction between the secular education and Islamic education system, which has come to stay in Muslim societies as a result of the introduction in the colonial context of a post-Reformation understanding of religion; he therefore treats education as a singular, organic, holistic process of understanding and underlines the fact that in Islamic cosmology there does not exist separate realms of secular (public, world) and religious (private, other world), but rather *din subsumes dunya*, and so Muslims are accountable in the next world for their conduct and actions in this world.

Third, the net effect of the interaction of Islam with the West during the colonial period, including the trend of Islamic modernism, was that Islam closed itself, erected a boundary around itself, became defensive, reactive, and past-oriented in outlook, feared to interact with the outside world, and engaged with this world on its own terms and conditions. In the process of closing itself, it strongly identified itself with spirituality and internalized the colonial discourse of "spiritual East" vs. "material West." It sought to compensate its material deprivation by contrasting its "vibrant spirituality" against the moral, spiritual, and ethical bankruptcy of Western materialism. Islam became the discourse of the "other world" (the Hereafter) and the West and modernity became the discourse of this world!

In contrast, Gülen's Islamic discourse aims to end this defensive, fearful, reactive outlook of Islam through the discourse of education and dialogue and injects a sense of motivation and confidence among Muslims to interact with the world without being fearful of losing their Islamic faith and identity. Writing in the context of Turkey he stated, "Our society had to be introduced to the modern age and be reconciled with its meanings and inspirations. We could in no way stay in retreat inside our small shell while the rest of the world was rapidly progressing."[3] The volunteers in the Movement often quote the Rumian dictum of "having one foot in the center of Islam while the other travels in seventy-two realms (nations) like a compass" in order to buttress this conception of Islam and express their new-found confidence.

Fourth, a crucial difference between the two approaches lies in the very conceptualization of education. For the Islamic modernists, "education" and "educational reform" was primarily an instrument for catching up with the West. Hence, the focus was on the reform of the university or creation of new universities as a site for the resolution of conflict between Islam and modernity by amalgamating both educational traditions. In other words, the focus was on conceiving education in the "realm of higher education" only. All proponents of Islamic modernism attempted to address the issue of "educational crisis" in Muslim societies by veering around the idea of reforming the existing Islamic educational institutions or creating new ones. Thus, the approach underlying educational reform to regenerate Muslim society was top-down, mechanical, rather technical in nature and one in which the juxtaposition of Islam and Western science was premised on a fixed, technical understanding of each other.

On the other hand, Gülen conceives education primarily as "social value," which is an open-ended, life-long process beginning with family and school. The underlying approach in Gülen's educational discourse is bottom-up, moral, and ethical, rather than technical, and concerned with the inculcation of universal values (such as altruism, elements of sacrifice, honesty, truthfulness, justice, peace, etc.) and ethics of social responsibility and individual accountability. Although conceptually Gülen's educational discourse comes closer to the perspective of "values education" in terms of its emphasis on character building, it goes beyond that, as it is geared towards creation of a holistic but balanced personality or achieving a balance by avoiding excess. By implication, the focus of educational discourse of Islamic modernists were and are institutions and structures, whereas the focus of Gülen's discourse is human agency: the raising of action-oriented, moral and ethical beings. Moreover, whereas all shades of Islamic modernism were hostile to Sufi Islam, Gülen attempts to retrieve the principles and practices of Sufism for the purpose of endowing Muslims with God-consciousness to develop an active, self-disciplining, moral and ethical being dedicated to the cause of humanity. This emphasis on human agency has led Fabio Vicini (and many others) to detect in Gülen's educational discourse a "strongly 'secular' faith in human ability to make this world better."[4] Certainly, Gülen through his discourse of education, entrepreneurship, and dialogue is developing a conception of Islam as "developmental discourse" by harnessing the transformative potential of Islam to make the world hospitable, but the underlying faith and motivation to transform the world has nothing to do with the "secular," either directly or indirectly, but is deeply Islamic in orientation, as it is linked with the notion of the Judgment Day in the next world; this is unlike the secular imagination, in which the individual is the measurement of everything, and life ends with this world only.

Thus, in view of the above differences, it can be safely argued that the educational discourse of Fethullah Gülen is not intended to reconcile Islam and modernity or "Islamize" modernity. Any resultant perception of the successful resolution of the paradox of being "Muslim and modern" together in Gülen's Islamic discourse is at best an *unintended* consequence of the trajectory of the Gülen Movement or an expression of a dominant collective desire of a section of literate Muslims. It may be noted that Gülen-inspired institutions—educational, media, publishing houses, charity works and interfaith dialogue centers, both within and outside Turkey—have become practical sites of demonstrating the harmony and unity of religion and science as well as mind and heart without pronouncing a discourse of "Islamic modernity."

It is interesting to note that none of the prominent protagonists of Islamic modernism (Afghani, Abduh, Sir Syed and others) has caught the imagination of Gülen; neither have they found a place in the list of Gülen's heroes of Islam that ranges from Prophet Muhammad to Bediüzzaman Said Nursi and which includes not only Islamic religious scholars but such diverse personalities as Sinan (the famous architect of Ottoman times) and some rulers of the Seljuk and Ottoman Empires.[5] With hindsight, it can be argued that the political overtones of these Islamic intellectual trends must not be appealing to Gülen, as he firmly believes that any form of politicization of religion harms Islam itself. Given Gülen's comprehensive, non-ideological, flexible, and inclusive understanding of Islam he must have found these models of Islamic resurgence not only fragmentary and exclusionary but ideologically and politically loaded and therefore insufficient to address the challenges of humanity.

Gülen's discourse and classical Islamic education

A second explanation identifies the success of Gülen's educational initiative with a resurrection of "classical Islamic education" that combines the study of transmitted sciences (Qur'an, Hadith, theology, jurisprudence, etc.) and natural sciences (logic, mathematics, etc.). In other words, Gülen's educational success lies in the harmony and unity of sciences (religious science and secular science) that was prevailing during the period of classical Islamic education (from the eighth to the tenth century CE).[6] However, such an understanding of Gülen's educational discourse does not correspond to the empirical reality of Gülen-inspired schools that have spread all over the globe. Nowhere in his writings has Gülen referred to such Islamic educational practices in history, nor has he mentioned the Nizamiyya *madrasas* or Ibn Khaldun's scheme of education or al-Farabi's philosophy of education that highlighted such distinctions and unity between the two knowledge systems. Further, the purported linkage of classical Islamic education with the Gülen Movement implicitly asserts the greater role of Islam in the education process that has brought success to the Gülen schools without demonstrating in any way how and in what manner Islam has played the decisive role in the success of Gülen schools. In other words, it entails an "Islamic point of view" in Gülen's educational discourse and the success of Gülen-inspired educational institutions.

However, as Farid Panjwani points out, "If one were to comb through the extant works from the first few centuries of the history of Muslims to find a book entitled, 'Islam and…', one would likely be searching in vain. For example, the bibliographical work of al-Nadim (1970, original in the tenth century) does not carry any such title. If a similar search were made today, however, one could fill an entire library with books carrying titles such as Islam and Democracy, Islam and Capitalism, Islam and Science, Islam and the West, and, certainly, Islam and Education."[7] Further, if one were to detect the Islamic point of view, in the modern sense of the term, in Gülen's educational discourse one might be tempted to stretch Gülen's educational philosophy to represent the current ideological project of the "Islamization of knowledge" that flows from the discourse of political Islamism, which is antithetical to Gülen's understanding of Islam and Islamic history. Moreover, the notion of "classical Islamic education" retains a "hierarchy of values" (that entails superiority of transmitted sciences over natural sciences), which is completely missing in Gülen's educational thought, notwithstanding the fact that Gülen draws inspiration from the classical period of Islam, particularly the period of Prophet Muhammad and Four Rightly Guided Caliphs.

Any attempt to bring Gülen's education discourse under the rubric of "Islamic education" would be gross injustice to Gülen's Islamic thinking; for it is the paradigm shift from "seeking Islamic education to education as an Islamic universal value" in Gülen's Islamic epistemology that partly explains what appears to be a paradox in modern thinking about an Islamic movement running secular educational institutions. The Kemalist law in Turkey that prohibits the opening of religious schools or *madrasa*s might have played a role in directing Gülen's attention towards the establishment of secular schools; however, the proliferation of Gülen-inspired schools abroad and in those countries (such as India) that do not place any ban on the opening of religious schools testifies to the "paradigm shift" in Gülen's Islamic thinking that flows from Gülen's understanding of Islam, rather than to the shift occurring due to the constraints of law. As Eşref Potur pointed out, "There were no *madrasa*s during the times of Prophet Muhammad and His Companions,"[8] thus not only deriving the legitimacy from Islam for such initiatives but also underlining the point that education does not have any color (religious or secular). Also, Gülen points out that Islam must be in tune with the contemporary age: "[W]e must raise generations who comprehend their time, who are able to consider the past, present, and future together. Otherwise, God forbid, our nation will be crushed in the merciless gears of history. Just as species become extinct when they fail to adapt to their environment, nations also pass away when they do not respond to the demands of their age."[9]

In sum, the key to the success of his educational discourse lies in his formulations that can be broadly deduced from his philosophy of education. First, he shifted the discourse from "seeking Islamic education" to "education as the most noble Islamic value" and an essential condition for securing one's own Islamic faith. Thus, he establishes the connection between education and Islamic faith. In this relationship education, and its various facets such as science, becomes an instrument to perfect one's own faith (*iman*) and explore God's creation. Gülen repeatedly emphasizes that Knowledge is but the first step on the way towards a true love of God.[10] Second, Islam, according to him, is essentially a discourse, not a matter of identity. Thus, Muslims can maintain their faith even while operating in a hostile, secular milieu without restricting the form in which Islam has to be practiced. Third, by teaching a very comprehensive but flexible understanding of Islam that makes God, the Qur'an, the universe and humanity manifestations of the same, single Truth and by emphasizing Islamic values in terms of "good moral and ethical conduct," he opens the door for the Muslim community to secure faith in multiple ways. Based on these three formulations, Gülen's philosophy of education, which is mostly derived from his balanced, organic, holistic understanding of Islamic foundational texts, values, events, and history, provides an alternative to both the classical Islamic education system and the Western-modern education system.

Dimensions of Gülen's educational discourse

In Gülen's scheme of education, subject to the truth of Islamic faith as envisaged in orthodox, mainstream, Sunni Islam, one is free to pursue the infinite domain of knowledge. Unlike materialist philosophy, Islam recognizes four sources of knowledge: revelation, reason, experience, and intuition. Education, according to Gülen, is required to ensure a balance between all these sources of knowledge.[11] For Gülen, knowledge is knowledge, and its utility is measured by its approach to serving humanity. He is thus representing the legacy of such Islamic scholars as al-Farabi, al-Baqillani, Ibn Sina, al-Juwayni, al-Ghazali, Ibn Rushd, and others, who believed that knowledge was knowledge, and its provenance did not detract from its legitimacy. It was belief in the universal value of education whatever its sources that allowed for the borrowings from Greek science which drove the explosion of scientific achievement that characterized medieval Islam and later traveled in translated form to Europe, where it played an important role in bringing the Reformation, the Renaissance, and Industrialization in Western Europe.

By considering the study of the Qur'an or history or physics or mathematics or any other discipline as essentially an Islamic universal value, Gülen envisions a similar, forward-looking, integrated knowledge system that draws inspiration from the Islamic past and attempts to obliterate the false distinction between "Islamic education" and "secular education," which has come to stay in the modern era. Education in the hand of Gülen is primarily an Islam-led, universal, ethical and moral discourse to guide human actions in various fields of life. The primary objective of Gülen's educational discourse is to produce an action-oriented, ethical and moral being. General interaction with the volunteers working in the Gülen-inspired schools and other fields confirms this prescription of Islam, as summed up by Nihat Can "We do not teach religion in our school. We provide our service to all irrespective of religious and other identities with an intention to contribute in making him or her a good human being; albeit, we consider our actions to be Islamic ones."[12]

General features of Gülen's educational discourse

Within this structure of Gülen's educational discourse, there are broadly two inter-related dimensions of his educational thought: general and particular. In the general, he first identifies education as a universal democratic value that "empowers" people to achieve the goal of freedom and development. As he emphatically states, "If you wish to keep the masses under control, simply starve them of knowledge. The only escape route from tyranny is through the attainment of knowledge."[13]

Second, Gülen highlights the significance of education for the vitality and longevity of nations and warns that "when nations neglect the moral and intellectual education of their children, they abandon their society to decadence and chaos."[14] In this context, he calls upon the present generation to work for the next generation and consider education as "the greatest gift that we have to offer."

Third, he identifies an "educational deficit" worldwide and provides a critique both of the dominant Islamic education system and of the Western, modern, scientific education system. He finds Islamic schools (*madrasas*) and Sufi brotherhoods (*tariqa*) to be too obsessed with the legal and ritual dimension of Islam and other issues of Islamic identity while ignoring the inner spiritual and scientific dimension of Islam; hence, they were incapable of addressing the challenges of contemporary society. On the other hand, he sees in the Western-modern educational system the development of high professionalism but without the culture of spirituality. Further, he detects violence and destruction in the positivist, materialist philosophy of life: "if allowed to run unchecked it will lead to nihilism and the survival of humanity will be at stake." Thus, he remarked that

> due to humanity's growing arrogance and egoism, arising from its accomplishments, we have lived through worldwide colonialism, immense massacres, revolutions that cost millions of lives, unimaginably bloody and destructive wars, racial discrimination, immense social and economic injustice, and iron curtains built by regimes whose ideology and philosophy sought to deny humanity's essence, freedom, merit, and honor.[15]

In an interview, he declared that "my main objective is to create global education, which will become an alternative to the Western model of cultural imperialism."[16] Thus, in Gülen's view, both forms of education system—traditional Islamic and modern-Western—have failed to produce a "perfect moral being" that combines "mind and heart" or a balanced understanding of materialism and spirituality.

Fourth, he diagnoses the problem of education systems in the modern world in terms of lack of moral and ethical education and educators. He maintains a distinction between a teacher and an educator: "Education is different from teaching. Most people can teach, but only a very few can educate."[17] He encouraged students to go into the field of education in order to fill the gap of "educators" in Turkish educational institutions. Sezai Sakarya (born in 1933) narrated his encounter with Gülen on this issue: "When I sought his advice about the education of my child after finishing high school, Gülen suggested to send him to the education faculty but later, looking at my face, he advised for medicine."[18] A pro-hizmet academic from Sakarya University of Turkey also confirmed that Gülen encouraged and motivated students to pursue careers in the field of education by obtaining Bachelor's and Master's degrees in education.[19]

The difference between the two lies in that both teachers and educators impart information and teach skills, but the educator is one who has the ability to assist the students' personalities to emerge, who fosters thought and reflection, who builds character and enables the student to internalize qualities of self-discipline, tolerance, and a sense of mission. He describes those who simply teach in order to receive a salary, with no interest in the character formation of the students, as "the blind leading the blind."[20] In short, by "educator" he means teachers not only qualified in their subject but also embodying good, moral and ethical conduct, being humane and compassionate, and representing the values of humanism in general.

Fifth, education is required for the balanced growth of all aspects of human beings. Unlike the materialistic conception of the human being, Gülen's understanding of the human being is holistic:

> We are creatures composed of not only a body or mind or feelings or spirit; rather we are harmonious compositions of all of these elements… Each individual is all of these. When a man or a woman, around whom all systems and efforts revolve, is considered and evaluated as a creature with all these aspects, and when all our needs are fulfilled, we will reach true happiness. At this point, true human progress and evolvement in relation to our essential being is only possible with education.[21]

Highlighting how the Islamic conception of education nurtures the balanced personality of the human being, he says,

> The Messenger's method of education does not just purify our evil-commanding selves; rather, it is universal in nature and raises human hearts, spirits, minds, and souls to their ideal level. He respected and inspired reason; in fact, he led it to the highest rank under the intellect of Revelation… His universal call encompasses, in addition to the rules of good conduct and spirituality, all principles of economics, finance, administration, education, justice, and international law. He opened the doors of economic, social, administrative, military, political and scientific institutions to his students, whose minds and spirits he trained and developed to become perfect administrators, the best economists, the most successful politicians and unique military geniuses.[22]

Sixth, Gülen's educational discourse seeks to achieve the goal of the "perfect moral being" or what he calls "a movement from potential human to perfect human" based on the model of Prophet Muhammad by combining the scientific temperament with Islamic universal ethics of "love," "compassion," and "selfless service"—the dimensions that many, particularly Western scholars, have (mistakenly) identified with the Sufi form of Islam and thus attributed the success of the Gülen Movement to his practice and exposition of Sufism. The idea of the perfect human (*insan-i kamil*) as embodied in Prophet Muhammad requires a balance and harmony between the functions of mind, heart, spirit, and body, which in turn entails balance and moderation among the three faculties of the human being: reason, anger, and desire, each of which consist of two opposite extremes, each of which is harmful.[23]

In short, he envisions an educational system which synthesizes religious and scientific values that inspire each other, and which binds the two in harmony in order to serve humanity, the universe, God and Islam—all manifestations of a single Transcendental Truth—rather than mechanically closing the gap between the two by offering simultaneous teaching of religious and science subjects in an educational institution, a trend in Muslim society in the past that continues today. As Gülen has said,

> In a new style of education, fusing religious and scientific knowledge together with morality and spirituality will produce genuinely enlightened people whose hearts will be illuminated with religious sciences and spirituality. Their minds will be illuminated with positive sciences, characterized by humane merits and moral values, and cognizant of current socioeconomic and political conditions."

The scope of Gülen's educational project is thus to form individuals with strong, inner, Islamic ethics which can guide humanity toward the appropriate use of scientific laws, discoveries, and innovations. It was this lack of proper understanding of the relationship between religion and science in the West, Gülen believes, that led to the production of bombs and other lethal weapons.[24]

Turkey and Muslim societies in Gülen's discourse

Gülen's educational discourse first took firm root within Turkish society and gradually spread to other parts of the world. In particular, his educational discourse primarily aims to secure the "Islamic faith," particularly of the Muslim youth whom he saw as becoming enslaved to the culture of materialism and hedonism of the high modernism represented by Kemalism in Turkey. In Kemalist Turkey the government placed a ban on all forms of Islamic education institutions that remains in force to date. This created a serious institutional crisis not only in imparting Islamic education but also in secular education as large numbers of Muslim parents in Turkey, particularly in Anatolia, refused to enroll their sons and daughters in the Kemalist state school for fear that their children would be influenced by the secular philosophy of the school and might in the process become "un-Islamic." In other words, they found these schools lacking in Islamic moral values, and hence refused to send their children to them.

Gülen saw in Kemalist Turkey a nation internally torn between two worldviews: an aggressive, ideological, secular worldview and a defensive, insular, Islamic worldview, with each being distrustful of the other and therefore resulting in the "stunted growth" of Turkish society. This situation developed, according to Gülen, partly due to centuries of misunderstanding of the idea of progress by a dominant section of modern secularists, that is, scientific progress is possible only by dominating and eliminating religious values, and partly due to hurried attempts by the Kemalist state to "modernize Turkey" along European lines, which led to the state's strict control and regulation of religious life and Islam in particular; this in turn gave the impression that science and secularism are inimical to Islam. Although almost all Muslim countries saw the growing gulf between the ascendant secular minority and the descendant religious majority under the modernization program of Muslim states, the degree of intolerance and hostility on the part of the ruling secular minority against the religious majority was much higher in "Republican Turkey" because of their understanding of modernity as a "progressive, ideological project" and of Islam and religion as a "backward, reactionary ideology."

By the end of the 1970s Gülen could see the emerging "national crisis" that was acquiring violent shape and threatening the social fabric of Turkey, as well as the relative underdevelopment of the Muslim world as a consequence of a serious educational deficit that included "lack of ideals," "lack of Islamic ethics and morals," and "lack of educators." Sezai Sakarya recalling his days with Gülen in Edirne, states that "among other things we also used to talk about the condition of education in Turkey, but Gülen was more concerned about the small number of educators."[25] In this context, although Gülen broadly agrees with the Nursian prescription that there are three fundamental enemies to Muslim society—poverty, ignorance, and disunity—and education is a powerful means to overcome these enemies, he differs with him in terms of solution. First, education for Gülen is a "totalizing discourse," which is concerned with the moral and ethical regeneration of human societies, particularly Muslim societies, and of the individual, particularly the Muslim individual. It is not limited to addressing a set of problems in society. As Gülen states, "all problems start and end with people. The most effective for a well-functioning and (almost) defect-free social system, or for the grave and beyond, is education."[26] Second, unlike Nursi, Gülen did not seek to secure "the Islamic faith" or "the teaching of Islam" by withdrawing from the Kemalist state education system into private houses, notwithstanding the fact that the unity of theological, spiritual and scientific knowledge was taught in such private Nurcu houses. Rather, he sought the solution in the public sphere by reconfiguring the meaning of Islam in moral and ethical terms in accordance with the demands of the modern age and by representing Islam in the dominant public form of modernity.

Since education is the most dominant agency of modernity and the Kemalist republic rules by monopolizing the educational and other public spaces, Islam has to be expressed and represented through the modern education system and other non-political public agencies. Gülen recognized the fact that the secular form of educational institutions has become hegemonic and the most acceptable form to impart education in society. Any other institutional form, including the *madrasa*, lacks legitimacy to provide a "good quality education" in accordance with the demands of the modern world. He soon recognized the futility of confining educational ideals to Islamic circles, and this led him, unlike many contemporary Islamic scholars and movements, to advocate the necessity of elite secular schools rather than mosques and *madrasa*s inside and outside Turkey.

Gülen repeatedly affirms, "If there is no adaptation to new conditions, the result will be extinction."[27] In his understanding, the previous attempts to reinterpret the Islamic texts fail to understand the mood, temperament, and requirements of the modern age. In order to achieve the goal of education and serve Islam, Gülen shifted the discourse from "Islamic education" (as exemplified by the *madrasa* and *tariqa*, which focus on the theological dimension of Islam) to "education as Islamic value." He argues, "Just as education and teaching are the most sacred professions, the best service to a country or a nation is made through education. Our Prophet esteemed teaching more than another way of serving people."[28] Thus, by investing education with the "noblest Islamic value to pursue," he makes Islam relevant to this world as well as to the other world. Although Gülen partly owes this shift in his approach to education to Nursi, who advocated that studying and learning science was an Islamic act, it is Gülen who not only institutionalized this discourse in the public sphere but also revolutionized the Islamic conception of spaces within which Muslims can travel and represent Islam within the nation-specific legal structure without restrictions on the "Islamicness" of structure, institutions, and environment where Muslims are located.

Therefore, for Gülen, what matters is not the secular orientation and physical space of the educational institutional but the "cognitive map" of the teacher who interacts with and retains the power of transmitting knowledge and values to students. It is for this reason that he did not provide any critique of the state, secular educational institution but identified the lack of "educators" in these schools. Rather, he preferred to implant in the secular educational institution teachers with Islamic sensibilities, who can impart Islamic universal values through their ethical and moral conduct even in the hostile, secular atmosphere of the institution or even while teaching secular subjects. In this sense, a teacher of any discipline becomes a living representative of Islam, humanism, and universalism. In other words, the focus in Gülen's philosophy of education is on *tamsil* (example), not *tabligh* (preaching). Preaching alienates; it does not attract. Teachers should embody universal values, know their learners well, and appeal to their minds and their hearts. In short, Hizmet with its educational core is a *tabligh* in the form of *tamsil*. Islamic faith (*iman*) is thus secured by seeking "good education" (irrespective of the field) or setting "good example" or "good conduct" which was hitherto confined to the paradigm of "Islamic education" that was being imparted by *madrasas*, *makhtab*, *khankha*, *tariqa*, and *tekke* or any other structure that was/is considered "Islamic" in the Muslim public imagination.

In this sense, his advocacy for opening secular education institutions partly derives from his understanding of Islam as essentially a realm of discourse, not an identity to be preserved in a particular form, behavioral or institutional. Therefore, he is reported to have remarked that if hijab becomes an obstacle in seeking education, a girl should still seek alternative ways to continue her education. From this perspective Gülen reminds that the veil or the beard are not among the essential elements of faith (*usul*) or as primarily indispensable to the accomplishment of Muslim life. As he remarked, "I see the robe, turban, beard, and loose trousers as details (*furu'*).[29] Muslims should not be drowning in detail… Choosing not to wear them should not be construed as weakening the Muslim Turkish identity. No one should be categorized as a sinner because of such things."[30]

It was due to the dominance of the conception of "Islamic education" among religious Turkish (Anatolian) Muslims that initially Gülen encouraged Anatolian Muslim parents to send their children to Imam-Hatip schools. Additionally, the underlying reason for Gülen to exhort Muslim parents to send their children to Imam-Hatip was for them to get access to at least some education rather than no education at all. It was only later, when the sharp differences between "Islamic education" and "secular education" began to become diluted and the idea began to filter through that one would remain Muslim despite receiving secular education or studying in government secular education institutions, partly due to Gülen's discourse on Islam and education, that many Muslim Turkish parents began to send their children, mostly sons, to state secular educational institutions. However, it was only when the option for Hizmet-linked *dershanes*, hostels, coaching institutes, dormitories, schools, and other education institutions became legally available after 1980 that Anatolian Muslims began to enroll their children, including girls, in large numbers in secular education institutions as parents trusted Hizmet-linked institutions for "security of faith" and to provide a morally and ethically safe environment for their children.

Thus, with this diagnosis of Turkish society, he first embarked upon delivering a series of lectures mostly related to the principles and history of Islam, the life of Prophet Muhammad, Islamic ethics and conduct, and the relationship between religion and science in his capacity as imam in order to restore recognition and respect to Islam, motivate and sensitize Muslims about the value of education, and to dispel the perception that Islam is opposed to science, progress, and development in the public sphere. Towards this aim he employed the Nursian framework of making Islam, God, humanity, and the universe as coterminous, inseparable, and interchangeable in having the same meaning, value, and goal. The human being as vicegerent on the earth is expected to improve things on the earth in order to serve humanity. To serve humanity means serving God. Education and knowledge is required to serve humanity in the most effective manner, which in turn amounts to serving God. As vicegerent on Earth, human beings are required to improve their educational capacity so as to understand and discover the signs of God. In particular, Gülen directed his energy through speeches and writings to dispelling the misconception in the public domain that Islam and science are contradictory. To do this, he even launched a magazine called *Sızıntı*, which became very popular within a short time of its publication. Following Nursi he described science as *one* among many methods of explaining or discovering the secrets and signs of God. He blamed the science-religion controversy on a section of European scientists who had elevated science to the status of ultimate "Truth": "the danger does not lie with science and the new world but with ignorant, irresponsible scientists, and others who exploit it for their own selfish interest."[31]

Gülen acknowledges the contribution of science in human life but believes that scientific truth must be subjected to divine belief as the former is of transient value and keeps changing with every new experiment, while the latter is ultimate, permanent, and transcendental in nature. For this reason, scientific applications and investigations must be subjected to moral and ethical consideration. In Gülen's words, "the real problem consists in the fact that we have been unable to assign a true direction to science and thus confused revealed knowledge with scientific theories and sometimes scientific knowledge with philosophy... One result is that the younger generation became alienated from their society. After a while these inexperienced generations lost their religious and moral values, and the whole nation began to decline in thought, ideals, art, and life ... and evil aspects of modern civilization were propagated."[32] However, unlike Nursi and other Islamic modernists, he did not confine his teachings to the theoretical exercise of the compatibility or even complementarity of Islam and science, but expressed the conviction that Muslims must take the initiative to personify the unity of Islam and science by becoming science teachers and scientists. So Gülen actively encouraged Muslim students and young people to pursue science education in particular, in order to dispel the perception in the conservative section of the Muslim community that science education promotes atheism. In addition, his initial emphasis on science education was also meant to reconnect Muslims with the scientific legacy of Islam, to make them aware of the central role that science is playing in making the world better, and to sensitize them to the necessity to learn from the scientific and technological resources of the West in order to develop Muslim societies.

His sermons on Islam and advocacy for education along with the religious connotation of *hizmet* (service) attracted the critical public mind and those who were increasingly alienated from the Kemalist order because of the latter's perceived failure to manage the economic, social, and sectarian crises of Turkish society in the 1970s. He then successfully persuaded a section of Anatolian businessmen to invest in establishing preparatory coaching classes with hostels, dormitories, and light houses to enable the students, mostly from the Anatolian region, to enroll in secondary and higher education institutions of Turkey. It was with *dershane*s (the preparatory coaching institutes) that Hizmet secured a footing in Turkey. Next, he successfully appealed to his followers to open secular, modern, private schools to promote quality education, to dispel the wide perception that Islam is inimical to modern education, and to enable the present generation of Turkish society to grapple with the challenges of the future.

The Turkish education system and the role of Hizmet

Hizmet's success with *dershane*s and the establishment of chains of schools, and later a few private universities in Turkey was and is also linked with the nature of the education system and the emerging political economy of contemporary Turkey. A brief analysis, therefore, of the nature of the education system and the emerging political economy since the mid-1980s is required in order to place the success of the Hizmet Movement in education in the larger setting of "modern" republican Turkey.

Turkey has a strong tradition of a centralized education system, which goes back to the Ottoman era and continues to date despite a decade of democratization under the political dispensation of the AKP, the ruling party in Turkey since 2002. From curriculum to examination to appointment of teachers in all kinds of education institutions ranging from school to technical institution to university, all is regulated, supervised, financed, and conducted by specific state agencies. Private educational institutions, mostly belonging to ethnic minorities or foreign missionaries, always existed, but their share in the educational production was negligible. However, these private schools were and are considered elite schools. The degree of centralization of education was increased during the Republican period as education, particularly school education, along with the military, police, and judiciary, was conceived as an integral part of an ideological project to transform Turkey into the European image, at least in the cultural frame, if not in the frame of political democracy. Thus, the Ministry of Education issued a circular on December 19, 1923 declaring, "*Schools are obliged to indoctrinate loyalty to Republican principles.*"[33]

Since the foundation of the Republic in 1923 the state initially provided free compulsory education for five years (till 5th grade), which was extended to eight years (till 8th grade) in 1997 and further extended to 12 years under the new "4+4+4" scheme since 2012. The education system is divided into elementary, middle and secondary high schooling; secondary schools comprise vocational, technical, and high schools. Imam-Hatip or religious schools come under technical/vocational education. Public high schools are further divided into three segments: super secondary/science school, Anatolian secondary school, and regular secondary school (Imam-Hatip). The first two are a recent addition with English, French, or German as the medium of instruction or imparting instruction in a certain group of subjects (preferably science) in a foreign language and are considered to provide better education in comparison to regular secondary schools, where the medium of instruction is Turkish, and English or German or French is taught as a foreign language. Higher education consists of a four-year undergraduate program, two-year Master's program, and four-year doctorate program. The military and police have their own separate education institutions wholly funded by the state.

There are two major entrance examinations that are conducted for the upward mobility of students: the entrance examination at the end of eighth grade to enter secondary high school and at the end of secondary high schooling (twelfth grade) to enter university. The educational system worked well until 1960 because of the low participation of Turkish population, which was mostly confined to the minority, secularized segments of Turkish population, including the Alevi religious minority, as a large majority of Sunni Turkish and Kurdish Muslims had shunned the government schools for fear of their corrupting influence on their Muslim faith and also could not enroll elsewhere in the absence of alternative private schools managed by Turkish and Kurdish Sunni Muslims. The education system therefore managed to cater for the small in-flow of students. Until the 1960s, entrance examinations were conducted in a decentralized way by each high school and by institutions of higher education, including the technical education institutions.

However, the increase in population and the demographic shift from rural to urban and the rapid industrialization process starting in the 1950s, as noted in the preceding chapter, created educational demands, which were beyond the capacity of existing educational institutions to accommodate. It is in this context that Gülen's sermons on education as Islamic value and its relevance in the modern world resonated with the larger Muslim public and motivated people to enroll their children and invest in secular education institutions. Combined, this resulted in a phenomenal growth in the demand for education in Turkish society. Thus, the number of students enrolled in secondary-level education, grew from 34,000 in 1950 to 55,000 in 1960, to 152,000 in 1970, to 321,000 in 1980 and to 387,000 in 1990.[34] The increase in the number of secondary schools also led to an increase in the number of students seeking admission to higher education, including university, which led to an increasing gap between demand and supply in higher educational institutions. Thus, in 1960, 19,197 of 23,535 students who graduated from high school were able to register in a higher education institution, but as the years passed the situation became worse. In 1973, only 41,789 of 89,359 high-school graduates were able to obtain the right to enroll in higher education institutions.[35]

In order to deal with the "mess" in the education system, in the mid-1960s the government created an administrative agency called the Student Selection and Placement System (ÖSYS), now affiliated with the Higher Education Council (YÖK), to conduct centralized entrance examinations at both elementary school and high school for entry to high school and university respectively. This examination requires a minimum mark for a student to be eligible to be admitted to a high school or particular departments of a university depending upon the quota in each educational institution, failing which the student's educational career comes to an end. Students are admitted to different educational institutions in accordance with their marks and the corresponding preference in the ranking order as drawn up by ÖSYS. In order to ensure the admission of their children to branded private schools or government high schools and to university, parents started paying for intensive private tutoring at home or putting their children in specialized coaching/preparatory institutes (*dershane*).

It was at this stage that Gülen started motivating Muslim entrepreneurs from Anatolia to establish *dershane*s and dormitories to coach the children of Muslim parents to compete in the national entrance examination at both high school and university level. Like other coaching centers, the Movement accepted students based on their admission test scores from private and public schools, including Imam-Hatips and even provided financial help to those students who could not afford to pay *dershane* fees, trained them, and succeeded through a combination of hard work, dedication, and the ideal of creating a new generation for the benefit of the Turkish nation, Muslims, and Islam. Soon the Hizmet *dershane*s became branded educational institutions because of their ability to ensure the admission of a good number of students into the top-ranking private secondary schools, government schools, and public universities. The total number of these private coaching institutions was 2,984 in 2005, which increased to 3,650 in 2006.[36] At the time of writing, the Movement was considered to run 25% of all *dershane*s within Turkey.

The shift towards a neo-liberal economy in the early 1980s under the Turgut Özal government resulted in the reduction of government spending on education and left a greater role to market forces in the field of education. Gülen, utilizing the newly gained recognition from *dershane*s, appealed to the emerging Anatolian Muslim Tigers and other local, Muslim, medium-scale businessmen to invest their money, as a part of *zakat*, *sadaqa*, or voluntary donations in kind or cash, in establishing quality schools and other education institutions. As the expanding, urban Muslim middle class and Muslim industrial class were wary of the poor performance of state education institutions and of their indifference, if not antagonism, to religion, they supported Gülen's endeavor to establish "secular schools" which would provide a safe moral and ethical environment in addition to quality education.

Thus, a combination of factors including faith and nation-wide demand for "quality education" led to the establishment of a chain of "Gülen-inspired schools" throughout the nation from the mid-1990s. Berdal Aral, a non-Hizmet academic with Fatih University, attributed the success of Gülen-inspired schools among a section of Turkish Muslims for providing "quality education with conservative morality."[37] Gradually Gülen-inspired schools came to be recognized as "branded schools" because of their success in national competitions and entrance examinations, and they attracted the children from all shades of people, including from the communist and Kemalist circles.

In order to popularize the schools, every year from 2003 to 2013, the Movement organized the "Turkish Olympiad" in different cities of Turkey—a mega event in which participants from Gülen-inspired schools from all over world competed in different activities in the Turkish language, the dominant medium through which Turkish nationalism expresses itself. Thus, the Turkish Olympiad served two purposes for the Movement: it demonstrates the high professionalism of the Movement and it conveys the message that the Gülen Movement is serving a national cause by promoting the Turkish language abroad. Both helped to increase acceptance of the Movement within Turkish society and to dilute secular and Kemalist opposition to the Movement.[38]

The privatization of education grew rapidly after 1980 in Turkey. From 164 primary schools and 76 secondary schools in 1965, it grew to 642 and 487 in 2001 to 728 and 650 in 2005 respectively. The number of students increased from 25,727 primary school students and 12,867 secondary school students in 1965 to 171,623 and 73,136 in 2001 to 180,090 and 76,670 in 2005 respectively.[39] It is not clear what percentage share the Gülen schools has in the total numbers of private schools in Turkey; however, until recently, the Movement was considered the dominant player in the private schools market in both primary and secondary schools. Nonetheless, private schools cater for a very low percentage of student enrolments in comparison with state schools. Thus, in 2012, private schools could cater for only 3 percent of all elementary school students and 3.1 percent of all secondary education students.[40] Informally, Movement participants express the belief that the Gülen-inspired schools constitute 5–7% of the school education system and 25–30% of private schools in Turkey.[41]

Similarly, in the field of higher education the number of private foundation universities has grown steadily since 1986: 3 in 1995, 17 in 1997, 23 in 2003, and 28 in 2006,[42] and reaching 72 in 2014. Today Turkey has a total of 190 higher education institutions, including 104 public universities, 72 private foundation universities, 8 private foundation higher education institutes other than universities, and 6 public higher education institutes other than universities.[43] Although there is no precise figure for the involvement of the Gülen Movement in the field of higher education, the Movement launched a number of universities, and it is estimated that the Movement ran approximately 17 universities inside Turkey with a more or less equal number outside Turkey. With the expansion of higher education institutions including private foundation universities and the increase in quotas for university, a substantially greater number of students is admitted to the university system every year than in the 1970s and 1980s, when less than half of the total number of high-school students managed to reach university. Today approximately 900,000 high-schools students are admitted to higher education every year.[44] However, despite significant increase in higher education institutions, a gap between demand and supply in Turkish higher education continues to exist.

The fallacy of the neo-liberal argument

There is a general tendency in academia to understand the success of the Gülen Movement in the field of education merely in terms of the logic of the emerging market economy in Turkey. Certainly, the increase in demand for education, particularly quality education, combined with the inefficiency of the public education system, the emergence of a Muslim-entrepreneur class, and the expansion of the middle class, tax benefits and so on, has pushed the pace of privatization of education in the country. However, to reduce the educational initiatives of the Gülen Movement to market forces or the role of private capital would amount to crude reductionism and a gross simplification of the Gülen Movement. It is true that almost all Gülen-inspired education institutions, including *dershanes*, schools, and universities within and outside Turkey charge relatively high fees and thus mostly children of families of good means have access to them. Although these institutions do provide scholarships for brighter students and other kinds of support to those coming from poorer backgrounds, overall participation of poor children in these institutions is rather low. Yet, although they operate on market principles, profit making is not the sole motive of these enterprises; rather, the surplus generated through the high fees is invested in other Hizmet-related works. The underlying economic model of Hizmet education institutions is the "trickle-down effect," in which attempts are made to influence elites and mobilize resources through them for a wider transformation of society. This inspiration comes from the Prophetic model, in which most of the Prophet Muhammad's initial Companions were "elite" in their respective fields. Looking from an Islamic perspective, the Gülen-inspired schools and other education institutions serve the same purpose: forging links with the elite of the society where the institution is located. As Bekim Agai says, "Gülen believed that a bureaucrat or businessman could do more to change society than could a preacher because the purely religious part of the society was so marginalized that people with solely religious knowledge were not in a position to influence the society."[45] Despite this market propensity what underlies the success of the Gülen Movement in the field of education is the shift in discourse from Islamic education to education as Islamic value and its gradual transformation into a service value or ethics that motivated thousands of Muslim teacher volunteers to work in Gülen-inspired schools for long hours at relatively low wages.

In the process, the Movement produced two significant and *unintended* consequences. The first broadly relates to the Turkish setting. It demonstrated that a religious student is capable of mastering secular knowledge and can achieve a high degree of professionalism in what are considered secular or worldly matters. In this the Movement broke the barrier between religious or Islamic studies and secular studies that had arisen in the modern world. This the Movement demonstrated by turning out large numbers of students from devout Anatolian families and directing them into the university system through rigorous coaching. This enabled them to secure positions in the state employment opportunity structure, which had hitherto been the monopoly of secularized segments of Turkey. Mehmet, a businessman trading in gold and diamonds in Izmir, underlines this contribution of the Hizmet Movement: "Because of [Gülen] most students from a theology background (Imam-Hatip) successfully moved to different science subjects and became engineers, doctors, architects, etc."[46] The transformative impact of educational initiative of Gülen among some Imam-Hatip students is also evident from a statement of a volunteer in Joshua Hendrick's work on Gülen Movement: ''We were Imam–Hatip students and natural outcome of such an education was to become an imam. We didn't dream of going to university. We didn't predict that we would have such an opportunity."[47] The association with the public employment structure provided to many hitherto excluded Turkish Muslims a new sense of identity, social recognition, respect and dignity, enhanced family status, and a new sense of identification with the nation. In part, the participants in Gülen's educational discourse and enterprise also visualized themselves as playing an important role in the "Muslim" transformation of Turkey through education.

As the Hizmet educational movement has long-term implications for transforming the power structure from below, the stake holders in "secular Republic of Turkey" tried to arrest this trend through the "post-modern" military coup in 1997, by blocking the access of Imam-Hatip school students to the university system by first reducing the quota for technical high school students (under which the Imam-Hatip School falls) and then introducing a "weighting system" in 1999 under which extra marks will be added to the marks obtained at the university entrance exam by the students of high schools (excluding technical high schools) so as to fill the quotas in various university departments. As a result, the enrolment in Imam-Hatip schools slumped after 1997.[48] The AKP government did not manage to overcome this inherent discrimination in the "secularized" Turkish educational system until 2012 when it introduced the "4+4+4" system.[49]

The second unintended consequence was that the Gülen Movement transformed the conception of education into an everyday Islamic value and service ethic of Turkish society. This created a "resource base" within Turkish society to support the educational activities of the Movement within and outside Turkey. As the sector of "Muslim Turkey" strongly came to identify with education as the most "noble Islamic cause" and one of the best ways to serve Islam, they generously funded and supported, even beyond their economic capacity, the Movement's initiatives in opening schools and other educational institutions abroad. Moreover, the larger number of teachers associated with the Movement was already religiously motivated to serve abroad, even in the most difficult situations, as they identified themselves with the role of the Sahaba (Companions of the Prophet) and thus undertook *hijrah* to perform the most fundamental duty of Islam: *dawa* through education. In addition, the Turkish volunteers in the Movement also found gainful employment. The emerging model of "*business-teacher-jihad-hijrah-dawa*," derived from the Prophetic model, transformed the Turkish Gülen Movement into a worldwide Islamic movement within a short span of time. It is through this process that education in the Gülen Movement has emerged as the prime instrument to serve the Turkish nation, Muslims, Islam, and people in the world. Enes Ergene, one of the prominent intellectuals associated with the Gülen Movement, stresses the unity of trade and Sufi Islam, which prevailed in the Selçuk and Ottoman periods, as the reason for the success of the Gülen Movement.[50]

Setting an example and the Golden Generation

Beneath the establishment of Gülen-inspired schools and university lies an Islamic imagination: to establish an "example" through deed and actions following in the footsteps of Prophet Muhammad and to create a "golden generation." As one academic from Atatürk university, Erzurum, puts it, "one should not compare this Movement with *namaz*, *hajj*, religion. This movement is about the creation of a golden generation on the principles of the original *tasawwuf* (Sufi Islam), original Islam (scholasticism), and science."[51] Thus, Gülen's educational discourse is intrinsically connected with the idea of a golden generation—a generation capable of becoming "inheritors of the Earth," who will combine the virtues of faith, love, science, mathematical thinking, freedom of thought, self-criticism, consciousness of responsibility, and a culture of the legal way of doing things.[52] Ali Ünal has described a member of the golden generation as "one who knows his age very well in which he lives."[53] The golden generation is expected to raise and prepare a better future for the next generation on the basis of Islam's universal values. This explains why, unlike commercial educational enterprises, all Gülen-inspired *dershanes*, schools, and universities have dormitories and light houses where students are socialized in the moral and ethical values that constitute the fundamentals of Islam, Sufi training in asceticism and living with God-consciousness, ethics of hard work and responsibility, and stress on acquiring knowledge, self-discipline, altruism, and so on through *sohbets* and the reading of the works of Said Nursi and Gülen.

Whether the idea of a "golden generation" is achievable or not, what is important here is to recognize that the formation of the golden generation in Gülen's thought process is part of a formal and informal process emerging from below through a rigorous system of education. In this way, Gülen fundamentally differs from many Islamic scholars and reformers, including Nursi, who have sought to "reform" Muslim society from above by conceiving of the "educational crisis" only in terms of a "crisis of higher education" and without attempting to reform Muslim society from within. Moreover, Gülen identifies education as the most effective source of socialization that has to be continuously carried out from childhood in order to inculcate strong moral and ethical values that will in turn provide the required social resources to bring overall reform in society. It is for this reason that he laid great emphasis on the opening of secular, modern schools within the framework of national law for the first two decades—the products of which today were/are serving in many institutions of higher learning including universities and other public fields within and outside Turkey. It would be a futile exercise to have an institution of higher learning or a university with a humanistic vision without a resource base of educators. This partly explains why previous attempts to establish universities or higher education institutions in Muslim societies failed in their desired goal of arresting the decline of Muslim society. It is indeed tragic and reflects the myopic vision of the Erdoğan regime that it has decided to close down all Gülen-inspired education institutions and arrested a large number of volunteers and sympathizers working in these institutions on the charge of being linked to "FETO" (Fethullahist Terrorist Organization), a dysphemism that the government uses for the Gülen Movement without any iota of evidence. Latterly, the government has discredited the success and high participation of students of these educational institutions in public service by linking their success with cheating in the examination system to benefit Hizmet-linked students. It is sheer absurdity, illogical and totally nonsensical to buy the argument of the Erdoğan government that the Gülen Movement through its educational institutions clandestinely generated the "elite human resources" over four decades with an objective to illegally topple the government through civilian (or judicial) or military coup as happened in Turkey on December 17, 2013 (corruption exposure) and the failed military coup of July 15, 2016.

CHAPTER 9

GÜLEN MOVEMENT IN ACTION: DIALOGUE AND INTERFAITH DIALOGUE

As outlined in the preceding chapter, the purpose of Gülen's educational discourse is to produce a "golden generation" or enable the goal of becoming *insan-i kamil* (the perfect human being modeled on Prophet Muhammad). However, this desired objective cannot be achieved without adopting dialogue as an article of faith. Thus, dialogue in Gülen's Islamic discourse is an integral part of moral, educational discourse and training which promotes love, peace, cooperation, and mutual understanding, recognizes diversity and pluralism as a natural or divine fact, and aims at peaceful resolution of conflict, where it exists. Enes Ergene confirms the link between dialogue and education: "The 'dialogue meetings' are an extension of Gülen's global educational activities; they also serve the education of humanity."[1] Thus, education and dialogue in Gülen's philosophy complement each other, and this partly explains the simultaneous origin of both discourses in Gülen's thinking during the 1970s and 1980s within the Turkish setting, as noted in Chapter 3. Thus, the Gülen-inspired dialogue centers also proliferated along with the spread of Gülen-inspired schools in the world, and their number is estimated to be around 150 or more on the basis of the existence of these schools in 150 countries.[2] Gradually, dialogue and education emerged as the two most important identities of the Gülen Movement.

Gülen's discourse of dialogue, particularly interfaith dialogue, has emerged in three inter-related contexts. Domestically, the Turkish milieu of the 1970s, characterized by intense political and ideological conflicts and violence, drove the idea in him of dialogue as an instrument to promote tolerance and understanding among Turkish peoples. In other words, the idea of dialogue begins with the recognition of the plurality of voices and lifestyles among Turkish people and within the predominantly Muslim community of the Turkish nation. Amidst chaos, conflicts, and violence in Turkey during the late 1970s, Gülen called for "national dialogue."

Internationally, it was the process of globalization that brought cultures, religions, and civilizations face to face and thus necessitated the need for interfaith and inter-cultural dialogue. As it becomes more globalized, inter-religious and inter-cultural encounter is increasingly becoming a part of the very fabric of modern life, the world faces a more daunting task in addressing the issue of pluralism and diversity. This has necessitated the inter-personal, inter-religious and inter-cultural understanding of each other in order to achieve the goal of living together. Thus, recent years have witnessed the emergence of a plethora of scholarship on interfaith and inter-cultural dialogue as a theoretical framework to deal with the multiple crises of modernity: cultural, religious, ethnic, and national conflicts. The recognition of the increasingly globalized world and the challenges of living together led Gülen to articulate both theory and praxis of interfaith dialogue from Islamic perspectives.

The third, and perhaps the most important context in which Gülen's discourse of dialogue emerged, was the issue of *representation of Islam* in modern times, about which he feels deep concern. As he reportedly remarked, "the task of "representing faith with its true values has gained an even greater importance than before."[3]

Muslim initiatives for dialogue and pluralism

What is the nature of Gülen's dialogue discourse? How does it differ from other conceptions of dialogue, including the dominant paradigm of interfaith dialogue? In what ways does Gülen's discourse of dialogue make a contribution to the existing paradigm of dialogue, particularly interfaith dialogue? In order to examine these questions a brief review of the existing model of interfaith dialogue will be required.

Recent years have witnessed a plethora of Islamic production on the issues of interfaith dialogue, individual freedom and conscience, tolerance, religious pluralism, and democracy. Some of the prominent representatives of this trend in the Muslim world are Muhammad Talibi (b. 1921), C. M. Naim, Asghar Ali Engineer (1940–2013), Maulana Wahiduddin Khan (b. 1925), Syed Zainal Abedin (1928–93), Farid Esack (b. 1958), Abdulaziz Sachedina, and Tariq Ramadan (b. 1962). It is therefore imperative to examine this emerging trend within the Muslim world in order to understand in what ways Gülen's discourse on these subject matters, which precedes much of the production by these scholars' and might have influenced their writings, converges with and differs from these Islamic scholars and thinkers.

Like Gülen, these scholars provide an ethical and moral re-reading of Islamic sources, texts, and history and broadly reflect on the "modern" discourses of freedom, individual conscience, tolerance, and democracy from Islamic ethical and moral perspectives. However, most of these Islamic scholarly writings have emerged out of a context of "minority Muslims" living in non-Muslim majority regions and countries such as Europe, the United States, India, and South Africa. These scholars and others are primarily addressing the issue of the integration of a Muslim minority in the democratic-secular setup of non-Muslim majority countries, particularly the Western nations. Many of them construct a powerful Islamic theological narrative on the basis of the Prophet's life in Mecca or what are known as the "Meccan verses" of the Qur'an, which mostly relate to patience, peace, tolerance, dialogue and non-violence, the Prophet's agreement with non-Muslims in Medina (what is called the "Medina Constitution");[4] they highlight the Qur'an's fair, equal, and just treatment of "non-Muslim others," particularly the "People of the Book" and women, and they demonstrate the just and fair system of rule of early Islam as represented by the Four Rightly Guided Caliphs, the relatively fair treatment of non-Muslims throughout the history of Muslim rule (particularly the *millet* system of Ottoman Empire), and the contribution of Islamic civilization to the European Renaissance in order to demonstrate the compatibility of Islam and liberal-democratic-secular orders, particularly of European varieties. In particular, these Islamic scholars provide powerful Islamic justification for the notions of "diversity," "pluralism," particularly religious pluralism, and "tolerance" with an implication for interfaith dialogue as a part of the wider objective of the integration of the Muslim minority in non-Muslim majority nations. Like Gülen, all these Islamic scholars assert that pluralism and diversity are divinely intended and respect for each other's religion and faith is an essential part of God's commandment. Tariq Ramadan goes farthest in this respect, to the extent of arguing for Islamic recognition of the plurality of Truth. As he remarks, "The intimate awareness of *tawhid* forms the perception of the believer, who understands that plurality has been chosen by the One, that He is the God of all beings, and that He requires that each be respected: "And say, 'We believe in what has been revealed to us and what has been revealed to you; our God and your God is the One.'"[5]

However, notwithstanding the good intention of these Islamic scholars in terms of providing Islamic justification for the Muslim minority community to integrate in the non-Muslim majority nation, the fact that these scholars primarily emerge from a "minority locale" and situate their discourses in a minority-majority relationship, which is often politically constructed, makes them suffer from the limitations of political pragmatism and apologetism and does not help much in advancing the agenda of intercultural and interfaith dialogue, which is otherwise crucial for the meaningful integration of a Muslim-minority community. Moreover, the "totalizing" and "apologetic" character of these writings has the unintended consequence of further sharpening the Islamic identity of Muslim communities at the cost of their diverse identity, which obstructs the "free movement" of dialogue and communication between the minority and majority in two significant ways. Firstly, given the asymmetry of the power structure at all levels between the minority and majority, and being overtly conscious of their own identity due to their minority status, minorities tend to become more insular or protective while interacting with the "imagined" collective majority personified in the dialogue partner (whether as an individual or institution) during the course of "structured negotiating or dialogic space." This in turn prevents the "Muslim self-representative" from learning about others or at least being open to the other's point of view. Secondly, it prepares the socio-psychological ground for the "politicization of religious identity" depending upon the context. Once this happens it further increases the "social gap" between the Muslim minority and non-Muslim majority, leading to the breakdown of negotiating space between the two. This is because most of these scholars start from the assumption that Islam is the final, superior, and most excellent religion of mankind and try to prove this while engaging with other religious traditions.

In the process, these liberal advocates of the Islamic conception of religious pluralism and tolerance failed to sharply differentiate themselves from a radical version of Islam under which the notion of *dawa* acquires an ideological overtone and emerges as the most important Islamic duty for Muslims living in a minority context with the eventual vision of transforming the non-Muslim majority into Muslims through the work of *dawa*, leading to the establishment of an Islamic state and society. This approach treats the minority status of Muslims as a "de facto situational reality," "a temporary phenomenon," and then proceeds to engage with the concepts of "pluralism," "multiculturalism," and "diversity" with an eventual conclusion: either to accept these concepts as "pragmatic necessity" or to reject them on the basis that they contradict the "Islamic" prescription of a good life. It is for this reason that various structured Muslim-Christian interfaith dialogues have failed to yield any positive results in terms of mutual understanding and trust. On the contrary, the gulf between the two is increasing, as reflected in the growing phenomenon of Islamophobia in much of the West and growing incidents of terrorism by a section of Muslim youth. A British Muslim Scholar, Shabbir Akhtar, while commenting on interfaith dialogue in 1991 noted, "the theme of inter-faith dialogue ... is likely to occupy the centre-stage of the theological concerns in this and the coming century' ... (however) most Muslim writers are yet to come to terms with the truthful claims of other faiths or with the ways in which these religions see themselves."[6] In this context Jacques Waardenburg has rightly observed:

> Most Muslim writings about other religions than Islam since World War II concern Christianity. A great number of them are refutations of it in one form or another, written from Muslim readers in the "Islamic" languages Arabic, Turkish, Persian and Urdu. As in earlier periods, the arguments are based on Quranic texts and common sense, and they are addressed specifically against such Christian doctrines as the sonship of Jesus, the Incarnation, the Trinity, and the Bible as Revelation. More recently, with the

presence of Muslim *dawa* centres in the West and elsewhere, Muslim publications critical of Christianity are now also printed and sold in the West. Besides such straightforward polemical literature, one also finds a more informative kind of literature that tries to compare Christianity with Islam, evidently concluding that Islam is superior.[7]

Interfaith dialogue in Gülen's thought

Unlike the several Muslim initiatives in the field of interfaith dialogue outlined above, Fethullah Gülen's discourse of pluralism, tolerance, and interfaith dialogue does not suffer from the limitation of political pragmatism, nor is it confined to the framework of minority-majority relationship. On the contrary, Gülen's discourse of interfaith dialogue is rooted in its Turkish Muslim majoritarian context[8] and thus relatively, if not completely, free of any political pragmatism; rather it flows from his ethical and moral re-reading of the universal message of Islam and is thoroughly grounded in a human-rights perspective.

Gülen first welcomes the role of the Church and Western nations in facilitating interfaith dialogue and identifies the structural constraints that prevented Muslims from being part of such an exercise for so long—factors which include Western domination over Muslim lands, the anti-Islamic polemics of the West, the emergence of political Islam, and suspicion from the Muslim community that the interfaith initiatives of the Church and Western nations are a ploy for conversion. He then encourages the Muslim community to be at the forefront of dialogue with a clear-cut commandment of Islam and its understanding of faith. As he emphatically states, "*the basic Islamic sources advise Muslims to engage in dialogue with other faiths.*"

Fethullah Gülen's philosophy of interfaith dialogue is set out in his seminal works—*Advocate of Dialogue* (Chapters 6 and 7), *Key Concepts in the Practice of Sufism* (Vols. 1, 2 and 3), *Towards a Global Civilization of Love and Tolerance*, and *The Necessity of Interfaith Dialogue: A Muslim Perspective*. Dialogue means, according to Gülen, "the coming together of two or more people to discuss certain issues, and thus the forming of a bond between these people. In that respect, we can call dialogue an activity that has human beings at its axis."[9] Thus, dialogue as human activity flows from the recognition of the humanness of a person without taking into consideration their sentiments and opinions. Gülen points out that Prophet Muhammad paid respect to the funeral procession of a Jew on the grounds that he was first human and hence deserved our respect.[10] My own interviews with several Turkish Muslims connected with the Hizmet Movement confirm they have this belief in establishing dialogue with anybody on the basis of their humanity. As Ahmet Said Pınar states, "to reach everyone without considering their identities."[11] Another senior volunteer quipped, "In Hizmet we can dialogue with everybody including atheists,"[12] and "Dialogue in Hizmet is a means to embrace all humanity," asserted a Turkish businessperson.[13]

Dialogue as "human-centric discourse," to use Frances Sleap and Ömer Şener's expression,[14] is embedded in Gülen's Islamic understanding of human beings as vicegerents of God on earth. As Gülen writes, "Human beings are at the center of creation; all other things, living or non-living, compose concentric circles around them. It could be said that the Exalted Creator has oriented every creature toward human beings."[15] This understanding of human beings creates moral equality of all human beings, which falls in the Saidian third possibility of the recognition of the moral equality of cultures that could learn from one another as equals.[16] Thus, by reserving the "Self" to God only and "Other" to all human beings, Gülen resolves the perpetual conflict between self and other that exists in positivist philosophy by upholding the moral equality of human beings. As vicegerent, humans are expected to reflect God's qualities and virtues such as peace, justice, compassion, love, merciful, cooperation, and respectfulness in order to live in harmony with each other. Gülen draws the attention of human beings in general and Muslims in particular to the repeated expression in the Qur'an of the phrase "the Most Merciful and the Most Compassionate" and interprets its meaning as calling for Muslims and other human beings to develop the values of cooperation, forgiveness, compassion, and love towards each other.

Further, Gülen highlights the necessity of cultivating these values in order to co-habit peacefully and develop common understanding as God has purposefully created "diverse creations with a unity of *din*." In the broadest sense, the balance in His "diverse creations" depends upon the cultivation of these values His creations—both living and non-living—are endowed with different capabilities. Western modernity—particularly its legacy of positivism and excessive materialism—has jolted the divine balance between Man and Nature and also bifurcated the unity of knowledge between religious science and secular science, which has resulted in continuing endemic conflict and violence between cultures, civilizations, and religions. Gülen's call for dialogue and interfaith dialogue is partly addressed to restoring the "divine balance" between Man and Nature and securing the unity of knowledge system. As he remarks, "Religion reconciles opposites: religion–science, this world–the next world, Nature–Divine Books, material–spiritual, and spirit–body."[17]

It may be cautioned here that Gülen's interfaith dialogue has not been conceived from the point of view of erecting "religious unity" of the faithful against "Godless modernity" and its associated materialism, positivism, and atheism. In this regard, his conception of interfaith dialogue fundamentally differs from Said Nursi's. In the Nursian framework, interfaith dialogue was essentially conceived as an instrument to secure the unity of Muslims and Christians against atheism and secularism, and one which will unleash the process leading to the transformation of Christianity into Islam. In contrast, Gülen is very much against the instrumentalization of faith or any other discourse, identity, or value for any objectives, whether political or non-political. Rather, for him the goal of interfaith dialogue is to retrieve "the fundamental essence and unity of (all) religions," echoing Gandhi's understanding of religion: "By religion, I do not mean formal religion, or customary religion, but that religion which underlies all religion, which brings us face to face with our maker."[18] Like Gandhi, Gülen identified common religious values with such moral and ethical values as love, tolerance, respect, trust, peace, freedom, human rights, mercy, cooperation, honesty, brotherhood, and so on. As Gülen states, "the goal of dialogue among world religions is not simply to destroy scientific materialism and the materialistic worldview that have caused such harm; rather, the very nature of religion demands this dialogue."[19] This dialogue is essential as religion as the moral and ethical repository of human civilizations "can erect a defense against the destruction caused by scientific materialism, put science in its proper place, and end long-standing conflicts among nations and peoples."[20] Moreover, unlike Nursi, Gülen does not seek the supremacy of one religion over another or the elimination of any religion. In fact, taking his cue from the Qur'anic mandate of diversity as divinely intended, in which religions are expected to compete among themselves in the "doing good" in order to please God, Gülen imagines the globalized world as a village in which peace and order will only be secured by adhering to the principles of respect and tolerance for difference and the freedom to express differences. As he states,

> "Different beliefs, races, customs, and traditions will continue to cohabit in this village. Each individual is like a unique realm unto themselves; therefore, the *desire for all humanity to be similar to one another is nothing more than wishing for all the impossible (emphasis mine).* For this reason, the peace of this (global) village lies in respecting all these differences, considering these differences to be part of our nature and in ensuring that people appreciate these differences."[21]

Sources of Gülen's interfaith dialogue

There are a large number of verses in the Qur'an that call for intra-individual and interfaith dialogue. Some of these verses are exclusively addressed to the "People of the Book" (Christians and Jews). Some of the important verses dealing with the issues of dialogue and interfaith dialogue, including those which refer to Christians and Jews, and which are frequently reflected in Gülen's discourse are as follows:

- O humankind! Surely We have created you from a single (pair of) male and female, and made you into tribes and families so that you may know one another (and so build mutuality and co-operative relationships, not so that you may take pride in your differences of race or social rank, or breed enmities). Surely the noblest, most honorable of you in God's sight is the one best in piety, righteousness, and reverence for God. Surely God is All-Knowing, All-Aware. (49:13)
- For each (community to which a Messenger was sent with a Book), have We appointed a clear way of life and a comprehensive system (containing the principles of that way and how to follow it). And if God had so willed, He would surely have made you a single community (following the same way of life and system surrounded by the same conditions throughout all history); but (He willed it oth-

erwise) in order to test you by what He granted to you (and thereby made you subject to a law of progress). Strive, then, together as if competing in good works. To God is the return of all of you, and He will then make you understand (the truth) about what you have differed on. (5:48)

- ... and for each people, there is a guide (appointed by God). (13:7)
- For every community, We have appointed a whole system of worship which they are to observe. So do not let those (who follow their own systems) draw you into disputes concerning this matter, but continue to call people to your Lord. You are most certainly on the straight way leading to pure guidance. (22:67)
- God will judge between you on the Day of Resurrection concerning what you used to differ on. (22:69)
- If your Lord had so willed (and, denying them free will, compelled humankind to believe), all who are on the earth would surely have believed, all of them. Would you, then, force people until they become believers? (10:99)
- Say: "Do you dispute with us concerning God, seeing that He is our Lord and your Lord?" (2:139)
- Say (to them, O Messenger): "O People of the Book, come to a word common between us and you, that we worship none but God, and associate none as partner with Him, and that none of us take others for Lords, apart from God." If they (still) turn away, then say: "Bear witness that we are Muslims (submitted to Him exclusively)." (3:64)
- You have your religion, and I have my religion. (109:6)
- Do not argue with those who were given the Book save in the best way. (29:46)
- God does not forbid you, as regards those who do not make war against you on account of your Religion, nor drive you away from your homes, to be kindly to them, and act towards them with equity. (60:8)
- It is not according to your fancies, nor according to the fancies of the People of the Book. (No one has a privilege in God's sight by virtue of being nominally a Muslim, or Jew, or Christian. Rather, the truth is this:) Whoever does an evil will be recompensed for it, and he will not find for himself, apart from God, a guardian or a helper. (4:123)

- Those who believe (i.e. professing to be Muslims), or those who declare Judaism, or the Christians or the Sabaeans (or those of some other faith) whoever truly believes in God and the Last Day and does good, righteous deeds, surely their reward is with their Lord, and they will have no fear, nor will they grieve. (2:62)

Thus, these and other Qur'anic verses not only clearly recognize religious diversity and invite to God but also underline the rewards for righteous deeds before God without any discrimination and even exhort believers to compete among themselves for His pleasure. However, modern Islamic scholarship—whether religious or secular—has been marked by the polemics of Meccan vs. Medinan verses and the theory of abrogation (which not only annulled the peaceful, non-violent message of the Qur'an by the later revelation of what are called the Sword Verses, but also asserts that all prophetic messages and revealed texts have been superseded by Medina Islam as the final revelation) that together have diluted the principle of religious pluralism of the Qur'an. On the other hand, Gülen avoids both the Mecca vs. Medina framework and instead unearths the unchangeable ethical and moral principles of the Qur'an in order to demonstrate that religious communities are divinely intended to compete among themselves for the pleasure of God and to achieve their common goal of *din*, a common humanity.

The Qur'an declares, "the same *din* was enjoined on Noah, Abraham, Moses and Jesus" and addresses Prophet Muhammad as "You are but a warner," and "every people has had its guide." In many Islamic exegetical works *din* is considered an active response to the will of God rather than an identification with the particular values of a particular religio-social group. Smith defines *al-din al-haq* (true *din*) as nothing but "obedience, submission, service to truth in terms of what God has made known in his *huda* (guidance) and *bayan* (discourse). This then is the *din* Allah (not the religion of God but the service of God), the total response to God Himself."[22] Making a distinction between *sharia* and *din*, al-Tabatabai emphatically stated, "*Sharia* is a path for a community among communities or a Prophet among Prophets who was sent with it… *Din* is a pattern, a divine and general path for all communities." Thus, *sharia* is amenable to abrogation, while this is not the case with *din* in its broad sense.[23] The import of these quotations is that the notion of *din* (even if interpreted exclusively or as coterminous with Islam as revealed in some verses of the Qur'an such as, "This day have I perfected for you your *din* and completed my favor unto you and chosen for you Islam as *din*" [5:3] or "Whosoever desires a *din* other than Islam will never have it [his or her choice] accepted" [3:85]), accommodates religious pluralism and reminds people about the doctrine of *tawhid*, ultimate accountability before God for their own deeds and enjoins all to do good in order to seek the pleasure of God.

How does Gülen interpret the notion of *din*? An analysis of Gülen's Islamic writings in many books, journals, and on websites clearly reveals that while upholding the doctrine of *tawhid* as the central pillar of *din*, he identifies it with a broader meaning of universal humanity expressed in the coterminous terms of Islam, the Qur'an, the universe, and humanity. Thus, he categorically states, "All Prophets came with the same doctrine, the fundamentals of which are believing in One God, Prophethood, the Resurrection, Angels, Divine Scriptures and Divine Destiny and worshipping God. All Prophets also conveyed the same moral principles. In this sense, all the Divine religions are one and the same."[24] As Gülen expounds the moral and ethical reading of "The Message" contained in the Qur'an, Hadith, and Sunna, his understanding of *din* is expressed in the notion of a "single, common humanity" formed on the principle of "moral and ethical goodness"—the very core of Islam or other religions. He repeatedly draws attention to the Qur'anic statement that "Those who are constant in praying and spend on others out of what We provide for them as sustenance, it is they who are truly the believers" and the Prophet's saying that, "Islam is the religion of good morals and deeds."

It is his inclusive understanding of *din* and religion that led Gülen to identify such values as love, compassion, freedom, tolerance, human rights, and other such values as common to all religious traditions. As he puts it, "Regardless of how their adherents implement their faith in their daily lives, such generally accepted values as love, respect tolerance, forgiveness, mercy, human rights, peace, brotherhood, and freedom are all values exalted by religion. Most of these values are accorded the highest precedence in the messages brought by Moses, Jesus, and Muhammad, upon them be peace, as well as in the message of Buddha and even Zarathustra, Lao-Tzu, Confucius, and the Hindu Prophets."[25] Thus, Gülen's doctrine of dialogue and interfaith dialogue flows directly from his idea of *din* as common destiny and common humanity. For this reason, Gülen emphasizes the "common" elements of religious traditions, civilizations, and cultures as the basis for dialogue and living together. As he stated, "what people have in common is far greater than what divides and separates them." The same approach also led Gülen to take an inclusive definition of Muslim: "As a Muslim, I accept all Prophets and Books sent to different peoples throughout history, and regard belief in them as an essential principle of being Muslim."[26] In this context, he not only includes the monotheistic religious traditions but even other world religions. This provides him with the basis for interfaith dialogue with adherents of non-monotheistic religions too.

In addition to the notion of *din* as common to humanity and the messages common to all religious traditions that Gülen utilizes for interfaith dialogue, Gülen nullifies the superiority claims of any religious community in the light of Qur'anic verses and the tradition of Prophet Muhammad so as to prepare "equal ground" for interfaith dialogue. For it is the assertion of "I" as "superior self-centered ego" against the presumed inferior "other" that has been historically the source of human conflict, misery, and suffering. Much of the Sufi doctrine, teaching and practice that constitutes an essential and integrated component of Gülen's understanding of Islam is directed to overcoming this human dualism of self vs. other—a theme that will be explored in detail later in this chapter. In fact, any superiority–inferiority complex is bound to affect the free flow of communication and thus inhibit the prospects of establishing a genuine dialogue among the members of humanity.

For this reason, Gülen does not emphasize *tabligh* (direct preaching) but values *tamsil* (setting an example); for *tabligh* is premised on the principle of inequality between preacher and the masses and invests superiority claims in preachers. As the practice of *tabligh* establishes power relations between the preacher and the rest, including lay Muslims, it hinders the prospects of dialogue among humans and also obstructs the prospect of understanding from other points of view. It is for this reason that Gülen emphasizes recognition of the moral equality, if not social, political, and economic equality, of all humans: it is this principle alone that can facilitate dialogue. Although social, political, and economic equality are certainly desirable goals and humanity must struggle to achieve them, no matter how utopian that sounds, the notion of social, economic, and political equality without moral foundation or moral equality is not capable of advancing the agenda of equality, mutual cooperation, and trust. This partly explains why, notwithstanding the call of modernity for social, political, and economic equality, in absolute terms inequality in the world has increased tremendously. As an academic colleague of Polish nationality told me in sheer desperation, "the older I grow, the more I realize that equality is a human fantasy."

Gülen draws attention to the normative structure of the Qur'an that addresses all humanity, recognizes the moral equal worth of all His creations, and strongly warns against the superiority claim of Jews and Christians that violates the mandate of God in whose eyes all humans are vicegerents of God on earth. Thus, against the claims of Jews and Christians that Prophet Abraham belongs to them, the Qur'an states, "Abraham was neither a Jew nor a Christian, but an upright person who submitted to Allah (3:67)." Similarly, the Qur'an decries the claims of *some* of Jews and Christians that they are the "chosen community of God" and that the afterlife (paradise) is for them and not for others: "And they say: 'None shall enter paradise unless he (or she) be a Jew or a Christian. Those are their vain desires… Nay, whoever submits his or (her) whole self to Allah and is a doer of good, will get his (or her) reward with his (or her) Lord; On such shall be no fear nor shall they grieve (2:111-112). In response to their claim of being "the children of Allah and His beloved" and that they "considered themselves Pure," the Qur'an says, "Nay, but it is Allah who causes whomsoever He wills to grow in purity; and none shall be wronged by even a hair's breadth" (5:49). At the same time the Qur'an repeatedly warns the Muslim community against claiming any superior status except being servants of Allah. As Gülen writes, "a servant (of God) must ascribe all material and spiritual accomplishments to God; not consider himself or herself as superior to anyone else; not pursue anything other than God and His pleasure."[27]

The Qur'anic expression about the Muslim community as the "best *umma*," according to Gülen, does not mean a "chosen community." Rather, Gülen interprets the said Qur'anic expression as: "You became the best of people, evolved for mankind, enjoining what is right, forbidding what is wrong, and believing in Allah" (3: 110).[28] Thus, the thrust in Gülen's interpretation is on *becoming*, not *being*, which means one has to constantly struggle to secure God's favor. Reflecting on Gülen's differentiation between "being and becoming," Gürbüz and Purkayastha rightly comment that "since becoming depends on conditions that should be fulfilled rather than being chosen *a priori*, we need to focus on attributes, duties and obligations. Thus, there are no God-favored people; instead, there are God-favored attributes."[29] Hence, Gülen's golden generation or what he called the "inheritors of the earth" are not a God-favored people but are expected to earn "God-favored attributes" through hard work and truthfully following the path of God. Further, the Prophet's Last Sermon obliterates any differentiation within the Muslim community on the basis of color, race, ethnicity, and tribe: an Arab has no superiority over a non-Arab, nor does a non-Arab have any superiority over an Arab; also, a white person has no superiority over a black person, nor a black person over a white person except in piety and good action. Gülen asserts the same Qur'anic ethics when he states that "a servant (of God) must ascribe all material and spiritual accomplishments to God; not consider himself or herself as superior to anyone else; not pursue anything other than God and His pleasure."[30]

Notwithstanding the Qur'anic emphasis on the moral equality of all and its strong denunciation of any claim by any community to superiority, some of its verses about non-believers, Christians, and Jews are considered very harsh and therefore are considered to obstruct the development of good faith, dialogue, and trust between Muslims and them. The Qur'an calls "Kafir" (loosely translated as "non-believer") all those who reject the signs of God, who slay the prophets and who slay people who enjoin justice. With regard to Jews and Christians, based on certain conditions, the Qur'an decries corrupt practices and oppression of the poor and illiterate in the name of Scripture and prohibits Muslims to make alliance with Jews and Christians.[31] Moreover, a part of Muslims' arrogance and sense of superiority flows from the claim of Islam that it is the last revealed religion and Prophet Muhammad is the last Messenger of God; hence, it alone possesses the truth by superseding all previous revealed religions.

Gülen dismisses such a pessimistic view about the prospect of interfaith dialogue between Muslims and People of the Book on four grounds. First, for Gülen, the Muslim arrogance and claims of superiority that supposedly flow from Islam as last revealed religion and Prophet Muhammad as last Messenger of God and that led to an exclusivist construction of Islam is totally misplaced. According to him, Prophet Muhammad being the "Seal of all Prophets" only confirms the religious truth of God as personified by various Prophets in different times and conditions, and Prophet Muhammad combines all the virtues and attributes of preceding Prophets. Hence, only by virtue of belief in Allah, Angels, all the Prophets and the Messenger of God can one attain the status of being "Muslim." Any dilution in this definition of Muslim would be tantamount to violation of "being Muslim." So, from this perspective, Muslims have no choice but to treat all Prophetic traditions with respect, piety, and humility.

Second, Gülen considers these so called "negative verses" as not something revealed against the entire community of Jews and Christians but as pertaining to those Jews and Christians that commit wrong: "the verses condemning and rebuking the Jews and Christians are either about some Jews and Christians who lived in the time of the Prophet Muhammad or their own Prophets such as Moses and Jesus, or those who deserved such condemnation because of their wrong beliefs or practices."[32]

Third, according to Gülen, these commandments of the Qur'an are general in nature as they are against wrongdoers, which includes even members of the Muslim community: "Rather than individual Christian and Jews, the Qur'an goes after wrong behavior, incorrect thought, resistance to the truth, creation of hostility, and non-commendable characteristics... The Qur'an's criticism and warnings regarding some of these attitudes and behaviors of non-Muslims also were made about Muslims whose faith did not prevent them from engaging in the same behavior."[33]

Fourth, Gülen points out the sayings of the Prophet and the Companions that call for treating of the People of the Book with justice and piety. As he narrates, "When the Prophet was dying and about to pass on to the next world, he stated: 'I place in your trust the People of the Book, the Christians and Jews.' When 'Umar was in the throes of death due to a dagger wound, he warned: 'I place the minorities among us in your trust. Fear God regarding them and treat them justly.'"[34] Further Gülen relies upon the general history of the rule of the Muslim community, particularly the Ottoman Empire, in order to demonstrate that Muslim rule has been relatively tolerant towards the People of the Book. Thus, he states, "Even non-Muslim, Western scholars, who often are hostile to Islam, acknowledge that Jews, Christians, and other non-Muslims ruled by Muslims generally enjoyed much greater economic prosperity, dignity, and prestige, and had far more freedoms than under non-Islamic rule—even that of their own co-religionists."[35]

Certainly, there is a grain of truth, which has also been attested by historians such as Bernard Lewis, in this view of Muslim empires as relatively tolerant in nature, particularly under the *millet* system of the Ottoman Empire, which guaranteed the exercise of personal law to each religious community in matters of religious practices. Ali Asani of Harvard University echoes this conclusion about the relationship between Muslim rule and non-Muslim subjects:

> From the earliest periods of Muslim history, we have examples of a great deal of respect for the rights of non-Muslims under Muslim rule. For instance, the fourth Caliph Ali ibn Abi Talib (d. 661) instructed his governor in Egypt to show mercy, love, and kindness for all subjects under his rule, including non-Muslims whom he declared to be "your equals in creation." Such tolerance is later reflected in the policies of the Arab dynasties of Spain, the Fatimids in North Africa, and the Turkish Ottomans in the Middle East granting maximum individual and group autonomy to those adhering to a religious tradition other than Islam. We can also cite the example of the Mughal Emperor Akbar (d. 1605), who—much to the dismay of the religious right wing of his time—promoted tolerance among the various traditions that compose the Indian religious landscape.[36]

However, the Qur'anic prescription of "*dhimmi* status" for "People of the Book," which calls for an extra tax to be paid by Jews and Christians for their protection by the Muslim state, has been the subject of scholarly controversy and dispute. Non-Muslim critics—whether religious or secular—have slammed this Qur'anic provision as an expression of Muslim arrogance and superiority and second-class treatment of the People of the Book and religious minorities that robs Islam of its claim to equality and justice. However, in the Muslim imagination the levy of extra tax (*jizya*) upon the members of the People of the Book or religious others for a guarantee of protection is just as the Muslim state does not call upon "*dhimmi* people" or "protected people" to fight on behalf of the Muslim state so it is paid in lieu of military service. Moreover, there has never been uniform application of *jizya* during the period of Muslim empire.

How does Gülen interpret the provision of *dhimmi* and *jizya* in modern times? It appears that Gülen has primarily looked upon the issue in the Gandhian frame of the moral responsibility of the majority community to ensure the safety and security of the well-being and identity of the religious minority. For Gandhi, a democratic state requires *sine qua non* the protection of the religious minority. As the democratic nation-state is essentially a "majoritarian state," Gandhi emphasized the necessity of a compassionate and generous attitude on the part of the majority community towards the minority community in order to instill the sense of confidence, trust, well-being and security to ensure their smooth integration into the nation.

Gülen, like Gandhi, looks upon the issue of *dhimmi* and *jizya* from a moral and ethical point of view and does not view *jizya* as a discriminatory law of Muslim rule, nor does it contradict the democratic principle of equality. For Gülen, what matters more in terms of treatment of People of the Book, religious others or religious minorities is not the principle of *jizya* (which legally binds the Muslim state—whether majority or minority in terms of demography—to protect the People of the Book/religious others/religious minorities) but prejudice, discriminatory attitudes, biases and intolerance. Even though the principle of *jizya* violates the principles of modern democratic rule in terms of political equality and equality before the law, the modern nation-state, too, has a poor record in protecting minority communities from the tyranny of the majority; worse, at times the democratic states has transformed itself into a majoritarian state and indulged in crimes against humanity targeting the members of minority communities.

For Gülen, what matters in governance is the principle of ethics and morals, without which the notion of political equality and freedom is empty rhetoric:

> Even in modern times, Western political constitutions typically make space for individual religious freedom, as opposed to collective and communal religious freedom. The Islamic polity recognizes the relevance and importance of community to the practice and

> continuance of religious beliefs and traditions. That is why … Muslims protected the lives and property as well as the rites and places of worship of their non-Muslim subjects. Also, non-Muslims were recognized as distinct communities with their own schools and institutions. The conditions for such a display of successful religious pluralism were a just, impartial, central authority and the discipline of non-provocation. A collective ethos of tolerance cannot be sustained without that discipline. For example, neither Muslims nor non-Muslims were allowed to blaspheme or otherwise mock and undermine each other's beliefs and rites.[37]

Conditions of interfaith dialogue

Having laid out an inclusive Muslim perspective and basis for dialogue, Gülen turns his attention towards excavating the minimal conditions for effective dialogue. For Gülen, the purpose of dialogue is to not to satisfy each other's ego but to help the truth to come out, which requires such principles as mutual understanding, respect, and dedication to justice.[38] The creation of this environment calls for a Muslim to develop what are considered Sufistic ethics or what Heon Choul Kim has described as "Gülen's Dialogic Sufism"[39] that has four inter-connected aspects: love, compassion, tolerance, and forgiveness. Lester R. Kurtz has called these dimensions of Sufi Islam "pillars of Gülen's conception of dialogue."[40]

Before elaborating these key Sufistic concepts of Islam it must be noted here that though Gülen acknowledges and takes pride in representing the humanistic legacy of Sufi Islam, one should not draw the inference, as many do, that Gülen considers the Sufistic dimensions of Islam as "the Islam" and therefore adheres to the modernist conception of religion as a private, personal entity or experience or accepts the Christian distinction between faith (the spiritual dimension of religion) and religion (the worldly dimension). In fact, Gülen's treatment of interfaith dialogue follows from his balanced, holistic, integrated understanding of Islam in which both the spiritual dimensions of Islam (*tasawwuf*—Sufi Islam) and worldly dimensions of Islam (institutional, political, social, economic and others) are complementary to each other. It is the institutional dimension of faith that sets boundaries and emphasizes differences, whereas it is the spiritual tradition that opens the heart to a force that obliterates difference. A neglect of any one dimension will result in a distorted understanding of Islam. According to Gülen, the two dimensions must never be separated:

> An initiate or traveler on the path (*salik*) never separates the outer observance of the *Sharia* from its inner dimension, and therefore observes all of the requirements of both the outer and the inner dimensions of Islam. Through such observance, he or she travels toward the goal in utmost humility and submission.[41]

Firuz Kul, an academic from Atatürk University, Erzurum, stresses this unity of Islam while describing the Hizmet Movement: "This Movement is not merely *tasawwuf*, not merely religion, but a combination of pure *tasawwuf*, original scholastic Islam and science."[42] Further, in many of his writings [Gülen] has stressed that Sufism must not remain a way of personal inner purification, but should be reflected in society. In fact, any distinctions between Sufi Islam and worldly Islam is a misnomer in the reformist traditions of Islam as most of the great Islamic reformers and personalities such as Abu Hanifa, Ahmad Yasawi, Mawlana Jalal al-Din al-Rumi, Yunus Emre, Imam Ghazali, and Imam Rabbani, Mawlana Khalid al Baghdadi, Shah Waliullah, Bediüzzaman Said Nursi and many others have combined both aspects of Islam. In this context Shah Waliullah, a nineteenth century Indian Islamic reformer, once remarked, "Sufis without knowledge of Qur'an and Sunnah, and scholars who are not interested in mysticism are brigands and robbers of the *din* (religion).[43]

Gülen represents this Islamic tradition and hence considers the interconnected notions of love, compassion, tolerance, and forgiveness as the core values of all religion, including Islam.

Love

Thus, the key word in Gülen's dialogue meetings is love. Philosophically speaking, Gülen considers love to be the essence of creation and an unquestionable condition for being human. According to Gülay, "The emphasis on 'love' and 'compassion' signals a departure point in Gülen's theological perspective compared to that of Nursi."[44] The Sufi emphasis on love as a central attribute of a believer shifts the focus from institution and ritual to the diffusion of love for God and for others. Love for Gülen is a self-sacrificing action that is motivated by obedience to God and the desire to promote the welfare of others. As creation is the reflection of God's love and mercy, human beings, as the vice-regent or vicegerent of God on earth, are expected to display love, care, and respect towards all creation—living and non-living. Thus, through love for humanity one attains the pleasure of God. The person who lives in this way is gradually growing in *marifah* or spiritual wisdom and in love (*mahabbah*, *'ashq*), both for God and for others. The Sufi notion of *marifah* is a "state of ecstasy," a kind of God-consciousness that allows the believer to dismantle all human based hierarchies and attain the "state of peace" by living in God's presence, irrespective of time and place. Without love, it is almost impossible to create an atmosphere conducive to dialogue and tolerance. For Gülen, a human can only communicate actively with all humans and other creatures through love, which leads her or him to help others. Relying on his own conviction and tradition, and on the global transmitters of love such as Abu Hanifa, Ahmad Yasawi, Mawlana Jalal al-Din al-Rumi, Imam Ghazali, and Imam Rabbani, Gülen describes love and tolerance as "the roses and flowers of our hill."

Compassion

Compassion, for Gülen, is another condition for being human:

> Compassion is the beginning of being; without it everything is chaos. Everything has come into existence through compassion and by compassion it continues to exist in harmony. Everything speaks of compassion and promises compassion. Because of this, the universe can be considered a symphony of compassion. All kinds of voices proclaim compassion so that it is impossible not to be aware of it, and impossible not to feel the wide mercy encircling everything. How unfortunate are the souls who don't perceive this. Man has a responsibility to show compassion to all living beings, as a requirement of being human. The more he displays compassion, the more exalted he becomes, while the more he resorts to wrongdoing, oppression and cruelty, the more he is disgraced and humiliated, becoming a shame to humanity.[45]

A person of compassion does not hesitate to be open to all and to enter into dialogue with all. Communication and relation with "the other" is not based on an abstract, unchanging model. According to Gülen, the desire to "communicate" with the world should lead Muslims to think and act in harmony with the changing conditions while preserving their essence at the same time: "If you seek to explain something to the world, you have to be in harmony with the world. In this respect, first of all, we have to get along well with our people; we have to be in dialogue with our own people." In this context Gülen refers to the metaphor of the famous Sufi poet Mawlana Rumi in order to explain how one can be both rooted in one's own tradition but open to diverse culture and interactions:

> Such a person is like a compass with one foot well-established in the center of belief and Islam and the other foot with people of many nations. If this apparently dualistic state can be caught by a person who believes in God, it is most desirable. So, deep in his or her own inner world, so full of love—so much in touch with God; but at the same time an active member of society.[46]

Tolerance and forgiveness

Gülen considers tolerance and forgiveness as the cardinal principle for dialogue and in most instances, he uses both expressions together. He draws numerous references from the Qur'an and Islamic history to demonstrate that these are deeply embedded Islamic values. Thus, he recalls the Qur'anic verse: "They swallow their anger and forgive people. God loves those who do good" (3:134) and similar other verses to buttress the Qur'an's call for forgiveness and tolerance. He cites the example of the Prophet's forgiveness to the House of Sufyan after returning to Mecca. The Medina constitution drawn up by Prophet Muhammad after migrating to Medina further testifies to Islam's commitment to tolerance of different viewpoints and life styles and the art of living together. Calling tolerance the "most essential element of a moral system and source of spiritual discipline,"[47] Gülen connects tolerance with love, compassion, and forgiveness because all require genuine feeling for the other. Just as love is an expression of empathetic feeling for the other, Gülen's more recent writings emphasize tolerance as a kind of sympathetic appreciation of the difference and uniqueness of the other.[48] Tolerance then, for Gülen, is both a moral demand by God and an invitation from God to a deeper place of devotion. Without tolerance grounded in love, we cannot be moral creatures. Gülen writes, "Be so tolerant that your heart becomes wide like the ocean. Become inspired with faith and love for others. Offer a hand to those in trouble, and be concerned about everyone."

Gülen's discursive field of tolerance is not only about unconditional acceptance of the principle of religious pluralism but also sensitive about expression in words. He draws attention to verses in the Qur'an and examples from Islamic history to show that a Muslim is one from whose tongue and hand others are secure. He believes that success of dialogue meetings is also contingent upon their performance in words. J. L. Austin's *How to Do Things with Words* provides a theoretical understanding of the performative relationships between words, actions, and the contexts of utterances. According to Austin,

> the performative element of speech is the effect that it has on the hearer, but this effectiveness occurs in a broader context than the explicit content of the words uttered. Utterances themselves may be illocutionary or perlocutionary. Illocutionary utterances are those that "'when saying, do what they say, and do it in the moment of that saying," hence amounting to deeds. Perlocutionary utterances lead to certain effects that are not the same as the speech act itself.[49]

The distinctive aspect of such performative utterances is that they do not merely name, they also perform what they are naming and represent it at the same time.

For this reason, Gülen is of the view that, in today's world, the task of "representing faith with its true value has gained an even greater importance than before." He attaches great importance to the issue of representation of Islam. He constantly refers to the Hadith (Prophet Saying) that defines a true Muslim as "one who harms no one with his/her words and actions, and who is the most trustworthy representative of universal peace." He notes that the Qur'an instructs believers not to respond to meaningless and ugly words or behavior with similar words, but to pass by in a dignified manner, as the Prophet himself did, showing tolerance and forgiveness even to his bitter enemies.

The underlying tone of Gülen's conception of tolerance and forgiveness is that human beings urgently need to cultivate these values in order to live together. This has assumed greater significance in the modern context of a relationship between Islam and the West marked by mutual distrust and fear. They can only overcome each other's prejudices, fear, and distrust by means of tolerance and forgiveness. Without tolerance and forgiveness, a genuine dialogue between two individuals or groups is not possible. It is for this reason that Gülen warns, "One who does not embrace humanity with tolerance and forgiveness will not receive forgiveness and pardon,"[50] and considers that

> the greatest gift that today's generation can give to its children and grandchildren is to teach them how to forgive, even in the face of the crudest behavior and most upsetting events. We believe that forgiveness and tolerance will heal most of our wounds only if this celestial instrument is in the hands of those who understand its language.[51]

It is through these four interconnected values of love, compassion, tolerance, and forgiveness, which a person internalizes by undergoing "rigorous systematic training of mind, heart and body," that he or she manages to overcome his/her selfish ego and discipline carnal desires for the greater good. It is under the effect of these values that the self is activated to serve the "other" in order to attain the pleasure of God. It is through this process that the self dissolves itself into the other without any expectation and thus creates a moral condition for dialogue and understanding of the other's perspective in order to find common ground. In fact, the entire purpose of Gülen's *Emerald Hills of the Heart* with its exposition of the principles of Sufism such as *dhikr* (remembrance of God), *zuhd* (asceticism), *muraqaba* (self-reflection) *muhasaba* (self-evaluation) and many more is to direct Muslims to undergo the spiritual training of Sufism in order that each may dissolve his/her "self" to overcome the carnal desires and to develop God-consciousness. In other words, for Gülen, a person must undergo the process of moral and ethical disciplining in order to participate in dialogue and interfaith dialogue with a view to promoting mutual understanding, peace, solidarity, and living together. The dershanes, and particularly the Light Houses, in the Gülen Movement are conceived as providing spaces for the volunteers to undergo such moral and ethical experience that combines reason (as taught in *madrasa*) with the heart (as practiced in *tekke*) in discipline (as in military academy). It is this entire gamut of processes that differentiates the Gülen model of tolerance from the Western liberal model of tolerance.

The Western liberal model of tolerance is premised on the principle of cultural homogenization and tolerance of individual difference. The tradition of Western liberalism, to a large extent, is theoretically equipped to handle the issues pertaining to individual differences. Commenting on the Western notion of tolerance Enes Ergene puts it bluntly: "This is my personal choice (accepted); this is my religious choice (not tolerated)."[52] Moreover, such individual difference is only tolerated, not accepted. Thus, the Western liberal framework of tolerance was found to be workable within a homogenized society and nation, as was the case with "old Europe," it is proving to be a failure in dealing with "new Europe" with its emerging multicultural and multi-faith spaces in the wake of Muslim migrants. Moreover, much of the discourse of multiculturalism that Europe witnessed in the early and mid-1990s vis-à-vis the immigrant communities beat a hasty retreat and Europe returned to its old tested liberal-assimilationist-model of integration.[53]

Gülen's model of tolerance is based on tolerance of difference—both individual and communal differences—and emphatic acceptance of others with all their religious, cultural, and secular traditions and irrespective of their identities. The "emphatic acceptance of others" in Gülen's framework of interfaith dialogue becomes possible as it is premised on what Alasdair MacIntyre, a Scottish moral philosopher, calls "tradition-bound rationality"[54] and negation of the Enlightenment's "universal reason." MacIntyre powerfully exposes the myth of a timeless, neutral, value-free conception of universal reason or rationality as argued by Enlightenment thinkers and demonstrates that reason or rationality is time-bound, and guided by the specific history, discourse, customs, and values of a community. The discourse of multiculturalism and post-modernism, which is dominant today, has more sharply exposed the relative nature of reason or rationality in various societies. It is this recognition of the relative nature of reason in Gülen's paradigm of interfaith dialogue that enables him to see the possibility and necessity of dialogue between cultures, histories, civilizations, and traditions in order to arrive at a common understanding of the core values of humanity, while retaining their distinctive religious, cultural, social and political identities.

The praxis of Gülen's interfaith dialogue

Having identified the Islamic basis and conditions for interfaith dialogue, Gülen declared, "Interfaith dialogue is a must today, and the first step in establishing it is forgetting the past, ignoring polemical arguments, and giving precedence to common points, which far outnumber polemical ones."[55] Towards this goal the Movement has established hundreds of dialogue centers in the world with a view to transforming dialogue, along with service ethics, into an everyday Islamic value. This contrasts Gülen's model of interfaith dialogue with the Church and Western model: in the latter paradigm, dialogue is a "structured phenomenon" and confined to important personalities, leaders, and religious functionaries, whereas in Gülen's paradigm it is "everyday discourse" and intends to involve all sections of societies. In this sense dialogue is an everyday, action-oriented program directed at enacting a common effort for the common good. Thus, Douglas Pratt has rightly stated that for Gülen, "dialogue is no rarefied academic pursuit; it is itself a praxis; a methodology; a struggle—even an *ijtihad*—in the pursuit of peace, harmony and justice."[56] Heon Choul Kim echoes this understanding of Gülen's model of dialogue:

> It is not a method reacting to problems, but a method acting harmoniously with any given context. As such a method, dialogic Sufism acts as a humanistic bridge between the past and the present, the East and the West, rationalism/materialism and spiritualism, and between different civilizations, religions and cultures, obliterating difference and distinction between "us and other."[57]

Çelik and Valkenberg identify three stages in Gülen's conception of dialogue. They describe the first stage as accepting the others in their own position. The second stage involves respecting the position of the other(s), and the third stage is the concept of sharing values in the context of the other(s).[58] In this dialogic paradigm Gülen does not create any hierarchy of values among believers or even between believer or unbeliever. As he states,

> Western thought has many useful aspects. For example, systematic contemplation/thinking is a quality of a *mü'min* (believer). In my opinion, every *mü'min* is not a believer with all his/her qualities. The one who has such a quality, whether he is a Christian, a Magian

> or a Buddhist, has the quality of a *mü'min*. Allah treats people, at least on earth, according to their qualities.[59]

Gülen's conviction is that humanity ultimately will be led to peace and unity by recognizing and accepting social, cultural, and religious diversity, an exchange of mutual values, and union in collaboration. Gülen sees diversity and pluralism as a natural fact. He wants those differences to be admitted and to be explicitly professed. Accepting everyone in their otherness, which is broader and deeper than the Western notion of tolerance, is his normal practice. In fact, the "self" and "other" in Gülen's thought, during the course of interaction incorporate each other and become one. Therefore, it is not surprising to observe that, as in Gandhian thought, there does not emerge the conception of "other" in Gülen's writings and thinking.

In terms of praxis and action Fethullah Gülen himself has taken a number of initiatives in meeting with representatives of other religious traditions, although so far this is confined to monotheistic religions. This includes his meeting with Pope John Paul II in Rome, the Ecumenical Patriarch of the Orthodox Church, and the Chief Rabbi of Israel in Turkey. In connection with the Parliament of the World's Religions, held in Cape Town, South Africa, Mr. Gülen delivered a major address on the theme: "The Necessity of Interfaith Dialogue: A Muslim Approach." In addition to this initiative, he has lent personal support to many interfaith meetings within and outside Turkey. Gülen's active advocacy for the praxis of dialogue and interfaith dialogue flows from his conviction that: (a) dialogue is intrinsically linked with the promotion of peace, harmony, cooperation, and solidarity in society; (b) interreligious and intercultural conflict is rooted in the misunderstanding of one's own religio-cultural traditions as well as the other's religious traditions. Dialogue greatly helps in removing such misunderstanding and promoting a sympathetic outlook towards each other; and (c) it is possible to resolve inter-communal, intra-individual, and inter-gender conflict, and associated violence through the combination of the correct representation of religious traditions and good moral education.

Thus, condemning the ghastly incident of 9/11 Gülen wrote right after the tragedy: "What lies behind certain Muslim people or institutions that misunderstand Islam getting involved in terrorist attacks that occur throughout the world should be sought not in Islam, but within those people themselves, in their misinterpretations, and in other factors. Just as Islam is not a religion of terrorism, any Muslim who correctly understands Islam cannot be thought of as a terrorist."[60] Before and after 9/11 Gülen has always been outspoken in condemning the terrorist attacks anywhere in the world with an the assertion that "a Muslim cannot be a terrorist and a terrorist cannot be a Muslim." It is in the context of the rise of religious extremism in the modern era that Gülen argues for that there is greater need than ever before now for the principles of tolerance, respect, and common understanding to be strengthened through interreligious and intercultural dialogue than ever before. For dialogue in general and interreligious and intercultural dialogue in particular as an everyday human value alone has the potential, if practiced properly, to serve as the antidote to the modernist trend of politicization and ideologization of social phenomenon that creates conflicts in the societies by transforming people into US vs. THEM.

Interfaith dialogue helps ones to learn about the religious beliefs and spiritual identity of the other while at the same time learning more about one's own religious beliefs and spiritual identity. It is about discovering oneself through otherness. Towards this goal various Hizmet dialogue centers have developed and conducted different programs according to the specific national, cultural, and religious traditions of the country where they are located in the form of seminars, lectures, interfaith trips, and so on. Interfaith trips are considered one of the most effective ways of sharing each other's religious experiences and developing a common outlook. The focus of engagement is not to indulge in theological discussion but to invite discussion of experience with the divine. Highlighting this aspect of interfaith activities, Kemal, associated with the Hizmet dialogue centers in the USA, informed me that one of their important interfaith programs is the Table of Abraham, at which speakers explore the common roots and aspects of Abrahamic faiths. Similarly, at the Interfaith Contemplative Prayer program the participants observe twenty minutes of silence in order to explore and experience faith.[61] The volunteers in the Hizmet Movement also believe in developing close interpersonal relationships in order to overcome internal prejudices towards the "other."

In my several interviews with Movement volunteers the "belief in dialogue with everybody" and "unconditional acceptance of others" came out strongly, but it appears to me that in terms of practice these principles are limited to believers only. As Halil Oztan, in charge of dialogue affairs in Konya puts it, "Hizmet is essentially a believer movement but others are welcomed. The main aim of Nursi, Hodjaefendi and Hizmet is to see humanity as believers, though not necessarily in accordance with Islam."[62] Cemal Uşak, former Vice President of the Journalists and Writers Foundation, the most important Hizmet think tank, told me that "the main purpose of a Gülen school is to produce "good Buddhists," "good Christians."[63] Thus, the idea of the "good human" is essentially conceptualized in religious terms. Further, in my conversations with many Movement volunteers, it emerged that there is a great deal of reservation at the individual level about "emphatic acceptance" of communists, atheists, Shia and members of what is called the community of LGBT (Lesbian, Gay, Bisexual and Transgender people). Reflecting on his understanding of pluralism and tolerance, Cemal Uşak candidly admitted that "for me pluralism and tolerance means respecting people's free will, free choice, but not necessarily agreeing with their values. In other words, I respect them as human beings without necessarily agreeing with their way of life. Anything sinful from an Islamic point of view, such as gays and lesbians, is not acceptable to me."[64]

However, in the same meeting, a young volunteer differed with Mr. Uşak and asserted that for him tolerance and pluralism amounts to respecting and accepting the other's way of life including that of LGBT people. This in part reflects an emerging generation gap within the Gülen Movement in which the older generation tends to subscribe to a relatively closed understanding of Islam, whereas the younger generation is subscribing to a more open understanding of Islam that takes into consideration modern sensibilities. My recent interviews with young volunteers of Hizmet in Germany also confirm this emerging trend, whereby they totally accept and respect people of different sexual orientation (LGBT) including them as members of their own family.[65] Referring to this emerging inter-generational divide over the meanings and discourse of Hizmet Movement, Osman, a USA-based volunteer rightly noted that one of the challenges before Hizmet now lies in negotiations between the generations.[66]

CHAPTER 10

THE "POLITICAL" IN THE MOVEMENT

The phenomenal growth of the Gülen Movement as an Islamic civic-social movement as detailed in the preceding chapters raises one pertinent question: Does the movement have a notion of "political" that has helped in attracting a large number of people cutting across ethnic, regional, and class identities? If yes, what is the nature of the "political"? Has Hizmet's conception of the "political" helped in facilitating the democratic transformation of Turkey? Or has it obstructed the process of democratic rule in Turkey?

This question has assumed significance from the two points of view. First, the dominant scholarship on social movements has mostly analyzed its appeal and growth in terms of the politics of "counter-mobilization" vis-à-vis the state. Thus, Gülen's Islamic discourse and the educational activities of the Movement have been seen as a "discourse of moral opposition" and "a counter site" for mobilization respectively against the Kemalist state system in Turkey that helped to attract people's attention.

Second, the literature on the relationship between the movement and the AKP is replete with narratives, though without much evidence, about a "political alliance" between the two, which is considered to have formally ended with the December 2013 exposure of a massive corruption scandal involving 52 officials, including family members of President Erdoğan.[1] This incident and later the failed military coup of July 15, 2016 led to the massive persecution of Gülen Movement volunteers within Turkey. After both incidents—the fraud corruption investigation and the coup attempt—the Erdoğan-led AKP government accused the Hizmet Movement of conspiracy to overthrow the legitimate government, called them a "parallel structure" and FETO (Fethullahist Terrorist Organization), and unleashed a witch hunt against movement participants of a kind never before witnessed in the history of the Republic.[2] Irrespective of allegations, claims, and counter claims from the Hizmet Movement and the government, the various developments since 2013 including these two incidents have mostly been seen in influential circles and among critics as a power-struggle between the Hizmet Movement and the AKP, thereby highlighting the political face of the Movement.

The Movement's critics—Kemalists, secularists, communists, and liberals—deeply suspect the Gülen Movement of a "hidden motive/agenda" to transform Turkey into an Islamic nation-state.[3] Since "education" has emerged as the *key* identity of the Gülen Movement, can this be considered a site of counter-mobilization against the secular state, the secular elite and their lifestyle in Turkey? Though a good number of scholars have pointed out the role of "moral opposition" inherent in Gülen's Islamic discourse, it is difficult to argue that Gülen conceived of education and encouraged the establishment of educational institutions as a "political project" to displace the Westernized status-quo. For Gülen, education is the most important Islamic value and the essential condition to ensure one's faith and hence needs to be acquired by everyone. However, one consequence of the spread of education is that it has an inherent tendency to break the monopoly of knowledge by a certain class, to advance equity, and to eliminate the income and status disparity within a country. The large transformation one is witnessing in today's Turkey in which the "black" Anatolian Muslim Turks are taking the center stage in all fields—economic, political and social—is at best an *unintended* consequence of Gülen's reconfiguration of fundamental Islamic principles and values to suit the present times.

The government's pejorative designation of the Gülen Movement as the "parallel structure" implies that the Movement is "purposefully hidden" so as to take over the state at a convenient time. Many others, who do not share the government's view of the Gülen Movement as a "parallel structure" or "FETO," point out its "non-transparent mode of functioning," which also implies that there is something "hidden" about the Movement. Further, a great deal of scholarship on the Gülen Movement primarily sees the Movement as an "essentially Islamist phenomenon" and hence not devoid of an orientation towards acquiring state power with the purpose of Islamizing the Turkish society and state. Thus, Michael Rubin, the influential editor of the *Middle East Quarterly*, once compared Gülen with Ayatollah Khomeini, the founder of the Islamic Republic of Iran, and drew a parallel between the possible return of Gülen to Turkey and Khomeini's return to Iran.[4] Even Ali Bulaç, one of the contemporary Islamist thinkers in Turkey, once compared the Gülen Movement with Hasan al-Banna's Muslim Brotherhood and stated that "there is a similarity between the two. Fethullah Gülen strongly recommends his students to read the books of Hasan al-Banna and Sayyid Qutb."[5] On the other hand, the Islamists in Turkey—whether the AKP variety or radical extremists like Hezbollah—accuse the Gülen Movement of collaborating with the United States and Israel to undermine the Muslim cause and unity. The government-invented term "FETO" serves the same purpose: to malign and rob the Movement's participants of their moral and ethical stance and to impugn the Gandhian legacy of Fethullah Gülen—the source of inspiration of millions of volunteers in the Movement.

In the above context, Gülen, like other Muslim leaders of Turkey, has been frequently accused by the secularists and Kemalists—mostly by those who treat Islamic social phenomena as "security threats"—to have a "hidden agenda" to topple down the secular regime with an Islamic revolution. This accusation is based on no evidence other than their age-old bias. They usually bring forward one alleged statement of Gülen in a video footage, in which he is allegedly asking his followers to "move in the arteries of the system without anyone noticing their existence."[6]

The above statement, apart from lacking an authentic source and not being free of suspicion of being doctored TV footage, was used to charge Gülen under the state's Anti-Terror Law with "attempting to change the secular characteristics of the Republic" on June 21, 1999—a charge of which he was eventually acquitted in 2008. Moreover, the reliance on a single passage amidst hundreds of thousands of pacific and non-violent written narratives, statements, interviews, passages, speeches and public actions of more than fifty years of Gülen's public life with clear intent to serve the greater humanity not only suffers from being a grave error of gross selectivity and shadowy scholarship but shows deliberate political intent on the part of such authors to malign and de-legitimize the Gandhian legacy of Fethullah Gülen in person and the Movement in general.

Nevertheless, it can be argued that there is a mostly non-written culture within the Movement. I even observed some consultative meetings went with no decisions written down and later circulated. This may appear as non-transparent from outside. However, being non-transparent does not mean that the Movement conducts its activities in an illegal way. None of the Movement's inspired volunteers, organizations, institutions, or business houses over the last fifty years within Turkey or abroad has been implicated or penalized for tax evasion or violation of any other rules and regulations. In fact, in the greatest travesty of justice, the Turkish Court justified the government's confiscation of Hizmet sympathizer Akın İpek's Koza İpek, a conglomeration of 22 companies, despite the government inspection report found no irregularities in the company records[7] and appointed "trustees" to it on the extraordinary grounds that its "documents are too perfect to find any single illegality in the functioning of the Company. This proves, in view of Turkish business practices, that the Company is conducting its business illegally (October 27, 2015)"![8]

In fact, there are two specific reasons for the development of the non-transparent mode of functioning in the Hizmet Movement. First, it emerges from the Movement's die-hard faith that human beings are trustworthy and that forging what Gandhi called "heart unity" is a noble goal, which the Movement must ceaselessly pursue. Second, the non-transparent culture within the Hizmet Movement has been shaped by specific characteristics of the Turkish state, which has a long tradition of *profiling, supervising, regulating, controlling, policing, and persecuting* the members and institutions of civil society. One consequence of such a political culture is that state has repeatedly identified, arrested, and harassed individuals affiliated with formal organizations despite their being legally registered in Turkish law under the constitution, in addition to shutting down such organizations (without any effective recourse to the justice system) as and when it feels threatened by any civil society groups. The Gülen Movement has repeatedly been the victim of this political culture. Individuals, institutions, associations, and business houses linked with the Movement were all targeted in the 1980 military coup as a threat to the secular character of the nation and again since 2013, including after the failed military coup of July 2016 in the name of being linked with "FETO."

In the aftermath of the December 2013 corruption exposure government inspectors conducted rigorous examinations of all documents of Hizmet-linked institutions such Bank Asya, Kimse Yok Mu, media organizations, teacher associations, business organizations, and so on, but failed to find any irregularity in the functioning of these institutions. Nonetheless, irrespective of belief and political orientation, individuals who had any formal/informal association with these institutions, even as little as holding a bank account in Bank Asya or being a subscriber to *Zaman* newspaper or being employed in their educational or other institutions, became the victims of the government crackdown on the Movement which commenced in December 2013, became more brutal after the failed military coup of July 2016 and surpassed all previous government repressions. Thus, despite the constitutional provision of fundamental rights, the specific political culture and poor governance in modern Turkey do not inculcate confidence in its citizens to live openly with non-state public identities, including their political identity, in the public sphere.[9]

Seen from the above perspective the presumption of a "power struggle" or breakdown in the "political alliance" between the AKP and the Gülen Movement is totally misplaced and at best a political construction rooted into two grounds. First it largely flows from the power-centric tradition of modern social science, which tends to treat every phenomenon from the perspective of power dynamics without much empirical evidence. Second, it brings the Gülen Movement within the fold of state power politics so as to empty it of its moral and ethical aura. However, what appears to be a plausible explanation is that the so called "power conflict" between the Hizmet Movement and the Erdoğan regime flows from the historical pattern of relationship between state and civil society, at least in the context of Middle East, in which the state is accustomed to using civil society forces for the purpose of its own legitimacy and consolidation, as well as to crushing it when it feels threatened—whether real or imaginary threat. Thus the late Mehmet Ali Birand, a keen observer of Turkish politics, prophesied in 2010 about the state's crackdown on Gülen Movement on account of its constructed image in public sphere as "too big/powerful," which made the Erdoğan government fearful of its existence.[10]

Thus, historically speaking, the political tradition in Middle Eastern countries including Turkey has been hostile to autonomous Islamic religious groups, as the state in the Middle East—whether secular or Islamist—suspects the political allegiance of various Islamic groups. The Middle Eastern states—whether democratic, secular, or Islamist—to a large extent rely on Islam as the most important source of legitimacy of their rule, which makes them wish not only to control and monopolize all "Islamic spaces" but also leaves them deeply suspicious of autonomous *visible* Islamic political and social organizations or groups, as the latter are perceived as potential legitimate political or social forces to challenge the legitimacy of the regimes. There are numerous examples of this trend in the state-civil society relationship. The Ikhwan al-Muslimin (Muslim Brotherhood) in Egypt has been the object of state repression in various degrees throughout the modern political history of Egypt since the Nasserite regime on the charge of being a "parallel state" or "state within state." The most recent instance of state repression against the Muslim Brotherhood took place in July 2013 when Mr Abdel-el Fateh Sisi, then Defense Minister and now President, overthrew the elected Muslim Brotherhood government led by the then-Prime Minister Mohammad Morsi, put him behind bars, and brutally crushed the protests of the Muslim Brotherhood, killing thousands, and declared the organization unlawful, illegal, and terrorist.

Modern Turkey has a similar political history. The modern Turkish state since the foundation of the Turkish Republic has displayed more or less the same political attitudes towards autonomous religious organizations and personalities. Despite the fact that Bediüzzaman Said Nursi participated in the Turkish War of Independence (1918–1921), later withdrew from any political engagement, and remained politically aloof and non-critical towards the Kemalist and post-Kemalist regimes, the regimes remained hostile to him, systematically harassed him, put him under house arrest, subjected him to trial on specious charges, and finally, after his death, disinterred his mortal remains from his burial site in Urfa, and buried him in an unknown place within Turkey so as to avoid the possibility of his burial site becoming a place where people might gather in future. The Nur movement in Turkey, inspired by Nursi's ideas, has been subjected to varying degrees of state repression throughout the greater part of modern Turkey.

Fethullah Gülen and the Gülen Movement too lived under the fearful shadow of the "deep state" and suffered from varying degrees of state repression. Today, the political hostility of the Turkish state under the AKP government, led by President Recep Tayyip Erdoğan, has turned on Gülen and the Gülen Movement in the harshest manner ever witnessed in the history of the Turkish Republic, despite the fact that they had been supportive of the AKP's democratic program in Turkey from its formation in 2002 until 2012. In the specific context of Turkey, the lack of autonomy of the bourgeoisie, the strong internal fragmentation of Turkish society along ethnic, sectarian, and ideological lines, the highly personalized/egoistic nature of politics, and the collective imagination of the state as "sacred institution" have provided additional impetus to the Erdoğan regime to deal harshly with the Gülen Movement and all institutions, volunteers, and business houses—whether small, medium or big—perceived to be associated with the Movement. In part, Erdogan's crackdown on Hizmet Movement is linked with his ambition of securing his "unfettered Islamicist Sultanic rule" without any internal and external constrains. Thus since 2012 onwards the Erdoğan regime started marginalizing the Hizmet Movement—the most powerful moral and ethical force and civil society actor—internally and externally moved away from adhering to Copenhagen criteria of securing membership in European Union, which he himself once championed between 2002-2012, in order to free himself from democratic pressure of European Union. Moreover as the institutionalization of Erdoğanism is linked with de-Kemalisation of Turkey, the process of which is very much under way, the "parallel structure" and "FETO," the two dysphemism for Hizmet, also served well in the hand of the Erdoğan regime to intensify the process of de-Kemalisation in the country.

It is noteworthy that the government has not backed its crackdown on Hizmet with any legal basis; nor has it come out with sufficient or convincing evidence of illegality committed by the individuals and institutions linked with the Movement that warrant the state's punitive action against them. This probably explains why the government decided to charge the Movement with being a "parallel structure" and a "terrorist outfit" (FETO), which would enable the government to crush the Movement violently without adhering to the existing national and international law on the subject. The fact that the government rejected the HDP's parliamentary resolution to constitute an investigation to identify the "parallel structure"[11] and has opted for parliamentary instead of judicial or independent national/international investigation of the corruption case[12] and the failed military coup[13] speaks volumes about the bad intentions and illegal and undemocratic practices of the government.

On the other hand, the Movement categorically denies any role in exposing the December 2013 corruption scandal and in the failed military coup of July 15, 2016. Gülen has demanded the setting up of an international commission to uncover the truth behind these developments and categorically stated that he will return to Turkey if such a commission finds he had even the slightest involvement in these incidents.[14] The Movement has avoided the temptation of launching a political party despite having a considerable social base to do so, as it has long held that politics has an inherent tendency to corrupt Islamic values. It has also eschewed any political role in terms of "direct political opposition" to successive regimes, except in terms of "guiding the political" without directly participating in the political. It is due to this nuanced, fuzzy engagement of the Movement with the "field of the political" that the question remains "what is the nature of 'political' in the Gülen Movement"? How is the political informed and understood in the Movement? What is Gülen's articulation of the political?

In conventional scholarship, the "political" in Islamic movements has been mostly derived from two dominant frameworks of understanding: state-centered Islamic discourse and society-centered Islamic discourse. In the former model, an Islamic movement is primarily concerned with the theorization of the state in an Islamic frame and securing the state either through peaceful democratic means (elections) or through undemocratic, violent means (such as military coup or armed struggle) with a view to Islamizing the society. In the latter model, the Islamic movement is primarily concerned with a gradual Islamization of Muslim society that will eventually lead to the development of a just Islamic rule or state. The Gülen Movement does not fit either of these understandings of Islamic movement.

While Islamic political movements such as Hasan al-Banna's Muslim Brotherhood, Maulana Maududi's Jammat-e-Islami and a host of Islamic militant organizations have been analyzed within the state-centered model of Islamic movements, Islamic social movements such as Tablighi[15] and the Gülen Movement have broadly been placed in the latter, society-centered, model of the movement, notwithstanding a mountain of differences between the two, which is not being elaborated here due to constraints of space. Ali Bulaç has constructed three Islamic models on the basis of his conception of Muslimhood—political Muslimhood, cultural Muslimhood, and intellectual Muslimhood—which roughly belong to the two models of Islamic movement referred to above.[16] Operating within this bipolar structure of Islamic movements, Bulaç and many others commit the mistake of drawing a parallel between the Gülen Movement and the Muslim Brotherhood. Similarly, many others see a parallel between the Gülen Movement and Tablighi Jamaat. The paradox here is that the Gülen Movement simultaneously becomes a "political" Muslim Brotherhood and an "apolitical" Tablighi movement. Part of the reason for this paradox lies in the very conceptualization of "political" in the Gülen Movement, which on the one hand rejects the "party-power politics" of the Muslim Brotherhood and on the other the "politics of withdrawal" of Tablighi Jamaat, yet participates in the political affairs of the country in a peaceful and non-confrontational manner. The Movement is neither political (a tendency that deals with power-politics), nor non-political (conscious withdrawal from politics), nor apolitical (indifference to politics), nor anti-political (against politics in any form). From this point of view, the political in the Hizmet Movement is confined to influencing the political process and public policies through various agencies such as media and other formal and informal networks.

In holistic terms, the issue of the political in Gülen's philosophy flows from his organic conception of Islam in which the parts of Islam are internally related to each other in a coherent manner so as to establish harmony among the various aspects of human life. Hence, Islam is bound to influence the political aspect of human life too. From this point of view, the political in the Gülen Movement emanates from its normative vision of Islam geared towards the moral-ethical-social transformation of society. To this extent, all religio-social movements are political in nature, which in part flows from their normative understanding of social change. The notion of a "golden generation" in the Gülen Movement is a discourse that aims at providing leadership to humanity, particularly the Muslim community, in all walks of life in order to achieve the goal of an Islam-led virtuous society. However, the nature of the political in Gülen's Islamic discourse is fundamentally different from all shades of

Islamic modernism: radical Islamism, liberal Islamism, and apolitical Islamism.

Thus, unlike radical Islamism, Gülen neither advocates the fusion of religion and politics nor, like liberal Islamism, endorses the principle of separation of religion and politics. In the former case he highlights the danger to Islam which ensues from the mixing of religion and politics. In his understanding, politicized religion has an inherent tendency to harm religion more than politics: politicizing religion ultimately does more damage, and does it more quickly, to religion than to the state.[17] This happens because an ideological understanding of religion, as in Islamism, not only serves sectarian interests but reduces religion to a political means to secure political objectives: state power, influence, political competition, money, and so on. Modern-day Islamist politics exhibits this instrumentalization of Islam for secular goals. In the process religion or Islam loses its moral and ethical principles and meanings and hence ceases to be religion or Islam. It is in this sense that Fazlur Rahman, the late celebrated Pakistani Islamic scholar, after surveying the relationship between Islam and politics in modern times, bitterly remarked, "instead of politics serving Islam, Islam has come to serve politics."[18]

On the other hand, politics, bereft of any of the moral and ethical regulations enshrined in the religious system, becomes an immoral phenomenon and in the process, has caused and continues to cause untold human misery, civil strife, violence, and destruction. The history of modernity with its separation of religion and politics testifies to this destructive facet of modern life as epitomized by the phenomena of colonization, holocaust, and countless inter-ethnic, interreligious, and inter-state wars. Hence, Gülen, like Gandhi, envisions a political space or act of the political or politics regulated by internal moral and ethical forces. It is only through such a mechanism that politics can be self-disciplined and be made accountable to the human life-process.

Similarly, the Gülen Movement fundamentally differs from the Tablighi model of the "politics of withdrawal" (a sort of apolitical Islamism) under which Muslims consciously withdraw from engaging in this world for the sake of "spiritualizing" or "Islamizing" themselves in order to attain God's pleasure in the next world. Thus, in the Tablighi model of Islam there appears to be a sharp demarcation between this world and the other world with the eventual consequence that Islam becomes primarily a discourse of the other world and not for this world. Gülen rejects such a demarcation, and while asserting the interconnectedness of both worlds, he stresses the primacy of the temporal life in Islam:

> One of the most important aspects of Islamic thought is its affirmation of the temporal life, which other philosophies too often treat with scorn. Islam prefers to relate every aspect of this world to God, envisioning this world as an enviable courtyard of the Hereafter. In this sense, the world can be viewed as a field ready for cultivation or a harbor at the boundary of the world to come.[19]

It is this conceptualization of Islam, unlike the Tablighi model, which has motivated Muslim volunteers in the Gülen Movement to unleash public action in various fields of life: education, dialogue, health, media, relief, and so on.

Thus, having rejected three models of interaction between religion and politics—fusion, separation, and withdrawal—Gülen subscribes to the functional autonomy of religion and state. In subscribing to this relationship between religion and state, Gülen is guided by the conception of Islam in which the secular is very much a part of the Islamic imagination of the life process as well as by the historical pattern of relationship between Islam and state in Muslim societies. In fact, secularism in terms of functional, if not legal, (which is at best a myth) separation of religion and politics[20] has historically been a part of the Islamic tradition of political governance in much of Islamic history.[21] In fact, contrary to popular perception, the functional separation between the two has existed since the inception of Islam. The perception of the doctrinal unity of religion and politics in Islam has been built by Orientalist historiography—both Western and Islamic varieties—which is derived from two non-Qur'anic sources: (a) the emphasis on Islam as ideological entity, and (b) the model of Prophet Muhammad that combined both roles.[22] Part of the doctrinal unity of religion and politics in Islam has also been reinforced by the dominant narratives in the West that conflate the *'ulama* with the institution of clergy. However, there is no institution of Church-clergy in Islam. Neither is the *'ulama* a monolithic entity; on the contrary, it is a decentralized entity marked by ideological, class, and sectarian cleavages. An *'alim* (member of the *'ulama*) could be a businessman, doctor, engineer, administrator, judge, and so on. In fact, Eickelman has lamented the absence of centralized religious authority in Islam and considers its absence a hindrance to democratic reform in Muslim societies: "When one begins to contemplate the idea of an 'Islamic Reformation,' we find that there exists no centralized religious authority either to lead such an effort or to serve as its target—no 'church,' in other words, to undertake reform or to be reformed."[23] The sociology of the *'ulama*, if not Islam, remains a neglected field of study in modern scholarship and the simplified reading of *'ulama* as the equivalent of Church or clergy has harmed understanding of Islam and Islamic traditions more than it has yielded any positive results. The current wave of Islamic movements—whether in the form of political Islam including militancy and terrorism or social Islam—is a pointer to the limitations of the framework of modernity in grasping and grappling with the reality of Islam and Islamic traditions.

Moreover, there are hardly any Qur'anic injunctions to support the indivisibility of religion and politics in Islam. In this context Gülen strongly underlines that "the Qur'an should not be reduced to the level of political discourse, nor should it be considered a book about political theories or forms of state."[24] He further states, "Islam establishes fundamental principles that orient a government's general character, leaving it to the people to choose the type and form of government according to time and circumstances."[25] While the religious commandments of Prophet Muhammad are infallible as they were and are part of revelation, many other decisions he took in his personal capacity and subsequently reviewed in consultation with his Companions. According to a Hadith, or what is known as the "date–tree tradition" in Islamic history, when the Prophet saw farmers who were trying to fertilize date trees he said he did not believe that would have any real effect, meaning that God is the only One with real influence over His creation. But the farmers took this as an advice and gave up on their fertilization. Eventually, they did not have the yield they were expecting. Upon this, the Prophet said, "I am only human. If I command something related to religion, then obey, but if I order you to do something on the basis of my opinion (*ray*), then I am only a human being."[26]

Certainly, Islam is a holistic creed, but its role is more to provide guidance for human life in different situations, roles, and conditions, as demonstrated in the Prophet's exemplary conduct and much of Islamic history, than to convey a fixed set of ideological principles; only the essential religious commandments clearly stated in the Qur'an are to be applied uniformly to all times and conditions. After all, Islam never developed theocracy, as happened in Christian medieval Europe. Though Islam has co-existed with states in various forms, ranging from the classical varieties like the Caliphate and Office of Sheikh ul-Islam in the Ottoman Empire to modern varieties like the Saudi-Wahhabi nexus in the Kingdom of Saudi Arabia, the institution of Velayat-e-Faqih in the contemporary Islamic Republic of Iran, Al-Azhar in Egypt, Al-Zaytuna in Tunisia and the institution of the Diyanet in "modern" Turkey, all reflect a variety of types of Islam-state relationship in the annals of Islamic political history, but not theocracy.

The secular aspect of political governance has historically been part of Islamic public reasoning, and the functional separation between religion and politics has been best exemplified in the Ottoman tradition of a separate civil (*kanun*) and *sharia* code. Hence, the modern idea of secularism in terms of the functional autonomy of religion and politics from each other was not a "new experience" for Muslim subjects, particularly in republican Turkey. What was and is "new" and "frightening" in the modern discourse of secularism for the Muslim subjects was not the issue of political governance on the basis of the principle of functional secularism but its modern thrust of *being anti-religion* (particularly in the Turkish context) and proposing secularism as "a way of life" without which one cannot become "modern." A great majority of Turkish Muslims therefore did not accept or internalize the Kemalist secular prescription of the "good life" at the level of self and continue to factor Islam or Muslimness into their social life.[27] Moreover, what has gone in the name of secularism and nationalism in most Muslim nations is neither the separation nor the functional autonomy of religion and politics but the state's ruthless domination and control over religious institutions and resources, which partly comes from the radical discourse of modernity that locates in religion a source of threat to the secular order. However, it may also be noted that all efforts of previous Muslim empires and present-day Muslim states to "officialize," "nationalize" or "institutionalize" Islam have met with little success. Similar attempts of many Western European governments to impose a "national representative body" upon their respective Muslim populations have also failed to achieve any positive results. The legitimacy of such processes has always been suspected among Muslims, as testified by the periodic recurrence of Islamic movements in diverse forms and orientations.

It is from within the historical tradition of Islam that Gülen considers the state primarily as a secular entity or a human construct for the purpose of governance within which the role of religion has historically been confined to the arena of informal consultation and advice. It appears that Gülen visualizes the Islam-state relationship not as a formalized or institutionalized relationship, but as this *liminal* form of relationship between Islam and state that has historically existed, in which Islam as "system of guidance" fulfils its voluntary duty to guide (that includes critique) state actions from legal, moral and ethical perspectives. Ahmet Kurucan, a theologian considered to be one of the leading interpreters of Gülen's views from an Islamic perspective, underlines this liminal conception of the political embedded in Gülen's Islamic discourse. According to him, Gülen represents a historical chain of Muslim scholars within which he belongs to the realm of the "Sultan of *'alim*," unlike the realm of the "*'alim* of Sultan" that has mostly been concerned with discourse on the Islamic legitimation of the state's action. Arguing from this perspective, he highlights three aspects of the "political" embedded in Gülen's integrated holistic thinking, which are typical of the tradition of the "Sultan of *'alim*": (a) a safe distance between themselves and politics, however much they are concerned with the result of politics. This instance of Gülen was also affirmed by another student of Gülen, who underlined Gülen's approach to politics as "a principled distance from all political parties but remaining engaged with the problems of Turkish society"[28]; (b) they carry the discourse above politics without expecting any governmental position so that they are engaged with the normative ideals of state governance without directly participating in the political affairs of the state; and (c) these "Sultans of *'alim*" speak about the "affairs of state" in the public interest according to their conscience and can go against the state's actions if the latter harms the public interest.[29]

For this reason, according to Kurucan,[30] Gülen differs from the pervasive Islamic understanding of the two Sunni Islamic dicta of "Obey God, obey the Messenger of God, and those in authority" and "bad government is better than no government" and insists that "(i)n Islam, ruling means a mutual contract between the ruler and the subject and it takes its legitimacy from the rule of law, and from the principle of the superiority of the law."[31] It appears that the formulation of the "political" in Gülen's thought comes from the Naqshbandi Sufi tradition, particularly as developed by Imam Rabbani and Khalid al-Baghdadi, that believes in cultivating a personal relationship with members of the elite, including the political elite, extending support, and influencing the ruler of the day in the interest of Islam and the community without directly participating in the affairs of government or expecting any favor from the government.[32]

But what is the notion of political opposition in Gülen's Islamic thinking? Kurucan[33] argues that there are three kinds of "Islamic opposition": (a) *sabr* (patience), (b) *tamkeen* (prudence), and (c) *khuruj* (revolution). Gülen subscribes to the first two and based on these two principles advocates the method of "passive resistance" to oppose illegal state actions. In this context, Kurucan, while highlighting Gülen's conception of Islamic opposition, stresses the distinction between the notions of civil disobedience and passive resistance in order to demonstrate the legal sensitivity of Gülen's Islamic thinking. Thus, according to him, in passive resistance one continues to offer internal moral-social opposition without violating the law, in civil disobedience laws are violated. Recognizing the role of the political in the Gülen Movement, İhsan Yılmaz also underlines the peaceful and non-violent form of political participation and opposition by the Gülen Movement when he states that "the Movement is against the notion of political injustice but *opposes* the politics of the street."[34]

The above Islamic understanding of the relationship between religion and state requires respect and recognition for each other's autonomy, which has totally collapsed in modern politics and the modern state system. It is for this reason, and speaking from within Islamic tradition, that Gülen demands the restoration of the functional autonomy of religion from the state, something that prevailed during most periods of Islamic history. Moreover, according to Gülen, this functional autonomy of religion is a necessity for the democratic functioning of the state. Thus, in Gülen's discourse, particularly within the Turkish context, more than anything it is the recognition of the principle of religious freedom, broadly envisioned within the framework of human rights, that qualifies a state as democratic. It may be noted that all the political reforms that the Gülen Movement within Turkey has supported since the mid-1990s have implications for extending the realm of religious freedom and human rights.

Hence, Gülen does not see any contradiction between Islam and democracy and unlike many Islamic scholars and theologians he does not indulge in the Islamic legitimation of democracy. For him, as an ideal, both Islam and democracy uphold the principles of rule of law, religious freedom, equality, accountability, transparency, human rights, political obligation, and justice. For Gülen, democracy becomes an ethical issue, which is closely linked with his understanding of religion in general and Islamic faith in particular. Thus, for him, politics is an ethical-normative value: "those who understand politics as political parties, propaganda, elections, and the struggle for power are mistaken. Politics is the art of management, based on a broad perspective of today, tomorrow, and the day after, that seeks the people's satisfaction and God's approval."[35] Mustafa Yeşil also argues the same: "Democracy as political arrangement should not only provide material satisfaction but spiritual satisfaction too."[36] The recent authoritarian turn in Turkey only confirm a fragile nature of democratic experiment in Turkey and a limit to the coexistence of Islamism and democracy,[37] if not Islam and democracy.

Gülen's conception of Islam focuses on tolerance, compassion, peaceful coexistence, and mutual harmony, which in turn demands the annihilation of "self" and "other" in one's self, leading to the construction of a humane and democratic personality. It is through the internalization of ethical Islam that one exhibits democratic behavior and values vis-à-vis the other—whether individual, community or state. It is from this point of view that Gülen declares that "*moderate interpretation of Islam and democracy meet each other*." However, he also maintains that the contentious issue of comparison between Islam and democracy is unwarranted; Islam as religion belongs to the domain of God, whereas democracy is a political doctrine and a human system of governance.

In fact, Gülen considers democracy a "process," ever-evolving, and not a self-contained ideological project to be pursued:

> Just as [democracy] has gone through many different stages, it will continue to go through other stages in the future to improve itself. Along the way, it will be shaped into a more humane and just sys-

tem, one based on righteousness and reality.... Islamic principles of equality, tolerance, and justice can help it to do just that.[38]

This partly explains why Gülen considers "consultation" the most important democratic value and a criterion to be recognized as a "full and perfect Muslim" and a "believing society." He devotes a full chapter to explaining the significance of the Qur'anic verse on Consultation for building a democratic society and state as well as for the future of Islam but does not, unlike the majority of late nineteenth-century modernist Islamic reformers, interpret the Islamic doctrines of *shura* (consultation), *ijma* (consensus), *qiyas* (analogy), and *maslaha* (public interest) as an Islamic basis for constructing representative democratic institutions.[39] Echoing this sentiment, Mustafa Yeşil, the President of Journalists and Writers Foundation, stated, "Islam endorses the idea of democracy but not necessarily representative institutions of democracy."[40] In the same breath he further remarked, "the benefits that come through democracy are more important than representative democratic administration." He further stated that, "only 3% of Islam [meaning the Qur'an] deals with matters of administration. It leaves the matters of administration in the people's hand. The '*ulama* never focused on the institution of democracy. They were mostly concerned with the issue of governance based on the principle of social justice."[41] Ahmet Kurucan concurs with Mustafa Yeşil that "Islamic history lacks the institutionalization of democracy."[42]

A part of the reason for the lack of serious engagement with the "democratization of polity," if not democracy, is due to the fact that the discourse of Gülen Movement is society—or community—and not state-centered. As a matter of fact, traditionally speaking, state and government have not been an object of speculation for Islamic theology, philosophy, or jurisprudence on account of the Islamic doctrine of *Hakimiyya* or the Sovereignty of God that excluded any serious engagement with the notion of political authority as God symbolizes all forms of authority in the Islamic imagination.[43] In this regard Şerif Mardin has rightly noted, "Islamic societies and their theoreticians had a tendency to see the state as an extension of the religious community, existing for the protection of the community. The emphasis was on the life of the community, not on the life of the state."[44] However, the colonial encounter and later dismemberment of the Muslim empire did bring "state" as an object of discourse in Muslim thinking, as reflected in the development of Islamic modernism in the late nineteenth and mid-twentieth century and political Islam in the latter half of the twentieth century, but it did not replace the "community" as central focus of Islamic discourses; rather, it reinforced it. Many theologians came to realize that the state is not a reliable partner to protect the community and Islam. Even if the state is a permanent entity, it cannot be relied upon due to its shifting orientations—secular, socialist, republican—in modern times. On the contrary, a strong community has greater leverage to influence the state and government even if the latter is not a neutral entity. Darul Uloom Deoband and Tablighi Jamaat in India were founded on such conceptions. Gülen in recent years has also moved from his former position that a strong state is needed for the protection of Islam and now advocates the necessity of strong, rich community for the preservation and promotion of Islam. Referring to his experience of living in the United States and visiting European countries, Gülen said,

> I realized the virtues and the role of religion in these societies. Islam flourishes in America and Europe much better than in many Muslim countries. This means freedom and the rule of law are necessary for personal Islam. *Moreover, Islam does not need the state to survive, but rather needs educated and financially rich communities to flourish. In a way, not the state but rather community is needed under a full democratic system*[45] (emphasis mine).

Society or community in the Islamic imagination is considered as a network of individuals in inter-personal relationships, and not a mechanical aggregate of individuals.[46] Therefore, an Islamic ethical and moral transformation of society, community, and individual—the focus and objective of all revivalist movements including Gülen Movement—would automatically bring positive change in the functioning of the state. In other words, an administration manned by good and moral individuals would provide good administration. Hence, it is not the nature of the state but the character of the individual who is heading the state, which is more important. In reply to a question about what value he ascribes to the state Gülen stated,

> Although the constitution and laws have some importance of their own in a good or bad administration, the real factor always lies in

> the administrators themselves. All problems begin and end with the human being. Thus, if the state is run by good people, it will be good. If it is administered by even better people, it will be even better. If it is administered by the Rightly Guided Caliphs, it will be perfect. But if now there are no such caliphs and the state is being run by the current administrators, it is better to approach the matter from the viewpoint that it is better to have this state than none at all... Of course, at the head of state I would prefer someone like Abu Bakr [the Prophet's first political successor], who is moral, virtuous, and evolved; whose purpose is to ensure the nation's continuation and life; who thinks not his own interest but only of the nation's welfare.[47]

In a later book, he says, "The state is like the captain on the bridge of the ship, whose crew is made of merits, virtues and morality."[48] In a more recent statement he reiterated the same: 'In my humble opinion, building peace means building the peace loving man. Unless man is not placed at the centre of the solution to the problems that emerged in and from the man, investing in political and legal systems will remain a waste of time and resources."[49]

Thus, what is clear from the above passage is that for Gülen it is not the "system of governance" (democracy, monarchy, republic, military, etc.) but the quality of the individuals in the office, which is the determining factor in governance: "According to different circumstances and eras, the conduct and the composition of the consultative committee might change, but the qualification and the attributes of those select people, such as people from knowledge, justice, social education and experience, wisdom, and sagacity, must never change."[50] This non-structural understanding of state and administration partly also explains the premium that Gülen places on the creation of a "golden generation" that will exemplify the "Muhammadi ethics" in all aspects of life and its presence in every institutions, field and sphere of society and state.

This probably explains apolitical outlook of Gülen towards Kemalist state in Turkey. Although Gülen had praise for Kemal Atatürk, the founder of the modern Turkish Republic, for saving the nation from disintegration, he remained silent on the functioning of the Kemalist state—neither supporting nor criticizing. The focus of the Gülen

Movement is the individual–centered discourse of human rights and civil liberty, not the state-centered discourse of political reform. The issue of democratization, political participation, and civil society in the discourses of the Gülen Movement is at best a derivative one. In this context, Berna Turam rightly remarked, "The Islamic networks of both the Gülen Movement and of the AKP have facilitated democratization not deliberately through their presumably pro-democratic projects but mostly accidentally."[51]

It is within the above derivative framework of "political" and "democratization" that Gülen's Islamic discourse of education, interfaith, intercultural dialogue, tolerance, compassion and service ethics has played a significant role in advancing the democratic space within Turkey, which is currently contracting due to the series of anti-democratic measures undertaken by the Erdoğan-led AKP government since 2013 in order to fight allegations of corruption as well as to institutionalize Erdoğan's personal rule. However, it should be made clear here that the notion of democratic space is only applicable to the realm of civil society without any serious implications for the democratization of Turkish polity. In fact, Gülen and the volunteers in the Gülen Movement have nothing to do with the larger issue of the "democratization" of Turkish polity. As the Movement is individual-, community-, and society-centered, it lacks any focus on the democratization of the state. By "democratization of polity" I do not mean merely political reform, which is indeed a significant aspect of the democratization of the state, but the development and institutionalization of a critical political culture and right discourses that shape and condition the behavior of the state towards the issue of governance. The Movement did strengthen civil society institutions and the building of democratic public opinion through the instrument of its media houses, Journalists and Writers Foundation, and Abant Platform, but did not develop critical discourses within the frame of Islam that challenged the "sacredness" of the Turkish state and its image of a historically constructed "father figure." It is this failure that partly accounts for the resurrection of an authoritarian structure of governance since December 2013 after a decade of democratic experiment by the Erdoğan-led AKP government without any serious opposition from the Turkish civil society sector. Not surprisingly, Fatih Demiröz has linked the return of authoritarianism under the AKP order with the absence of demands for the democratic functioning of the state in society:

> The political culture in the country acknowledges the state as a sacred authoritarian figure that needs to be protected (even from its own people). This image of the state eliminates protests against illegitimate state actions (e.g., clientelism, corruption, and discrimination against minorities).[52]

It is within the limited democratization of state polity in Turkey that the role of the Gülen Movement in expanding the democratic space was most visible in four inter-related socio-economic-political fields: the mobility of the marginalized Anatolian Muslim masses, political reform and the pluralization of the public sphere, majority-minority relationships, and the advancement of women.

Upward mobility of Anatolian Muslims

Any serious observer of the recent democratic transformation of Turkey would have noticed the upward rise of a good number of Anatolian Muslims. The success story of those called the "Anatolian Tigers" has been rightly traced to the economic liberalization program of the Turgut Özal government in the mid-1980s, which continued and intensified under the Erdoğan-led AKP government. The free-market economic process helped the development of "Islamic entrepreneurship" in Turkey, which emerged from provincial Anatolian cities such as Kayseri, Sivas, and Gaziantep. With the influx of capital from the Arab region and the mobilization of the savings of the Turkish diaspora, particularly in Europe, "green" or "Islamic" capital was invested first in the banking and tourism sectors. Gradually, their economic activities diversified and today, the Anatolian Tigers play a role in almost all modern economic sectors from manufacturing to commerce and the service sector. A large number of Muslim companies emerged that were able to establish themselves on the world market as producers and suppliers of export of goods in the textile, leather, construction, and engineering industries. The backbone of this new bourgeoisie is Muslim academics, family businesses, and small to medium-sized companies.

The growing economic strength of Muslim entrepreneurship was given an organized shape in the form of MÜSİAD (Müstakil Sanayici ve Işadamları Derneği – the Foundation of Independent Industrialists and Businessmen), TUSKON (Confederation of Businessmen and Industrialists of Turkey), representing small and medium-sized Islamic businesses and İŞHAD (Business Life Co-operation Association) representing large-scale businesses. TUSKON and İŞHAD were linked directly with the Gülen Movement. These associations have been formed in order to influence the Turkish state in their own interest and break the monopoly of TÜSİAD (Association of Turkish Industrialists and Businessmen - TÜSİAD)—the confederation of secularist business groups that had hitherto enjoyed the direct patronage of the Kemalist state. MÜSİAD had a membership of 2,600 companies in 2006, accounting for 12 percent of Turkey's gross national product.[53] Before its illegal take over by the Turkish government in the wake of 15th July failed military coup 2016, TUSKON had 55,000 members, organized 19 world trade summits and hosted 40,000 domestic and 30,000 foreign businessmen and industrialists with a trade volume of $30 billion between 2006 and 2013.[54]

The business associations' biggest achievement is having turned Islam into a strategic resource for strengthening their own identity, promoting networking among members and lobbying for their own interests with state authorities. These associations work as NGOs (non-governmental organizations) and aim to provide a suitable environment to unite the Turkish private business sector and stress the importance of cooperation, trust, and ethics. They arrange business trips all over the world to seek new opportunities for Turkish entrepreneurs. The businesspeople of these associations also finance the educational institutions of the Gülen Movement, considering it a social (or, in a sense, a religious) responsibility.

Behind this economic growth of the Muslim entrepreneur class lie five interrelated factors. The first is the diffusion of industrialization to provincial Anatolian towns and the rapid urban growth associated with the emergence of new metropolitan towns such as Kayseri, Sivas, and Gaziantep in addition to the older established cities of Izmir, Istanbul, and Ankara. Second, city economies gradually transformed with small and medium-sized enterprises (SMEs) integrated into regional and world markets. In 2011, SMEs contributed 60.1 percent to total exports.[55] This transformation process has resulted in the emergence of new urban classes, which combine capitalist practices with strong rural and religious ties. Third, in order to manage these emerging provincial metropolises, the process of political decentralization was initiated. The rapid increase in the number of municipal administrations has been dramatic. In 1929, there were only 467 municipalities. This number rose to 546 in 1947, then to over 1,700 in 1977 and reached 3,215 in 1998.[56] Fourth, the dominant Muslim political formations, such as the Erbakan-led Milli Görüş, MSP-Refah-Saadet Party, or the Erdoğan-led AKP party, extended political support to this class both to undermine the hegemony of the Kemalist and secularized "White Turks" and to expand and consolidate their Muslim social base.

Fifth, and perhaps most important, the Gülen Movement provided an "Islamic motivational structure" to the emerging Muslim bourgeoisie in particular and Muslims in general to compete and interact with the modern global structure. Gülen's Islamic discourse of education, dialogue, compassion, hard work, trust, solidarity, honesty, fairness, equity, and service ethics—mostly drawn from reference to the Islamic past, including the Ottoman Empire—provided strong motivation and self-discipline for the accumulation of wealth and productive investment and the equitable distribution of wealth in society and led to a belief that strengthening of the Islamic faith could ensure the progress of the Turkish state and economy.[57] As the Turkish economy grew—partly on account of its increasing exports to Central Asia, Russia, the Middle East and North Africa, Europe and Africa during the 1990s and much of the 2000s—the association between strong Islamic faith and economic development grew firmer and helped the Gülen Movement to become global with its expanding network of educational institutions, publishing houses, media outlets, and dialogue centers, which in turn also provided employment opportunities to thousands of volunteers and made them more visible in both the Turkish and international public sphere.

Political reform, pluralization, and relationship with the AKP

The emergence of a Muslim bourgeoisie, along with new global consumption patterns, led to the proliferation of independent TV, radio, and newspaper outlets, which, in turn, blurred the boundary between local and transnational. Islamic movements, particularly the Gülen Movement, succeeded in establishing a series of educational institutions—schools, colleges, and universities—hospitals, radio and television channels, newspapers and many other social institutions. As a result, an Islamic public sphere formed as a counter or an alternative public to the state-regimented public by utilizing the global discourse of human rights and democracy. In this new public sphere, "Islam was reinterpreted to meet the needs of a free market economy, democracy, globalization, and the discourse on human rights."[58]

The gradual pluralization of the public also led to the decline of radical Kemalism (militant secularism and nationalism) and radical Islamism towards the end of the 1990s. Behind the decline of radical "isms"—whether nationalism, secularism or Islamism—lies a cognitive shift at the national level that took place in Turkey as a result of the interaction between mainstream Islamic movements and discourses such as the Gülen Movement and the new socio-economic conditions generated by the processes of liberalization and globalization. These Islamic movements and discourses share the vision of post-modernism and thus strengthen the process of democratization at the level of state and society. The post-modern features of Islamic movements in Turkey, particularly the Gülen Movement, were reflected in their being non-ideological and in their adoption of universal discourses such as human rights, cultural rights, democracy, tolerance, pluralism, and rule of law in order to protect and negotiate their demands with the Kemalist secular state.

In this context the Journalists and Writers Foundation, particularly its Abant Platform, played an important role in shaping the national political orientation towards political reforms and the consolidation of democratic rule in the country. The Abant Platform, named after Abant Lake in Turkey, was formed in 1998 by the Journalists and Writers Foundation as a forum for dialogue. Before being closed down by the Erdoğan regime in 2016, the Platform had been organizing an annual meeting of Turkish intellectuals, academicians, businesspeople, journalists, writers, political and cultural personalities from across the ideological spectrum and diverse faiths to discuss the contentious issues and challenges facing Turkey, both internal and external, and to issue a joint consensus communiqué or declaration, which was openly arrived through mutual debate and discussion. I myself participated in two Abant Meetings (2013,

2014) and witnessed the open deliberations and preparation of the final declaration through mutual negotiations, debates, and agreements over wordings of the resolutions. Among the topics that were regularly deliberated were "Islam and Secularism," "Islam and Democracy," "Pluralism," "War and Democracy," "The Kurdish Question," "Turkey and the European Union" and "New Constitutions."[59]

It was under this evolving national political consensus that the AKP managed to implement some significant political reforms leading to the consolidation of civil-democratic rule in modern Turkey between 2002 and 2012. The European Commission noted the progress made by the AKP government in this direction and observed the following:

> The 2011 elections took place in a generally peaceful atmosphere. For the first time, political parties and candidates were able to purchase broadcasting time for political advertisements. In March 2011, the Supreme Election Board (YSK) ruled that, while political parties and candidates will principally use Turkish in their advertising, use of other languages, including Kurdish, is possible. Various parties tried to target Kurdish voters by running election campaign advertisements on TRT 6, the first national Kurdish language TV station.
>
> The Supreme Military Council of August 2011 was a step towards greater civilian oversight of the armed forces. Civilian oversight of military expenditure was tightened and a revised National Security Plan adopted. Additionally, Supreme Military Council decisions were opened to civilian judicial review.
>
> There has been progress in the reform of the judiciary, notably with implementing the 2010 constitutional amendments. As regards the independence of the judiciary, a Law on the High Council of Judges and Prosecutors was adopted in December 2010. This law, together with the constitutional amendments approved by referendum in September 2010, established a new High Council that is more pluralistic and representative of the judiciary as a whole.
>
> As regards freedom of expression, the media and public continued debating openly and freely a wide range of topics perceived as sensitive, such as the Kurdish issue, minority rights, the Armenian

issue, and the role of the military. Opposition views are regularly expressed.

Concerning freedom of thought, conscience and religion, freedom of worship continues to be respected. Ecumenical Patriarch Bartholomew celebrated in August, for the second time after almost nine decades, the Divine Liturgy of the Dormition of Theotokos at the Soumela monastery in the Black Sea province of Trabzon. In September, the second religious service since 1915 was held at the Armenian Holy Cross church on the Akdamar Island in Lake Van. A Protestant church was opened officially in June in the city of Van in Eastern Turkey. Turkish authorities, including a Deputy Prime Minister, held a number of meetings with religious leaders of non-Muslim communities. This included a visit to the Ecumenical Patriarchate, the first visit by a high-ranking official since the 1950s.

The Ministry of National Education has prepared new religious education textbooks containing information on the Alevi faith, too. These are to be used as of the 2011–2012 school year.

Limited progress can be noted also on women's rights and gender equality. As noted earlier, the gender gap in primary education at national level has been virtually eliminated and the proportion of women in Parliament rose from approximately 9 percent to 14 percent of its membership after the 2011 elections.

As regards cultural rights, the law on the establishment and broadcasting principles of radio and TV stations entered into force in March 2011. It permits broadcasts in languages other than Turkish by all nationwide radio and television stations.[60]

The "democratic push" of the Gülen Movement has largely been looked upon from within the frame of political pragmatism, which is partly true. For Gülen, democracy is preferable, if not the ideal, among the all existing forms of governance because at least it guarantees freedom, including religious freedom. A democratic, neutral state with a strong civil society is desirable not only for the Gülen Movement but for all religious actors, movements, and organizations in contemporary Turkey as they see these as a powerful bulwark against the hostile Kemalist political and military establishment that remains strong notwithstanding the erosion in their legitimacy in recent years. It was from this perspective that the Gülen Movement advocated the implementation of the European Union's standards of democracy in Turkey and supported AKP rule from 2002 till 2012, until the AKP turned hostile to the Gülen Movement, accusing the latter of orchestrating the corruption cases to oust the government. As both had been victims in the past to the politics of the "deep state," their interests converged on the implementation of democratic political reforms within the European Union framework so as to weaken and eliminate the threat from the Kemalist and military establishment.

The "political" of the Gülen Movement has largely been understood in terms of its relationship with the AKP as mentioned in the beginning of this chapter. It does appear that the Movement had developed a close, functional relationship with the AKP government until their relationship sharply deteriorated in 2013. Reflecting on the general political orientation of the Movement, İhsan Yılmaz noted that "Hizmet provides issue-based support to [a] political party and government."[61] However, from many other sources, it appears the Movement not only provided electoral support to the AKP government but also defended AKP policies in the public sphere through their media houses on many issues, including the controversial Ergenekon trial in the interest of the democratic progress of the country.[62] As Veli Turan, another Hizmet volunteer working in India, pointed out, "Hizmet and AKP views converge on the 90% of all national issues, including the Ergenekon case."[63]

It may be noted here that this stance of Hizmet was in sync with many liberal democratic voices within Turkey as well as the position of the larger West including many European governments and the European Union which saw Ergenekon trial as a right step in the direction of democratization of Turkey's polity.

Another serious issue that polarized Turkey was Gezi protest.[64] It appears that Hizmet did not have a unified approach to this issue. As a result, though a good number of Hizmet volunteers opposed the AKP government in this matter, a substantial subsection of Hizmet volunteers as well as Hizmet media outlets were uncritical or indifferent about the government's crackdown on Gezi protestors. As Selahattin Selvi, a volunteer working in India, stated, "The Gezi protest [referring to the role of the Western media] has shown that Turkey does not have any friend in the world."[65]

It may be noted that the Movement tacitly supported the arrest of a good number of journalists, writers, and publishers by the AKP regime on the grounds that they were/are part of the "Ergenekon gang" or what is called the "Deep State" in Turkey. Berna Turam also demonstrated the close functional relationship between the Islamic movements, particularly the Gülen Movement and the Turkish state under the AKP, which has mostly revolved around issues concerning national loyalties, ethnic politics, gender politics, education, and international politics.[66] The closeness of the relationship between the two is further testified to by the fact that two volunteers of Gülen Movement were elected to the 2011 Turkish Parliament on the AKP ticket for the purposes of liaison between the AKP government and the Gülen Movement. The two members subsequently resigned from the AKP on account of AKP hostility towards the Gülen Movement.

It can be argued, yet with no credible proof, that one consequence of political cooperation between the AKP government and Hizmet was that Hizmet-inspired aspirants/volunteers had an opportunity to enter into various sectors of state administration including the police, army, and judiciary. Although there is no direct evidence to suggest that the AKP government favored or helped Hizmet volunteers to enter the state administration in the way that the present AKP government is "staffing" the state administration with pro-AKP loyalists en masse with utter disregard for considerations of merit since the December 17, 2013 corruption scandal period. However the fact that the government remained neutral and was not hostile towards Hizmet for considerable period of time, despite the 2004 military dominated National Security Council's decision (jointly signed by then-Prime Minister Erdoğan and President Gül) to draw up a plan of counter measures against Nur communities and the Gülen Movement,[67] proved beneficial to Hizmet people, who were better educationally equipped than many others in Turkish society to find a place in the state administration. As Ali Bulaç noted, "The AKP was not supporting the Gülen Movement but also not blocking them. The Movement found a safe and secure haven under AKP rule."[68] Ömer Çaha concurs, "The AKP government did not discriminate against members of the Gülen Movement."[69]

Nonetheless, it is plausible to argue that the Movement, utilizing the favorable political conditions, would have focused on motivating their volunteers/aspirant candidates to enter the state administration, including the police, judiciary, intelligence, and armed forces, both as a matter of legal right for Turkish "Black" Muslims, who had otherwise been discriminated against and excluded by the Kemalist system,[70] and to establish the credential of their educational institutions, particularly the coaching institutes, in the competitive market—the process of which led to a good presence of Hizmet inspired persons in the state system. It may be noted here that the police, judiciary, intelligence, and armed forces are the priority sectors for all aspiring students, as they constitute the most important source of upward mobility for citizens of Middle Eastern countries including Turkey.

Thus, from various informal sources it appears that while the Hizmet-inspired individuals did establish a good presence in the police and judiciary, however, the same cannot be said about the intelligence wing and military. Though the secular-Kemalist hold over these institutions were weakened during the Erdoğan regime; however, they remained a sufficiently Kemalist fort, until the failed military coup of July 2016, to prevent students from Hizmet-linked or educational institutions from entering in considerable numbers. On the other hand, the AKP, lacking qualified people also needed the support of Hizmet to run the state administration.

Majority-minority relations

One consequence of the de-ideologization of the Turkish political process, which was set in motion in the mid-1990s due to multiple factors including the military coup of 1980, the integration of Turkey into the globalized economic order, and Gülen's inclusive Islamic discourse, was the decline of the former deep distrust that has traditionally marked the relationships in Turkish politics and society between the members of the majority Sunni Muslim Turks and members of ethnic and religious minorities such as the Shia, Alevi, Kurdish, Jewish and Orthodox Christian communities. This trend was further strengthened by the Gülen Movement. The Movement helped in building a democratic political culture of dialogue, compromise, accommodation, reconciliation, and negotiation for the resolution of conflict with the Kemalist and post-Kemalist state and social groups. There is no doubt that the Movement has been the leading social force and voice in establishing channels of communication and dialogue with the members of religious and ethnic minority communities. In establishing dialogue with and addressing the fears and concerns of minority communities, Gülen underlined the Gandhian approach in which the moral responsibility lies with the majority community to instill confidence and trust in members of the minority community, so that the latter will feel safe to live with dignity and without being fearful of threats to their identity and culture from the majority community. A second implication of this approach is that both members of majority and minority communities can represent themselves in the political arena and thus create a political culture of trust and tolerance.

Although the Alevi community has remained suspicious of the Gülen Movement on account of its Sunni majoritarian roots and sees it as threat to its identity and culture, the Movement does not harbor any discriminatory attitude towards the community. Rather the Movement supports the Alevis' demands for legal recognition of its religious places of worship (*cemevi*). Further, one does encounter a good number of people with an Alevi identity working in the Gülen-inspired educational institutions, particularly in the university, and media houses. Gülen in person even proposed the idea of establishing joint Alevi and Sunni Muslim mosque and cemevi side by side in the same place as a mark of national reconciliation between the two communities. Towards this goal a site in Ankara was identified and an architectural plan was even prepared; however, the building works could not be started because of stiff resistance from extremist sections of the Alevi and Sunni Muslim communities. Further, the Abant Platform organized a conference in December 2013 on "Alevi-Sunni Dialogue"[71] in order to identify and solve the contentious issues between the two groups. The author was present at the Conference and witnessed the lively debates among journalists, intellectuals, academics, religious figures, business persons from across the spectrum belonging to both communities and a final joint communiqué which identified the "Turkish state" as the biggest source of fomenting trouble and conflict between the social groups and which called upon members of both communities to work together for the wider democratization of the Turkish society and state.

In recent years, the Gülen Movement has made tremendous progress in reaching out to the Kurdish community and reducing significantly the trust deficit between the Turkish and Kurdish community, despite stiff opposition from the PKK and the Turkish state. Political reform under the AKP government that recognizes the Kurdish community's cultural autonomy as an ethnic minority and allows it to run television and radio channels in the Kurdish language and give instruction in school in Kurdish further helped to increase trust between the two communities. In 2014, the government abolished the mandatory pledge that had all school children, including ethnic minorities, chant at school every morning, "I am a Turk—and happy is the one who says he is a Turk."

This measure along with gradual movement toward the official recognition of Kurdish identity, which was anathema in Turkish public life till the late 1990s, when Kurds were still referred as "Mountain Turks," has further helped to integrate the Kurdish community into mainstream public life in Turkey. However, behind the series of political reforms that recognize the Kurdish identity lie the sustained Islamic discourse of the Gülen Movement about pluralism, multiculturalism, equity and justice, tolerance, human rights, peace, and brotherhood. This discourse has spanned more than three decades and has advocated meeting the Copenhagen criteria in order to become a member of European Union. Hence, it has helped to modify Turkish-centered national public life so as to accept the identities of linguistic, cultural, and religious minorities. The Gülen Movement was the first Turkish social movement to openly accept the Kurdish identity within the Turkish nation.

The Movement started working in the Kurdish-dominated South Eastern region of Turkey as early as mid-1980s by opening examination preparatory centers in Diyarbakır and Urfa. By 2009, the overall number of Hizmet education institutions in Kurdish-populated provinces was 289, with 84,282 registered students.[72] The Movement also established a Kurdish TV channel called Dünya in 2011 and in 2014 Selahaddin Eyyubi University in Diyarbakır. Participants have founded 17 high schools and Ishik University in Northern Iraq (now commonly known as Kurdistan). The Movement also organized an Olympiad (a competitive language and culture event) in the Kurdish language in the pattern of its Turkish Olympiads.

In addition, a large number of Kurdish students are educated in

Hizmet-affiliated education institutions all over Turkey. Over the years the Movement has succeeded in attracting a large number of Kurdish volunteers to the extent that the Turkish-Kurdish social composition of the Movement has blurred the Turkish identity of Hizmet and helped to significantly reduce the social distance and cleavages between members of the Turkish community and members of the Kurdish community.

As the Movement was increasingly becoming a significant social force and voice in the Kurdish part of Turkey, it was being perceived as threatening the influence and social base of the Kurdish Workers' Party (PKK), an outlawed, communist outfit headed by Abdullah Öcalan, who is currently in prison. As a result, PKK has launched systematic attacks on Hizmet institutions and has even set fire to Hizmet schools. It is widely believed that during the Peace Process launched by the Erdoğan-led AKP government, the PKK demanded the closure of the Hizmet schools in the Kurdish region. While present conjunctures put Hizmet in a very difficult situation, as both the government and PKK are hostile to it, Gülen had nonetheless lent his personal support to the peace process by quoting from Qur'an that "there is benefit in peace" and adding that "sometimes nations might need to accept bitter peace agreements."[73]

Similarly, the Movement took concrete initiatives to initiate interfaith dialogue with religious head of the Jewish congregation in Turkey and with the head of the Orthodox Church within Turkey, the detailed reference to which has been made in the chapter on Interfaith Dialogue.

Advancement of women

The Gülen Movement has been the subject of severe criticism for promoting an Islamic conservative discourse that inherently unleashes the process of domestication of Muslim women and discourages them from entering public life. Thus dubbed "conservative" Gülen has been accused of pursuing a "segregation policy on gender" and confining women mostly to domestic sphere. While reflecting on the role of women in Hizmet (in America), Webb noted that

> the women almost universally wear headscarves (*hijab*), and many group activities are gender-segregated—women do not seem to occupy public and visible roles of authority, except over other women—and the result is a compelling appearance of inequality that

> most American women cannot accept.[74]

Ebaugh, an American sociologist, commented that

> the one area that is problematic in terms of the lack of modernization in the movement, in my opinion, are attitudes toward the role of women in the world...Women tend to be in the background performing the tasks of childcare, housekeeping, cooking, teaching in the schools and mosques, and deferring to their husbands in public arenas.[75]

Yavuz also concurs with Ebaugh's observation on the subordinate position of women in the Movement: "The role of women is still subordinated to men, and women are esteemed more as mothers of the next generation than they are as the intellectuals and political equals of men."[76] An academic with Fatih University, while sharing on the issue of gender relationships in the movement stated that, "In the Gülen Movement men talk to men, women talk to women, and children talk to children." Klas Grinell also came to the same conclusion: "I still find that Gülen speaks from a place of patriarchal heteronormativity. Even his views of women's rights and women's worth are conservative, and it is one of the topics where I find it most difficult to respect his opinions."[77]

However, the above criticism appears to be unfair and directed at highlighting the non-democratic character of Gülen and the Gülen Movement. These criticisms are grounded in the liberal, individualistic-libertarian-modern philosophy that tends to conceptualize "freedom" and "equality" in terms of one's inalienable right to "freedom of choice" and ability to control and direct one's destiny and life process. A cursory look at Gülen's discourse reveals that there is nothing in his writings and ideas that indicates a contradiction or even a dilution of this principle. In fact, Gülen espouses a more inclusive understanding of equality. He, unlike many modern scholars, does not prescribe a mechanical, color-blind understanding of equality. The mechanical equality of the sexes is one thing; the equal treatment as well as treating equally of the sexes is another. Gülen tends to endorse the latter position. Certainly, Gülen emphasizes a moral code of interaction between the sexes; free mixing between the sexes is disfavored, if not completely banned, and more emphasis is placed upon the family role of women because of two factors: (1) the commandments of Islam from the Qur'an and various

Hadiths, and (2) the extreme form of individualism and equality that took a heavy toll on the family structure in the West and has also started affecting the family structure in many parts of the world including Turkey. The issue of family disintegration globally led the Journalists and Writers Foundation (JWF) to organize an international conference on "The Family" in Antalya in 2010.

It is absurd that his emphasis on the role of women in family affairs so as to preserve family as the moral foundation of human society should be interpreted as confining women to domestic affairs. It may be noted that Gülen has never prevented girls and women from having access to modern education and participating in the opportunity structures of society. He neither restricts girls from seeking education in a particular discipline or category of subjects (like the Islamic Government of Iran in the first decade of Revolution), nor imposes any dress code for women.[78] In fact, Gülen has advised the girls to prefer education even at times when they face discrimination because of their headscarf. According to Gülen, the headscarf is not an essential feature (*usul*) of Islam and it should not be allowed to become an obstacle in the path of seeking an education.

From 1980s onwards there has emerged a booming market throughout the Muslim world in fashionable *hijab* and veil outfits that allows Muslim women to retain their Muslim identity while remaining presentable according to the demands of modern lifestyles. In this context, the Tekbir company in Turkey set this trend (*tesettür*) without any significant opposition from Islamic quarters including the Gülen Movement.[79] Along with the women's apparel industry, the hotel and resort industry came up with segregated women's and family swimming pools with modern facilities. In providing flexibility in lifestyles to women, Hizmet demonstrated its doctrinal flexibility in changing times and conditions without compromising the core values of the Islamic faith.

It is due to the efforts of Gülen and its associated educational institutions that the enrollment of girls in the school, college and university has tremendously increased in the Turkey. Mine Göğüş Tan has noted the rise in participation of Girls in educational field. According to her, "In the years between 1930 and 2004 the ratio of female students increased from 35.6 to 47.8 percent in primary education, and from 23.9 to 43.0 percent in secondary education, to catch up with the boys' ratios

(SIS 1995; MONE 2005).[80] The reform in 1997, which finally extended mandatory education from five to eight years seems to have given a stimulus to positive development in girls' enrolments. In the first three years following the reform, enrolment rates at primary school level increased by 18.5 percent for girls and 11.3 percent for boys.[81] But the most remarkable change was recorded at the level of higher education. The ratio of females at this level increased from 16.3 percent in 1930 to 41.9 percent in 2004."[82]

Though the author has not done any research into the role of the Gülen Movement in the increasing participation of girls in education, it is plausible to argue that since it is the conservative Anatolian Muslim family that was reluctant to send their daughters to educational institutions under the secular dispensation of Kemalist Turkey, they might have found in Gülen's discourse the means and legitimacy to send their daughters to the education institutions. The gradual relaxation of state policies under the AKP government allowing women who wear hijab to study at university, sit in public examinations, and finally serve in public institutions (now includes police, judiciary and army)[83] has further motivated young women to enroll in educational institutions.

Parents of Muslim girls felt more secure in sending their daughters to Hizmet educational institutions as they are considered morally upright institutions, unlike other governmental and non-governmental educational institutions. It is true that all Gülen-inspired schools in Turkey were single sex school until 1998, when a new government regulation made co-education mandatory in Turkey. Probably, Hizmet participants would prefer single-sex schools to co-educational schools, as evident from the token presence of girl students in predominantly boys' schools and vice-à-versa (required to meet the legal obligation), but this does not make Hizmet an undemocratic movement.[84]

It is a mistake to believe that Gülen advocates segregation of the sexes. What he advocates is separate but equal treatment of the sexes that demands a respectable distance, even in a working environment, in order to provide a sense of security and safety to women. Though "segregation" and "separation" have a similar meaning in terms of differentiation, they refer to different sets of conditions and practices and therefore should not be confused. Segregation implies a denial of opportunity and perpetuating inequality on the basis of the "principle of inferiority" (female, black, low-caste, lower class, etc.), whereas "separate" implies a "differential treatment" or what the Indian constitution has called "positive discrimination" with a view to enabling a particular group or class to exercise its right to equality and freedom.[85] Thus, whereas the notion of segregated treatment is discriminatory and exclusive, the notion of differential/separate treatment is inclusive, as the latter is based on the idea of equality that demands a favorable treatment keeping into consideration one's special circumstances.

While modernity and capitalism have pushed women into the public arena, the capitalist market and state institutions, irrespective of form, have remained insensitive to the issue of the safety and security of women, as these institutions themselves were built on the "invisible" notion of patriarchy. It is only recently that due to a greater awareness of women's rights and the sustained campaigns of feminist movements that governments and states have started addressing safety norms for women in the public arena. Therefore, the notion of equality for women demands an approach that goes beyond the mechanical equality of the sexes and advocates a more compassionate treatment of women in view of their special circumstances—physiological as well as social. After all men do not suffer from the menstruation cycle and its effects upon body and mind. This will sound patronizing and hence intended to perpetuate inequality in the name of protection and care and to deny the conditions and opportunity to make women independent and equal. Theoretically, the argument holds its ground, but it also seems an extreme understanding of individualism. Independence, freedom, and equality are actualized only in safe and secure conditions, and that certainly requires a more compassionate treatment in addition to public safety and security norms for women. Compassion thus becomes an enabling factor for women to realize their freedom and equality. This is what, I believe, comes out in many of the writings of Fethullah Gülen on women, which are derived from the Qur'anic position that states, "And for women are rights over men similar to those for men over women."[86] Thus, this compassionate view becomes a *right* of each upon the other, and is not merely men's obligation or patronization of women. Taking into consideration their special circumstances, women deserve more compassionate treatment by men than vice-à-versa.

Thus, a professor from Fatih University told me, "My wife had to go to Bosnia for a conference. I arranged the ticket and hotel booking through a Hizmet tourist agency because I trusted the agency to provide security for my wife."[87] Other girls echo this position, "Our parents allow us to work in Hizmet as they trust Hizmet."[88] The sense of safety and security led one young girl to state, "I prefer a segregated [meaning separate] floor at the work place. The idea of segregation gives me more security and freedom."[89] Another woman, stressing the safety dimension of segregation, stated, "Segregation is permissible in Islam, so I follow."[90] Yet another women interviewee remarked, "Yes, in Hizmet there is strong religious training that shapes the gender choices but there is no red line."[91] In fact, in my interviews with many women and girls, mostly with a high level of education and associated with the Gülen Movement, what comes out is that they perceive Hizmet as an *enabling* factor, rather than a constraining factor, in the exercise of their freedom. Many empirical and ethnographic studies on the role of the Movement in the development of women have also more or less argued this. Thus, Elisabeth Özdalga, on the basis of her interviews with three Hizmet-linked women, similarly concludes that despite the mooring of conservatism in the Movement, "there is room for self-reflexivity as well as for individual initiative and autonomy."[92] Jassal in her study on "upper-class women's *sohbet*" linked with the Gülen Movement found that *sohbet* constitutes a modern space that empowers women to realize their Islamic way of life in modern form and also ensures the collective participation of women in conceiving, raising money for and executing projects leading to empowerment of women.[93] Thus, in Jassal's study, Muslim women emerged as self-confident, autonomous agents able to shape their own life and destiny within the frame of their understanding of Islam in the light of Islamic sources as well as of Gülen's Islamic discourse. Similarly, Maria Curtis in a detailed empirical, ethnographic study of Hizmet women highlights the diverse roles of women and decisively rejects the thesis of the domestication of women in Hizmet. She aptly captures the nature of participation of women in the Movement:

> Their narratives offer a unique "women in the center" perspective rather than beginning from a "women at the margins" point of departure, and their modes of exchange seek to create new religious-cultural imageries rather than striving to reach established

> social ideals. GHM women thereby reject somewhat both Kemalist feminism and its calls for prescribed forms of civic engagements, as well as traditional Turkish women ideals that stress women's central place in the home.[94]

Over the years there has been growing participation of women in the Movement in various fields, including going abroad in the service of humanity for education and relief work, a process that has produced a good number of Hizmet-affiliated female teachers, journalists, doctors, engineers, etc. Women are on the Board of Trustees of the Journalists and Writers Foundation, the most important institutional face of the Gülen Movement. Certainly, there is a "dominance of the masculine voice in the present Hizmet Movement," as one women interviewee puts it, but it has more to do with the overwhelming presence of men and their social background than it is the product of any design or planning. As an ethical and moral discourse Hizmet tends to be relatively conservative in its social manifestation in comparison to Western liberalized sexual mores but this does not amount to segregation of the sexes but rather interaction of the sexes with a respectable distance. Moreover, the social conservatism of the Gülen Movement has a pragmatic side. Reflecting on the conservative orientation of the Gülen Movement on gender relations, one senior female volunteer of the Movement stated that the Movement is very conscientious about three aspects of its functioning: (1) male-female relationship, (2) matters related to money, and (3) trust. She believes that the Movement would like to remain "clean" in all these three aspects as the majority of socio-political movements and institutions in the world are vulnerable to these three temptations.[95]

CHAPTER 11

In Lieu of Conclusion

FUTURE CHALLENGES FOR THE MOVEMENT

What emerges from my analysis of the Gülen Movement is that in terms of its core functionaries and leadership, it is a die-hard, orthodox, Sunni Islamic movement drawing inspiration from Nursi and Gülen's interpretation of the Qur'an, Hadith, and Sunnah in general, and Ottoman-Islamic history in particular. The visible civic-social aspect or secularity of the Gülen Movement is at most a function of or an embedded part of Gülen's interpretation of the Islamic value system. In this book I have attempted to illuminate how the interplay of larger objective forces and processes (social, economic, and political) and subjective forces (the individuality and vision of Fethullah Gülen) shaped the emergence of the Gülen Movement in Turkey.

Unlike the late nineteenth- and twentieth-century model of Islamic reformism or modernism, the Gülen Movement does not indulge in the Islamic legitimation of modernity nor does it seek doctrinal compatibility between Islam and modernity. Rather, as shown in the preceding chapters, the Movement aspires to reproduce what it considers Islam's universal moral and ethical values and principles (such as trust, peace, love, friendship, social responsibility, hard work, honesty, legal sensibility, dialogue, cooperation, service ethics, ethical accountability, etc.) both in the private and public sphere.

It is from within the paradigm of Islam's universal ethical and moral discourse that the Gülen Movement seeks to engage with the forces, ideologies, and value system of modernity and selectively appropriates what has come to be identified as the values of modernity. Thus, the Movement endorses and promotes such modern values as universal human rights, individual rights, civil liberty, democratic forms of governance, tolerance, religious freedom, equality, and freedom which it considers part of Islam's universal values. For the same reason the Movement demonstrates a strong reservation about, if not outright rejection of, such modern political values or ideologies as individualism, secularism, and nationalism. To this extent, the Movement provides a moral and ethical critique of modernist-materialistic-individualized lifestyles and seeks to strike a balance between materialism and spirituality for the balanced growth of the individual and between the individual self- identity and the social self-identity as reflected in family, community, nation, and *umma*. The "rule of the golden mean" sums up Gülen's Islamic discourse, which is different from the Western projection of the Gülen Movement as "liberal" or "moderate" Islam. However, notwithstanding its emphasis on striking a balance, the Movement exhibits a strong preference for a collectivist value system over an individualized value system as a part of their "imagined good life."

In terms of its relationship with modernity, the issue of whether the Gülen Movement represents a liberal democratic trend is keenly debated among scholars. The critics normally see the liberal democratic positioning of the Gülen Movement in its championing of civil and political liberty, particularly within the Turkish context, as a "mask" and a pragmatic political choice due to its marginal representation in the power structure, which the Movement needed to build its social capital and social alliances and as a tool for political survival while operating within the secular-authoritarian political order. The critics suspect that with the achievement of dominance in the power structure, the Movement, like any Islamic movement, will abandon its liberal posturing and will return to its original, authoritarian Islamic moorings.

The fear is more palpable from the point of view of gender justice, where it is expected, particularly within the Turkish context, that the material gains that women achieved under the Kemalist modernization and secularization program would be lost under a hegemonic leadership of the Gülen Movement. The fear is not groundless considering the fact that women are considered a custodian of morality—both in the public and private realm in religious discourses and hence all religions including Islam—there is an inherent tendency to regulate, conscript and restrict women's action in the physical, social, economic, and political dimensions. On the other hand, several scholars have detected a secularizing process in Gülen's discourse of universal humanism. They expect that Gülen's humanistic discourse and actions will inevitably lead to weakening the faith and thus contributing to the process of secularization and democratization. This group of scholars also applies the Weberian thesis of Protestantism to the Movement.

However, as I have pointed out earlier in this work, these scholarly positions and debates on the Gülen Movement are totally misplaced as they evaluate the Gülen Movement from the perspective of the Western form of modernity, in which religion is imagined as a negative force unless it undergoes the process of secularization. This work has shown how the Gülen Movement empowers Muslim women, enhances their mobility in the public sphere, and ensures their relative autonomy. Further, there is no evidence of the weakening or dilution of the Islamic faith or the transfiguring of Islamic doctrines and principles leading to a more secularized conception of faith due to Gülen's Islamic emphasis on humanism. On the contrary one finds a strengthening of Islamic consciousness and a very strong observance of Islamic values in everyday life, a tendency that has only become stronger among its volunteers with the persecution of the Movement since December 2013.

The empirical reality of strong religious consciousness among the Movement volunteers and its advocacy of a secular, rather neutral, state has led some scholars to conceptualize the Gülen Movement in terms of the notion of "civic religion" and to draw a parallel between the Gülen Movement as a symbol of "Turkish Exceptionalism" and what is called "American Exceptionalism," which, unlike European varieties of modernity, embodies strong religiosity in society and strong secularity of the state. The comparison between the two is erroneous on several grounds, including the differences in the religious and political traditions of each country; however, what it does recognize is the strong religious element of the Gülen Movement with the desire to see Turkey moving in the direction of American Exceptionalism.

In this regard, this work implicitly also questions the pervasive thesis that the success of the Movement is due to its nationalist refashioning of Islam. In other words, the success is due to the packaging of Islam in nationalistic idiom and value as symbolized once by the official discourse of the Turkish-Islam synthesis. Turkey does have a strong nationalist tradition, but in Gülen's Islamic cosmology nation, Islam, community, universalism, and humanity are coterminous, overlapping terms without privileging one over another. In fact, Gülen addresses the problems and challenges of Turkey and offers solutions in terms of Islamic history. Further, most of my interviewees, as well as my observations, testify that for the volunteers the first marker of their self-identity is Muslim/Islam, followed by other identities. Similarly, this study debunks the growing trend of compartmentalizing the life of Gülen and the Gülen Movement into two periods: the Turkish-Islamo-nationalist phase till 1999 and the Islamo-Universalist phase after Gülen's move to the United States in 1999. Instead, it demonstrates the unity and continuity of moral thought and praxis with forward-looking approach in Gülen's Islamic discourse and actions.

In fact, the liberal democratic values that the Gülen Movement appears to represent flow from the variety of its social actions and practices, as well as from its moral and ethical mores. As an ethically oriented religio-social movement, it eschews the process of ideologization of social and political phenomena and rejects any categorization of itself or other with any kind of "ism" and thus contributes to the process of democratization of society and state without having any direct agenda or program for the same. The Abant Platform has not gone beyond building public opinion in favor of democratic governance. In fact, the Movement excludes the role of the "politics of street mobilization" in the democratic transformation of Turkish state and society, although it does contribute to a similar "political" process indirectly through its educational, media, and other institutions. As a result, the Movement has not developed the kind of critical discourses, which is needed to bring change in the social imagination that tends to see the Turkish state as "paternalistic Father Figure"—a collective imagination that helps the state to retain its authoritarian political culture. This partly explains why the Turkish state under the Erdoğan regime managed to portray the Movement as "anti-state, anti-national forces" in the wake of December 2013 corruption exposé and the failed military coup of July 15, 2016 and to forcefully crush it despite its history of good works and its pro-state and pro-nation outlook.

On the contrary, the Movement in its overall functioning, leadership and thought process tends to *promote a culture of conformism* within its rank and files and therefore lacks the requisite human resources and conceptual tools to advance the agenda of the democratization of state and society. Even when the Movement is facing an existential threat from the Erdoğan-led AKP government, one is struck at finding that volunteers are adopting an Islamic discourse that justifies the ongoing victimization by the Turkish state on the grounds that (1) this proves that Hizmet is a genuine Islamic movement as all genuine Islamic movements in Islamic history have faced persecutions; (2) this helps to remove the public perception that Hizmet and the AKP are the same and thus increases Hizmet's Islamic credentials (3) Allah is testing the *iman* of Hizmet volunteers and (4) Hizmet must have committed certain mistakes or sins and is hence facing the displeasure of God: "We hope to overcome this crisis through our prayer!" One hears an argument within the Movement as stated by one doctor, associated with Gülen movement, "that if Hizmet belongs to Allah, He will take care of it under any circumstances."[1]

In this regard Gülen and the Movement appears to fall back on the traditional Islamic method of dealing with crisis: providing a conservative interpretation of event or understanding the event in terms of "deviation from correct practice of Islam." As a result the balance between reason and faith, the very defining feature and strength of Gülen Movement, is breaking down. All across the Gülen fraternity one observes the more hardened practice of Islamic faith with an objective of pleasing Allah to overcome the present crisis. Nowhere have I come across a site where Hizmet is building a rights-based discourse (a feature of post-Islamism, which has been predominantly applied to understand and explain the Movement) against state authoritarianism except for two or three days of silent protest in 2014 against the government's action of having Ekrem Dumanlı, Editor–in-Chief of *Zaman* Newspaper and Hidayet Karaca, CEO of Samanyolu TV, arrested.

Herein lies a paradox: the Movement has been advocating the "principle of neutrality" in the functioning of the government institutions but does/did little to mobilize social forces or through their respective programs for the democratization of the state beyond building public opinion through (once strong) media, and holding seminars, conferences, and other academic events. This is one of the serious challenges that the Gülen Movement is currently facing within Turkey. The Movement has been the victim of the authoritarian Turkish state in the past and is currently facing an existential dilemma on account of severe illegal persecution of its volunteers and institutions. Its reluctance to directly participate in the program of democratization of the state comes from an understanding that, beyond its advocacy role, such an action demands a "political role" which is deeply antithetical to the non-party-political sensibilities of the Movement as well as from the Movement's firm belief in the principle that the politicization of Islam is bound to harm the ethical and moral spirit of Islam. A second reason for the reluctance of the Gülen Movement to advance the agenda of democratization through a direct political role is rooted in an understanding that with a moral and ethical restructuring of society, the state would automatically function on democratic principles as it is members of society that compose the state.

However, what emerges from this analysis is that the Gülen Movement neither considers itself a liberal, moderate Islamic movement nor subscribes to the trajectory of a Western form of modernity nor conforms to the pattern of a tradition-bound, past-oriented, literalist Islamic movement but is a future-oriented, authentic, Sunni Islamic movement based upon the Mujaddidi model of Islamic renewal that seeks to engage reflexively with tradition and modernity as discursive space. As such it exists in a non-traditional and non-modern framework under which tradition and modernity do not appear as closed entities but as a dynamic, interactive process. One consequence of this dynamic, interactive process inherent in Gülen's Islamic discourse and actions is the successful resolution of the paradox of "living as Muslim and modern together"—a paradox whose resolution has eluded many Islamic scholars and philosophers. The reason for this success lies in Gülen's ability to avoid the "discourse of reform of Islam" or "identity-centered Islamic discourse," thereby allowing his Islamic discourse to retain the image of "unadulterated, pure and authentic Islam" that motivates, provides flexibility, and gives confidence to the Movement's volunteers to interact with the structure of modernity without fear of dilution of their Islamic faith, unlike the modernist and traditionalist conceptualizations of Islam. The Mujaddidi model of Islamic renewal that lays down the framework of Islamic essence (content/within himself or herself) and non-Islamic forms (changing societal-political structure) further equips the volunteers of the Movement to move in all kinds of structures and settings.

This work, following Talal Asad, Jose Casanova and other political sociologists, has demonstrated the limitation of the post-Reformation understanding of religion as an essentially private, personal entity and its application to Islamic movement, particularly the Gülen Movement. However, as noted in the preceding chapters, traditions of Islam have their own sets of reasoning, conceptions of the public sphere and the secular, and the Islam-state relationship, which prescribe neither complete separation nor fusion of religion and state but various forms of consultative association between Islam and the nation-state in which Islam remains a part of imagined nationhood. Unlike in modernized Christianity, in the Islamic cosmology there is no disjunction between this and the other world and no private-public dichotomy—a Western discourse that has become universal to frame the discussion on the role and status of religion in most societies and polities of the world. On the contrary, Islam's worldview including Hizmet's understanding of Islam is premised on the integral linkage between this world and the other world, in which the actions and conduct of human beings in this world will be counted for their place in hereafter. Thus Islam, probably more than any other religion, as a complete value system reserves its right to participate in societal affairs, generate the social good, intervene in public debates concerning the state's policies and actions, and finally aims at the moral and ethical re-ordering of individual lifestyles in accordance with its imagined good life for the sake of Allah. Broadly speaking, by following this trajectory of Islam, the Gülen Movement has generated a remarkable level of "human and social capital" and a host of modern socio-educational institutions to serve Islam, universal values and humanity. It differs from other Islamic movements in its emphasis on the rejection of ideologization and politicization of Islam on the one hand and refusal to withdraw from the public sphere on the other, as well as on its method of representing and serving Islam: by setting an example through exemplary action and conduct (*tamsil*) instead of direct preaching about Islam (*tabligh*). Over the years the Movement has significantly contributed to the cause of humanity by not only transforming the principle of *hizmet* or altruism into an everyday value but also by continuously expanding the scope and activities of the Hizmet Movement, creating innovative organizational structures and means to implement this service to humanity.

As the Movement has become global and spread to more than 170 countries, it has raised the question of the democratization of decision-making processes within the Movement. The Movement has demonstrated a remarkable level of flexibility in terms of strategies, organizational structure, and its combination of centralized and decentralized mode of functioning within the overall hegemonic Turkish leadership that has so far served the intended purpose of integrating the non-Turkish volunteers within the Hizmet Movement. The Movement has also devised various consultative mechanisms at an informal level, if not the formalized ones, to facilitate the interaction with members of host societies; however, the participation of non-Turkish Hizmet volunteers in the decision-making structure at the level of leadership is rare, if not negligible. The region of Central Asia is the exception in this regard with whom, unlike other parts of the world, Sunni Muslim Turks feel they share an emotional, racial, cultural, and religious bonds. Certainly, people of Turkish origin continues to provide major human and material support to Hizmet activities (which has drastically declined following the post 2016 failed military coup); however, if the Movement aspires to be representative of the plural faces of the globe, a gradual "de-Turkification" of Hizmet leadership and development of an Ottoman-like multicultural frame of collective leadership respectful of inter- and intra-Islamic differences is needed, both from the point of integration of non-Turkish volunteers into leadership and the smooth functioning of Hizmet Movement at global level, as well as for the democratic representation of the Hizmet.

Finally, although Nursi has remained relevant as a source of Islamic inspiration among many, it is Fethullah Gülen whose individual character personifies the collective Islamic aspirations and sentiments of the millions of volunteers, predominantly Turkish, across the globe and motivates them to social action. This veneration of Gülen-in-person among the Turkish volunteers partly may be on account of the fact that unlike Nursi, Gülen's primary identity is Turkish and one of the rare Islamic figures of global stature with non-state Turkish identity in contemporary times, which blends well in the political context of Muslim Turks' search for an Islamic way of life in post-Kemalist modernized setting. Given the unshakable belief that volunteers display in the words, action, and integrity of Gülen it appears that Gülen, particularly for Turkish Muslim volunteers, has come to signify the "authentic Muhammadi path" in the present age. As Gülen embodies an inspiring figure with a spiritual charismatic authority among the volunteers of the Movement, notwithstanding his denial of such attributes and preference for identifying himself as a "humble teacher" or "humble servant of God," the Movement is indeed pregnant with issues related to its future in the post-Gülen period.

However, it is extremely difficult to transfer charisma to another person. Hence, the prospective leadership in the post-Gülen phase—whether an individual or a collective body—would certainly lack Gülen's charisma and authority. Following the death of Nursi, the Nur movement fragmented into several Nur Jamaats on the basis of interpretation of his text, the *Risale-i Nur*. Will the Gülen Movement follow a similar trajectory? One sees a growing trend of multiplicity or pluralization of Hizmet discourses, a process that has been intensified since December 2013 Corruption Exposé. While there are many who believe Hizmet should leave behind the experience in Turkey – which had evolved for decades under the undemocratic conditions of a repressive regime – there are two clear-cut emerging trends of thought within Hizmet in the light of developments since 2013.

The first is a group of Hizmet scholars with social science background and some volunteers in different fields, mostly living in Western hemisphere, who have recently emerged to publicly *criticize the Abi and imam culture* within the Movement. This group claims to advocate for a more transparent mode of functioning which is in line with liberal and secular values while preserving the Islamic discourse. This is still a minority trend within the Hizmet Movement. The second group is the vast majority of Hizmet volunteers who seem to have consolidated their convictions about Hizmet values, and choose to remain active in their defense and promotion. This does not mean that they do not have any critical opinion with regard to certain policies within Hizmet. Regardless of their own opinions, they continue to be active in their respective Hizmet activities and try to reach conciliation between their ideals and the current conditions. The approach of this second group seems to be the guiding culture of Hizmet within Turkey and outside. Some individuals from within this second group also tend to develop a more closed and conservative discourse apparently with an impulse to protect Hizmet against criticisms.

Hizmet has always been in conformity with the diverse legal and cultural environments and they have been successfully active for many years in different countries under different regimes. Yet, it can also be argued that they have continued to carry along with them certain reflexes – like extreme cautiousness to avoid Turkish state's persecution – in other parts of the world, too. Criticisms that are recently arising from within Hizmet can be considered as a reaction to this baggage that some senior Hizmet members cannot fully save themselves from. It also has to be noted that, aside from some of their unconditional criticisms, the resentment among the first group also has to do with their disappointment and sense of failure that arose after the Erdoğan regime's persecution of Hizmet members since 2014, especially after the coup attempt in 2016. Many are seeing this a lost battle against a tyrant, and the leaders of Hizmet have to account for this loss.

Notwithstanding this emerging fissure within the Movement, it appears to me that since the Gülen Movement lacks any central text like the *Risale-i Nur*, the chances of the fragmentation of the Movement into various factions is less. As tradition, not the text, is the signifier of the Gülen Movement, the Movement will continue to grow. Further, the Movement has demonstrated remarkable resilience to all kinds of illegal persecution of its volunteers and destruction of its institutions by the Erdoğan-led AKP government, and continued its altruistic activities within and outside Turkey. This is indicative of a strong spiritual bond that volunteers have developed with the Movement and with Gülen in person, which will continue to inspire future Hizmet volunteers to work for humanity for the sake of Allah.

POSTSCRIPT

THE PREDICAMENT OF THE GÜLEN MOVEMENT IN THE AFTERMATH OF THE JULY 15TH COUP ATTEMPT

The Gülen Movement has been subjected to intense scrutiny by the international community about any possible role or linkages, direct or indirect, to the failed military coup in Turkey on July 15, 2016. Within hours of the incident, President Erdoğan personally accused Gülen and the Gülen Movement with orchestrating the failed military coup. He launched a nationwide effort to hunt down the volunteers of the Gülen Movement. This rash judgment – made without any evidence – excluded any possibility of a fair and just internal inquiry on the subject matter. The subsequent, arbitrary state crackdown on the volunteers of the Movement, which continues to this day, has served only to reveal the regime's deep antipathy and biases towards the Movement, and is the final act in its effort to consolidate authoritarian power in its hands.

Externally, the intelligence departments of the United States, Germany, and the United Kingdom, conducted their own respective inquiries on the event and ruled out the possibility of Gülen's personal involvement in the coup, while questioning the larger Movement's supposedly non-transparent mode of functioning. In the absence of compelling evidence, the United States did not pay heed to the repeated requests of the Erdoğan government to extradite Gülen. It found the evidence and records submitted by the Turkish government as "inadequate" and "lacking in evidence" to proceed on the matter. It further rebuffed the blackmailing diplomacy of the Erdoğan regime: the exchange of a US pastor, imprisoned in Turkey, for Gülen.

Germany and other European countries also refused to cooperate with the Erdoğan regime and its requests for the extradition of alleged members of FETO (the Turkish government's dysphemism for the Gülen Movement). Most countries, in fact, remained skeptical of the Turkish government's claims about the coup attempt, though a few rogue states, mostly the non-democratic, Muslim-majority nations, could not resist the Turkish government's pressure and shut down Gülen-inspired schools and other institutions associated with the Movement. They were "rewarded" with personal, economic, and political benefits.

Critics on the Gülen Movement

In recent months, a few scholarly publications have surfaced in the public domain offering fresh appraisals of the Gülen Movement. Important among them are M. Hakan Yavuz and Bayram Balci (2018)[1] and a collection of articles in a special volume of *Politics, Religion & Ideology* (2018)[2] *Volume 19, 2018 - Issue 1: Ruin or Resilience? The Future of the Gülen Movement in Transnational Political Exile.* A majority of the articles in these two volumes take three primary positions: (a) to blame, directly or indirectly, Gülen for orchestrating the failed military coup; (b) to supposedly "discover" the *real, violent, immoral, hidden, clandestine, terrorist face of* the Movement, a face what they consider successfully "concealed" over the last five decades under the Movement's hegemonic soft discourse of education, human rights, interfaith dialogue, democracy, and civil society; and (c) to make the Western world believe about the direct or indirect role of Gülen and the Gülen Movement in the failed military coup, about which the West remains deeply skeptical.

In other words, many of these scholars, particularly Hakan Yavuz, one of the acclaimed scholars on Turkish affairs, believe that they were totally deceived in their earlier, relatively positive evaluation of the Movement, which they now want to correct by bringing a fresh perspective in light of "post-coup new evidence." Re-visiting one's own assumptions is a good academic exercise as it often helps in refreshing one's own perspective on a given theme. However, if the re-visit proceeds from an assumed conclusion, the text then suffers from "tailor-made analysis," being polemical, and loses its academic neutrality and integrity.

This is what appears to be the case with a majority of the aforementioned scholarly productions. Thus in order to highlight what they believe to be the "inherent power obsession" of the Gülen Movement, these scholarly texts are littered with the deliberate, repeated pre-fixing/insertion of certain terms, such as Hakan Yavuz's description of light houses as "sacred secretive,"[3] *without demonstrating how these terms are relevant for the description of the Movement.* Among these terminologies are: *infiltration, secretive, hidden, deceptive, parallel, Janus-faced, takiyya, hidden religious dimension, para-political, ambiguous, violent, terrorist, power-seeking organization, FETO, legally considered terrorist outfits*, etc.

Bayram Balci poses a good, serious question to be probed: whether the Gülen Movement was/is inherently violent from its inception or has a violent capability developed at a later stage? However, the whole narrative of his article has nothing to do with this question.[4]

Another article takes note of the absence of a violent legacy within the Gülen Movement and is even dismissive of state's nomenclature of FETO to designate the Gülen Movement a terrorist organization, for there has never been a single act of terrorism connected to the Gülen Movement; yet the author considers it far more dangerous than Al Qaida, ISIS, and other terrorist outfits on account of its invisible capacity to "infiltrate" state institutions.[5] The same author, without providing any evidence or indicating any sources, noted, "Contrary to what many early accounts in the West intimated, the plotters mobilized over ten thousand armed men … with a vision of religious struggle."[6]

Returning to Hakan Yavuz and his account, he described three stages of the Gülen Movement's development: religious, educational, and political, as a well thought out, *systematic strategy* to acquire political power in the Turkey.[7] Towards the latter, he, along with many others, takes into consideration the following factors: (1) the presence of the Gülen Movement volunteers in the police, intelligence, judiciary, and army, and the power of their media and their combined role in defaming and delegitimizing the "secular opponents, particularly the decorated military officers" through what they consider to be the fictitious Ergenekon and Sledgehammer conspiracy cases;[8] (2) Hizmet's opposition to "Oslo Peace Process";[9] (3) Gülen's statement on the Mavi Marmara Turkish Flotilla to Gaza;[10] (4) the judicial summoning of Hakan Fidan, the chief of Turkish Intelligence (MIT); and (5) attempting to overthrow the legitimate Erdoğan government first through what the government and critics called the Judicial Coup (the December 17 and 25, 2013 corruption probes, which directly implicated the the Erdoğan government, including his family members, in crimes) and later through the failed military coup of July 15, 2016.

Yavuz and a few others in the referred texts also came to the conclusion that the alleged corrupt and immoral practices (illegal wiretapping, bugging, videotaping, blackmailing, corruption etc.) of "Gülenist" police and judges alienated the civil and political society to such an extent that hardly anybody or any group came forward to support or help the Gülen Movement when the Erdoğan regime brutally targeted them.

Counter narratives

The arguments, analyses, and narratives of the majority of these articles, mostly based upon the above enumerated terminologies and factors, amount to an uncritical acceptance of the discourse of the Erdoğan regime. Such uncritical acceptance of state discourse by a section of "credible intelligentsia" lends legitimacy to the authoritarian regime and contributes to the weakening of democratic rule of law. The bare listing of a few facts would sufficiently demonstrate how some of these narratives are totally lacking in *critical examination of the established procedure of inquiry and assessment of evidence to arrive at their conclusions about the complicity of the Gülen Movement in the failed military coup.* A few of these are as follows:

First, the fact that the Erdoğan government called the "2013 Corruption Exposé" and the "2016 Failed Military Coup" conspiracies to topple the government; in investigating these incidents, the government preferred a Parliamentary Commission, which is normally politically motivated, rather than an independent judicial investigation. Such a preference speaks volumes about the mal-intentions and malpractices of the Erdoğan regime. These decisions ran contrary to the democratic discourse of governance, which *minimally* demands an independent judicial investigation of such serious charges.

Second, the two crucial witnesses in the failed military coup, Hulusi Akar, the Chief of Army Staff, and Hakan Fidan, the intelligence Chief (MIT), were not deposed before the Parliamentary Commission for cross examination. Oddly enough, both were retained in their respective jobs despite monumental lapses of duty on their parts.

Third, the Turkish government and the critical media and scholarship on the Gülen Movement *zeroed in* on Mr. Adil Öksüz as the "point man" of Fethullah Gülen, and later used him to implicate the larger Gülen Movement network in the failed coup. They further emphasized Gülen's admission of meeting this person as *proof* of involvement by Gülen and the Movement in the failed coup. As an ethical and moral person of the highest order, Gülen rightly upheld the truth of meeting Öksüz, despite suspicion around the latter. However, such an admission cannot be proof, by any stretch of the imagination, of committing wrong. However, the arrest of Mr. Öksüz in the immediate aftermath of the coup – he was near a military base – and then his quick disappearance and state's inability to hunt him down to date, is most intriguing. One wonders how the Turkish government, which once arrested Mr. Öksüz, a prized possession, could be so reckless as to allow him to flee and disappear from its control. The possibility of Mr. Öksüz working for the Erdoğan regime cannot be ruled out, for he would not be the first former member of Hizmet to work for Erdoğan.

Fourth, any academic narratives that accepts the "2013 Corruption Exposé" as part of a larger conspiracy to topple the government simply on the ground that it targeted the first family (Erdoğan's) of Turkey, *and hence was politically motivated*, proceeds from assumption that the *First Family is above the law.* Such a premise theoretically precludes the possibility of honesty, sincerity, integrity, ethics, and morality in performing official functions.

A critical figure in the 2013 corruption probe was Reza Zarrab, an Iranian-born businessman who was arrested in Turkey and charged with bank fraud, money laundering, and helping the Turkish and Iranian governments evade US sanctions against Iran. In 2016, Zarrab was arrested in Miami and charged by the US government with exactly the same crimes along with Mehmet Hakan Atilla, a manager at Turkey's majority state-owned Halkbank.[11] While Erdoğan dropped all charges against Zarrab and 53 other suspects,[12] released and awarded him the best business person of the year, Zarrab turned approver during the Court trial in the US, accepted all charges, and implicated Ministers and Erdoğan, the then Prime Minister, in what is infamously called the "Oil for Gold Trade."[13]

Fifth, the Gülen Movement being labeled "terrorist" or FETO is given credence only in the context of the deaths of 255 Turkish citizens during the failed military coup. However, the forensic and ballistic reports for those deaths were never investigated by an independent body. If the government has a strong case backed by the evidence, it should not shy away from conducting forensic and ballistic reports and an independent investigation. Hence the question "who killed 255 civilians" remains an open one, with the possibility of this crime being committed by Erdoğan's supporters – the entire coup a ploy to further consolidate support for Erdoğan.[14] Since Turkey has now been reduced to "one man rule" and the justice system has collapsed, it is fair and reasonable that a UN-led international investigation, or an investigation by any neutral country under the watch of the international community, must be conducted to unearth the truth. This has been proposed by Fethullah Gülen.[15]

Sixth, the history of most Middle Eastern countries, including Turkey and other postcolonial nations, has been riddled with governments killing their own people for the "*security of the regime." In such countries, national security, for all practical purposes, means regime security*. In this context, the possibility of the failed military coup being a "self-military coup" orchestrated by the regime itself – or allowed to play out for the regime's benefit – is what Kemal Kılıçdaroğlu, the leader of Turkey's leading opposition party, the CHP, has termed "the Controlled Coup."[16] Considering Erdoğan's ruthless governance, at least since 2012, such an option can not be ruled out.

Seventh, despite being subjected to brutality, oppression, and dehumanization by the Erdoğan regime in the aftermath of the failed military coup, there is no evidence that the Gülen Movement has ever opted for any kind of "street opposition" – peaceful or violent – to the government's repression. Nor is there any history of any kind of "street opposition" by the Gülen Movement. It is difficult to accept that a movement with fifty years of "*civil society discourse of peace and non-violence*," both in theory and practice, would raise a generation intent on taking over the state – either peacefully or violently. Retaining the moral right to guide the political the Gülen Movement, unlike many Islamic movements around the world, has not built any state-centered Islamic discourse. The Movement has always stayed out of politics and never expressed any political ambitions.

Eighth, it has been repeatedly mentioned in the public domain that the failed military coup originated from within a faction of the army, and not from the "chain of command," to demonstrate a point: that the failed coup was the handiwork of a clandestine, terrorist, secretive, subversive Gülenist network in the Army intent on harming the Turkish nation. Though one must condemn the culture of the military coup, as this is one of the most undemocratic ways of acquiring state power, a coup led by junior and young officers, inspired by idealism to serve the nation, against the wishes or opposition of the chain of command, is nothing new in the annals of political history. In recent memory, Kemal Atatürk in Turkey, Gamal Abdul Nasser in Egypt, and Muammar Gaddafi in Libya, to varying degrees, represent this trend. According to the narrative of the Turkish government and critics of the Gülen Movement, this was an attempt by lower ranking officers, thus an illegitimate and a terrorist act. This sounds as if it would have been a legitimate one if it had originated within Chain of Command. It's entirely possible that some junior officers, acting on their own, without aid or support from Gülen or any other network, attempted the failed coup.

Ninth, even if assuming, but without accepting, that the failed military coup was a desperate and panicked response on the part of supposedly Hizmet-linked military officers to the looming threat of losing their jobs or being demoted following the mandatory yearly military review meeting in August 2016, the Turkish government, to a large extent, is responsible for contributing in shaping the illegal, illegitimate reaction on the part of a section of its military officers. It is no secret that, following the 2013 Corruption Scandal, the Erdoğan regime created a climate of fear and made the security and dignity of life of people associated with the Gülen Movement "insecure."

Tenth, within a few days of the failed military coup, the Erdoğan regime indulged in massive purges, dismissing and arresting thousands of government employees from their jobs; shutting down educational, charitable, medical, banking, and other private institutions; confiscating the private property of businesses and seizing individual bank accounts; and detaining and jailing thousands of people without trial. It is astonishing that all these illegal coercive measures were carried out on the charge of merely having "suspected" association with the Gülen Movement. This fact alone is sufficient to indicate that the Erdoğan regime had for long nursed strong biases and grudges against, kept watch over, systematically profiled, and strategically built a "hostile national mood" against the Movement, with accusations of Parallel State and FETO before hitting them hard with all state's might. Under the pretext of a failed military coup, the government thus tried to eradicate the Movement from Turkey. This also unmasked the "theatrical politics" of Erdoğan, wherein he could ask the nation's forgiveness for "being misled" by the Gülen Movement while still remaining in power, while others would continue to languish in jail or face harassment in different forms, with no luxury to claim that they too were "misled" by the Gülen Movement!

It is no secret that both then-Prime Minister Erdoğan and then-Foreign Minister Abdullah Gül signed the 2004 MGK (National Security Council) in order to liquidate the Gülen Movement and other religious groups.[17] In 2006, Erdoğan tried forcefully to introduce a "terrorism" bill in Parliament. This bill included a provision on "terrorism without weapons" but was modified, due to opposition from within AKP, to treat such people as "part of a gang." Nonetheless, the 2006 Anti-Terrorism Law defines terrorism as any kind of act aimed at "[W] eakening or seizing the authority of the State, eliminating fundamental rights and freedoms, or damaging the internal and external security of the State, public order or general health by means of pressure, force and violence, terror, intimidation, oppression or threat,"[18] which leaves the interpretation of terrorism, per this Act, open enough to even include the peaceful, lawful activities of ordinary citizens.

Why didn't Erdoğan strike against the Gülen Movement following the 2004 MGK decision? Why did he wait more than a decade? Not out of love or having any programmatic alliance with the Movement, but for two specific reasons: (a) he himself was not then powerful enough to contemplate such outrageously illegal actions; and (b) he discovered in Hizmet a helpful hand in projecting himself as a "democrat" and much needed bureaucratic support, which enabled him to survive the still-heavily Kemalist establishment.

Eleventh, if the period between 2002-2012 is considered one of the golden periods of modern Turkey – and if it is true that during this period the Hizmet-inspired volunteers had a real presence in the state sectors (as has been repeatedly stated by critics of the Gülen Movement) – then surely some of the credit for these "good days" of democratic governance must go to the Gülen Movement. Thus the charges of corrupt practices among Hizmet-linked state personnel, particularly in the police and judiciary, which has alienated the Movement from a majority of Turks, does not hold much weight. It may be noted that Erdoğan's hostility towards the Gülen Movement began to manifest openly only in post-2012, when he himself was becoming corrupted and began to display his dictatorial ambition.

Finally, while people sacrificed their lives to save democracy from the possible military coup, Turkey under President Erdoğan, within just two years of the failed coup, has slipped into authoritarian polity. Thus, much like the Islamic revolution in Iran, Turkey's authoritarian government was born under the auspices of the democratic mobilization of the people!

Decoding the assumptions of Gülen Movement critics

Besides these fallacies, the underlying assumptions of the critics, upon which rest their whole critical narratives about the Gülen Movement, suffers from the following flaws:

First, a good majority of these articles on the AKP-Gülen Movement relationship constructs their narratives on the assumption that both of them, predominantly representing so-called "Black" Turks (that is, the Muslim majority of Turks who were, for decades, denied access to halls of power), were united only to marginalize the "White" Turks, particularly their domination of the military establishment. Once this purpose was achieved, both fought each other for a greater share of power, which eventually led to their brutal split. This dominant assumption, though prevalent in a large number of critical works on the Gülen Movement, is deeply problematic and flows from three sources:

A) It derives from the framework of "power-centered, western, and modern social science," which tends to treat every social phenomenon in the context of power dynamics. Thus, by framing the Gülen Movement merely in the context of power dynamics, this scholarship suffers from the "limitation of power-centered modern social science" in addition to reinforcing the Orientalist myth that Islamic movements cannot be divorced of power aspirations.

B) In part, it flows from "theory of the Deep State," an invisible, non-empirical, conspiracy discourse, which is very pervasive among a predominant majority of Turkish intellectuals – whether secular, Kemalist, Gülenist, Muslim, laicist, or other. This view is used to understand the events and developments in "modern" Turkey. On one hand, the critics of the Gülen Movement apply the discourse of "a deep state" – secretive, invisible, non-transparent – to portray the Gülen Movement as a "secretive *dangerous entity*" working against the Turkish Republic, society, state, people, government, and national interest; on the other hand, many – including high level functionaries within the Gülen Movement – subscribe to this theory in order to explain that the failed military coup is the handiwork of the "Deep State" attempting to implicate the Gülen Movement to weaken it and prevent the "rising Turkish Muslim nation." High profile cases such as Ergenekon or Sledgehammer, or discourses on the Parallel State or FETO – whether real or fictitious – all have their origin in the theory of the Deep State. They represent a conspiratorial frame of mind, which continues to enjoy legitimacy among a substantial section of the Turkish public, intellectuals, media, and even the government establishment. In short, the conspiracy discourse remains popular within Turkish society, and the state can easily mobilize public opinion in its favor by conjuring up the picture of an external threat to its existence.

C) Many Muslim Turkish scholars, who are critical of Gülen and the Gülen Movement, have a strong reservation regarding Islamic scholarship of Gülen and believe that he is not at the level of many outstanding Islamic figures, such as Bediüzzaman Said Nursi. They believe Gülen's rise and fame to be accidental and was, at best, due to conjectural support of the Turkish state.

The sum total of these three fallacies are that the heavy reliance upon the "framework of power dynamics" among critics of the Gülen Movement served two crucial intended functions: (a) the modern mind is susceptible to the "power discourse" and therefore it is easy to convince a western, modern mind of certain conclusions if the Gülen Movement is presented through the prism of power dynamics; and (b) by placing Gülen and the Hizmet Movement within the framework of power, it robs Gülen of his ethical and moral persona and reduces him to the level of a lesser mortal subject susceptible to ordinary human caprices: greed, manipulation, money, lies, power, etc.

However, a brief glimpse at human history reveals a large number of figures and movements that have rejected the human impulses of ego, greed, and power. In more recent history, Mahatma Gandhi, Martin Luther King, Jr., Daisaku Ikeda, and many others have inspired non-powered, service-oriented, religio-social and political movements. If Fethullah Gülen would have been motivated by power considerations, he had a number of opportunities to use his proximity to Turkish Prime Ministers and Presidents to either acquire state offices or use the social capital of the Gülen Movement to influence the government for personal gains. However, the fact remains: he neither used his personal charisma and influence to acquire wealth for himself or for any of his family members, or even to help their sons and daughters to secure positions within the state, nor is he surrounded by family loyalists to keep his "power" intact and transfer the same to his close relatives as successor, as often happens in the political world. He has not demonstrated any kind of tendency toward hobnobbing, and he has not compromised with the Erdoğan government to end or dilute the government's hostility against the Hizmet Movement.

The bitter truth in this regard is that when such people of high moral and ethical character *refuse* to cooperate with the government on high moral, national grounds or to get co-opted/accommodated within the power structure of the state, the state, particularly in the context of Middle Eastern authoritarian regimes, takes recourse to its traditional, time-tested methods of coercion and violence to finish off such figures and movements. The modern history of Middle Eastern states, including Turkey, is littered with such examples. These states have rarely tolerated relatively autonomous religio-social movements.

This partly explains why the Erdoğan regime, having failed through inducement, slander, and coercion (in the form of appointing trustees to and taking over pro-Hizmet institutions, foundations, and corporations, confiscating their assets, etc.) to persuade the rank and file of volunteers and institutions of the Movement to dissociate themselves from Gülen, finally decided to violently crush the Movement and shut down the educational, charitable, dialogue, media, health, finance, and other institutions inspired by Gülen.

The second flaw in the critics' logic has to do with the relationship of a civil society movement with the government. This relationship traditionally takes three dominant forms to the policies and programs of the government: neutral, supportive, or oppositional. However, the Gülen Movement did not fall within these three traditional forms. The Movement preferred to keep itself "autonomous," maintaining a safe distance from the government without being either too critical or too openly supportive of it. To the extent the Erdoğan regime expanded and strengthened the "zones of democracy" in Turkey, albeit as a part of the regime's own survival strategy, the Hizmet Movement supported such constitutional reforms, policies, and programs. Its support of the AKP government or other governments in the past flowed from its understanding of itself as a patriotic and nationalist force of "Muslim Turkey." Such cooperation took many forms, including Gülen's personal appeal to the Turkish volunteers of the Hizmet Movement across the world to travel back to Turkey to vote in favor of the 2010 Constitutional Reforms, which a great many of them did (it may be noted that this is the only time Gülen expressed his political opinion openly). It is true that some Hizmet volunteers joined AKP rallies; that some Hizmet-led media supported the AKP's democratic policies and programs; and that Hizmet-inspired businesses and volunteers extended crucial bureaucratic support to the AKP government both to thwart the politics of the "Deep State" and to implement the AKP's policies and programs.

One unintended consequence of this general democratic process, at least until 2012, was that it led to the expansion and strengthening of civilian authority in many spheres of public life, including the military, which is the hallmark of democratic rule. Following 2012, Hizmet refused to support Erdoğan's pursuit of what he called an "Executive Presidency." Erdoğan was seeking for himself a leading role for all Muslims at a global level, and Hizmet's network of schools and reputation around the world could have helped immensely. It is this refusal that made Erdoğan and his regime deeply suspicious of the Movement's loyalty. By this point, Erdoğan had become increasingly paranoid, and perceived any opposition – imaginary or real as an existential threat.

The third flaw stems from another social development: the expansion, since the mid-1980s, of education among Muslim/Anatolian "Black" Turks. This has had the unintended consequence that threatened the vice grip "White" Turks have had on Turkey's most powerful institutions. The Gülen Movement significantly contributed to this process and encouraged students, predominantly from conservative pious Anatolian Muslim families, to participate in the state opportunity structure. This trend, aided by relatively friendly, Muslim-majority governments, inspired Black Turks to compete for government positions – a process that eventually broke the monopoly White Turks had in the state sectors. Thus, the relative decline in representation of White Turks in different institutions of state administration including the police, judiciary, military, and intelligence, is a part of the general process of democratization of the Turkish state and society, and not the result of any programmatic alliance between the Gülen Movement and the AKP, as many critics have sought to assert, sans any credible evidence.

It is true that Hizmet-inspired institutions did focus on motivating students to compete for the opportunities in different government branches, including the police, intelligence, judiciary, and military (though their success rate in military institutions was much lower compared to the other branches). This was more to do with enhancing the brand value of Hizmet-led institutions and attracting students towards Hizmet, as these governmental opportunities constituted the highest upward mobility in Turkish society.

In this regard, *the Movement has been accused of forging examination questions over the last four decades, enabling students from Hizmet-inspired schools to get higher scores. These are preposterous claims, considering the amount of government oversight that goes into such examinations.* If the claims were to be believed, one has no other alternative but to believe that Turkey with a history of one of the most centralized state system is a "land of Bantustan," where anybody is free to do anything for any great length of time and state – its president, prime minister, vigilance department, bureaucracy, prosecution, anti-corruption bureau etc. – remained a helpless spectator for long to suddenly woke up one fine morning to discover the hidden culprit and crush it with all its might to save the nation.

The domestic isolation of the Gülen Movement

How did the Erdoğan government succeed in transforming the Gülen Movement, within Turkey, into an anti-national force? Alternatively, why have the Gülen Movement's good works of the last five decades failed to generate solidarity or support from Turkish civil society? This is more puzzling considering the fact that the Movement has, by and large, espoused the Turkish ethnic-territorial nationalism and overall carried the Turkish state agenda. In specific terms, the Movement carried the state agenda in four ways: (a) employment generation; (b) promotion of secular education; (c) creation of a generation both disciplined and loyal to the Turkish state; and (d) promotion of Turkish culture and identity abroad.

A tentative answer to the domestic isolation can be as follows:

First, the state remains a sacred institution in the eyes of a majority of Turks, who also have a high degree of faith in that state. It has historically been at the center of and has pervaded most aspects of people's lives: religious, social, educational, economic, and political. Therefore, all good works are considered to be either done directly by state leadership itself or with its blessing. A survey on the "work done by Hizmet, particularly with reference to Turkish Olympiad" in 2013 by Hizmet institutions showed that people considered these events to have either been organized by the government itself or with its support. One consequence of this process is that the formation of civil society in the region, including Turkey, has been historically weak, which allows the state to govern without conforming to the constitutional principle of the rule of law.

Another consequence is the development of governing norms under which the state is considered the legitimate owner of societal resources, including individual's private property. Thus, the Turkish state – from the Ottoman era to the present day – has acted like a "patriarchal father figure," with the inherent right to look after its subjects; own and distribute societal resources; and dole out discipline, punishment, or rewards, depending upon the political context. The hegemonic presence of the state in people's lives has produced the "politics of clientism and patronage" and the ever increasing struggle among social groups to become a beneficiary of the state's patronage. Thus, a person's dignity, respect, and influence are determined by virtue of access to state resources or his/her location in the pyramidal structure of state.

To this extent, it is statism, rather than Turkish nationalism, which defines people's identity. After all, statism was one of the six enshrined principles of Kemalism. One consequence of statist tradition in modern Turkey is that people in general as well as a good section of intelligentsia have *undifferentiated* understanding of government, state, nation and community. As a result a perceived threat to government easily gets transformed into a perceived threat to community, state and nation and easily flock in solidarity towards the state regime on latter's call. This partly explains why a significant section of Black Turks rallied behind Erdoğan and his call to defend democracy against the failed military coup and turned against the Gülen Movement. For them, Erdoğan continues to signify the hope of Anatolian Black Turks (religious Muslims) against the fear of the return of White Turks (Kemalist, secular). This fact, along with Erdoğan's legacy of economic development, tilts the balance of social and political forces in favor of the regime.

A third consequence of Turkey's historical relationship between state and society is a relative *lack of culture of opposition* to the state. The Sunni Islamic historiography has systematically frowned upon the right to dissent, particularly against the patriarchal figure of father or state. Moreover, in the relationship between *'ulama* and state in predominantly Sunni Muslim societies, the former has historically been subservient to the state authority. The subordination and bureaucratization of the Sunni *'ulama* in Sunni Muslim societies is a historical reality; so is the fact that any form of dissent against (Muslim) political authority is considered illegitimate in Sunni Islamic traditions. Thus, the principle of dissent lacks effective legitimacy in Turkey's predominantly Sunni Muslim society.

Given this Islamic/Muslim tradition, in the ensuing conflict between Erdoğan and Gülen, whether perceived or real, the overwhelming majority of Turkish Muslims sided with the former and considered the latter's opposition as illegitimate and anti-nationalist. Similarly, the Kemalist regime's "policy of Europeanisation," which included switching to Latin script, changing the dress code, the "Turkification of Islam," and its general anti-Islam thrust, hardly invited any significant opposition from Turkish society, except localized protests in pockets of the Kurdish region. During my stay in Turkey, from September 2013 through June 2016, I myself did not find any effective opposition from any quarter of society to the growing authoritarianism of the Erdoğan regime, save Kemal Kılıçdaroğlu's 25-day-long Justice March in 2017.

Second, the current domestic isolation of the Gülen Movement is deeply connected with the birth and consolidation of Erdoğanism. Despite the country's authoritarian turn following the quashing of the 2013 corruption probe, Erdoğan couldn't fully establish his hegemony and control over all state institutions and thus mold Turkey in his own vision. The failed military coup conferred such legitimacy, opportunity, and authority upon him. It generated an "unprecedented national crisis" and provided a "God-sent opportunity" (as he himself admitted) to emerge as the "savior of (Muslim) Turkish nation" – something parallel to the emergence of Kemal Atatürk as the "savior of the Turkish nation." The regime succeeded in creating this scenario by portraying the Gülen Movement, an internal enemy, as collaborating with the Western powers, particularly the US (the İncirlik military base, where US forces are stationed, was allegedly used during the coup attempt, and its former Turkish commander has been arrested for alleged connection with the Movement). This paralleled Kemal Atatürk's fight with his internal enemy – the Ottomans – in collaboration with an external enemy – Western forces (British, France, Greece, and others).

Erdoğan needed such legitimacy to shape the Turkish nation according to his vision, much as Kemal Atatürk did. The failed military coup thus strongly appears to be a case of a "Controlled Coup," which allowed Erdoğan to overcome his "dented image" caused by the 2013 Corruption Exposé and to easily convince the majority of Turks that both events were essentially a "deep western conspiracy" to block the rise of (Muslim) Turkey – a perception shared by a substantial section of Turkish Muslims. It is only through such political motions that Erdoğan could realize his long suppressed, hidden desire: becoming, like Atatürk, the "Leader of the Nation" and overseeing all institutions of governance.

Erdoğanism was to emerge at the demise of the Gülen Movement. The relative autonomy of the Gülen Movement and its public visibility situated it as the dominant Muslim bloc in post-Kemalist Turkey. Erdoğan's futurist, Islamicist goal therefore required not only the physical elimination of the Gülen Movement but to thoroughly delegitimize and criminalize the Movement in the public's view, with a goal of permanently eliminating it from the public memory. The process of physical and cognitive elimination of the Gülen Movement had begun following 2010 and culminated with the 2013 December corruption probe and the failed military coup. To this effect, the regime has already made the Gülen Movement, albeit in negative way, and the failed coup part of the school curriculum.

Third, the Gülen Movement gradually came to acquire its status as a political actor in the public's perception due to the position it took on several critical issues, like the Ergenekon and Sledgehammer investigations; the Turkish Mavi Marmara flotilla to Gaza (an aid expedition organized by the extremist IHH organization, with the indirect support of the Turkish government);[19] lobbying the government to replace Hakan Fidan, the MIT Chief, and later a prosecutor summoning him in connection with the Oslo Peace Process of 2012; and finally the December 2013 corruption probe. All of these contributed to the image of the Gülen Movement as a "political actor" within the Turkish setting. To the extent that the Gülen Movement was perceived as a political factor in the public domain, it alienated a section of Turkish Muslims, including a few from within the Movement, which used to understand Hizmet as a purely spiritual movement.

Fourth, the government may not have succeeded in demonizing Hizmet were it not for the fact that the other three major national political parties – the CHP, MHP, and HDP – joined the government in blaming the Gülen Movement for the failed military coup. They did so for their own respective reasons.

The secularist CHP supported the Erdoğan regime's crackdown on the Gülen Movement for two reasons: first, it provided a golden opportunity for the CHP and other Kemalist forces to disassociate themselves from the Kemalist legacy of military coups and thus to become the leading force of democracy. As the Erdoğan government has already embarked on an authoritarian mode of governance since 2012 (Gezi Protest), the CHP saw an opportunity to project itself as Turkey's "real democratic force." Moreover, the CHP and other Kemalist and secular forces saw the development as a political fight within the Islamic forces (among the Black Turks themselves), which might weaken the "Islamic alliance."

The nationalist MHP primarily backed the government due to its understanding that the US, with the help of Gülen, was instrumental in carrying out the military coup, and thus posed a danger to the Turkish nation. Hence the Gülen Movement must be liquidated.

For the Kurdish HDP, the Gülen Movement is primarily a pan-Turkish nationalist movement with inbuilt biases, prejudices, and political hostility towards the Kurdish movement.

Moreover, all three national political forces considered the Gülen Movement more dangerous than the AKP. They considered the Gülen Movement as an ultra-Islamic, ideological-political movement with an educational and intellectual base and a considerable presence in state institutions and civil society. For this reason, they found that it was more difficult to dislodge them or wipe out their influence than that of the AKP, which they view as an Islamic pragmatic political party without much of an educational and intellectual base.

Fifth, the Turkish society is very polarized along secular, religious, and ethnic lines. A large number of secular, Kemalist, and atheist forces within the society and state simply despise the role of religion or religious figures. For them it is simply impossible that an imam of mosque (i.e. Fethullah Gülen) can inspire such a global educational movement; there must be some forces working from behind with a hidden agenda. Hence this group with their media power has systematically attacked the educational legacy of the Gülen Movement and tried to undermine the Movement's success in competitive examinations by allegations of fraud over the last forty years!

Sixth, other Islamic groups were also happy with this demonization and marginalization of Hizmet Movement. This is due to two reasons: first, they primarily saw Hizmet as "political entity" and found Hizmet's opposition, irrespective of its form, to the Erdoğan regime as contrary to Islamic tradition and value. Second, they found Hizmet's advocacy of secular education, its visibility in public sphere and calls for participation in opportunity structure of Turkish republic as deviation from true teaching of Islam. In addition, they found an opportunity to fill the social vacuum created by the marginalization of the Gülen Movement and to come closer to Erdoğan regime.

Finally, the marginalization of Hizmet-affiliated business groups pleases the secularists and the Islamic nationalists. This marginalization has removed one of the biggest competitors in the market for both the non-Hizmet associations like MÜSIAD (Muslim) and TÜSIAD (secular).

While the fear from the state is the most important reason, it is this combination of factors that explain why the Gülen Movement faced complete isolation and could not attract any support from different quarters of society. Hakan Yavuz and others, who analyzed the lack of societal support for Gülen and the Movement in terms of "corruption," have been, at best, too narrow in their summations; at worst, they have been lopsided and lacking in analytical merit.

To be precise, there are two tentative conclusions that can be drawn with regard to the Gülen Movement and to why it has been so vulnerable despite decades of good work:

a) The Movement lacks the assessment of Turkish political tradition and therefore it could not prepare itself to prevent the forthcoming existential challenges to itself. It saw the issue more in terms of individual problems (Erdoğan's jealousy), rather than structural ones.

b) During the course of its evolution, the Movement could not settle its identity firmly: whether religious, civic-social, or political. It became a combination of all three. This undifferentiated picture of the Gülen Movement in the public domain is itself a product of a mismatch between its conscious representation of itself within the liberal-modern Islamic tradition but without internalizing the discourse of modernity, which requires the "strict privatization and spiritualization" of religion while also avoiding politics. As a result, it created different perceptions about itself to different social, religious, and political groups in Turkish society and thus helped strengthen the negative public perception, built by the government and critical scholarship, that the Movement has a "hidden agenda" or "something to conceal." Thus, many found Erdoğan's dysphemism of a "parallel structure" to be real, which added legitimacy to Erdoğan's coercive action against the Movement.

International dimensions: the intriguing silence

If the domestic opposition to the regime's brutality vis-à-vis the Gülen Movement is negligible and voices of solidarity too limited to make any impact on the government, the response of the international community has been neither too positive nor strong enough to pressure the Erdoğan regime to halt its current policy of repression. The international community, except a few voices, has remained skeptical, rather silent, on the Erdoğan government's crackdown. What has made the international community a silent spectator despite the fact the Erdoğan government has become more authoritarian and perpetrated all kinds of human rights violations?

Some of it has to do with how the Movement is perceived abroad.

The perception, especially in the Western world, has not always been very positive for the Movement due to the following reasons:

First, the Gülen Movement continues to suffer from an "image deficiency" in international arena on account of its being perceived as non-transparent. If the West does not approve of Erdoğan's repressive actions against volunteers of the Gülen Movement, it also does not have a positive view of the Movement. The international community has expressed tepid resistance to the Turkish government's human rights violations against Hizmet; some countries have cautiously granted refugee and asylum status to some of the fleeing Hizmet members.

It is important to mention that almost all Hizmet affiliated or inspired institutions – educational, health, recreational, relief, dialogue, etc. – function within the established laws, rules, and regulations of their host nations. They keep accounts and records, as required in accordance with local laws. However, the informal structure of Hizmet is a non-written culture. It consists of leadership and *sohbet* gatherings (weekly informal reading circles where participants read and discuss a text, usually religious, and at times discuss future developmental projects) at all levels, which provide guidance to the members and volunteers of the institutions. As it is a trust and faith driven movement, Hizmet functions more on oral tradition than on written ones. As a researcher on the Gülen Movement, I have not once come across a meeting at which minutes were being recorded.

Moreover, Hizmet does not have a constitution detailing the objectives of the Movement, the rights and duties of its core volunteers/members, and means of achieving its objectives, etc. This is quite normal, especially due to the informal structure of most non-Western social movements. The roots of Hizmet's non-written culture can also be traced to its origins in Sufism, where the "discourse of the heart" is considered more important than the "discourse of the mind." The Movement was also born when the Kemalist-secular political culture was particularly repressive, especially when it came to Islamic groups. In Turkey, there has always been a high degree of abuse, manipulation, and misinterpretation of written words by the state. Writings have been used to implicate and punish the state's perceived enemies, which throughout the history of the modern Turkish republic has been mostly religious groups and individuals.

Due to its informal structure and the abovementioned reasons, the Movement does not have – and has always avoided – a formal system of membership. Though these explanations are convincing, plausible, and rational, the Movement is not helping itself by continuing to embrace its non-written culture. The sooner the Movement fills this gap in its functioning by making affiliations more visible and public, the better it will be able to meet the concerns of the international community about transparency. It is heartening that there is a growing trend in this direction, as evident from the large number of Hizmet-linked institutions like the Journalists and Writers Foundation, the Alliance for Shared Values (USA), Dialogue Society (UK), Indialogue (India), Affinity Intercultural Foundation (Australia), etc. These groups publicly announce that they are inspired by Fethullah Gülen.

Second, the international community, particularly Europe and the West, has serious reservations about the possibility of a religious movement transforming itself into a social movement. The Euro-centric theories of social movements hardly take into consideration religion as factor in building social movements. A large part of secularized Europe/the West distrust religion, especially as part of the state, and doubt that religious organizations are capable of promoting social good. A part of the reason for European distrust of religious groups is their particular historical experience in which the "idea of the good life," material progress, and scientific and technological achievement, have been shaped by secularization and religion has ceased to be factor or is accorded a very limited role in the construction of modern civil society and state. The dominant narrative of the principle of religious liberty on the European continent is freedom or liberty *from* religion and not *of* religion. Given such historical context – and also considering the widespread Islamophobia in the West – an overwhelming segment of European citizenry is not inclined to understand the Gülen Movement as a social democratic movement. Such a skeptical attitude towards Islamic movements and towards their capacity to produce social good also stems from the relative absence of Islam-driven "secular development" in modern times.

Third, the international community, particularly Europe, in the light of Hitler, has become increasingly uncomfortable with the idea of individual-centered discourse and loyalty. Europe itself has consciously moved from an era of mass democracy to a very individualized conception of democracy. For Europe and the greater West, taking inspiration from individual philosophy and philosophers is one thing; being a slave of a particular idea or professing unflinching group loyalty to an individual – whether a political leader or spiritual guru – is another thing. A large majority of Europeans associate the latter with aspects of fascism/Nazism. However, the Gülen Movement remains an individual-centered phenomenon, mostly revolving around the personality of Fethullah Gülen. The Movement, despite its many achievements in various fields, tends to promote a conformist viewpoint and appears willing to implement the vision of Fethullah Gülen – without sufficient critical reflection, notwithstanding Gülen's emphasis on the principle of self-criticality and reflectivity.

Fourth, the Gülen Movement's distinction from other Islamic movements is not always very clear. Like many other Islamic movements, including the political ones, the Movement has re-conceptualized the role of Islam in social field, if not in political field, leading to the building of institutions in various fields, including education, health, media, relief services, child care, business, and others. Though not wedded to the idea of an Islamic state, or even the role of Islam in the realm of governance except advocating the re-centering of universal moral and ethics in public life, the fact that the Gülen Movement generates public opinion about public policies and performs like a "moral watchdog" over the affairs of the government through its media and various associations may cause some in the international community to have apprehensions about a possible hidden political agenda. The Movement can do better to counter this perception and define its primary identity: religious, social, or political.

Fifth, the current conflict between the Gülen Movement and the Erdoğan government has mostly been viewed as internal struggle for power between the two erstwhile former allies. Though there had never been a programmatic alliance between the two beyond the Movement's support for the government's democratic measures, such dominant perceptions about the Movement have pushed the international community to perceive the Movement as a political actor instead of a social actor within Turkey. A good number of critical intellectuals in the West believe that what matters in the context of Turkey is not Prime Minister or President but the control over the judiciary, military, and bureaucracy, including the police. In the past the civilian Prime Minister and President have been ousted through the intervention of the judiciary and military. Moreover, political parties have been banned by court order. Therefore, Gülen's motivating his volunteers to join state institutions have been looked upon with suspicion.

However, what was considered more problematic than the presence of a few Gülen followers in the state institutions is the linkage between the Movement and state personnel through the informal structure of the *sohbet*, *himmet*, and other forms of socio-spiritual gathering. The Movement retains this structure both horizontally (societal institutions) and vertically (state institutions) at various levels, usually under the supervision of a volunteer/abi/imam. The possibility that information concerning state affairs might change hands during the course of these informal meetings cannot be ruled out, despite the Movement's followers being morally and ethically upright. They may share information concerning state affairs with an ethical and moral intention to serve the larger common good of Turkish society. However, it is this organic connection between the Movement and state institutions, which has raised some concern within the international community, particularly in Western Europe, and has caused people to question whether the Gülen Movement is truly a social movement without any desire for power.

These concerns and questions of the international community are not difficult to understand: they have primarily arisen from within the western-modern discourse of governance, which either demands a complete dissociation of religion and politics at the level of ideas and practice, or ensures state control over, and marginalization of, religion. However, the Gülen Movement, in its activities and discourse, cuts the binary of modernity and tradition and seeks an ethical and moral transformation of every individual, including the re-centering of ethics and morals in public life in order to address to the "corruption" of *Godless modernity*, which has resulted from (in the Movement's understanding) the divorce of the moral and ethical from the political. The Gülen Movement reserves its moral right to forge linkages with each and every individual, including state officials, and did not consider it problematic, illegitimate, or inappropriate to forge such linkages. Though there is no hard evidence that points out misuse of official power arising from such linkages, the Movement must, sooner or later, address this concern of the international community.

Finally, the international community is constrained in its efforts to acknowledge the plight and victimization of the Gülen Movement in international forums partly due to the geo-strategic significance and good economic health of Turkey. Europe, for all practical purposes, is dependent upon Turkey to control the flow of Syrian refugees and other migrants to Europe and to combat the spread of Islamist militants into the West. At a time when Erdoğan's assertive Islamism is posing a threat to Europe, given the Turkish government's linkage with the large Turkish diaspora, particularly through institutions like the Diyanet (the Presidency of Religious Affairs), the European governments prefer to engage Erdoğan within the framework of the European Union, rather than to antagonize and isolate him further.

Similarly, for international investors, Turkey continues to be a good destination for investment, given its current rate of economic development and overall political stability, and therefore they are willing to ignore the "domestic wrongdoings" of the Erdoğan government. After all, a capitalist West has long lived and done business with all kinds of authoritarian and semi-authoritarian rulers around the world.

NOTES

CHAPTER 1

1 The term *hizmet* is derived from the Arabic root *khidma*, meaning "the act of service."

2 "*Hodja* (in Turkish, *hoca*) is a title of imams, religious scholars, or religiously knowledgeable people. Hodjaefendi (in Turkish, *Hocaefendi*) is a combination of the titles *hoca* and *effendi* (a title of respect for men of knowledge or position)" (Ünal and Williams 2000:17, footnote 21). However, the word *hodja* or *hodjam* is everyday usage in Turkey to address the other with respect. Gülen prefers to call himself "a humble teacher in the service of humanity." He continues to provide Islamic teaching from his present home in Pennsylvania, USA, to students, mostly Turkish.

3 Estimate of the number of participants varies. Some estimate around six million in Turkey alone (Turam 2007, 13; Hermansen 2005). İhsan Yılmaz, a volunteer in the Movement, finds this exaggerated and puts the number at around one million within Turkey. Others, who are critical of the Movement, put the figure at around 16–22 million globally (Jager 2016).

4 The precise number of Hizmet institutions is not known and varies from one author to another. However, following the failed military coup on July 15, 2016, the Erdoğan government shut down more than 5,000 Hizmet-linked institutions within Turkey due to the alleged role of the Movement in the coup.

5 Agai 2003, 54. It may be noted that the movement strongly resists any characterization in terms of "-ism."

6 The Movement does not see itself as a representative of social Islam or even subscribes to this notion. Gülen himself does not believe in any compartmentalization of Islam. For him, Islam is a holistic way of life and it should be understood in a balanced and holistic way only. He rejects the contemporary debate over Islam vs. Islams. He espouses the organic understanding of the social phenomenon where the parts are interrelated to each other and establishes the relationship between whole and parts.

7 Lewis 1994; Lerner 1958.

8 Some of the volunteers in the Movement, working in India, confided to me

that many Muslims in India, while appreciative of their initiatives in the field of education, suspect their Islamic authenticity. Part of the reason for this is that under the long spell of "Arab-Wahhabi Islam" a large number of South Asian Muslims are accustomed to identifying Islam in this particular format. The Gülen Movement differs drastically in its bodily and institutional representation of Islam and thus creates suspicion about its Islamic authenticity.

9 Post-Islamism reflects a shift from state-centered Islamist discourse to a civic-society-centered discourse of individual rights, democracy, freedom, political participation, and religious modernity. On post-Islamism see Bayat 2007 and 2013. See more at: http://pomeps.org/2014/02/07/rethinking-post-islamism-hezbollah/.

10 Esposito 1983; Kurzman 1998; Esposito and Voll 2001; Abu-Zayd 2006.

11 Esposito, Haddadi, and Voll 1991.

12 For Yesilova this perceived alliance is overstated and that "Erdoğan and Gülen only came together when Erdoğan's stated goals reflected deeply held beliefs by Gülen." See Yesilova 2016.

13 Interview with Kerim Balcı, editor of *Turkish Review*, Istanbul, December 15, 2010.

14 In Yavuz 2013, quoting Brian Knowlton's interview with Gülen in the *Turkish Review*, Jan–Feb 2011, 52.

15 Interview with Kerim Balcı, editor of *Turkish Review*, Istanbul, December 15, 2010.

16 Walton 2013, 157.

17 Ibid.

18 Interview in Atlanta, April 12, 2015, with Akin, a volunteer associated with the Alliance for Shared Values, a Hizmet institution based in New York.

19 *Asharq Al-Awsat* 2014.

20 Gülen 2005, 27.

21 However, I must make it clear here that Hizmet, unlike *tabligh*, is not a proselytizing movement; the act of *tamsil* is for the sake of Allah without any expectation in return and so coming to the fold of Islam would be completely a voluntary act without any external inducement or influence.

22 Yılmaz 2003.

23 Quoted in Ergil 2012, 27.

24 Gülen 2012.

25 Interview with Berdal Aral, formerly with Fatih University, Istanbul, December 31, 2010.

26 There is a debate in Turkey about the youth turning away from Islam, which one may relate to AKP's autocracy and corruption that, obviously, contradict its outward Islamic rhetoric. See Girit 2018.

27 For an explanation of the "root paradigm" see Mardin 1989, 3–4.

28 In a chance meeting with a young Turkish serving Air Force military officer in Üsküdar, Istanbul, in April 2011, when I informed him that I was working on the Gülen Movement he stated, "The Gülen Movement is very powerful, more powerful than the army in Turkey. I do not know where they get the money from. They run many schools and other charitable works." Expressing his helplessness at the growing profile of the Movement he said, "But what to do? They are very legal," meaning all their activities are legal. It may be noted here that it is to the credit of the legal tradition and sensibilities of the Hizmet Movement that the Turkish government miserably failed to find any illegal wrongdoing on the part of Hizmet institutions and volunteers and thus resorted to the fictitious charge of the "parallel structure" and "FETO" against the Movement in order to crush it.

29 The term "orthodox" here refers to the mainstream Sunni Islamic tradition of *Ahl al-Sunnat wal-Jamaat,* the ones committed to upholding the basic tenets of Sunni Islam.

30 See Asad 2003.

31 Casanova 1994; 2006, 12-30, 2008, 101-19.

32 Today all these institutions have been confiscated or shut down by the government on the allegation of their linkage with what the Turkish government calls FETÖ, one of the two terms, the other being "parallel structure" invented by the Erdoğan-led government to malign and criminalize the Hizmet movement in the aftermath of December 17, 2013 exposé of government corruption.

33 Yavuz 2013, 10.

CHAPTER 2

1 Among the most important are: Esposito and Yılmaz 2010; Yavuz and Es-

posito 2003; Ebaugh 2009; Çetin 2010; Ergene 2008; Carroll 2007; Hunt and Aslandoğan 2007; Balci and Miller 2012; Yavuz 2013; Hendrick 2013. In addition, there exists a good quantity of resource material in the form of conference proceedings, dissertations, theses and numerous articles in the press and in online internet sources.

2 Yavuz 2013, 66.

3 Ergil 2012, 19.

4 Aras and Caha 2000, 38.

5 Gülay 2007a, 59.

6 Kuru 2003.

7 Yılmaz 2015.

8 Özdalga 2003, 72.

9 Interview with Yusuf and other senior volunteers, Istanbul, March 8, 2011.

10 Ergene 2008, 96–113.

11 Bulaç 2007.

12 Gülay 2007b.

13 Togoslu 2008.

14 Yavuz 2013, 47.

15 Undated and unpublished and meant only for internal circulation; a copy was given to me by the then Director of the Journalists and Writers Foundation, Mustafa Yeşil, during a conversation with him in March 2011.

16 Özdalga 2006.

17 Ibid. 564

18 The term "Turkish Muslimness" had gained currency among the Hizmet-oriented Turkish intelligentsia in the last two decades, partly because while Islam cannot be compartmentalized, "Muslimness" reflects the subjectivities of a Muslim population living in a particular area.

19 Yavuz has propounded a theory of "zones of Islam" and argues that its Sufi origins, Sunni Hanafi liberalism, and Kemalist reform succeeded in achieving modernity, unlike Persian, Arab, and South Asian Islam. See Yavuz 2004a.

20 Mardin 1997; Silverstein 2010.

21 Though one may argue that it is the threat from the military, the custodian of Kemalism, that deters the government from revisiting the issue of Kemalism,

the argument is not well founded for two reasons. First, the military no longer enjoys the legitimacy that it enjoyed during the heyday of Kemalism: civilian control over the military has increased tremendously and the military institution has much weakened, if not completely eliminated, its capacity to engineer a military coup. The 15-16th July failed military coup does not qualify as a "military coup." Second, no state or organ of state can permanently prevent its subjects from raising their voice.

22 A total of 8,985 new mosques were constructed throughout Turkey between 2005 and 2015, an average 1,000 mosques per year. "Turkey builds nearly 9,000 mosques in 10 years," *Hürriyet Daily News*, Sept 16, 2016. http://www.hurriyetdailynews.com/turkey-builds-nearly-9000-mosques-in-10-years-.aspx?PageID=238&NID=103950&NewsCatID=341. Accessed February 20, 2017.

23 The purpose of Imam-Hatip schools [Imam – prayer leader, Hatip – preacher] was to produce religious professionals (whose number was steadily declining under the Kemalist regime) to perform Islamic religious rituals under state supervision. The number of Imam-Hatip schools steadily multiplied to deal in part with the communist threat from the Soviet Union and due to the introduction of multiparty democracy in Turkey in the late 1940s. All political parties and governments have made significant contributions to the proliferation of Imam-Hatip schools in order to ensure the electoral support of religious Turkish Muslims. Thus according to Yavuz (2003b, 127), "the number of middle *imam-hatip* schools and high *imam-hatip* schools rose from 7 in 1951 to 604 and 558 in 2001 respectively. The number of student enrollments in middle and high *imam-hatip* schools also rose from 876 and 889 in 1951 to 219,890 and 134,224 in 1999 respectively while the combined strength of teachers in both middle and high *imam-hatip* schools went from 27 to 15,922 during the same period." They are partly funded by the state, but 60-70% of the funds for their construction comes from donations from the Muslim population. The schools cover the secular state curriculum, in addition to Islamic subject (Qur'an, Hadith, Sunni Islamic history, etc.). Since the AKP came to power in 2002, the number of Imam-Hatip middle schools and Imam-Hatip high schools increased from 0 and 450 in 2002–2003 to 1,597 and 1,017 in 2014–2015 respectively, while the number of students in these schools went up from 0 and 84,898 in 2002–2003 to 385,830 and 546,443 in 2014–2015 respectively. See Makovsky 2015. On the role of Imam-Hatip

school in shaping the Islamic political discourse in the country, see, Ozgur 2015.

24 A national attribute, though subject to varied interpretation but one that has to be respected, either symbolically or in practice, by all mainstream political actors, irrespective of their ideological colors. See Gupta 2000.

25 Gülen 1998, 71–3.

26 Interview with Şeref Hancı, Bursa, February 23, 2010.

27 Referring to the objective of the Nur movement, of which he claims the Gülen Movement is one faction, Yavuz (2003c,308) categorically writes, "Its main goal is not to return to an Islamic past but to Islamicize modernity by reinterpreting the shared language of Islam."

28 Interviews with Dr. Özkan Bahar, Dr. Korhan Tan, Dr. Kahraman Ahıskalı, and Dr. Çiğdem Atay in Edirne, March 3, 2011.

29 The Movement has been at the forefront in mobilizing public opinion in favor of Turkey joining the European Union and drafting a Turkish constitution on the basis of the Copenhagen criteria of the European Union. The openness displayed by Hizmet Movement towards the European Union results from an understanding that membership to the EU would open opportunities for cross cultural dialogue between Islam and the West leading to strengthen the process of democratization within the Muslim world including Turkey and in the West. In part, it was guided by the political pragmatism to counter the Kemalist establishment at home as well as to reap the economic benefits that would come through being a part of the Union. However, save a few intellectuals in the Movement, most volunteers do not prescribe a vision of the "good life" based on the European model of individualism upon which rest European economic, social and political values. After all, the AKP, the ruling party of Turkey since 2002 and which once championed the democratization process, did not witness any significant loss in its support base in the wake of its shift towards an authoritarian mode of governance in violation of the basic values of European Union. It may be noted that the social constituencies of the Movement and the AKP often overlap.

30 Interview with Tahsin Koral, New Delhi, January 2, 2011.

31 Others have undertaken similar attempts to retrieve the ethical and moral values of Islam in recent years. See Ramadan 2007 and Abou El Fadl 2006.

32 Kuru 2003.

33 Toguslu 2007.

34 Pew Forum on Religion and Public Life 2010, 18.

35 Çetin 2010, 244–5.

36 Ibid., 242.

37 Ergene 2008, 17.

38 Interview with Dr. Berdal Aral, formerly with Fatih University, Istanbul, December 31, 2010.

39 Yavuz 2013, 33.

40 Quoted in Yavuz 2013, 21.

41 Journalists and Writers Foundation n.d.

42 A few people I interviewed said that Gülen was Syed, mentioning about Gülen's family origins that go all the way up to the Prophet. During my research I never came across any such self-attribution by Gülen in any written source.

43 One senior volunteer associated with the Gülen Movement told me that according to a Prophetic tradition Christians and Muslims will unite against disbelief. Since Christians in Europe and America can understand Islam only through democracy and secularism, it is then important for the Gülen Movement to represent Islam in secular and democratic terms. The same was echoed by another senior volunteer associated with Journalists and Writers Foundation (JWF): "Sufi way of Islam is a means to approach the West, i.e. the materialist world" (interview with Cemal Uşak, now deceased. June 14, 2011. JWF, Istanbul).

44 See, Hendrick 2013.

45 See Casanova 1994.

46 Asad, 1993, also see Salvatore 1997; Eickelman and Piscatori 2004; Zaman 2002; Hoexter, Eisenstadt, and Levtzion 2002; Sachedina 2006.

47 Ebaugh 2009, 2. At the release of her book in Turkey Helen Rose Ebaugh explained that the phrase "moderate Islam" in the title of the English edition was retained considering the Western audience in mind, and the Turkish edition does not have those words in the title. Journalists and Writers Foundation, Istanbul, January 12, 2011.

48 Yılmaz 2005, 397.

49 Gülen 2009a, 145.

50 For an insightful work from this perspective, see, by El Fadl 2005.

51 Sevindi 2008.

52 For a collection of writings by Gülen on this subject matter, see Gülen 2016.

53 Yavuz 2013, 8.

54 Ibid. 9.

55 The violence and destruction generated by the modern discourse of development has led a large number of scholars to reject the European liberal model of tolerance and return to its religious roots of tolerance. See Nandy 1988.

56 Interview, Istanbul, April 8, 2011.

57 Ünal and Williams 2000, 172.

58 Journalists and Writers Foundation n.d., 5.

59 Conway 2014.

60 Ünal and Williams 2000, 314.

61 Kuru 2003, 130.

62 Interview with Kerim Balcı, Istanbul, April 8, 2011.

63 Ünal and Williams 2000, 64.

64 Ibid. 157, quoting Sevindi's *Fethullah Gülen ile New York Sohbeti.*

65 Ibid. 120.

66 Nandy 1988

67 See Yılmaz, 2010, 2011, Kucukun 2007, Ugur 2007.

68 Putnam 1993.

69 Kömeçoğlu 2014; Yılmaz 2015.

70 It may be noted here that the expression "zone of cooperation" does not refer to any alliance in terms of public policy between the Gülen Movement and government, nor does Turam demonstrate such an alliance in terms of specific public policy.

71 Wickham 2002; Wiktorowicz 2004.

72 Şimşek 2004; Yavuz 2004b. For other references see *International Conference Proceedings: Muslim World in Transition: Contributions of the Gülen Movement* 2007.

73 Dreher 2013, 258.

74 Wood and Keskin 2013.

75 Yavuz 2004b; Kuru 2005.

76 Yavuz 2003b, 273.

77 Interview, Istanbul, 2011.

78 Çetin 2010, 5.

79 Eickelman and Piscatori 2004.

80 Besides Yavuz (2013), some of the other works that have applied the Weberian framework of "Protestant Works" to explain the linkage between the Gülen Movement and the economic development of Turkey are Özdalga 2000; Uygur 2007; Arslan 1999; 2000, 2001; Yousef 2001; Topal 2012.

81 The issue of recognition of Islamic contribution to modernity has resurfaced in Europe. Tariq Ramadan and many others have strongly raised this issue and consider such recognition crucial for the integration of Muslim immigrants in Europe.

82 Selahattin Selvi, a Turkish volunteer working in India, revealed this during an informal conversation.

83 Quoted in Gülay 2007a.

84 Interview with Kerim Balcı, Istanbul, 2011.

85 Separate from and over or above society, the very institutional location of Christianity, along with the Biblical dictum "render unto God which is of God and render unto Caesar which is of Caesar," is highlighted as a factor contributing to the development of secularism in the West.

86 In recent years a number of writings have stressed the role of the print and communication revolution—mass media and new media—that has resulted in the democratization of Islamic knowledge, erosion of legitimacy and fragmentation of the authority of the '*ulama*, leading to the democratization of Muslim societies (Eickelman and Piscatori 2004; Mandaville 2007). Yavuz (2003, 2013), highlights the role of Nursi's Textual Islam and its subsequent vernacularization by the Gülen Movement in the democratization of Turkish society and polity. Though this process may have played some role, the modern-day Turkish Islamic outlook—characterized by strong distaste for the direct political role of Islam or rule of Sharia—is more a product of the long history of gradual secularization of Turkish polity and society that was intensified by Kemal Atatürk than of any print revolution which the Otto-

mans had already introduced in the eighteenth century. (See Berkes 1964.) Zaman (2002) has also demonstrated that it is naïve to think that the print revolution and mass media weakened the '*ulama*'s authority; on the contrary, it has helped to increase its influence and has strengthened its authority.

87 "Arabic to be offered as second language in Turkish elementary schools." November, 23, 2015, http://www.hurriyetdailynews.com/arabic-to-be-offered-as-second-language-in-turkish-elementary-schools-.aspx?pageID=238&nID=90244&NewsCatID=341 , accessed on November 25, 2015.

88 Interview, Istanbul, 2011.

89 Dreher 2015.

90 Bernards 2015, 124-145.

91 Mardin 1989, 56, quoting Friedmann 1971, 15-6. Also, Friedmann 1966, 20-1.

92 Turner 1974, 2.

93 Ibid. 144.

94 Lapidus 1997, 454.

95 Interview, Istanbul, 2011. In addition to my interviews with Turkish scholars in which the notion of Turkish Islam frequently occurred, some important works dealing with the notion of Turkish Islam are: Aras and Caha 2000; Yavuz 2004, 2013, Ch. 2; Ugur 2008, 84-8. For a critical analysis of Turkish Islam, see Özdalga 2006.

CHAPTER 3

1 Asad 1986, 20.

2 See, Geertz 1968.

3 Asad 1986, 12.

4 MacIntyre 1988, 45.

5 Asad 1993, 29.

6 Asad 1986, 12.

7 MacIntyre 1988, 345.

8 Brown 1996, 3.

9 Voll 2008.

10 Haj 2009, 5.

11 Gülay 2007b, 8.

12 Gülen 2005, 4–5.

13 Karabaşoğlu 2003, 263.

14 Eisenstadt 2000. For the application of the conception of multiple or alternative modernity to Muslim societies, see, Göle 2000.

15 Navaro-Yashin 2002; Mahmood 2005; Göle 1996.

16 Abu-Lughod 1998; Gole 2002; White 2002; Salvatore 1997, 2007; Salvatore and Eickelman 2004.

17 Bacık and Kurt 2011.

18 Interview with Eşref Potur, 70, considered a close associate of Gülen and associated with Hizmet since 1969. March 17, 2011, Izmir.

CHAPTER 4

1 Giddens 1991, 1-70.

2 Smith 1957, 162.

3 For a critical reading of this discourse and its linkage with power and knowledge, see Said 1978.

4 Smith 1957, 47.

5 See Nandy 1983.

6 The earliest encounter of modernity in Muslim society was usually traced to the Napoleonic invasion of Egypt (1798-1801). However, it was short-lived and without much impact on the Egyptian society.

7 Sir Syed Ahmad Khan had visited Britain and France before embarking on the Aligarh Project. It is said that the physical structure of Anglo-Muhammadan College, which now stands as Aligarh Muslim University, is very much based on the pattern of Oxford University. Muhammad Iqbal pursued his higher education in Germany. Afghani and Abduh published their journal *al-⊠Urwa al-Wuthqāal* from Paris. Abduh frequented Europe many times and discovered "hope" in his visit to Europe for the regeneration of the Islamic *ummah*.

8 Al-Azmeh 1993, 28. For details, see chapter 4, "Islamic Revivalism and Western Ideologies," 77-88.

9 On the political life and activities of Jamal al-Din Afghani, see Adams 2013,

4-17; Keddie 1968, 1972; and Belkeziz 2009, 28-33.

10 See Kurzman 1998.

11 One recent example of this imbalance between state and civil society in Turkey is the decision of the Prime Minister Erdoğan-led AKP government to close down private preparatory schools in 2013. The decision was particularly to target the rising profile of the Gülen Movement that controlled 25% of all preparatory schools in Turkey as these were the most crucial institutions for attracting young minds to the Gülen Movement. Criticism from several quarters could not move the government to re-consider this decision. On the contrary, the government since then has hardened its position toward the Gülen Movement. Following the December 2013 corruption case the Erdoğan government intensified its crackdown on the Gülen Movement resulting in the arrest and detention of police officers and harassment of supporting business people—a trend that culminated in closing down more than 5,000 educational, relief, charitable, and health institutions along with the dismissal of more than 100,000 public officials after the failed military coup of July 15, 2016. Recently, the government has arrested even more police officers it suspects of working on behalf of the Gülen Movement against the state. On the Turkish purge see, https://turkeypurge.com

12 On Muhammad Abduh, see Adams 1968 and Haj 2009, 67–109.

13 On Sir Syed Syed Ahmad Khan, see Malik, 1980.

14 Iqbal 2012, 124.

15 Ansari 1995, vii–ix.

16 Ibid.

17 Ibid.

18 Iqbal 2012, 101.

19 Adams 2013, 86.

20 See his *Risale-i Nur*.

21 Brown 1996, 33.

22 Sir Syed Ahmad Khan, 'Lecture on Islam,' in Kurzman, 2002, 296.

23 Abu-Zayd 2006, 30.

24 Ibid, 32.

25 Brown 1996, 37.

26 Abu Zayed, 2006, 35.

27 For instance, An-Na'im, following his teacher Mahmoud Mohammed Taha, sought to reconstruct the meaning of Islam based upon Meccan verses and rejecting Medinan verses by invoking the Islamic theory of abrogation in order to bring Islam closer to modern-day concepts of civil liberty, human rights, and international law. See An-Na'im 1990, 1994.

28 Iqbal 2012, 129.

29 Rahman 1979.

30 Iqbal 2002, 312.

31 Gökalp 2002.

32 Rahman 2002, 309.

33 Shabestari 2004, 116-28; Keddie 1981, 13.

CHAPTER 5

1 Yavuz 2013, 33.

2 Ibid.

3 See Casanova 1994.

4 Rahman 1995, 86.

5 Gülen 2005, 20.

6 Gülen 1998, 87.

7 Though there is a strong link between *Islah* (Reform), *Ijtihad* (Reasoning) and *Tajdid* (Renewal), the literature on *tajdid* or the *mujaddidi* tradition is scarce. For a few useful analyses of the *mujaddidi* tradition in Islam, see Landau-Tasseron 1989, 79-117; Friedmann 1966, 17-29. On *Ijtihad* and *Islah*, see Voll 1983 32–45; Rahman 1970, 1995.

8 Gülen 1998, 91.

9 Gülen 2005, 19.

10 Interview with M. Enes Ergene, Istanbul, December 28, 2010.

11 Acar 2012, 70.

12 Ibid.

13 Interviews with M. Enes Ergene, Istanbul, December 28, 2010, with Veli Turan, Delhi, December 25, 2011, and with Hasan Kaya, Mardin, February 23,

2011.

14 For the reason-revelation divide in Islamic history, see Gülay 2007b, 1-10.

15 Lapidus 1997, 454.

16 Ergene 2008, 111.

17 Alam 2004, 25-85.

18 Gülen 2009b, 117-119.

19 Yusuf Kartal, a volunteer in the Hizmet movement told me in an informal conversation that to a query by one of his students Hodjaefendi said he considered Bediüzzaman Said Nursi as one of the *mujaddids*. Zirve University, Gaziantep, October 15, 2015.

20 Iqbal 2012, 3.

21 Al-Ghazali's *Incoherence of Philosophers* and his *Revival of the Religious Sciences* are considered, primarily in Western literature, as the culmination of the historical conflict between Islamic theology and philosophy. It is contended that al-Ghazali's thesis put an end to further evolution of Islamic philosophy and resulted in the stagnation of Muslim thought and growth which proved fatal to the growth of science and independent thinking, leading to the decline and backwardness of Muslim civilization.

22 Lapidus 1998, 192-224.

23 A great majority of reformers in the annals of Islam has displayed this approach towards Islam, though elements of Salafism and Sufism vary from one Islamic reformer to another. It is the balancing act between the two that has differentiated Ghazali, Imam Rabbani, and Said Nursi from other Islamic reformers. All Islamic reformers, ranging from Abdul Bin Wahhab to Jamal al-Din Afghani, Muhammad Abduh, Hasan Al Banna, Sayyid Qutb, etc., have retained the association with Sufism, while being critical of many aspects of Sufi traditions. However, under the spell of modernity, contemporary Islamic scholars and reformers gravitated more towards Salafism (a legal-scripturalist tradition) at the cost of Sufism, leading to the development of a kind of neo-Salafism often marked by a very high level of indulgence of violence.

24 Lapidus 1998, 448.

25 Mahmood 1996, 8.

26 Michel 2014, 76, quoting Gülen, 1998, 122-23.

27 On these aspects of Ghazali's thought, see Griffel 2009.

28 Ansari 1986, 17, 230.

29 Devji 2011.

30 Friedmann 1971; also Alam 2010, 160-65.

31 Hourani 1972, 89-103.

32 Gülen 2005, 74.

33 On the life, times and thought of Bediüzzaman Said Nursi, see Mardin 1989; Nursi 2006; Abu-Rabi 2003; Vahide 2005.

34 The Hanafi school arose from the teachings of Abu Hanifa (d. 150/767), who lived in Kufa in Iraq. Since the school originated in Iraq, the Abbasid caliphs, who were based in Iraq, gave it their support. However, this support declined over time and the school had to wait until the emergence of the Ottoman Empire to become influential again. This school, particularly in the early stages, was associated with an emphasis on reason (much more than other schools of law). Today, Hanafi law is the dominant form of Islamic law in the Indian subcontinent, Central Asia, and Turkey". See Saeed 2006, 50-51. "A Hanafi in law, al-Maturidi used reason within the limits of orthodoxy, and shunned literalism. Maturidism occupies a position between Asharite and Mu'tazilite. No writings of Al-Maturidi appear in published form. It is thus easier to speak of Maturidism than to speak of al-Maturidi himself. The creed of Najm al-Din al-Nasafi (d. 537/1142) and its commentary by Taftazani are renowned Maturidi sources to this day. Maturidism also maintains that God endows human beings with both choice and power to act. See Saeed 2006, 70.

35 Gülay 2007b, 71-72.

36 Ibid. 12.

37 Gülen 2009a, 145.

38 Ibid. 49.

39 This paragraph is based on the following sources: Albayrak 2011 1-39; Tuncer 2006; Gülen 2005; interview with Ali Ünal, Istanbul, March 2, 2011.

40 Çalış 2011, 46.

41 Gülen 2009.

42 Volunteers in the Hizmet had informed me during this research that Gülen had plans of writing a *tafsir* of the Qur'an.

43 Mardin 1989, 56, quoting Friedmann 1971, 15-6. Also, Friedmann 1966, 20-1.

44 Albayrak 2011, 26-7.

45 There are three chief features of Naqshbandi Sufi discourse that make it different from other Sufi orders (*silsala* or *tariqa*). First, the Naqshbandi trace their source of inspiration and genealogy to Prophet Muhammad through Abu Bakr, and not through Ali, with whom almost all other Sufi Orders are affiliated. Second, it is more action-oriented than other Sufi orders. Third, in comparison to other orders, Naqshbandi strictly emphasizes the separateness of Allah from everything—living and non-living things—and gives a much greater role to the Prophet's Sunna in their life. Fourth, unlike other Sufi orders, the Naqshbandi practices the silent mode of *dhikr* (remembrance of God). For general reading on Sufism, see Geoffroy 2010.

46 Gülen 2009b, 2007.

47 Özübüyük 2013.

48 Değirmenli 2013.

49 Ünal and Williams 2000, 358.

50 According to Metin Şahin, who was a student of Gülen from 1992-1999, Gülen does *dhikr* for about five hours in addition to reading Qur'an every day in a silent manner. Interview with Metin Sahin, Istanbul, December 28, 2010. Imam Rabbani, who opted for the Naqshbandi *tariqa*, called the loud, musical and dance form of *dhikr* practice a "deviant Sufi practice that contravenes the Sunna" and upheld Naqshbandi form of *dhikr* as correct practice. See Alam 2010.

51 Gülen 1998, 20.

52 This description is attributed to Fethullah Gülen as he was seen to remain aloof even if interacting with people. See Seker 2011, 115.

53 This account of Gülen's exposition of Sufism is based on the following sources: Gülen 1999; Gülen 2005; Ünal and Williams 2000, 352-69; Michel 2005, 341-359, Aslandogan 2007, 663-682; and Ergene 2008, 158-186.

54 Interview with Ali Ünal, Istanbul, March 2, 2011.

55 There appears to be some confusion with regard to period of *al-asr al-saadah [Age of Happiness*]. For, some it strictly refers to the period of Prophet Muhammad. For others, like Ahmet Kurucan, one of the foremost interpreters of Gülen's ideas, consider the period of Prophet Muhammad and the Four Rightly Guided Caliphs as the period of *al-asr al-saadah* as during this period the ideas and principles of the Prophet were fully developed, practiced,

and institutionalized. In this way, the concept of *al-asr al-saadah* differs from the Islamic modernist construction of the "Golden Period of Islam." Ahmet Kurucan opines that the fact that three of the four caliphs were assassinated during this period dilutes the sense of a golden period of Islam. Interview with Ahmet Kurucan, April 12, 2015, Atlanta, USA.

56 However, there is growing perception among Muslim social scientists that while the "Christian doctrine of Sin" has led to focus on the building of democratic institutions in the West in order to regulate unbridle desire and ego of the human beings, the Islamic understanding of human nature in terms of its goodness has not produced the democratic institutions in the Muslim majority country. Hence there is a need to rethink this proposition of Islamic discourses about the mankind.

57 Ünal and Williams 2000, 315.

58 Ibid. 242.

59 Gülen 2006, 75-6.

60 Gülen 1998c, 106.

61 Quoted in Çalış 2011, 7.

62 Since October 2013 the AKP government has gradually allowed the wearing of the headscarf in all public institutions including the judiciary and military. Wearing Muslim headscarf has been a big debate in Turkey for decades. Especially in late '90s when the secularist military had a tough grip on the government, university students were banned to wear the Muslim covering. This ban polarized the society to an extreme social unrest. In that period, Gülen tried to ease the tension by emphasizing the importance of education, and that Muslim women should pursue their education despite the ban. His message was never meant to undermine the religious principles regarding the headscarf or the way Muslim women chose to dress.

63 Çalış 2011, 82.

64 Ibid. 80.

65 Ibid. 79-81.

66 Ünal and Williams 2000, 62.

67 Interview with Tahsin Koral, New Delhi, January 2, 2011.

68 For Soroush, whereas religion (the foundational text which in the case of Shia Islam includes the Qur'an and Hadith related to the Prophet, Ali, and Shia

Imams) is infallible, religious knowledge is the corpus of interpretation of the foundational text; hence it is historically contingent and in need of constant re-evaluation. See Souroush 2000, 30-80.

69 Habermas 2010, 17-18.

70 Gülen 2005, 28-9.

71 Ünal and Williams, 2000, 52-3, 56.

72 Sevindi 2008, 79.

73 Sevindi 2008, 79.

74 Quoted in Ergene 2008, 113-4

75 Friedmann 1971, 82-3, referring to *Maktubat* Vol. 3.

76 Kömeçoğlu 1997, 45.

77 Rahman 1995, 97.

78 Quoted in Kömeçoğlu 1997, 44.

79 Gülay 2007a, 42, quoting Gülen, *Prizma*, Vol. 2. p. 12 (1997).

80 Ergil 2012, 27.

81 Quoted in Ergene 2008, 183.

82 Gülen 2012.

83 Quoted in Ergene 2008, 184.

84 Özübüyük 2013, 88-9.

85 Lapidus 1997.

86 Yılmaz 2003.

CHAPTER 6

1 Interview with İhsan Yılmaz, December 31, 2010, Fatih University, Istanbul.

2 Yavuz 2013, 26–29, Yavuz and Esposito 2003, 20.

3 Agai 2007, 166.

4 Yavuz 2013, 43.

5 Interviews with Professor Dr. Recep Kaymakcan, Sakarya University, Sakarya, February 28, 2010, and İhsan Yılmaz, Fatih University, December 31, 2010.

6 Agai 2007, 162-163.

7 Ibid.

8 Yavuz 2013, 31.

9 Balci 2012, 81.

10 Modern scholarship is replete with a debate on Islam vs. Islams. In this debate an essentialized, textual, urban and Great Tradition form of understanding of Islam is contrasted with localized, varied, and plural forms of understanding of Islam(s). In other words, Textual or Essential vs. Sociological or Lived Islam compete with each other in the realm of interpretation of Islam and its associated values and traditions. In this debate, the question is whose Islam, class, ethnicity, tribe, etc., assumes a major role in experiencing and interpreting Islam. Notwithstanding the merit of this debate, I do not see any oppositional polarity between Islam and Islams but the two have been continuously interacting and negotiating with each other and it is through this process that an "Islamic" position is arrived at on various subject matters concerning human life.

11 Asad 1986, 14.

12 "Syed" is an honorific in Muslim society through which the genealogy of a person and his family is traced to Prophet Muhammad. In modern terminology, it is an important indicator of social capital. However, some senior volunteers of Hizmet Movement did refer to Gülen as "Syed" there is no record of Gülen using the title before his name.

13 There appears to be a little confusion with regard to the exact year in which Gülen was born. In many English-medium books on the Gülen Movement, his year of birth is recorded as 1938 or 1941. However, Seyfullah Gülen (retired as driver from Atatürk University in 1990), now deceased, who was the younger brother of Gülen, identified his own year of birth as 1941. As Seyfullah was two and half years younger than Gülen, I presume Gülen's year of birth is 1938 (interview with Seyfullah Gülen, Erzurum, February 26, 2011). One volunteer associated with Hizmet I spoke with put his date of birth as November 11, 1938, a day after the death of Kemal Atatürk, indicating a degree of divine plan in Gülen's birth. However, İhsan Yılmaz strongly disagrees with such a formulation, calls it a myth prevailing among some movement volunteers, and puts his date of birth as 1941 on the basis of a minimum age of 18 years required to become an imam in the public mosque. In 1960 the Court increased his age by one year to make him eligible for the position of imam, considering his special knowledge of Islam, which would have been

otherwise denied to him as his father had registered his date of birth as 1942. The issue of increasing Gülen's age for the purpose of giving him the position of Imam in the mosque was also confirmed to me to by an interviewee who is a contemporary of Gülen during my field trip in Edirne in 2011.

14 Interview with Seyfullah Gülen, Erzurum, February 26, 2011.

15 Interview with Yaşar Gülen, cousin of Gülen, Korucuk, Erzurum, February 25, 2011.

16 The name of the mosque now has been changed to Millet mosque following the July 2016 failed military coup for which the Erdoğan government directly blamed the Gülen Movement.

17 Interview with Seyfullah Gülen, Erzurum, February 26, 2011.

18 Interview with Yaşar Gülen, cousin of Gülen, Korucuk, Erzurum, February 25, 2011, and interview with Seyfullah Gülen, Erzurum, February 26, 2011.

19 Ibid.

20 Ibid.

21 M. Ünal 2004, 23.

22 In this region *madrasas* and Sufi lodges continued to operate despite the official ban.

23 Interview with Yaşar Gülen, Korucuk, Erzurum, February 25, 2011.

24 M. Ünal 2004, 25.

25 Interview with Yaşar Gülen and others, Korucuk, Erzurum, February 25, 2011.

26 Interview with Seyfullah Gülen, Erzurum, February 26, 2011.

27 Interview with Yaşar Gülen, Korucuk, Erzurum, February 25, 2011.

28 Interview with Mehmet Kırkıncı, Erzurum, February 26, 2011.

29 Adhan, call to prayer, which is called in Arabic all over the Muslim World, was banned in Turkey from 1932 to 1950. Imams were allowed to call it in Turkish only.

30 Ibid.

31 Ibid.

32 Interview with Prof. Fehmi Namlı (Bosphorus University), Hacı Gani Kutdereli (Businessmen), Prof. Firuz Kul (Ataturk University), Mehmet Kırkıncı and others, Erzurum, February 26, 2011.

33 Interview with Mehmet Kırkıncı, Erzurum, February 26, 2011.

34 Ibid.

35 In addition to these traits, according to several of my other interviewees, Gülen appeared to his contemporaries to live an ascetic life, value time, be meticulously organized, have a high level of legal sensitivity, very particular about his sense of dress, have a sensitive heart and mind, keep in touch with his contemporaries and family members, and have a natural propensity to helping others. He never wore a creased pair of pants (trousers). In the absence of an iron, he used to put them under the mattress at night so as to make them appear pressed in the morning. His wearing of this garment is considered by many to show his ease with modernity.

36 Based on interviews with more than 50 volunteers associated with Hizmet, including volunteers closely associated with Gülen during 1960s, 1970s, 1980s and 1990s.

37 Interview with Seyfullah Gülen, Erzurum, February 26, 2011.

38 Ibid.

39 Ibid.

40 Interview with Sezai Sakarya (born 1933), Edirne, March 4, 2011, a contemporary of Gülen and a close associate.

41 Interview with Fahri Hayırlı, 71 (served as muezzin and later imam in Selimiye mosque for 41 years as an employee of Diyanet), Edirne, March 4, 2011.

42 Gülen 2010, 27.

43 Sezai Sakarya put the age of Gülen as 18-19 when he took the position of imam in Edirne. He was thus under-age to be eligible for the position of imam. After considering his religious knowledge, his age was increased by the decision of the Court. Interview with Sezai Sakarya, Edirne, May 10, 2011.

44 Ibid.

45 Ibid.

46 Interview with Seyfullah Gülen, Erzurum, February 26, 2011.

47 Interviews with Sezai Sakarya, Fahri Hayırlı, and Hüseyin Ertem, 65. Edirne, March 4-5, 2011.

48 Interview with a group of doctors from central Anatolia associated with Hizmet (Özkan Bahar, Korhan Tan, Kahraman Ahiskalı, and Çiğdem Atay).

Edirne, March 4, 2011.

49 Interview with Fahri Hayırlı and Sezai Sakarya, Edirne, March 4, 2011.

50 Interview with Muin Adıgüzel, age 70, and others, Izmir, March 16, 2011. Today the practice of Islam in Edirne and other Western cities is a hundred times greater than in the 1950s and 1960s, asserted these interviewees. Another noticeable feature about the Friday gatherings in the mosque, according to these interviewees, is that whereas during 1950s and 1960s it was mostly people of an older age who frequented the mosque, today it is youngsters who fill the mosque. My own observation while in Turkey from 2010-2011 and from September 2013-June 2016 onward confirmed this trend.

51 Interview with Hüseyin Ertem. 65, Edirne, March 5, 2011.

52 A biography of Fethullah Gülen, Gülen Institute, http://dialogin.dk/pages/wp-content/uploads/2013/04/Biography_of_Gülen.pdf, accessed September 24, 2014.

53 http://en.cihan.com.tr/news/1153496-Diyanet-tops-the-budget-league-CHMTE1MzQ5Ni81. Accessed August 31, 2014.

54 The founder of the Muslim Brotherhood in Egypt that served as the prototype of Political Islam throughout the Muslim world.

55 The radical ideologue of the Muslim Brotherhood executed in 1966 by the Nasserite regime.

56 Founder of Jamaat-e-Islami in South Asia.

57 Leader and founder of Islamic Republic of Iran (1979).

58 See Jenkins 2008, Yavuz and Esposito 2003, Yavuz 2003; Yılmaz 2005.

59 On the general process of secularization and modernization in Turkey see Berkes 1964; Ahmed 1993; Lewis 2002.

60 Casanova 1994.

61 Yavuz, 2003, 46.

62 Interview with Prof. Dr. Suat Yıldırım, Istanbul, June 13, 2011.

63 Ibid.

64 Hermann 2014, 97.

65 Ibid. 97-99.

66 Ibid. 46-52.

67 In a very rare interview Gülen accused Erdoğan as "not fit" for rule. See,

"Fethullah Gullen: Erdogan Is not Fit to Be President" Wednesday, 26 July, 2017 | 21:10 WIB, https://en.tempo.co/read/news/2017/07/26/241894729/Fethullah-Gullen-Erdogan-is-not-Fit-to-be-President, accessed February 4, 2018.

68 Sayyid 1997.

69 See Mardin 208–9.

70 Gülay 2007b, Chapter Three: Said Nursi and the Modern Philosophy of Islamised Science.

71 See Michel 2014, 85–95.

72 This was confirmed by many of my interviewees.

73 Interview with Muin Adıgüzel, 70, close associate and contemporary of Gülen, Izmir, March 16, 2011.

74 Ibid also Yusuf, 73, Seyfi Kara, 53, Eşref Potur, 70, and others, Izmir.

75 Ibid.

76 Ibid.

77 The author has personally witnessed Gülen weeping while conducting *sohbet* at his residence in Pennsylvania, October 14, 2017.

78 As Seyfi Kara, 57, says, many people in the Movement, as in the cases of many other spiritual leaders and movements, have personal convictions that Gülen has a strong connection with God and the Prophet Muhammad, and that he is spiritually guided by them. Some businessmen that I spoke with said their business actually has grown after they started giving in charity for Hizmet, pointing to what Muslims call *baraqa*, an abundance that God gives in return for good service, worship, etc. This perception is not specific to Gülen; similar sociological processes are visible in other cases of religious-spiritual personalities across societies and cultures.

79 Interview with Yusuf Pekmezci, 73, Izmir, March 16, 2011, a close associate of Gülen and Hizmet since the arrival of Gülen in Izmir in 1966, and who lived in Kazakhstan for 15 years from 1991, where he helped to establish 28 schools and one university.

80 I attended one such camp in a resort, near Ankara, as part of an India-based Hizmet group comprising 43 families led by Tahsin Koral, in May, 2011. In India, the schools re-open in July after the summer holiday in May and June. The Asya resort was three-star hotel with separate swimming facility

for men, women, and family. It was a week-long program. Apart from the daily book-reading program, two senior Abis (Ali Bayram and Mehmet Ali Şengül) visited the camp to deliver lectures. I was told that Ali Bayram was one of the earliest faces of Hizmet, played a crucial role in spreading Hizmet and the development of schools in Central Asia, and today enjoys an advisory position in the Hizmet. Mehmet Ali Şengül has been a close companion of Gülen and is considered next to him in terms of understanding of Hizmet. The lectures mostly focus on subject matter like "The Necessity of Religion for the younger generation," "Being Just – Unique Feature of Islam" and "Importance of the Family in Islam."

81 Muin Adıgüzel, age 70, close associate and contemporary of Gülen, March 16, 2011.

82 Interview with Şeref Hancı, student of Hodjaefendi, December 23, 2010. Bursa.

83 Private houses for university students to live, study, and practice their religion together.

84 Interview with Mustafa Yeşil, Journalists and Writers Foundation. Istanbul June 8, 2011.

85 However, Ömer Caha, an academic at Fatih University, in a survey on the "Turkish perception of the Gülen Community" in 2010, found only 56% of Turkish population were familiar with the name "Gülen." Interview with Ömer Caha, Fatih University, Istanbul, April 27, 2011.

86 Yavuz 2003, 69, quoting *Milliyet* newspaper, September 12, 1998.

87 Interviews with Mehmet, Izmir, March 16, 2011, Ahmet Dal, Gaziantep, March 18, 2011, Şeref Hancı, Bursa, December 23, 2010.

88 Interviews with Suat Yıldırım, Istanbul, June 13, 2011, Şeref Hancı, Bursa, December 23, 2010.

89 Interview with two industrialists associated with the Gülen Movement, Sivas, March 18, 2011 and March 2, 2011, Kayseri.

90 Interviews with Ahmet Dal and Halis Yurtsever Gaziantep, March 18, 2011.

91 Interview with Kerim Balcı, *Zaman* office, Istanbul, December 15, 2010.

92 Pamuk 2007, 291.

93 In the Turkish context, the distinction between Islam, nation and community is blurred. A large number of literatures have focused on the adoption

of nationalist language for the rise of Turkish Islamic groups and primarily casts Gülen within the "Islamo-nationalist paradigm"; however, the distinction between Turkish and Islamic identity is not very sharp and they subsume each other. Moreover, any empirical survey today in Turkey would reveal that many Hizmet volunteers or Muslims in general prefer Islam as the first marker of their identity, then Turkish and others. It may also be stressed here that for Gülen, nation as secular formation and Islam as religious identity do not contradict but complement each other. For Gülen, nation is principally an Islamic concept and natural artifact that flows from the Qur'anic dictum that God has created different nations so that humans can understand each other and live together by respecting difference, pluralism, and diversity (Hujurat 49:13).

94 See Hendrick 2013.

95 Interview with Suat Yıldırım, JWF, Istanbul, June 13, 2011.

96 Özdalga 2010, 85.

97 İhsan Yılmaz, n.d, *From Kemalism to Erdoğanism* (unpublished English translation).

CHAPTER 7

1 The political role of the mosque under Erdoğan-dominated AKP rule became increasingly manifest when the imams of mosques began to recite the *adhan* every half hour very shortly after the start of the coup attempt on July 15, 2016 and started mobilizing people on the street against the military and coup plotters. Later, the Diyanet under its then-head Mehmet Görmez declared Gülen and the Hizmet Movement as "excommunicated," meaning he placed Gülen and the volunteers of the Movement beyond the pale of Islam. He also dismissed a total of 1,618 Diyanet officials and functionaries, the majority of whom were imams of mosques. Later, imam of Diyanet-controlled mosques within and outside Turkey were pressed to identify Hizmet followers and report them to the government authorities. The obedience to this order by imams outside Turkey invited the ire of the German, French, and Austrian governments and led to the expulsion of Diyanet imams back to Turkey. See, Eddy 2018.

2 Thijl Sunier, Nico Landman, Heleen van der Linden, Nazlı Bilgili and Alper Bilgili, 2011, 51-52.

3 Ibid.

4 Today this opportunity is closed in Turkey, and discussion about Islam or religion in public spaces is strictly prohibited.

5 Soltes 2013, 61.

6 Mardin 2006, 218.

7 TURKSTAT, Turkish Statistical Institute. www.tuik.gov.tr.

8 Tas and Lightfoot 2005, 267.

9 This situation was something that hardly occurred in the history of nations, at least not in Muslim nations. The nation-building process everywhere, including the communist countries, has preserved its linguistic and cultural past. The present-day Secular Europe transformed her non-secular past into the cultural legacy of the various European nations. Each of the different states in the Arab world gave more primacy to its part of Islamic history in the process of its nation-building. See Choueir 2001. The Kemalist government's decision to switch to the Latin alphabet in 1928 was not merely a complete substitution of the Turkish language for the Arabized Ottoman language in order to express the newly established Turkish nationalism but was intended to permanently disconnect people from the memory of the Ottoman-Islamic past that had components of Arab Islam. This was also partly to do with Atatürk's project of the "Europeanization of Turkey" and partly due to fear that the Ottoman legacy might pose a threat to his rule at a later juncture. See Yavuz 1999.

10 Mardin 2006. p. 224.

11 "In 1951, the Turkish National Parliament passed a law on 'Crimes Against Atatürk'. Law Number 7872, still on the books in the 1990s, punishes all those who 'insult the memory of Atatürk' through words or actions to three years in prison. Those who damage busts or statutes of Atatürk are similarly punished with confinement." See Navaro-Yashin 2002, 202–203.

12 Kramer 2000, 90.

13 For why Islamism filled the national vacuum or emerged as an alternative to Kemalism, see Sayyid 1997.

14 Gülen 2005, 35.

15 See Mardin 2006, chapter, "Youth and Violence in Turkey," 205-224.

16 It has been suggested that the re-centering of Islam in the Turkish public do-

main is in part due to articulation of Islamic interest by the Muslim social and political forces within the *nationalist* language and idioms in the 1980s or what is called the Turkish-Islam synthesis, unlike in the 1940s, when the Islamic opposition to Kemalism was couched in Islamic terms and hence failed. However, one needs to be cautious about the idea that the success of the Gülen Movement is due to Gülen's skillful use of nationalist trappings because Gülen does not juxtapose Islam in opposition to nation: service to Islam means service to individual, community, state, and nation and vice-à-versa. Moreover, most of the volunteers of the Gülen Movement that I have interacted identify their first identity as Muslim/Islamic followed by other identities. In an interview in 1995, Gülen identified himself as a "Muslim Turk," saying that "the Turks became a nation after they became Muslim." See Balci 2012, 81, quoting *Medya Aynasında Fethullah Gülen*, 22.

17 Quoted in Kömeçoğlu, 2014, 29.

18 It may be noted here that the formation of Turkey as a homogenized Sunni Turkish Muslim nation was a long drawn process. It began with the Tanzimat modernization program under Ottoman rule between 1839 and 1876 and continues today. As the Ottoman Empire began to decline, the politics of nationalism resulted in the secession of large ethnic and religious minorities, predominantly Christians from its body politic during the late nineteenth century. The politics of "Turkification (read Muslim) of Ottoman Empire" pursued by the CUP and Young Turks further resulted in alienating Armenians, Greeks and Arabs and their eventual secession from the Empire at the end of the First World War. The Kemalist regime witnessed an even more vigorous process of homogenizing the Muslim nation through systematic marginalization of all other ethnic minorities and the exchange of populations with the Greeks under the ideology of Turkish nationalism. See Çağaptay 2006.

19 Kömeçoğlu 1997, 45.

20 Gülen's Anatolian background, his appearance in western dress without beard and his Islamic credentials went a long way in helping and assuring the people to live under the modern condition without being fearful of losing the faith. As Mr. Unal Cantimur while narrating his transformation from past irreligious and alcoholic life to becoming a Muslim, stated: "As I was suffering from personal internal crisis I had started going to local, Naqshbandi-Qadiri Sufi order for guidance but without any success. In 1995, after 9 months of

consulting the local Sufi person, I met a person from the Gülen Movement, attended a gathering with them and found the outlook of *jamaat* (Gülen Movement) different from traditional Islam. One day I watched along with my wife Fethullah Gülen on a local TV channel who appeared in western dress and speaking about Islam including 'hostel for students.' 'Imam with western dress' was something new for me. I had never imagined Islam in this form. I felt comfortable and assured of my Muslim identity even if I practice my Islam in western form. Since then I am associated with the Movement and contribute in my own way. With the support from the Gülen Movement, I also overcame all my bad habits" (Interview with Mr. Unal Cantimur, a businessman, born 1968. Mardin, February 26, 2011).

21 In my more than 50 structured interviews and countless informal interaction with volunteers of Hizmet, never did I find them carry the notion of 'other' while being committed for the Islamic vision of nation and the world.

22 An indicator of the growing economic assertion of Muslim entrepreneurship was the formation MÜSİAD (Müstakil Sanayici ve İşadamları Derneği). According to Yavuz, (2003, 65) "2,600 companies were members of MÜSİAD in 2006, accounting for 12 percent of Turkey's gross national product.

23 Many practicing Muslims, laymen and intellectuals, including many from the Hizmet Movement, consider Özal, not Atatürk, to be the real architect of modern Turkey.

24 Interview with Mustafa Yeşil, Journalists and Writers Foundation, Istanbul, June 8, 2011.

25 Since Turkey does not carry out an ethnicity-based national survey of public employment, it is difficult to find the degree of various forms of exclusion and marginalization of Anatolian Muslims. However, it is widely believed that the Center [meaning Administration, Army, Police, Bureaucracy, Judiciary, Education, Media and Business] has traditionally been dominated by minority Westernized "White Turks" with a large intake of the Alevi ethnic minority. This has begun to change recently as Anatolian Muslims have made tremendous progress in almost all sectors except the Army and Judiciary—the two most powerful institutions since the Kemalist era.

26 Toprak 1999, 5.

27 The disparity between those educated in French-medium and Arabic-medium schools in access to public employment opportunities, prestige, iden-

tity, and recognition was an important factor in the civil war of Algeria. The Francophone sector monopolized all governmental opportunities, while the state legally barred those with a background in Arabic-medium study from pursuing science courses, which was only possible in the French medium. See Martinez 2000

28 The digital divide between the *madrasa*-educated and secular-educated is extremely wide. The students taught in *madrasas* without any access to market opportunities were politicized under General Zia's Islamization program, and later sections of them became the victims of Islamic terrorism in the volatile political situation of Afghanistan (Malik 1996, 85–119).

29 Quoted in Yavuz 2013, 79.

30 Interview, Istanbul, June 8, 2011.

31 Yavuz 2013, 78.

32 Mardin 1989, 3.

33 Ibid, 4. Those taking part in the process of conquest are called as *gazi* and their activity *gaza*.

34 Interview, Fatih University, December 31, 2010.

35 Interview, Fatih University, Istanbul, April 27, 2011.

36 Copeaux 1996.

37 Bilici 2006, 4.

38 Interview with Mehmet Alp, Sema Hospital, Istanbul, March 9, 2011.

39 Gocmen 2014.

40 T. Yılmaz 2014.

41 Dinçer, et al. 2013.

42 Yılmaz 2003, 234.

43 Gülay 2007, 48.

44 Pandya and Gallagher 2012; Balci and Miller 2012.

45 The Olympiads are annual, competitive, cultural and educational festivals for Hizmet schools across the world.

46 In the aftermath of July 15 failed military coup, the Erdoğan government also froze a large number of individual bank accounts, particularly in Bank Asya, for being suspected to be part of the Gülen Movement.

47 Ebaugh 2009, 83-107.

48 Interview, Istanbul, May 12, 2011.

49 Interview, Akademi, Istanbul, December 12, 2010.

50 Interview, Izmir, March 17, 2011.

51 Gülen 1997 *Prizma 2*. Istanbul: Nil, p. 12, http://fethullahgulen.com/en/home/1338-fgulen-com-english/conference-papers/the-fethullah-gulen-movement-i/25505-discursive-and-organizational-strategies-of-the-gulen-movement#1 Accessed on July 12, 2018.

52 Findley 2015, 7, 5-18.

53 However, Gülen's lawyer used the expression "leader of the Gülen Movement" in order to acquire a US Green Card for Gülen in a petition submitted to the US Court. Hendrick (2013) has used this piece of evidence to show the culture of strategic ambiguity and non-transparency that surrounds the Movement. It must be pointed out here that the legal petition containing the expression of "leader of the Gülen Movement" was merely a functional necessity for a modern judiciary which is accustomed to understanding clearly defined modern language and roles, and which cannot understand non-modern expression such as the *ustad* or *Sufi* as the source of educational inspiration.

54 Interview, Istanbul, June 23, 2011.

55 Yavuz 2013, 64.

56 Gülay 2007, 42.

57 Gülen 2005, 43–58.

58 Ibid. 5.

CHAPTER 8

1 Michel 2010, 135. A large number of these educational institutions were in Turkey and were closed down by the government following the July 15, 2016 military coup attempt.

2 I am not arguing that there is a single educational system in the Western world. Every nation within the Western hemisphere has designed its education system based on its specific national history, traditions, and culture. I refer here to the common philosophical foundations and values to which almost all educational institutions in the West are wedded: individualism and secularism.

3 Gülen 2005, 82.

4 Vicini 2007.

5 Gülen 2005, 68-83.

6 See Afsaruddin 2005.

7 Panjwani 2004, 1.

8 Interview with Eşref Potur, businessman and Gülen Movement volunteer, Izmir, March 17, 2011.

9 Quoted in Kurt 2014, 126.

10 Gülen 2004b, 123-27, 2010b, 42-46.

11 Interview with Mehmet Alp, Istanbul, March 9, 2011.

12 Interview with Nihat Can, a volunteer who worked in Gülen-inspired schools in Kenya and Madagascar for about 10 years. Gaziantep, November 12, 2014.

13 Quoted in M. Ünal 2004, 33.

14 Kurt 2014, 126.

15 Quoted in M. Ünal 2004, 43.

16 Sevindi 2008, 74.

17 Ünal and Williams 2000, 312.

18 Interview, Edirne, March 4, 2011.

19 Interview, Sakarya University, February 28, 2010.

20 Quoted in M. Ünal 2004, 43.

21 Ünal and Williams 2000, 315.

22 Gülen 2000a, 3.

23 Gülen draws the classification of human faculties from Ibn Miskawayh, a tenth-century Muslim philosopher. For details, see Ünal and Williams 2000, 306-8.

24 Gülen 2002, 83.

25 Interview, Edirne, March 4, 2011.

26 Quoted in Ünal and Williams 2000, 325.

27 Thomas Michel, S.J. 2002. *Gülen as Educator and Religious Teacher*, https://fgulen.com/en/press/review/24902-gulen-as-educator-and-religious-teacher, accessed on 12.07.2018.

28 Ünal and Williams 2000, 325-6.

29 *Usul* and *furuu'* are the two main categories that outline the literature of Islamic jurisprudence. While *usul* explores the main sources for the essentials of faith and qualifies whether one is a believer or not, *furuu'* covers secondary issues that relate to worship, practice, etc.

30 "The Beard and the Turban Issue," https://fgulen.com/en/home/1305-fgulen-com-english/fethullah-gulen-life/gulens-thoughts/25051-the-beard-and-the-headscarve-issue, accessed on 12.07.2018.

31 Ünal and Williams 2000, 81.

32 Ibid. 97.

33 Gök 2007, 248, quoting Akyüz 1993, 286.

34 Cekerol 2012, 344.

35 Ibid.

36 Gök 2007, 253, quoting TED 2006, 6.

37 Interview, Istanbul, December 31, 2010.

38 I witnessed this mega event in 2011 in Ankara. However, since 2014 the Movement has been organizing the Turkish Olympiad as the "International Festival of Language and Culture" outside Turkey on account of the government's hostility and for fear of security problems that could be created by government agencies. The success of the Turkish Olympiad can be gauged by the fact that it not only attracts hundreds of thousands of Turkish visitors from all different walks of life but also it is estimated that "since the first [Gülen-Inspired Schools] were established outside Turkey, approximately 300,000 people have taken language classes at these institutions (Dreher 2013, 265, quoting TÜRKÇEDER 2012: 14). The number of countries represented by students at the [Turkish Language Olympiad] has increased from 17 in 2003 to 140 in 2012" (Dreher 2013, 265). For details on Turkish Olympiad, see Wulfsberg 2015.

39 For these data, see Gök 2007, p. 252.

40 Çelik and Gür 2013, 165.

41 In the wake of the July 15, 2016 military coup attempt, the government shut down all Gülen-linked educational institutions for their alleged role in it.

42 Gök 2007, 253, quoting YÖK 2006 www.yok.gov.tr, 10 August 2006.

43 Günay n.d.

44 Çelik and Gür 2013.

45 Agai 2003, 55.

46 Interview, Izmir, March 16, 2011.

47 Quoted in Hendrick, 2013, p. 86.

48 Following 1997 military intervention the imam-hatip school was targeted. As a result, only 2,000 students applied to these schools in 1997, compared with 35,000 in 1995. The number of students decreased from 396,677 in 1998 to 71,583 in 2002. See, Yavuz, 2003b, 124, 128.

49 By 2011-2012 the total number of Imam-Hatip High Schools was 493 while students and teachers numbered 235,639 and 112,608 (Aslanargun, Kılıç and Bozkurt 2014, 138). According to *Hürriyet Daily News*, the number of Imam-Hatip schools has increased from 493 in 2010-2011 to 854 in 2013-2014, which is a 73% jump in comparison to vocational High Schools and Anatolian High Schools, which have registered increases of 23% and 3% respectively (Yinanç 2014).

50 Interview, Istanbul, December 28, 2010.

51 Interview, Erzurum, February 26, 2011.

52 Gülen 2005, Chapter: "The Statue of Our Souls."

53 Interview, Istanbul, March 2, 2011.

CHAPTER 9

1 Interview, Istanbul, December 10, 2010.

2 Sleap and Şener 2013, 94.

3 Gülen 2004a, quoted in Pratt 2007. However, it may be noted that the focus on educational and dialogue activities varies from country to country. Thus, dialogue is the major face of the Movement in the advanced countries like USA, Europe, Australia, and even India, as these nations do not suffer from a chronic shortage of quality education. The emphasis on dialogue in these countries has the purpose of explaining the Hizmet Movement, forging institutional links, and building favorable public opinion. On the other hand, the Movement focuses more on building educational institutions in less advanced regions such as Central Asia, Asia, Africa, parts of South East and South Asia, etc., as there is demand for such educational institutions, and with a view to establishing links with the elites of those countries. In other words, it is primarily through dialogue centers in advanced countries and

educational institutions in less advanced countries that the task of *dawa* is performed by the Hizmet Movement.

4 For the full text of the Medina Constitution, see Bulaç 1988, 169–78. Many scholars have hailed the Medina Constitution as the first multicultural constitution in the world.

5 Ramadan 2004, 203.

6 Akhtar Shabbir, 1991, 197.

7 Waardenburg 1999, 88.

8 The dialogue discourse emerging in the Turkish Muslim majority context is often celebrated among the Hizmet scholars and practitioners in Turkey to buttress the thesis of "Turkish Exceptionalism" as well as to point out that there is no inherent political pragmatism in this initiative. However, it may be noted that "the religious Muslim majority in Turkish setting" during Kemalist era has been politically, economically, and socially marginalized.

9 Gülen 2004a.

10 Ünal and Williams 2000, 195.

11 Interview, Konya, March 20, 2011, student of Fethullah Gülen (from 1997-2007).

12 Interview with Cemal Uşak, Vice President, Journalists and Writers Foundation, Istanbul, June 14, 2011.

13 Interview with Hakan Cihangir, one of Hizmet inspired industrialists from Konya, March 21, 2011.

14 Sleap and Şener 2013, 88.

15 Gülay 2007b, 93, quoting Fethullah Gülen, "The Inner Profundity of Humankind," *The Fountain* (2005).

16 Said 1978, 78, 199, 112.

17 Gülen 2000b in Pratt 2007.

18 Gandhi 1938, 30.

19 Gülen, 2000b in Pratt 2007.

20 Ibid.

21 Gülen 2002b; 32-33, quoted in Pearson 2012, 206.

22 J. Smith 1975, 74, in Esack 1997, 133.

23 Al-Tabatabai 1973 in Esack 1997, 167.

24 Ünal and Williams 2000, 269

25 Ibid 242.

26 Gülen 2000b, 242.

27 Walton, 2013, 151.

28 Gülen, *İrşad Ekseni*, 1998, quoted in Gürbüz and Purkayastha 2013, 44.

29 Ibid.

30 Quoted in Walton 2013.

31 As with the entire Qur'an, these verses on Jews and Christians should not be studied exclusively, but according to the overall message of the scripture and the context of revelation (*asbab al-nuzul*).

32 Ünal and Williams 2000, 260.

33 Ibid. 261.

34 Ibid. 203.

35 Gülen 2001.

36 Asani 2002.

37 Gülen 2001.

38 Ünal and Williams 2000, 259.

39 Kim 2008.

40 Kurtz 2005, 378.

41 Gülen 1999.

42 Interview, Erzurum, February 26, 2011.

43 In Sarıtoprak and Griffith 2005.

44 Gülay 2007b, 75.

45 Gülen 1998, 40-2.

46 Ünal and Williams 2000, note 9, 207.

47 Ibid. note 9, 207.

48 Yavuz 2003, 45.

49 Gülen 2006, 34.

50 Ünal and Williams 2000.

51 Ibid.

52 Interview, Istanbul, December 28, 2010.

53 See Joppke 2004.

54 See MacIntyre 1988

55 Gülen 2010a, 38.

56 Pratt 2007.

57 Kim 2008.

58 Çelik and Valkenberg 2007.

59 Ünal and Williams 2000, 206-7.

60 Ünal and Williams 2000, n.9, 207.

61 Interview, Atlanta, April 13, 2015.

62 Interview with Oztan, 51, Konya, March 20, 2011.

63 Interview, JWF, Istanbul, June 14, 2011.

64 Ibid.

65 Interviews with Ömer, Kemal, Selçuk, Ersin and others (age: 30-42) Freiburg, Germany, June 14, 2017 and July 7, 2017.

66 Interview, Atlanta, April 4, 2015.

CHAPTER 10

1 This primarily concerns the "oil for gold" trade, under which, during the Ahmadinejad period, Iranian oil was being illegally sold in the international market via Turkey in exchange for gold. This violated US and United Nations economic sanctions on Iran imposed in 2006. The key facilitator of this illegal trade, Babak Zanjani, was convicted and sentenced to death by an Iranian court on March 6, 2016, while Reza Zarrab, with dual Iranian-Turkish nationality, is currently in custody awaiting trial in US jail accused of exporting gold from Turkey to Iran. The scandal led to resignation of three key Cabinet Minister in Turkey in 2014. Later the then Prime Minister Erdoğan personally intervened in the matter, scuttled the judicial trial, arrested the prosecution and investigating police staff and put them behind the bar. Zarrab was released from jail after three months of detention, got the confiscated money back to him with interest and was later awarded Turkey's best businessperson. Zarrab has now turned approver for the prosecution in the ongoing US trial for the same charges for which he was arrested in Turkey, admitted his guilt and told the Court the involvement of high officials including President Er-

doğan in facilitating this illegal trade.

2 After the eruption of the corruption scandal in late 2013, the government attempted to finish off the Hizmet Movement by labeling it a "parallel structure" and even a terrorist organization. It took a series of illegal measures including systematically identifying and profiling critical individuals in particular and Hizmet in general, the sacking and illegal transfer of thousands of police officers, closing down the Movement's preparatory coaching institutions and schools, harassing and financially draining off all Hizmet-linked institutions such as Bank Asya, Samanyolu TV, and *Zaman* newspaper and their associates. The government "criminalized" the mundane activities of the Movement and defamed Gülen, pressurizing individual businessmen to withdraw their financial support from the Movement. It has attempted to mobilize international opinion against the Hizmet Movement, particularly pressurizing African and Central Asian governments to close down the Movement's schools there. Following the failed military coup of 2016, the government confiscated all Hizmet-linked institutions and associated business groups, amounting to 50 billion US dollars, according to government sources, and dismissed more than 135,000 government employees, particularly from the police, judiciary, bureaucracy, and military. There have been countless illegal arrests and detentions and several kidnappings by security forces. On the recent anti-democratic moves of the Erdoğan regime and its illegal crackdown on Hizmet, see Bozkurt 2015; Yılmaz 2015; Woolf C.H., Jowell KCMG QC and Garnier QC MP 2015. For latest report in this regard see, http://turkeypurge.com/purge-in-numbers.

3 Critical works on the Movement include: Jager, 2016; Sharon-Krespin 2009; Gözaydin 2009, Holton and Lopez, 2015. This is also based on my interaction with some of these secular critics about the Movement in Turkey.

4 Later, Rubin (2016) revised his opinion.

5 Interview, Istanbul, May 26, 2011. However, of late Ali Bulaç has moved away from his framework of political Islamism and his views today resonate more with the Hizmet understanding of Islam and its role in the social and political life of the country. Ali Bulaç has been jailed for almost two years and was recently released (May 11, 2018) pending trial in the government crackdown on Hizmet volunteers in the wake of the failed military coup. A student from India currently receiving Islamic education under Gülen has confirmed me that Gülen recommends reading Sayyid Qutb's book for the purpose of un-

derstanding the Qur'an. Also, Ergün Çapan has provided a detailed list of books taught by Gülen that includes Sayyid Qutb's (1966) *Fi Zilal-al Qur'an* (6 vols). See Çapan 2011.

6 For the full statement of this alleged accusation against Gülen, see, Sharon-Krespin 2009.

7 Murat Yetkin, "What does the Koza-İpek case mean?" http://www.hurriyetdailynews.com/opinion/murat-yetkin/what-does-the-koza-ipek-case-mean-90426 October 28, 2015.

8 "Koza İpek Holding ve şirketlerine kayyum atanmasına avukatlardan tepki," HABER TURK, 27.10.2015, http://www.haberturk.com/gundem/haber/1145466-koza-ipek-holding-ve-sirketlerine-kayyum-atanmasina-avukatlardan-tepki, accessed on 12.04.2018.

9 During my stays in Turkey from 2010–2011 and September 2013–June 2016 I often found that students and faculty members were evasive about disclosing their political preference or association with political parties and any other religious or secular associations.

10 Mehmet Ali Birand, "Gülen movement becoming victim of its own legend," *Hürriyet Daily*, October 5, 2010, available at http://hizmetnews.com/18992/gulen-movement-becoming-victim-legend/#.WtMqoBRBU9d, accessed on April 15, 2018.

11 "HDP 'Paralel yapı araştırılsın' dedi, AK Parti kabul etmedi," *Hürriyet*, February 18, 2015, http://www.hurriyet.com.tr/gundem/hdp-paralel-yapi-arastirilsin-dedi-ak-parti-kabul-etmedi-28234803

12 "Turkey's parliamentary commission on graft queries ex-ministers' wealth," *Hürriyet Daily News*, November 29, 2014, http://www.hurriyetdailynews.com/turkeys-parliamentary-commission-on-graft-queries-ex-ministers-wealth-74981 , also "Parliament acquits four ex-ministers on corruption, but vote stirs ruling AKP," *Hürriyet Daily News*, January 20 2015, http://www.hurriyetdailynews.com/parliament-acquits-four-ex-ministers-on-corruption-but-vote-stirs-ruling-akp-77188 accessed on December 12, 2018.

13 Turkey's coup commission wraps up work with little outcome, January 04, 2017, *Hürriyet Daily News*, http://www.hurriyetdailynews.com/turkeys-coup-commission-wraps-up-work-with-little-outcome--108125, accessed on December 12, 2018.

14 Sanchez 2016.

15 On Tablighi Jamaat see Sikand 2002.

16 Interview with Ali Bulaç, Istanbul May 26, 2011.

17 Ünal and Williams 2000, 36.

18 Rahman 1998, 309.

19 Quoted in Kurt 2014, 175-176.

20 Demerath III 1991, 22.

21 Lapidus and Burke 1990 .

22 In this context it may be noted that whereas the Western Orientalists constructed the doctrinal unity of religion and state in Islam to explain the perpetual backwardness and violence in the Muslim societies in contrast to the principle of separation of Church and State that accounts for the progress and development in Western societies, the Islamic Orientalists and their political progeny–the radical Islamists–are demanding the return to the doctrinal unity of Islam and state they consider to have prevailed during the period of Prophet Muhammad and the Four Rightly Guided Caliphs in order to retrieve the era of Islamic happiness, development, and progress which was lost due to the separation of Islam and State in the post-Caliphal period. Oddly enough a good number of Turkish intellectuals highlight this functional separation as specific to the notion of Turkish Islam and hence its successful transition to modernity as opposed to the backwardness of Arab Islam due to its principle of the fusion of Islam and politics. Thus, the Gülen Movement, whose success is traced partly to the historical formation of Turkish Islam, continues to inadvertently reinforce the Orientalist paradigm of self vs. other, notwithstanding its desire to transcend it.

23 Eickelman 1998, 105.

24 In Sarıtoprak and Ünal 2005, quoted in Yılmaz 2012, 47.

25 Quoted in Yılmaz 2012, 47.

26 Quoted in Brown 1996, 18.

27 While the abolition of the Caliphate in 1924 by the Kemalist regime created ripples through a large part of Muslim world, the near silence of Turkish Muslims on the issue appears to be a puzzle for many scholars. A.J. Silverstein (2010, 82) and many others consider this long silence, with its smooth switch over from Ottoman-Arabic to Latin script, to be a sign of the "flexibility" of Turkish Muslimness/Islam, and there may be truth in this explanation. How-

ever, a combination of other factors, such as fear of the authoritarian regime, the strong tradition of the legitimacy of the state, and the gradual transformation of the Caliphate and Arabic language from being an Islamic institution and Islamic language into an Arab institution and the language of Arabs in the changed political context, as well as the identification of Arab and Islam with "backwardness" should not be discounted. More than anything, it was the "anti-Arab" perception among Turkish Muslims, which developed during the course of the alliance of Sharif Hussain of Mecca with the British and French (what is called "Arab Revolt" of 1916) against the Ottomans, that shaped the outlook of Turkish Muslims towards the Caliphate and the transition to the Latin script.

28 Interview, Akademi, Istanbul, February 23, 2010.

29 For point a, b, and c interview with Ahmet Kurucan, Atlanta, USA, April 11, 2013.

30 Ibid.

31 In Sarıtoprak and Ünal 2005, quoted in Yılmaz 2012, 47.

32 Gülen has personally admitted that he had had good personal relationship with many Turkish Presidents and Prime Ministers and at times gave them advice in the larger public good. However, it is true that Gülen never used his influence to secure any kind of government favors and kept a safe distance from public authorities.

33 Interview with Ahmet Kurucan, Atlanta, USA, April 11, 2013.

34 Interview, Istanbul, December 31, 2010. However, in December 2014 the Movement did mobilize its volunteers and came out openly on the street to protest the state's action against *Zaman* newspaper throughout the major parts of Turkey. This was the first time since its inception that the Movement organized a "street demonstration with placards," albeit in a peaceful manner. This was the single occasion when I witnessed Movement volunteers indulging in a "street demonstration." Since then, until the writing of this book, the government has further stepped up its pressure and even carried out illegal atrocities against the Movement, yet the Movement volunteers have not organized any similar kind of protest again.

35 Quoted in Grinell 2015, 182.

36 Interview, JWF, Istanbul, June 8, 2011.

37 See, Alam 2013.

38 Quoted in Yılmaz 2003, 224.

39 Gülen, 2005, the chapter "Consultation," 43-58.

40 Interview, JWF, Istanbul, June 8, 2011.

41 Ibid.

42 Interview with Ahmet Kurucan, Atlanta, April 11, 2015.

43 On the doctrine of *Hakimiyya*, see Madampat 1995; also, for its political construction, see Belkeziz 2009, Chapter 9, "Pseudo-Theocracy in the Rule of Allah— 'al-Hakimiyyah'", 195-219.

44 Mardin 1989, 18.

45 Quoted in Akyol 2007, 31.

46 Mardin 1989, 11

47 Ünal and Williams 2000, 171-2.

48 Gülen 2005, 114.

49 Gülen 2017.

50 Gülen 2005, 55.

51 Turam 2007, 25.

52 Demiröz 2015, 17-23, referring to Pasini and Morselli 2010, 341-355.

53 Yavuz 2003, quoting *Cumhuriyet*, July 12, 1997 and July 21, 1998.

54 Hizmet Movement News Portal, 2014.

55 TurkStat 2010.

56 Gül 2000, 201.

57 On the role of Islamic ethics and morality in the emergence of Islamic entrepreneurship in Turkey, see Arslan 1999, 2000, 2001; Türkdoğan 2005; Yousef 2001; Özdemir 2006; Ocal 2007.

58 Yavuz 2004a, 224.

59 Uğur 2013.

60 European Commission 2011, 5-28.

61 Interview, Fatih University, Istanbul, December 31, 2010.

62 Among Hizmet circles the term "Ergenekon" was/is used to refer to a concealed, illegal, criminal organization/gang with its members widely spread in the military, the political class, media houses, academia, industry, etc., and mostly belonging to the secularist camp that was working clandestinely to

preserve the political status quo in the country. The group was rumored to use all its power and means, including violent methods, to eliminate its perceived enemies. However, the critics believe that Ergenekon was a "fictitious case" fabricated by Gülen Movement to target its opponents across the state and civil society.

63 Interview, Istanbul, May 26, 2011.

64 The Gezi protest (May 2013) was initially an environmentalist protest led by leftist and secular students against government's decision to construct a historical barracks building together with a shopping center and luxury flats at the site of Gezi Park/Square and transitioned into an oppositional movement against the Erdoğan government. Erdoğan called the participants in the protest "terrorists" and a "Western conspiracy to destabilize Turkey."

65 Informal conversation, June 5, 2013.

66 Turam 2007.

67 "Gov't-endorsed MGK plot against Gülen exposed by daily," *Today's Zaman* on 29 November 2013, https://fgulen.com/en/press/news/37444-todays-zaman-govt-endorsed-mgk-plot-against-gulen-exposed-by-daily, also, Sedat Ergin "Why was the National Security Council's Gülen decision not implemented?" *Hürriyet Daily News*, June 30, 2017, http://www.hurriyetdailynews.com/opinion/sedat-ergin/why-was-the-national-security-councils-gulen-decision-not-implemented-114932 , accessed on December 12, 2018.

68 Interview, Istanbul, May 26, 2011.

69 Interview, Fatih University, Istanbul, April 27, 2011.

70 There has been countless stories in Turkey, which I have personally heard during the course of informal interaction with members of various religious groups and sects, apart from Hizmet volunteers, how members of "black Turk" were discriminated and denied the entry into these elite segments of state administration, particularly the military, despite having possessed the requisite qualification and having successfully passed the required examination on account of being perceived as coming from religious background.

71 "Aleviler ve Sünniler: Barışı ve Geleceği Birlikte Aramak," organized by Abant Platform, Bolu, Turkey, December 13-15, 2013.

72 Gürbüz 2015, 6.

73 "Islamic scholar Gülen backs peace talks between government and PKK," *Today's Zaman*, Jan 8, 2013, in Gürbüz 2015.

74 Webb 2012, 160-1.

75 Ebaugh 2009, 120.

76 Yavuz 2013, 105.

77 Grinell 2015, 165.

78 The Islamic government of Iran under Imam Khomeini imposed severe restrictions on women pursuing education in many fields. It is only in post-Khomeini period that laws have been amended to allow female students to pursue a career in various subjects.

79 For details see Yashin 2002, 78-113.

80 Tan, 2007, 109, referring to SIS 1995; MONE 2005.

81 Ibid, referring to MONE 2005.

82 Ibid, 109-110, referring to, SIS 1995, MONE 2005.

83 Patrick Kingsley, *Turkey Allows Women in Military to Wear Hijabs, in Cultural Shift, New York Times, Feb. 22, 2017, https://www.nytimes.com/2017/02/22/world/middleeast/hijab-turkey-military.html*, accessed on 14.04.2018.

84 In the West some new studies on educational efficacy have yielded positive results for single-sex schooling in comparison to co-educational schooling, though the debate is far from over. Melinda D. Anderson, The Resurgence of Single-Sex Education,: The benefits and limitations of schools that segregate based on gender, The Atlantic Daily, 22 December 2015, https://www.theatlantic.com/education/archive/2015/12/the-resurgence-of-single-sex-education/421560/ , accessed on 14.04.2018, ‘ The Single Sex Education : The Connecticut Context, the Technical Report, SERC, 2013, http://ctserc.org/documents/news/2013-03-12-single-sex-education.pdf, accessed on 14.4.2018, Peter McGuire, Single-sex or mixed: what's best for your child?, https://www.irishtimes.com/news/education/single-sex-or-mixed-what-s-best-for-your-child-1.2893612 , accessed on 14.4.2018.

85 The term refers to constitutional provision and governmental measures for the advancement of marginalized classes, including women.

86 Quoted in Iqbal 2012, 35.

87 Interview with a professor at Fatih University, Istanbul, 2011.

88 Interview with a group of girls and women, JWF, Istanbul, March 23, 2011.

89 Ibid.

90 Ibid.

91 Ibid.

92 Özdalga 2003.

93 Jassal 2014.

94 Curtis 2012, 121.

95 Interview with Fatma, Şanlıurfa, January 15, 2015.

CHAPTER 11

1 Interview with Feyzullah Aslan, Adana, Turkey, September 15, 2015.

POSTSCRIPT

1 Yavuz, M. Hakan and Balci, Bayram, 2018. (ed). *Turkey's July 15th Coup: What Happened and Why*. The University of Utah Press.

2 *Politics, Religion & Ideology (2018)* Volume 19, 2018 - Issue 1: Ruin or Resilience? The Future of the Gülen Movement in Transnational Political Exile.

3 Yavuz and Balci 2018, 28.

4 Ibid. 196.

5 Ibid. 100, 98-129.

6 Ibid. 99.

7 Ibid. 20-45. Also Yavuz, "A Framework for Understanding the Intra-Islamist Conflict Between the AK Party and the Gülen Movement," *Politics, Religion & Ideology,* Volume 19, 2018 - Issue 1: Ruin or Resilience? The Future of the Gülen Movement in Transnational Political Exile, 11-32.

8 These cases refer to an attempted "secular coup" against the AKP government. A good number of high profile secular military officers, bureaucrats, and others were prosecuted, punished, and jailed on these charges. In 2014, the Erdoğan government withdrew many of the charges and released a good number of these secularists pending further trial. The critics alleged that both these cases were fictitious in nature, with the evidence brought and manipulated by the Gülen Movement to denigrate and delegitimize the secular legacy of the nation and weaken the dominance of so-called "White" Turks in the state institutions, particularly the military.

9 The Erdoğan government initiated secret peace talks with the PKK – the

Kurdistan Workers Party, which has been at war with the government since 1980s – in 2010, in Oslo. It is alleged that the Gülen Movement opposed this move, as it might lead to the secession of the Kurdish dominated part of Turkey. The summoning of Hakan Fidan, the MIT Chief, to a court of law in 2010 is considered, by critics, a ploy of the Movement to derail the Peace Process. It was alleged that the summoning was in relation to many MIT operatives caught among PKK members and accused of conducting some of its terrorist attacks.

10 Mavi Marmara Turkish Flotilla was a Turkish aid ship, organized by IHH with an indirect support of AKP government, to participate in the global campaign against the Israeli blockade against Gaza in 2010. The incident led to the killing of 10 Turkish citizens on boat by Israeli Defense Force, followed by diplomatic breakdown of the relationship between the two government. Turkey resumed diplomatic relationship with Israel on the condition of apology and due compensation. Gülen had criticized the expedition on the ground that the said expedition should have not been undertaken without the legal permission of the government of Israel. The government took serious note of Gülen's statement and thought it as interference in the foreign policy domain of the government. However, it must be stated here that much later in 2017 the Erdoğan government castigated the IHH for launching expedition without the permission of the Turkish government. The IHH then submitted an unconditional apology to the government and agreed to the terms and condition of Israeli compensation, which was funneled through an Israeli NGO.

11 "Mehmet Hakan Atilla gets 32-month sentence in Iran sanctions case," May 17, 2018, https://www.aljazeera.com/news/2018/05/mehmet-hakan-atilla-32-month-sentence-iran-sanctions-case-180516175154849.html. Accessed on June 19, 2018.

12 "Turkish prosecutors drop graft charges against ex-ministers' sons," http://www.dw.com/en/turkish-prosecutors-drop-graft-charges-against-ex-ministers-sons/a-18005157, accessed on July 19, 2018.

13 Shaheen, Kareem, "Erdoğan knew of alleged Iranian scheme to evade sanctions via Turkey, court told," November 30, 2017, https://www.theguardian.com/world/2017/nov/30/us-court-alleged-iran-scheme-avoid-sanctions-turkey , accessed on June 19, 2018.

14 Jacinto, Leela, "Turkey's Post-Coup Purge and Erdoğan's Private Army," July

13, 2017, http://foreignpolicy.com/2017/07/13/turkeys-post-coup-purge-and-Erdoğans-private-army-sadat-perincek-Gülen/, accessed on June 19, 2018.

15 "Gülen resorts to UN to investigate Turkey's coup," September 27, 2017, http://hizmetnews.com/23376/Gülen-resorts-un-investigate-turkeys-coup/#.Wy-ibthRBVlA, accessed on June 19, 2018.

16 Ayasun, Abdullah, "Turkish Opposition Leader: July 15 Was A Controlled Coup," April 4, 2017, https://www.theglobepost.com/2017/04/03/opposition-leader-july-15-was-a-controlled-coup/, accessed on June 19, 2018.

17 For 2004 Hizmet NSC document, see, "PM's order echoes 2004 MGK decision [to undermine the Gülen Movement]," January 16, 2014, http://hizmetnews.com/9517/pms-order-echoes-2004-mgk-decision/#.WyilGRRBVn0, accessed on June 19, 2018.

18 *Amnesty International, Turkey: Briefing on the Wide-Ranging, Arbitrary and Restrictive Draft Versions to the Law to Fight Terrorism (2006)*, quoted in Turkey's Anti-Terrorism Law: Protecting the Republic or Violating Children's Rights? Available on https://www.americanbar.org/content/dam/aba/publishing/criminal_justice_section_newsletter/crimjust_juvjust_newsletter-june09_june09_pdfs_turkey.authcheckdam.pdf , accessed on June 19, 2018.

19 Gülen criticized the flotilla on the grounds that necessary permission from the Israeli authorities should have been sought for the delivery of the aid. Unfortunately, 10 people were killed on the boat by Israeli soldiers.

BIBLIOGRAPHY

Abou El Fadl, Khaled. 2006. "The Ugly Modern and the Modern Ugly: Reclaiming the Beautiful in Islam." In *Progressive Muslims: On Justice, Gender, and Pluralism*, edited by Omid Safi, 33–78. Oxford: One World.

Abu-Lughod, Lila. 1998. "Introduction: Feminist Longings and Postcolonial Conditions." In *Remaking Women: Feminism and Modernity in the Middle East*, edited by Lila Abu-Lughod, 3–31. Princeton University Press.

Abu-Rabi, Ibrahim M., ed. 2003. *Islam at the Crossroads: On the Life and Thought of Bediuzzaman.* Albany: State University of New York Press.

Abu-Zayd, Nasr. 2006. *Reformation of Islamic Thought: A Critical Historical Analysis.* Amsterdam: Amsterdam University Press.

Acar, Ismail. 2012. "A Classical Scholar with a Modern Outlook: Fethullah Gülen and His Legal Thought." In *Mastering Knowledge in Modern Times*, edited by Ismail Albayrak, 65-84. New York: Blue Dome.

Adams, Charles C. 2013. "Al Sayyid Jamal al-Din al-Afghani." In *Islam and Modernism in Egypt: A Study of the Modern Reform Movement Inaugurated by Muhammad 'Abduh.* New York: Russell and Russell.

Afsaruddin, Asma. 2005. "The Philosophy of Islamic Education: Classical Views and M. Fethullah Gülen's Perspectives" in *Islam in Contemporary World I: The Fethullah Gülen Movement in Thought and Practice, Conference Proceedings*, 1–25. The Boniuk Center for the Study and Advancement of Religious Tolerance at Rice University of Houston.

Agai, Bekim. 2007. "Islam and Education in Secular Turkey: State Policies and the Emergence of the Fethullah Gülen Group." In *Schooling Islam: The Culture and Politics of Modern Muslim Education*, edited by Robert W. Hefner and Zaman Muhammad Qasim, 149–169. Princeton and Oxford: Princeton University Press.

——. 2003. "The Gülen Movement's Islamic Ethic of Education." In *Turkish Islam and the Secular State: The Gülen Movement*, edited by M. Hakan and John L. Esposito Yavuz, 48-68. Syracuse: Syracuse University Press.

Ahmed, Feroz. 1993. *The Making of Modern Turkey.* New York: Routledge.

Akhtar, Shabbir. 1991. *A Faith for All Seasons: Islam and the Challenges of the Modern World*, Chicago: Ivan R. Dee.

Akyol, Mustafa. 2007. "What Made the Gülen Movement Possible?" Edited by İhsan Yılmaz, Eileen Barker, Henri J. Barkey, Muhammad Abdul Haleem, George S. Harris, Michel Thomas and Simon Robinson. *Muslim World in Transition: Contributions of the Gülen Movement, 22-32.* London: Leeds Metropolitan University Press .

Akyüz, Y. 1993. *Türk Eğitim Tarihi.* Istanbul: Kültür Koleji Yayınları.

Alam, Irshad, trans. 2010. *Faith Practice Piety: An Excerpt from the Maktubat-i Imam-i Rabbani Original: The Great Mujaddid Ahmad Sirhindi* . Dhaka: Aklima Akter Sufi Peace Mission.

Alam, Anwar. 2013. "Limits of political Islam: the other face of AKP" http://www.todayszaman.com/op-ed limits-of-political-islam-the-other-face-of-akp-by-anwar-alam- 334722.html, dated. 2013-12-22, "Limits of political Islam: the other face of AKP (2)" http://www.todayszaman.com/op-ed limits-of-political-islam-the-other-face-of-akp-2-by-anwar-alam- 334721.html , dated. 2013-12-23. The government illegally took over *Zaman* and *Today's Zaman* in 2015 and was later shut down.

Alam, Muzaffar. 2004. *The Languages of Political Islam in India C. 1200-1800*. Permanent Black, Delhi.

Al-Azmeh, Aziz. 1993. *Islams and Modernities*. London, New York: Verso.

Albayrak, Ismail. 2011a. "Fethullah Gülen's Approach to Quranic Exegesis." In *Mastering Knowledge in Modern Times: Fethullah Gülen as an Islamic Scholar*, edited by Ismail Albayrak, 1-38. New Jersey: Blue Dome Press.

——. ed. 2011b. *Mastering Knowledge in Modern Times: Fethullah Gülen as an Islamic Scholar*. New Jersey: Blue Dome.

Al-Tabatabai, Muhammad Hussain. 1973. *Al-Mizan fi Tafsir al Quran*. Vol. 21. Qum: Al-Hawzah al-Ilmiyyah.

An-Na'im, Abdullahi Ahmed. 1990. *Towards an Islamic Reformation: Civil Liberties, Human Rights, and International Law,*. New York: Syracuse University Press.

——. 1994. "Towards an Islamic Reformation: Islamic Law in History and Society Today." In *Shari'a Law and the Modern Nation-State*, edited by Norani Othman. Kuala Lumpur: SIS Forum.

Ansari, Bazmee. 1995. "Foreword." In *Islamic Methodology in History*, by Fazlur Rehman. Islamabad: Islamic Research Institute.

Ansari, Muhammad. 1986. *Sufism and Shari'ah: A Study of Shaykh Ahmad Sirhindi's Effort to Reform Sufism* . Leicester: The Islamic Foundation.

Aras, Bulent, and Omer Caha. 2000. "Fethullah Gulen and his Liberal "Turkish Islam" Movement." *Middle East Review of International Affairs* (Rubin Center for Research in International Affairs) IV (4).

Arslan, M. 1999 . *A Cross Cultural Comparison of the Work Ethic of the Protestant, Catholic and Muslim Managers*. PhD Thesis, Leeds University, Leeds: Leeds University.

——. 2000. "A Crosscultural Comparison of British and Turkish Managers in Terms of PWE Characteristics." *Business Ethics: A European Review* 9 (1): 13–9.

——. 2001. "The Work Ethic Values of Protestant British, Catholic Irish and Muslim Turkish Managers ." *Journal of Business Ethics* 31: 321–39.

Asad, Talal. 2003. *Formations of the Secular: Christianity, Islam, Modernity* . Stanford, CA: Stanford University Press.

——. 1993. *Genealogies of Religion: Discipline and Reasons of Power in Christianity and Islam*. Baltimore, MD: John Hopkins University Press.

——. 1986. "The Idea of an Anthropology of Islam." Occasional Papers Series, Center for Contemporary Arab Studies, Georgetown University, Washington, DC.

Asani, Ali S. 2002. "Pluralism, Intolerance, and the Qur'an." *The American Scholar* 71 (1): 52-60.

Asharq Al-Awsat. 2014. *In Conversation with Fethullah Gülen*. March 24. Accessed May 28, 2017. http://fgulen.com/en/press/1796-interview-by-asharq-al-awsat/43590-in-conversation-with-fethullah-gulen.

Aslanargun, Engin, Abdurrahman Kılıç, and Sinan Bozkurt. 2014. "Parental Expectation and Religious Education in State Schools in Turkey: The Case of Imam Hatip High Schools' ." *International Journal of Instruction* 7 (1): 135–149.

Aslandogan, Y. Alp. 2007. "Present and Potential Impact of the Spiritual Tradition of Islam on Contemporary Muslims: From Ghazali to Gülen ." *Muslim World in*

Transition: Contributions of the Gülen Movement. Dialogue Society. 663-682

Austin, J. L. 1975. *Doing Things with Words.* Cambridge, Mass.: Harvard University Press.

Bacık, Gökhan, and Umit Kurt. 2011. "New Islamic Movements and Amodern Networks." *Culture and Religion* 12 (1): 21–37.

Balci, Tamer. 2012. "Islam and Democracy in the Thought of Nursi and Gülen." In *The Gülen Hizmet Movement: Circumspect Activism in Faith-Based Reform*, edited by Tamer Balci and Christopher L. Miller. Newcastle: Cambridge Scholars Publishing.

Balci, Tamer, and Christopher L. Miller, . 2012. *The Gülen Hizmet Movement: Circumspect Activism in Faith-Based Reform.* Newcastle: Cambridge Scholars Publishing.

Bayat, Asef. 2007. *Making Islam Democratic: Social Movements and the Post-Islamist Turn.* Stanford: Stanford University Press.

——. 2013. "Post-Islamism at Large." In *Post-Islamism: The Changing Faces of Political Islam*, by Asef Bayat. New York: Oxford University Press.

BBC News: Middle East. 2016. *Iran billionaire Babak Zanjani sentenced to death.* March 6. Accessed September 30, 2017. http://www.bbc.co.uk/news/world-middle-east-35739377 .

Belkeziz, Abdelillah. 2009. *The State in Contemporary Islamic Thought: A Historical Survey of the Major Muslim Political Thinkers of the Modern Era.* New York: I.B. Tauris.

Berkes, Niyazi. 1964. *The Development of Secularism in Turkey.* Montreal: MacGill University Press.

Bilici, Mücahit. 2006. "The Fethullah Gülen Movement and Its Politics of Representation in Turkey." *The Muslim World* 96: 1–20.

Birand, Mehmet Ali. 2010. "Gulen movement becoming victim of its own legend," *Hürriyet Daily*, 5th October available at : http://hizmetnews.com/18992/gulen-movement-becoming-victim-legend/#.WtMqoBRBU9d, access on 15.04.2018

Bozkurt, Abdullah. 2015. *Turkey Interrupted: Derailing Democracy.* New Jersey: Blue Dome Press.

Brown, Daniel W. 1996. *Rethinking Tradition in Modern Islamic Thought.* Cambridge: Cambridge University Press.

Bulaç, Ali. 1988. "The Medina Document." In *Liberal Islam: A Source Book*, edited by Charles Kurzman. Oxford: Oxford University Press.

——. 2007. "The Most Recent Reviver in the Ulama Tradition: The Intellectual 'Alim, Fethullah Gülen." In *Muslim Citizens of The Globalized World: Contributions of the Gülen Movement*, edited by Yuksel A Aslandogan Robert A. Hunt, 101–120. New Jersey: Tughra Books.

Cagaptay, Soner. 2006. *Islam, Secularism and Nationalism in Modern Turkey: Who is a Turk?* London: Routledge, Frank Cass.

Calis, Halim. 2011. "Fethullah Gülen's Thought on Hadith." In *Mastering Knowledge in Modern Times: Fethullah Gülen as an Islamic Scholar,* edited by Ismail Albayrak,39-64. New Jersey: Blue Dome Press.

Çapan, Ergün. 2011. "Teaching Methodology in His Private Circle." In *Mastering Knowledge in Modern Times: Fethullah Gülen as an Islamic Scholar* , edited by Ismail Albayrak,127-56. New Jersey: Blue Dome.

Carroll, Jill. 2007. *A Dialogue of Civilizations: Gülen's Islamic Ideals and Humanistic Discourse.* New Jersey: Tughra Books.

Casanova, Jose. 1994. *Public Religions in the Modern World.* Chicago: University of Chicago Press.

——. 2008. "Public Religions Revisited." In *Religion: Beyond a Concept*, edited by Hent de Vries, 111–19. New York: Fordham University Press.

——. 2006. "Secularization Revisited: A Reply to Talal Asad." In *Powers of the Secular Modern: Talal Asad and his Interlocutors*", edited by David Scott and Charles Hirschkind, 12–30. Stanford: Stanford University Press.

Cekerol, Kamil. 2012. "The Demand for Higher Education in Turkey and Open Education ." *The Turkish Online Journal of Educational Technology* 11 (3): 344–56.

Çelik, G, and P. Valkenberg. 2007. "Gülen's Approach to Dialogue and Peace: Its Theoretical Background and Some Practical Perspectives." *International Journal of Diversity in Organizations, Communities and Nations* 7 (1): 29–38.

Çelik, Zafer, and Bekir S. Gür. 2013. "Turkey's Education Policy During the AK Party Era (2002–2013)." *Insight Turkey* 15 (4): 151–76.

Çetin, Muhammed. 2010. *The Gülen Movement: Civic Service Without Borders.* New Jersey: Blue Dome Press.

Choueir, Youssef M. 2001. *Arab Nationalism: A History: Nation and State in the Arab World* . Oxford: Wiley-Blackwell.

Conway, Trudy D. 2014. *Cross-Cultural Dialogue on the Virtues: The Contribution of Fethullah Gülen.* Springer.

Copeaux, Etienne. 1996. "Hizmet: A Keyword in Turkish Historical Narrative." *New Perspectives on Turkey* 13: 97–114.

Cumhuriyet. 2015. "Koza İpek'e bilirkişi raporu: Şirketin suçu mükemmellik" [Koza Ipek expert report: company's fault is perfection. October 27, 2015. http://www.cumhuriyet.com.tr/haber/turkiye/396647/Koza_ipek_e_bilirkisi_raporu__Sirketin_sucu_mukemmellik.html. Accessed on March 4, 2017.

Curtis, Maria. 2012. "Among the Heavenly Branches: Leadership and Authority Among Women ın the Gülen Hizmet Movement." In *The Gülen Hizmet Movement: Circumspect Activism in Faith-Based Reform*, edited by Tamer Balci and Christopher L. Miller, 119–54. Newcastle: Cambridge Scholars Publishing. Değirmenli, Fatih. 2013. *Inner Dynamics of People of Hizmet.* Tughra Books.

de Vries, Hent, ed. 2008. *Religion: Beyond a Concept.* New York: Fordham University Press.

Demerath III, N. J. 1991. "Religious Capital and Capital Religions: Cross Cultural and Non-Legal Factors in the Separation of Church and State." *Daedalus* 120 (3): 21–40.

Demiröz, Fatih. 2015. *Government Reforms in Turkey: Is There a Demand?* Turkey Country Report, Rethink Institute, Washington, DC: Rethink Institute, 17-23.

Devji, Faisal. 2005. *Lanscapes of the Jihad: Miltancy, Morality, Modernity.* Ithaca: Cornell University Press.

——. 2011. "Muslim Universality." *Postcolonial Studies* 14 (2), 231-41.

Dinçer, Osman Bahadır, Vittoria Federici, Elizabeth Ferris, Sema Karaca, Kemal Kirişci, and Elif Özmenek Çarmıklı. 2013. *Turkey and Syrian Refugees: The Limits of Hospitality Thursday, November 14,.* Policy Brief, Brookings Institution and USAK, Brookings Institution.

Dreher, Sabine. 2015 "Islamic Capitalism? The Turkish Hizmet Business Community Network in a Global Economy." *Journal of Business Ethics* (129): 823–32.

——. 2013. "What is the Hizmet Movement? Contending Approaches to the Analysis of Religious Activists In World Politics." *Sociology of Islam* (Brill) 1 (3–4): 257–275.

Ebaugh, Helen Rose. 2009. *The Gülen Movement: A Sociological Analysis of a Civic Movement Rooted in Moderate Islam*. Springer.

Eddy, Melissa. June 8, 2018. "Austria Closes Seven Mosques and Seeks to Expel Imams Paid by Turkey," The New York Times. https://www.nytimes.com/2018/06/08/world/europe/austria-islam-mosques-turkey.html

Eickelman, Dale F. 1998. "Inside the Islamic Reformation." *Wilson Quarterly* 22 (1): 80–89.

Eickelman, Dale F., and James Piscatori. 2004. *Muslim Politics*. Princeton: Princeton University Press.

Eisenstadt, S. N. 2000. "Multiple Modernities." *Daedalus* 129 (1): 1–29.

El-Banna, Sanaa. 2014. *Resource Mobilization in Gülen-Inspired Hizmet: A New Type of Social Movement*. New York: Blue Dome Press.

El Fadl, Khaled Abou. 2005. *The Great Theft: Wrestling Islam from the Extremists*. Perfect Bound,

Ellis, Robert. 2017. *Reza Zarrab: Erdogan's Ticking Bomb*. September 20. Accessed September 30, 2017. https://intpolicydigest.org/2017/09/20/reza-zarrab-erdogan-s-ticking-bomb/.

Ergene, Mehmet Enes. 2008. *Tradition Witnessing the Modern Age: An Analysis of the Gülen Movement*. New Jersey: Tughra Books.

Ergil, Doğu. 2012. *Fethullah Gülen and The Gülen Movement in 100 Questions*. New Jersey: Blue Dome Press.

Esack, Farid. 1997. *Qur'an, Liberation, and Pluralism*. Oxford: Oneworld.

Esposito, John L. 1983. *Voices of Resurgent Islam*. New York: Oxford University Press.

Esposito, John, Yılmaz, İhsan. 2010. *Islam and Peacebuilding: Gulen Movement Initiatives*. New York: Blue Dome.

Esposito, John, Voll, John O. 2001. *Contemporary Islam*. New York: Oxford University Press.

Esposito, John, Haddad, Yvonne Y., and Voll, John O. 1991. *The Contemporary Islamic Revival: A Critical Survey and Bibliography, annotated edition*. Westport, CT: Greenwood.

European Commission. 2011. *The Report of European Commission Staff Working Paper: Turkey 2011 Progress Report*. Commission Staff Working Paper, European Commission, Brussels: European Commission, 1–115.

Findley, Carter Vaughn, 2015. *Hizmet among the Most Infl uential Religious Movements of Late Ottoman and Modern Turkish History*, in *Hizmet Means Service: Perspectives on an Alternative Path within Islam*. Edited by Martin E. Marty, 5-18. University of California Press.

Friedmann, Yohanan. 1971. *Shaykh Ahmad Sirhindi. An Outline of his Thought and a Study of his Image in the Eyes of Posterity*. Montreal and London: McGill-Queens University Press.

Geertz, Clifford. 1968. *Islam Observed: Religious Development in Morocco and Indonesia*. New Haven and London. Yale University Press.

Geoffroy, Eric. 2010. *Introduction to Sufism: The Inner Path of Islam*. Translated by

Roger Gaetani. Bloomington, Indiana: World Wisdom Books.
Giddens, Anthony. 1991. *The Consequences of Modernity.* Cambridge: Polity Press.
Girit, Selin. 2018. "The young Turks rejecting Islam," BBC News. www.bbc.com. May 10.
Göçmen, İpek. 2014. "Religion, politics and social assistance in Turkey: The rise of religiously motivated associations." *Journal of European Social Policy* 24 (1): 92–103.
Göğüş Tan, Mine. 2007. *Women, Education and Development in Turkey.* Vol. 18, in *Education in 'Multicultural' Societies: Turkish and Swedish Perspectives*, edited by Marie Carlson, Annika Rabo and Fatma Gök, 109–24. Swedish Research Institute in Istanbul.
Gök, Fatma. 2007. *History and Development of Turkish Education.* Vol. 18, in *Education in 'Multicultural' Societies: Turkish and Swedish Perspectives*, edited by Marie Carlson, Annika Rabo and Fatma Gök, 247–55. Swedish Research Institute in Istanbul.
Gökalp, Ziya. 2002. "Islam and Modern Civilization." In *Modernist Islam, 1840–1940: A Sourcebook*, edited by Charles Kurzman. Oxford: Oxford University Press.
Göle, Nilüfer. 2002. "Islam in Public: New Visibilities and New Imaginaries." *Public Culture* 14: 173–90.
. 2000. "Snapshots in Islamic Modernities." *Daedalus* 129 (1): 91–119.
——. 1996. *The Forbidden Modern: Civilization and Veiling.* Ann Arbor: University of Michigan Press.
Gözaydın, İştar B. 2009. "The Fethullah Gülen Movement and Politics in Turkey: A Chance for Democratization or a Trojan Horse?" *Democratization* 16 (6).
Gran, Peter. 1979. *Islamic Roots of Capitalism: Egypt 1760–1850.* Austin: University of Texas Press.
Griffel, Frank. 2009. *Al-Ghazali's Philosophical Theology.* Oxford: Oxford University Press.
Grinell, Klas. 2015. *Reflections on Reason; Religion and Tolerance: Engaging With Fethullah Gülen's Ideas.* New York: Blue Dome.
Gül, Berna Özcan. 2000. "Local Economic Development, Decentralization and Consensus Building in Turkey." *Progress in Planning* 54: 199–278.
Gülay, Erol N. 2007a. "The Gülen Phenomenon: A Neo-Sufi Challenge to Turkey's Rival Elite?" *Critique: Critical Middle Eastern Studies* (Taylor & Francis Online) 16 (1).
——. 2007b. The Theological Thought of Fethullah Gulen: Reconciling Science and Islam, MPhil Thesis, Oriental Studies/Modern Middle Eastern Studies, St. Antony's College, Oxford University.
Gülen, Fethullah M. 2017. "Jerusalem Deserves Unique International Status," Speaking Trees, Times of India Dec.14. https://blogs.timesofindia.indiatimes.com/toi-edit-page/jerusalem-deserves-unique-international-status/. Accessed on 11.02.2018
——. 2016. *Muslims' Responsibility in Countering Violence: A Perspective.* Edited by Ergün Çapan. Leuven: KU Leuven Gülen Chair for Intercultural Studies.
——. 2012. "Violence is not in the tradition of the Prophet," *Financial Times*, September, 27, https://www.ft.com/content/6ac625c0-07c6-11e2-9df2-00144feabdc0. Accessed on December 15, 2014.
——. 2009a. *Muhammad, The Messenger of God: An Analysis of the Prophet's Life.*

New Jersey: Tughra Books.

——. 2009b. *Key Concepts in Practice of Sufism: Emerald Hills of the Heart.* Vol. 1 and Vol. 3.Trans. Ali Unal. New Jersey: Tughra Books. Vol 2. 2007.

——. 2007. *Key Concepts in Practice of Sufism: Emerald Hills of the Heart.* Vol. 2. Trans. Ali Unal. Tughra Books, New Jersey.

——. 2006. *Towards A Global Civilization of Love and Tolerance.* New Jersey: Light.

——. 2005. *The Statue of Our Souls: Revival in Islamic Thought and Activism.* Translated by Muhammed Çetin. New Jersey: Tughra Books.

——. 2004a. *Dialogue in the Muhammadan Spirit and Meaning.* July 22. http://en.fgulen.com/content/view/1811/33/ .

——. 2004b. *Emerald Hills of the Heart: Key Concepts in the Practice of Sufism.* Vols. 1 & 3. New Jersey: Light.

——. 2004c. *The Two Roses of the Emerald Hills: Tolerance and Dialogue.* July 22. https://fgulen.com/en/fethullah-gulens-works/toward-a-global-civilization-of-love-and-tolerance/1297-forgiveness-tolerance-and-dialogue/25223-the-two-roses-of-the-emerald-hills-tolerance-and-dialogue.

——. 2002. *Fethullah Gülen: Essays, Perspectives and Opinions.* New Jersey: The Light, Inc.

——. 2001. *The Qur'an says: There is no compulsion in religion (2:256) what does this mean?* September 2001. Accessed September 29, 2017. https://fgulen.com/en/fethullah-gulens-works/faith/questions-and-answers/24500-the-quran-says-there-is-no-compulsion-in-religion-2256-what-does-this-mean

——. 1999. "Sufism and Its Origins." *The Fountain*, July-September.

——. 2000a. *Prophet Muhammad: Aspects of His Life.* Vol. 2. New Jersey: The Fountain.

——. 2000b. "The Necessity of Interfaith Dialogue." *The Fountain*, July-September.

——. 1998a. *İrşad Ekseni.* Izmir: Nil.

——. 1998b. *Prophet Muhammad as Commander.* Kaynak.

——. 1998c. *Towards the Lost Paradise.* 2nd Edition. Izmir: Kaynak.

Günay, Durmuş. n.d. *Turkish Higher Education System: New Developments and Trends.* Accessed November 20, 2014. http://int-e.net/kis2014ppt/DurmusGunay.pdf .

Gupta, Dipanker. 2000. *Culture, Space and the Nation-State.* New Delhi: Sage.

Gürbüz, Mustafa. 2015. *Turkey's Kurdish Question and the Hizmet Movement.* Rethink Paper 22, 1-27, Washington, DC: Rethink Institute.

Gürbüz, Mustafa E. and Purkayastha, Bandana. 2013. "From Gandhi to Gülen: The Habitus of Non-Aggressive Action." In *The Muslim World and Politics in Transition: Creative Contributions of the Gülen Movement*, edited by Greg Barton, Paul Weller and İhsan Yılmaz. London: Bloomsbury.

Habermas, Jurgen. 2010. *An Awareness of What is Missing: Faith and Reason in a Post-Secular Age.* Translated by Ciaran Crown. Cambridge: Polity Press.

Haj, Samira. 2009. *Reconfiguring Islamic Tradition: Reform, Rationality, and Modernity. Cultural Memory in the Present.* Stanford, CA: Stanford University Press.

Hendrick, Joshua. 2013. *Gülen: The Ambiguous Politics of Market Islam in Turkey and the World.* New York: New York University Press.

Hermansen, Marcia. 2005. "Understandings of 'Community' within the Gülen Movement." November 12. Accessed December 15, 2014. http://gyv.org.tr/content/userfiles/pdf/makale-hos-marcia_hermansen.pdf.

Hizmet Movement News Portal. 2012. *Financial Times Publishes Fethullah Gulen's Op-Ed.* September 27. Accessed May 28, 2017. http://hizmetnews.com/589/financial-times-publishes-fethullah-gulens-op-ed/#.WSr2LcaZNUM.

——. 2014. "TUSKON-led trade volume reaches $30 billion," http://hizmetnews.com/12704/tuskon-led-trade-volume-reaches-30-billion/#.WoP9exRBU9c. Source: Cihan, June 16, 2014. Accessed on 14.02.2018

Hoexter, Miriam, Eisenstadt, Shumuel N. and Levtzion, Nehemiah. 2002. *The Public Sphere in Muslim Societies.* Albany, New York: State University of New York Press.

Holton, Christopher and Lopez, Clare. 2015. *The Gulen Movement: Turkey's Islamic Supremacist Cult and its Contributions to the Civilization Jihad*, The Center for Security Policy Washington.Accessed December 27, 2017 https://www.centerforsecuritypolicy.org/wp-content/uploads/2015/12/Gulen_Final.pdf

Hourani, Albert. 1972. "Shaikh Khalid and the Naqshabandi Order." In *Islamic Philosophy and the Classical Tradition* , edited by S. M. Stern, Albert Hourani and Vivian Brown. Columbia, South Carolina: University of South Carolina Press.

The Holy Quran (Koran): 1987. English Translation of the Meanings by Abdullah Yusuf Ali. From a version revised by the Presidency of Islamic Researches, IFTA, Call and Guidance. Published and Printed by the King Fahd Holy Quran Printing Complex in 1987. http://www.streathammosque.org/uploads/quran/english-quran-yusuf-ali.pdf accessed on 24.12.2017

Hunt, Robert A. and Yüksel A. Aslandoğan (ed.). 2007. *Muslim Citizens of the Globalized World: Contributions of the Gülen Movement.* New Jersey: The Light, Inc.

Hürriyet Daily News. 2015. *AKP rejects proposal to probe 'paralel state'.* February 18. Accessed March 6, 2017. http://www.hurriyetdailynews.com/akp-rejects-proposal-to-probe-parallel-state.aspx?pageID=238&nid=78551.

Iqbal, Muhammad. 2002. "Islam as a Moral and Political Ideal." In *Modernist Islam, 1840–1940: A Sourcebook*, edited by Charles Kurzman, 304–13. Oxford: Oxford University Press.

——. 2012. *The Reconstruction of Religious Thought in Islam.* Stanford, California: Stanford University Press.

Jager, Jeff. 2016. "Understanding the Gülen Movement." *Small Wars Journal.* August 5. Accessed May 28, 2017. http://50.56.4.43/jrnl/art/understanding-the-gülen-movement.

——. 2016. *Understanding the Gülen Movement.* August 5. Accessed February 20, 2017. http://smallwarsjournal.com/jrnl/art/understanding-the-gülen-movement.

Jassal, Smita Tewari. 2014. "The Sohbet: Talking Islam in Turkey." *Sociology of Islam* (Brill) 1 (3–4): 188–208 .

Jenkins, Gareth. 2008. *Political Islam in Turkey: Running West, Heading East* . New York: Palgrave Macmillan.

Joppke, Christian. 2004. "The Retreat of Multiculturalism in the Liberal State: Theory and Policy." *The British Journal of Sociology* 55 (2): 237–57.

Journalists and Writers Foundation. n.d. *Note on the Gülen Movement.* Internal, Istanbul: Journalists and Writers Foundation.

Kömeçoğlu, Uğur. 1997. *A Sociologically Interpretative Approach to the Fethullah*

Gülen Community Movement. MA Thesis, Sociology Department, Istanbul: Boğaziçi University.

——. 2014. "Islamism, Post-Islamism, and Civil Islam." *Current Trends in Islamist Ideology* 16: 16–32.

Karabaşoğlu, Metin. 2003. "Text and Community: An Analysis of the Risale-i Nur Movement." In *Islam at the Crossroads: On the Life and Thought of Bediuzzaman Said Nursi*, edited by Ibrahim M. Abu-Rabi. State University of New York Press.

Keddie, Nikki R. 1968. "The Life and Thought of Sayyid Jamal al-Din." In *An Islamic Response to Imperialism*, 1–98. Berkeley: University of California Press.

——. 1981. *Roots of Revolution: An Interpretive History of Modern Iran.* Yale University Press.

——. 1972. *Sayyid Jamal al-Din al-Afghani: A Political Biography.* Berkeley: University of California Press.

Kim, Heon Choul. 2008. "Gülen's Dialogic Sufism: A Constructional and Constructive Factor of Dialogue." *Islam in the Age of Global Challenges: Alternative Perspectives of the Gulen Movement*, 374-406. Washington DC: Rumi Forum.

Kramer, Heinz. 2000. *A Changing Turkey: The Challenge to Europe and the United States.* Brookings Institution Press.

Kucukcan, Talip. 2007. "Social and Spiritual Capital of the Gülen Movement." Edited by İhsan Yılmaz, Eileen Barker, Henri J. Barkey, Muhammad Abdul Haleem, George S. Harris, Thomas Michel and Simon Robinson. *Muslim World in Transition: Contributions of the Gülen Movement.* London: Leeds Metropolitan University Press. 187–197.

Kurt, Erkan M., ed. 2014. *A Fethullah Gülen Reader: So That Others May Live.* New York: The Gülen Institute and Blue Dome Press.

Kurtz, Lester R. 2005. "Gülen's Paradox: Combining Commitment and Tolerance." *The Muslim World* 95 (3).

Kuru, Ahmet T. 2003. "Fethullah Gülen's Search for a Midlle Way: Between Modernity and Muslim Tradition." In *Turkish Islam and the Secular State: The Gülen Movement*, edited by M. Hakan Yavuz and John L. Esposito, 113–130. Syracuse: Syracuse University Press.

——. 2005. "Globalization and Diversification of Islamic Movements: Three Turkish Cases." *Political Science Quarterly* (Academy of Political Science) 120 (2): 253–74.

Kurzman, Charles. 1998. *Liberal Islam: A Source Book.* New York: Oxford University Press.

——. 2002. "Modernist Islam, 1840–1940: A Sourcebook." Oxford: Oxford University Press.

Landau-Tasseron, Ella. 1989. "The "Cyclical Reform": A Study of the mujaddid Tradition Source ." *Studia Islamica* (Maisonneuve & Larose) 70: 79–117.

Lapidus, Ira M. 1998. *History of Islamic Societies.* New York: Cambridge University Press.

——. 1997. "Islamic Revival and Modernity: The Contemporary Movements and the Historical Paradigm." *Journal of the Economic and Social History of the Orient* 40 (4): 440–60.

Lapidus, Ira M., and Edmund Burke, . 1990 . *Islam, Politics and Social Movements (Comparative Studies on Muslim Societies Series).* Vol. 5. Berkeley: University

of California Press.
Lerner, Daniel. 1958. *The Passing of Traditional Societies: Modernizing the Middle East.* Glencoe, Illinois: Macmillan.
Lewis, Bernard. 2002. *The Emergence of Modern Turkey.* New York: Oxford University Press.
——. 1994. "Why Turkey Is the only Muslim Democracy." *Middle East Quarterly* 41–49.
MacIntyre, Alasdair. 1988. *Whose Justice? Which Rationality?* Notre Dame, Indiana: Notre Dame University Press.
Madampat, Shajahan. 1995. *The Concept of 'Hukm' in the Islamist Writings and in Classical Works of Exegesis: A Comparative Study', M.phil Dissertation, Centre for West Asian and African Studies, Jawaharlal Nehru University, New Delhi.* M.Phil. Thesis,
Mahmood, Saba. 2005. *Politics of Piety: The Islamic Revival and the Feminist Subject.* New York: Princeton University Press.
——. 1996. "Talal Asad: Modern Power and the Reconfiguration of Religious Traditions." *SEHR: Contested Polities* 5 (1).
Makovsky, Alan. 2015. *Re-Educating Turkey: AKP Efforts to Promote Religious Values in Turkish Schools* . Accessed February 20, 2017. https://www.americanprogress.org/issues/security/reports/2015/12/14/127089/re-educating-turkey/.
Malik, Hafeez. 1980. *Sir Sayyid Ahmad Khan and Muslim Modernization in India and Pakistan.* New York: Columbia University Press.
Malik, Jamal. 1996. *Colonization of Islam: Dissolution of Traditional Institutions in Pakistan,.* Delhi: Manohar.
Mandaville, Peter. 2007. *Global Political Islam.* Oxford: Routledge.
Mardin, Şerif. 1971. "Ideology and Religion in the Turkish Revolution." *International Journal of Middle East Studies* 2: 197–211.
——. 1997. "Projects as Methodology: Some Thoughts on Modern Turkish Social Science." In *Rethinking Modernity and National Identity in Turkey*, edited by Sibel Bozdogan and Resat Kasaba. University of Washington Press. Pp
——. 1989. *Religion and Social Change in Modern Turkey: The Case of Bediuzzaman Said Nursi.* New York: University of New York Press.
——. 2006. *Religion, Society and Modernity in Turkey.* Syracuse, New York: Syracuse University Press.
Martinez, Luis. 2000. *The Algerian Civil Wars, 1990–1998* . New York: Columbia University Press.
Michel, Thomas. 2014. *Insights from the Risale-i Nur: Said Nursi's Advice for Modern Believers.* New Jersey: Tughra Books.
——. 2014. *Peace And Dialogue in a Plural Society: Contributions of the Hizmet Movement At a Time of Global Tension* . New York: Blue Dome.
——. 2005. "Sufism and Modernity in the Thought of Fethullah Gülen." *The Muslim World* (Hartford Seminary) 95 (3).
——. 2010. "The Thinking Behind the Gülen Movement." *International Fethullah Gülen Conference: The Gülen Model of Education.* Jakarta. 19–21.
MONE 2005. *Milli Eğitim Istatistikleri (National Education Statistics)* 2004-2005. Ankara: Devlet Kitapları Müdürlüğü Basımevi.
Nandy, Ashis. 1983. *Intimate Enemy: The Loss and Recovery of Self under Colonization.*

Oxford University Press.
——. 1988. "The Politics of Secularism and the Recovery of Religious Tolerance." *Alternatives* (Sage) XIII: 177–94.
Navaro-Yashin, Yael. 2002. *Faces of the State: Secularism and Public Life in Turkey.* New York: Princeton University Press.
Nursi, Bediüzzaman Said. 2006. *The Words: The Reconstruction of Islamic Belief and Thought.* Translated by Huseyin Akarsu. New Jersey: Light.
Ocal, A. T. 2007. *Corporates' Social Responsibility: An Ethical Evaluation (Isletmelerin Sosyal Sorumlulugu: Ahlaki bir degerlendirme).* Istanbul: Beta.
Ozgur, Iren. 2015. *Islamic Schools in Modern Turkey: Faith, Politics, and Education.* Cambridge University Press.
Özdalga, Elizabeth. 2003. "Following in the Footsteps of Fethullah Gülen: Three Women Teachers Tell Their Stories." In *Turkish Islam and the Secular State: The Gülen Movement* , edited by M. Hakan Yavuz and John L. Esposito, 113–130 . Syracuse : Syracuse University Press.
——. 2006. "The Hidden Arab. A Critical Reading of the Notion of Turkish Islam." *Middle Eastern Studies*, July: 551–70.
——. 2003. "Secularizing Trends in Fethullah Gülen's Movement: Impasse or Opportunity for Further Renewal?" *Critique: Critical Middle Eastern Studies* (Taylor & Francis Online) 12 (1): 61–73.
——. 2010. "Transformation of Sufi Based Communities in Modern Turkey: The Nakşibendis, the Nurcus, and the Gülen Community." In *Turkey's Engagement with Modernity: Conflict and Change in the Twentieth Century*, edited by Celia Kerslake, Kerem Öktem and Philip Robins, 69–91. Palgrave Macmillan.
——. 2000. "Worldly Asceticism in Islamic Casting: Fethullah Gülen's Inspired Piety and Activism." *Critique* 17: 84–104.
Özdemir, S. 2006. *MÜSİAD: Anadolu Sermayesinin Donusumu ve Turk Modernlesmesinin Derinlesmesi (Musiad: The Transformation of Anatolian Capital and the Deepening of Turkish Modernity).* Ankara: Vadi.
Özübüyük, Ibrahim. 2013. *Qualities of a Devoted Soul: A Portrayal of the Hizmet People. The Essential Guide for Volunteers.* New Jersey: Tughra Books.
Pamuk, Sevket. 2007. *Economic Change in Twentieth-Century Turkey: Is the Glass More than Half Full?* Working Paper No. 41, American University of Paris, Paris: Trustee Fund for the Advancement of Scholarship. PP
Pandya, Sophia and Nancy Gallagher, ed. 2012. *The Gülen Hizmet Movement and Its Transnational Activities: Case Studies of Altruistic Activism in Contemporary Islam. Brown Walker Press.*
Panjwani, Farid. 2004. "The 'Islamic' in Islamic Education: Assessing the Discourse." *Current Issues in Comparative Education,* 7 (1): 1–11.
Pasini, Stefano, and David Morselli. 2010. "Disobeying Illegitimate Requests in a Democratic or Authoritarian System." *Political Psychology* 31 (3).
Pearson, Thomas D. 2012. "Is Genuine Interfaith Dialogue Impossible? Alasdair MacIntyre and Fethullah Gülen in Conversation." In *The Gülen Hizmet Movement: Circumspect Activism in Faith-Based Reform*, edited by Tamer Balci and Christopher L. Miller, pp. London: Cambridge Scholars Publishing.
Pew Forum on Religion and Public Life. 2010. *Muslim Networks and Movements in Western Europe.* Washington: Pew Research Centre.
Pratt, Douglas. 2007. "Islamic Prospects for Inter-Religious Dialogue: The

Contribution of Fethullah Gülen." In *Muslim World in Transition: Contributions of the Gülen Movement*, edited by İhsan Yılmaz, Eileen Barker, Henri J. Barkey, Muhammad Abdul Haleem, George S. Harris, Thomas Michel and Simon Robinson. London: Leeds Metropolitan University.

Putnam, Robert. 1993. *Making Democracy Work. Civic Traditions in Modern Italy.* Princeton: Princeton University Press.

Rahman, Fazlur. 1979. *Islam.* 2nd Edition. Chicago: Chicago University Press.

——. 1998. "Islam and Modernity." In *Liberal Islam: A Source Book* , edited by Charles Kurzman, 304–318. New York: Oxford University Press.

——. 2002. "Islam and Modernity." In *Modernist Islam, 1840–1940: A Sourcebook*, edited by Charles Kurzman. Oxford: Oxford University Press.

——. 1995. *Islamic Methodology in History.* 3rd reprint. Islamabad: Islamic Research Institute,.

——. 1970. *Revival and Reform in Islam.* Vol. 2, in *Cambridge History of Islam*, edited by Peter Holt, Ann K. S. Lambton and Bernard Lewis, 632–42. Cambridge: Cambridge University Press.

Ramadan, Tariq. 2007. *The Messenger: The Meanings of the Life of Muhammad.* New York: Oxford University Press.

——. 2004. *Western Muslims and the Future of Islam.* Oxford: Oxford University Press.

Rashid Rida, Muhammad. 1980. *Tafsir al-Manar* . Vol. 12. Beirut: Dar al-Marifah.

Rodinson, Maxim. 1978. *Islam and Capitalism.* Austin: University of Texas Press.

Rubin, Michael. 2015. *Reconsidering Fethullah Gülen.* May 20. Accessed June 16, 2015. https://www.commentarymagazine.com/foreign-policy/middle-east/reconsidering-fethullah-gulen/.

Sachedina, Abdulaziz. 2006. "The Role of Islam in the Public Square." *ISIM Papers.* Leiden, Amsterdam: Amsterdam University Press.

Saeed, Abdullah. 2006. *Islamic Thought: An Introduction.* London: Routledge.

Said, Edward. 1978. *Orientalism,* New York: Pantheon Books.

——. 1994. *Culture and Imperialism,* Amsterdam: Atlas.

Safi, Omid, ed. 2006. *Progressive Muslims: On Justice, Gender, and Pluralism.* Oxford: One World.

Salvatore, Armando. 1997. *Islam and the Political Discourse of Modernity.* Ithaca: Garnet Publishing.

——. 2007. *The Public Sphere: Liberal Modernity, Catholicism, Islam.* New York: Palgrave Macmillan.

Salvatore, Armando, and Dale F. Eickelman, . 2004. *Public Islam and the Common Good.* Leiden: Brill.

Sanchez, Ray. 2016. "Fethullah Gulen on 'GPS': Failed Turkey coup looked 'like a Hollywood movie.'" July 31. Accessed March 6, 2017. http://edition.cnn.com/2016/07/31/world/fethullah-gulen-turkey-fareed-zakaria-gps/.

Sarıtoprak, Zeki, and Ali Ünal. 2005. "An Interview with Fethullah Gülen." *The Muslim World* 95 (3): 447–67.

Sarıtoprak, Zeki and Sidney Griffith. 2005. "Fethullah Gülen and the People of the Book: A Voice from Turkey for Interfaith Dialogue." *The Muslim World* 95 (3): 329–40.

Sayyid, Bobby S. 1997. *A Fundamental Fear: Eurocentrism and Emergence of Islamism.* London: Zed Books.

Scott, David, and Charles Hirschkind, . 2006. *Powers of the Secular Modern: Talal Asad and his Interlocutors.* Translated by Powers of the Secular. Stanford, CA: Stanford University Press.

Seker, Mehmet Yavuz. 2011. "Sufism and Fethullah Gülen." In *Mastering Knowledge in Modern Times: Fethullah Gülen as an Islamic Scholar*, edited by Ismail Albayrak. New Jersey,97-126: Blue Dome Press.

Sevindi, Nevval. 2008. *Contemporary Islamic Conversations: M. Fethullah Gülen on Turkey, Islam and the West.* New York: State University of New York Press.

Shabestari, Mohammad Mojtahed. 2004. *Ta'amulati dar Qira'at-e Ensan-i az Din [Reflections on the Human Reading of Religion].* Tehran: Tarh-e Naw.

Sharon-Krespin, Rachel. 2009. "Fethullah Gülen's Grand Ambition Turkey's Islamist Danger." *Middle East Quarterly* 16, no.1 (2009): 55-66.

Sikand, Yoginder. 2002. *The Origins and Development of the Tablighi Jama'at: (1920–2000). A cross-country comparative study* . New Delhi : Orient Longman.

Silverstein, Adam J. 2010. *Islamic History: A Very Short Introduction.* Oxford: Oxford University Press.

Silverstein, Brian. 2010. *Islam and Modernity in Turkey.* New York: Palgrave Macmillan.

Şimşek, Sefa. 2004. "New Social Movements in Turkey Since 1980." *Turkish Studies* (Taylor and Francis) 5 (2): 111–39.

SIS 1995. *Women in Statistics 1927-1992.* Ankara: SIS Printing Division.

Sleap, Frances, and Ömer Şener. 2013. "Fethullah Gülen." In *Dialogue Theories*, edited by Paul Weller, 83–100. London: Dialogue Society.

Smith, Jane. 1975 . *A Historical and Semantic Study of the Term 'Islam' as Seen in a Sequence of Quran Commentaries* . Montana: University of Montana Press.

Smith, W.C. 1957. *Islam in Modern History.* Princeton: Princeton University Press.

Soltes, Ori Z. 2013. *Embracing the World: Fethullah Gülen's Thought and Its Relationship to Jalaluddin Rumi and Others.* New Jersey: Tughra Books.

Souroush, Abdolkarim. 2000. *Reason, Freedom and Democracy in Islam.* Translated by Mahmoud Sadri and Ahmad Sadri. New York: Oxford University Press.

Sunier, Thijl, Landman, Nico, Linden, Heleen van der, Bilgili, Nazlı and Bilgili, Alper. 2011. *Diyanet: The Turkish Directorate for Religious Affairs in a Changing Environment.* VU University Amsterdam Utrecht University, available at https://pdfs.semanticscholar.org/ae90/33c7130bad834e6b2968f18b2f9c3ed96195.pdf. Accessed on July 11, 2018.

Tan, Mine Gögüş. 2007. Women, Education and Development in Turkey. *Education in 'Multicultural' Societies – Turkish and Swedish Perspectives*, eds. Marie Carlson, Annika Rabo and Fatma Gök, Swedish Research Institute in Istanbul, Transactions, vol. 18 Stockholm. 107-122.

Tas, Halil I., and Dale R. Lightfoot. 2005. "Gecekondu Settlements in Turkey: Rural-Urban Migration in the Developing European Periphery." *Journal of Geography* (Taylor & Francis Online) 104 (6): 263–271. http://www.tandfonline.com/doi/full/10.1080/00221340508978648.

TED. 2006. Hayat 195 dakikaya sığar mı? (Can Life Be Put in 195 Minutes?). İstanbul.

Türkdoğan, O. 2005 . *Islami Degerler Sistemi ve Max Weber (The Islamic Value System and Max Weber).* Istanbul: IQ Yayincilik .

Toğuslu, Erkan. 2007. "Gülen's Theory of Adab and Ethical Values of Gülen Movement." In *Muslim World in Transition: Contributions of the Gülen Movement* , edited by İhsan Yılmaz, Eileen Barker, Henri J. Barkey, Muhammad Abdul Haleem, George S. Harris, Michel Thomas and Simon R. Robinson, 445–457.. London: Leeds Metropolitan University Press..

——. 2008. "Hizmet: From Futuwwa Tradition To The Emergence Of Movement In Public Space." In *Islam in the Age of Global Challenges, Alternative Perspectives of the Gulen Movement*, 711-729. Rumi Forum, Washington D.C., 2008.

Topal, Semiha. 2012. "Pursuit of Piety in the Public Sphere: A Weberian Analysis of the Gülen Hizmet Movement." In *The Gülen Hizmet Movement: Circumspect Activism in Faith-Based Reform*, edited by Tamer Balci and Christopher L. Miller, 189–99. Cambridge Scholars Publishing.

Toprak, Binnaz. 1999. "Religion and State in Turkey." *Africa Portal*. Accessed September 12, 2017. http://dspace.africaportal.org/jspui/bitstream/123456789/22465/1/Religion%20and%20State%20in%20Turkey.pdf?1.

Turam, Berna. 2007. *Between Islam and the State: The Politics of Engagement.* California: Stanford University Press.

TurkStat. 2010. *Press Release: Trade Statistics By Entreprise Characteristics 2010.* September 27. Accessed June 26, 2012. http://www.turkstat.gov.tr/HbPrint.do?id=10714.

Turner, Bryan S. 1974. *Weber and Islam: A Critical Study.* London: Routledge and Kegan Paul.

TÜRKÇEDER. 2012. "20 yılda 300 bin kişi Türkçe öğrendi." *Türkçe Olimpiyatları 10. Yıl, Mayıs-Haziran 2012*, Istanbul: Uluslararası Türkçe Öğretimi Derneği

Uğur, Etga. 2004. "Intellectual Roots of 'Turkish Islam' and Approaches to the Turkish Model." *Journal of Muslim Minority Affairs* 24 (2): 327–45.

——. 2013 . "Organizing Civil Society: The Gülen Movement's Abant Platform." In *The Muslim World and Politics in Transition: Creative Contributions of the Gülen Movement*, edited by Greg Barton, Paul Weller and İhsan Yılmaz, 47–64. London: Bloomsbury.

——. 2007. "Religion as a Source of Social Capital. The Gülen Movement in the Public Sphere." In *Muslim World in Transition: Contributions of the Gülen Movement,* Edited by İhsan Yılmaz, Eileen Barker, Henri J. Barkey, Muhammad Abdul Haleem, George S. Harris, Thomas Michel and Simon Robinson, 152-62. Leeds Metropolitan University Press..

Ünal, Ali, and Alphonse Williams. 2000. *Fethullah Gülen: Advocate of Dialogue.* Edited by Ali Ünal and Alphonse Williams. New Jersey: The Light, Inc.

Ünal, Mehmet. 2004. *In the Service of Peace: A Short Biography of Fethullah Gülen.* Istanbul: Ufuk Books.

Uygur, Selcuk. 2007. "'Islamic Puritanism' As a Source of Economic Development: The Case of Gülen Movement." *International Conference Proceedings: Muslim World in Transition: Contributions of the Gülen Movement.* London: Leeds Metropolitan University Press. 176–97 .

Vahide, Sukran. 2005. *Islam in Modern Turkey: An Intellectual Biography of Bediüzzaman Said Nursi.* Albany: State University of New York Press.

Vicini, Fabio. 2007. "Gülen's Rethinking of Islamic Pattern and Its Socio-Political Effects." In *Muslim World in Transition: Contributions of the Gülen Movement,* edited by İhsan Yılmaz, Eileen Barker, Henri J. Barkey, Muhammad Abdul Haleem, George S. Harris, Thomas Michel and Simon Robinson pp. London: Leeds Metropolitan University Press.

Voll, John O. 2008. *Islam, Continuity and Change in the Modern World.* 2nd Edition. Syracuse, New York: Syracuse University Press.

——. 1983. "Renewal and Reform in Islamic History: *Tajdid* and *Islah* Oxford University Press." In *Voices of Resurgent Islam*, edited by John Esposito, 32–47. New York: Oxford University Press.

Waardenburg, Jacques. 1999. *Muslim Perceptions of Other Religions: A Historical Survey.* Oxford: Oxford University Press.

Walton, Jeremy F. 2013. "Is Hizmet Liberal? Mediations and Disciplines of Islam and Liberalism among Gülen Organizations in Istanbul." *Sociology of Islam* 1: 145–164.

Webb, Mark. 2012. "The Genius and Vulnerability of the Gülen Hizmet Movement." In *The Gülen Hizmet Movement: Circumspect Activism in Faith-Based Reform*, edited by Tamer Balci and Christopher L. Miller, 155-164. Newcastle: Cambridge Scholars Publishing.

White, Jenny B. 2002. *Islamist mobilization in Turkey: a study in vernacular politics.* Seattle: University of Washington Press.

Wickham, Carrie Rosefsky. 2002. *Mobilizing Islam: Religion, Activism and Political Change in Egypt.* New York: Columbia University Press.

Wiktorowicz, Quintan, ed. 2004. *Islamic Activism: A Social Movement Theory Approach.* Bloomington, Indiana: Indiana University Press.

Wood, Gary, and Tugrul Keskin. 2013. "Perspectives on the Gülen Movement." *Sociology of Islam* (Brill) 1 (3–4).

Woolf C. H., The Rt. Hon. The Lord, Professor Sir Jeffrey Jowell KCMG QC, and The Rt. Hon. Sir Edward Palin, Sarah Garnier QC MP. 2015. *A Report on the Rule of Law and Respect for Human Rights in Turkey Since December 2013.* Law & Human Rights, One Brick Court, Journalists and Writers Foundation.

Wulfsberg, Joanna Christine. 2015. *Singing Turkish, Performing Turkishness: Message and Audience in the Song Competition of the International Turkish Olympiad*, The University of Arizona, USA. Available on https://repository.arizona.edu/bitstream/handle/10150/556223/azu_etd_13760_sip1_m.pdf?sequence=1&isAllowed=y , accessed on 12.07.2018.

Yavuz, M. Hakan and J. L. Esposito. 2003. *Turkish Islam and the Secular State: The Gülen Movement.* Syracuse: Syracuse University Press.

Yavuz, M. Hakan. 1999. "The Assassination of Collective Memory. The Case of Turkey." *The Muslim World*, 89 (3–4): 193–207.

——. 2003a. "The Gülen Movement: The Turkish Puritans." In *Turkish Islam and the Secular State: The Gülen Movement*, edited by M. Hakan Yavuz and J. L. Esposito, pp. 17-45. Syracuse: Syracuse University Press.

——. 2003b. *Islamic Political Identity in Turkey.* Oxford: Oxford University Press.

——. 2003c. "Nur Study Circles (*Dershanes*) and the Formation of New Religious Consciousness in Turkey." In *Islam at the Crossroads: On the Life and Thought of Bediuzzaman Said Nursi*, edited by Ibrahim M. Abu-Rabi, 297–316. State University of New York Press.

——. 2004a. "Is There a Turkish Islam? The Emergence of Convergence and Consensus." *Journal of Muslim Minority Affairs*, 24 (2): 213–23.

——. 2004b. "Opportunity, Spaces, Identity, and Islamic Meaning in Turkey." In *Islamic Activism: A Social Movements Theory Approach*, edited by Quintan Wiktorowicz, 270–89. Bloomington, Indiana: Indiana University Press.

——. 2013. *Towards an Islamic Enlightenment: The Gülen Movement.* New York: Oxford University Press.

——. 2018. "Ruin or Resilience? The Future of the Gülen Movement in Transnational Political Exile," in *Politics, Religion & Ideology*, Volume 19, 2018 - Issue 1.

Yavuz, M. Hakan, Bayram Balci (ed). 2018. *Turkey's July 15th Coup: What Happened and Why.* The University of Utah Press.

Yeşilova, Hakan. 2016. "Debunking the Gülen-Erdoğan Relationship," *The Daily Caller*. September 22.

Yılmaz, İhsan, Eileen Barker, Henri J. Barkey, Muhammad Abdul Haleem, George S. Harris, Thomas Michel, and Simon Robinson. 2007. *Muslim World in Transition: Contributions of the Gülen Movement.* London: Leeds Metropolitan University Press.

Yılmaz, İhsan. 2011. "Beyond Post-Islamism: A Critical Analysis of Turkish Islamism's Transformation toward 'Civil Islam' and its Potential Influence in the Muslim World." *European Journal of Economic and Political Studies,* 4 (1): 235–80.

——. 2003. "Ijtihad and Tajdid by Conduct." In *Turkish Islam and the Secular State: The Gülen Movement*, by M. Hakan Yavuz and John L. Esposito, 208–237. Syracuse, N.Y.: Syracuse University Press.

——. 2015. *Kemalizmden Erdoğanizme: Türkiye'de Din, Devlet ve Makbul Vatandaş.* Istanbul: Ufuk Yayınları.

——. 2005. "State, Law, Civil Society and Islam in Contemporary Turkey." *The Muslim World* (Wiley Online) 95 (3): 385–401.

——. 2012. "Towards a Muslim Secularism? An Islamic 'Twin Tolerations' Understanding of Religion in the Public Sphere." *Turkish Journal of Politics* 3 (2).

——. 2010. "Utilization of Social Capital for Sustainable Development and Peace Building in Global Conflict Zones by Faith-Based Movements." *European Journal of Economic and Political Studies* 3 (1): 189–99.

——. n.d. *From Kemalism to Erdoğanism* (unpublished English Translation).

Yılmaz, Turan. 2014. *Turkey ranks third most generous donor country.* October 4. Accessed October 6, 2014. http://www.hurriyetdailynews.com/turkey-ranks-3rd-generous-of-donor-countries-.aspx?pageID=238&nID=72519&NewsCatID=510.

Yinanç, Barçın. 2014. *Rise in imam-hatips shows AKP's favoritism for religious education.* August 11. Accessed October 14, 2014. http://www.hurriyetdailynews.com/rise-in-imam-hatips-shows-akps-favoritism-for-religious-education.aspx?pageID=238&nid=70225.

Yousef, D. A. 2001. "Islamic Work Ethic: A Moderator between Organizational Commitment and Job Satisfaction in a Cross-cultural Context ." *Personnel Review* 30 (2): 152–169.

Zaman, Muhammad Qasim. 2002. *The Ulama in Contemporary Islam: Custodian of Change.* Princeton: Princeton University Press.

INDEX

O

P

Q

R

Z